THE COLOURS
OF THE 7th (CITY OF LONDON) BATTALION THE LONDON REGIMENT

THE KING'S COLOUR   THE REGIMENTAL COLOUR

PRESENTED BY
HIS MAJESTY KING EDWARD VII
AT WINDSOR CASTLE
19th JUNE, 1909

(FOR HONOURS OF THE GREAT WAR 1914–18 see page 243)

Blocks kindly lent by S. Straker & Son, Ltd.

PRIVATE IN THE
LOYAL LONDON VOLUNTEERS, 1804

Blocks kindly lent by Pocket Publications, Ltd.

The History
of the
"Shiny Seventh"

Printed and Bound by Antony Rowe Ltd, Eastbourne

COL. EDWARD FAUX, C.M.G., V.D.

Frontispiece

HISTORY

of the

7TH

(CITY OF LONDON)

BATTALION
THE LONDON REGIMENT

*Embracing the 3rd London and the 32nd
Searchlight Regiment, R.A. (7th City of London)*

COMPILED BY

C. DIGBY PLANCK

With a Foreword by
Brig.-Gen. The Right Hon. VISCOUNT HAMPDEN
G.C.V.O., K.C.B., C.M.G.

PUBLISHED BY
THE OLD COMRADES' ASSOCIATION, 24, SUN STREET, E.C.2.

A FOREWORD

*I*T is now 30 years since I took over command of the 140th Infantry Brigade in France and to be asked, after all these years, to write the Foreword to the History of the 7th Battalion London Regiment is a compliment which cannot be over estimated, and is very much appreciated by me, notwithstanding feelings of inability to do justice to the part my old friends of the 7th London Regiment played in the 1914-1918 war.

Memory in respect of events so long gone by is apt to be defective, but the admiration, pride and indeed affection I felt for all ranks in the 140th Brigade of which the 7th Battalion formed a part can never pass away.

The chief event in which the 7th London Regiment took part during the period I was with the Brigade was the Battle of the Somme, where on Sept. 15th, 1916, they captured High Wood, which had for many weeks held out against all British attacks, a feat which the Brigade can ever be proud of taking part in.

HAMPDEN.

9th June, 1946.

PREFACE

I waited twenty years for the history of the " Shiny Seventh " to be produced, and with the approach of the World War I commenced the task of placing on record the history of the Regiment ; conscious all the while that many with greater knowledge and more active experience of the Regiment, and others capable of a greater literary effort than I, could have performed the task.

Research work to obtain material has covered a long period and provided much food for thought, particularly when comparing transport, equipment and armour of early days, the Great War 1914-1918 and the World War.

The text of this history was first prepared in draft form and read through by my colleagues Mr. W. Horley, M.M., and Mr. C. Luck. After making their corrections, the draft was typed and each part was sent to members of the Regiment who were most concerned with the period covered.

Following their valuable alterations and additions, the draft was revised and then checked through by Lieut.-Col. C. J. Salkeld Green, D.S.O., M.C., T.D., and finally passed to Mr. F. Scothorne to " dot the I's and cross the T's." From the list of acknowledgments it will be gathered that many have assisted in the preparation of these pages.

I have been greatly helped in preparing the early portion by Mr. C. Luck, and also by Mr. B. Fryer, who provided me with copies of the 3rd London Regimental Gazette, from which much information has been obtained.

My thanks are due to our President, Major H. D. Barnes, O.B.E., T.D., D.L., and Major Allan D. Laurie, T.D., for their very great help, and also to Major P. B. Berliner, M.C., and Mr. H. Lydiart, M.M., for their assistance. The greater portion of the narrative covering the Ypres period of the 2/7th is based on material supplied by them.

I am also indebted to Major Sir K. O. Peppiatt, K.B.E., M.C., and his brother, Major L. E. Peppiatt, M.C., who have been of great assistance to me throughout, particularly the latter in connection with the Reserve Battalion, and to Lieut.-Col. L. S. Davis, T.D., for writing the chapters " Further Reorganisation," and the " Second World War."

Lieut.-Col. C. J. Salkeld Green, D.S.O., M.C., T.D., who, apart from checking the history, has throughout assisted me with important details and the work has benefited greatly by his guidance and advice.

In compiling this work every care has been taken to confirm dates and to check positions, names of individuals and place names, and I

PREFACE

request the indulgence of the reader for any error which may have crept in.

My endeavour has been to avoid making this work a "telephone directory," but names have been mentioned with a view to keeping memories alive. Those mentioned are so quoted because they have been brought to my notice or have occurred in diaries or correspondence.

I trust those whose names and deeds are not recorded will understand and forgive the omission. I am fully alive to the fact that many more are deserving of mention. My other worry has been that I should fail to do justice to the "Shiny Seventh."

Generally, in describing actions, the official side has been put first, followed by an endeavour to describe what actually happened, and completed by descriptive accounts and extracts from letters of members of the Regiment. Throughout I have avoided all matters dealing with strategy.

The foreword, so kindly written by Brig.-Gen. the Right Hon. Viscount Hampden, G.C.V.O., K.C.B., C.M.G., will be read with pleasure by all Old Comrades, and I am grateful for the interest he has shown.

I appreciate the assistance of those who placed their diaries at my disposal and of which I have made good use. I also appreciate the help rendered by all those who corresponded with me, including Mr. S. Weaver, who has prepared the sketches included in this book.

My sincere thanks to the Honorary Colonel, Col. J. Trevor, and my old friend of the 6th London Regiment, Mr. F. S. Stapleton, the former for his help in enabling us to go to print, and the latter for his advice and for supervising the printing of these pages.

The dates preceding the chapter headings refer to the period covered by the chapter.

It is in memory of those killed in action during 1914-1918 and in respect for men of the 32nd, who helped to make victory possible in the World War, that this book is written.

We who survive can feel proud that we have served in either the 3rd, 7th, or 32nd, and should endeavour to maintain that fine spirit that has prevailed in the past, always remembering that "Once a Seventh, always a Seventh."

C. D. P.

ACKNOWLEDGMENTS

"British Campaign in France and Flanders, 1917," by A. Conan Doyle. "British Official History," "Leader and Saturday Analyst," "The Times," "History of the 6th London," "3rd London Regimental Gazette," "I Lived These Years," by Mr. Eric Baume.

"Songs of the Shiny Seventh," by Mr. E. Mudge. "The Fighting Territorials," by Sir Percy Hurd. "Country Life." "The Volunteer, 1899." "Supplement to the Army List, October, 1919." "So Few," by Mr. David Masters, "News of the World," London "Evening News," and "The 47th (London) Divisional History."

Diaries of the following have been consulted :
Maj. Sir K. O. Peppiatt, K.B.E., M.C. ; Maj. H. D. Barnes, O.B.E., T.D., D.L. The late Maj. R. Danford Thomas. The late Capt. and Q.M. G. D. Roche. The late Lt.-Col. C. E. Johnston, D.S.O., M.C. The 1/7th Battalion War Diary. Messrs. F. Dunham, R. Ashley, H. Bond (Cambridge), H. Hunt, H. Lydiart, M.M., W. Horley, M.M., and S. Weaver.

Assistance has been rendered by the following :
Mr. G. Addison, Brig. E. E. F. Baker, C.B.E., D.S.O., M.C., T.D., D.L. A.D.C., Lt.-Col. A. E. F. Barnes, Col. J. G. Budd, Lt. G. E. Bradfield. Messrs. R. Bond, M.M., W. G. Browning, M.M., F. Brooks, D.C.M., M.M., H. Bacon and S. Blackmore.

Capt. C. Cartwright, Mr. J. Chetland, M.M., Sir L. B. Freeston, K.C.M.G., O.B.E., Capt. D. G. Fearnside-Speed, Capt. C. L. Faux, Lt.-Col. S. L. Hosking, Capt. H. G. Head, Lt. G. Hill, M.C., D.C.M. Messrs. F. Haxell, M.M., H. Hughes, M.S.M., B. Hare, J. Jordan and M. Kerr, M.M., Capt. Lang (The Right Rev. Lord Bishop of Woolwich), Lt. W. J. Lucas, M.C. Messrs. H. Morris, T. Middleton, F. Mannock and W. M. C. Norie, Lt.-Col. K. J. Pearce, R.S.M. F. J. Payne, M.C., Mr. J. J. Patrickson, Capt. V. H. Raby, M.C. Messrs. F. Redway, A. Robinson, W. Robertson, R. Rayner and R. C. Richards. Maj. N. G. Straker, Capt. P. L. Smout, M.C., Lt. E. J. Simons, Lt. E. C. Stringer. Messrs. G. Summers, F. Scothorne, F. J. Smith and F. Trigg, Capt. R. W. Thomas, M.C., Capt. H. C. Woolner. Messrs. L. Williams, D.C.M., W. Pye, K. M. Wood and Mr. F. C. Atkins.

Royal United Services Institute. Imperial War Graves Commission. Historical Section War Cabinet Secretariat. The British Broadcasting Corporation. The Librarians of Hendon and Westminster Libraries and the War Museum.

CONTENTS

CHAPTER		PAGE
1	Early Days.	1
2	Mobilization. August, 1914—March, 1915.	12
3	Arrival in France and Initiation to Warfare. March—May, 1915.	17
4	Festubert. May, 1915.	21
5	Three " Cushy " Months. June—August, 1915.	27
6	Loos. September, 1915.	31
7	Wet Days. October, 1915—January, 1916.	44
8	The Affair at the Copse. February—March, 1916.	51
9	Carency and Souchez. March—May, 1916.	57
10	Vimy. May 21st, 1916.	61
11	Souchez Again. May—July, 1916.	72
12	The Trek to the Somme. July—September, 1916.	75
13	High Wood. September 15th, 1916.	77
14	Butte de Warlencourt. September—October, 1916.	83
15	Ypres. October, 1916.	91
16	The Bluff, Craters and Hill 60. October 19th—December 26th, 1916.	93
17	Winter in the Salient. December 27th, 1916—April 8th, 1917.	102
18	The Spoilbank. April 9th—May 11th, 1917.	109
19	Trek and Training. May 12th—June 5th, 1917.	112
20	Messines, White Chateau and Foret Farm. June 6th—September 7th, 1917.	114
21	Glencorse Wood and Cryer Farm. September 8th—September 16th, 1917.	122
22	Arras. September—November 26th, 1917.	128
23	Bourlon Wood. November 27th, 1917—February, 1918.	130
24	2/7th Battalion. Formation and Training. 1914—January, 1917.	143
25	Trenches and Working Parties. January, 27th—May, 1917.	150
26	Bullecourt. May—June, 1917.	157
27	Croisilles, Cherisy and Metz. June 16th—August 24th, 1917.	162
28	Ypres, Poelcappelle and Passchendaele. August 24th, 1917—January 31st, 1918.	165
29	Amalgamated Battalion. February—April 3rd, 1918.	184
30	Villers Bretonneux. April, 1918.	187
31	Henencourt and Baisieux. May 2nd—July 31st, 1918.	192
32	Malard Wood and Chipilly Ridge. August 2nd—August 13th, 1918.	197
33	War of Movement. August 13th—September 26th, 1918.	202

CHAPTER	CONTENTS	PAGE
34	Final Months. October—November, 1918	209
35	Peruwelz.	215
36	7th (Reserve Battalion) The London Regiment.	217
37	Epilogue to 1914–1918.	219
38	Post-War Activities. 1920–1935.	221
39	Further Reorganisation. 1935–1939.	225
40	Second World War. 1939–1945.	228
41	The Old Comrades' Association.	239

APPENDICES

A	Honorary Colonels of the Regiment.	243
B	Regimental Colours and Battle Honours.	243
C	Officers and Men Who Died in the Great War.	245
D	Honours List.	253
E	Memorials and Standards.	256
F	Letter from Viscount Hampden to Lieut.-Col. Green.	257
G	Regimental Titles and Commanding Officers.	258
H	Commanding Officers and Battery Commanders. 32nd Searchlight Regiment.	259

LIST OF ILLUSTRATIONS

Colonel Edward Faux, C.M.G., V.D.	*Frontispiece*
A Private in the 3rd Loyal London Volunteers, 1804.	*Facing page* 6
7th London Officers at Watford, 1914	39
7th London Sergeants at Eastney, 1914.	39
Regimental Colours.	86
Lieut.-Col. C. J. Salkeld Green, D.S.O., M.C., T.D.	102
Lieut.-Col. C. W. Berkeley, T.D.	102
Lieut.-Col. S. L. Hosking.	102
Maj. H. D. Barnes, O.B.E., T.D., D.L.	102
7th London Officers of the Reserve Battalion.	134
7th London South African Officers.	134
7th London Officers of the 2nd Battalion.	150
7th London N.C.O.'s of the 2nd Battalion.	150
Maj. Sir K. O. Peppiatt, K.B.E., M.C.	166
Maj. Allan D. Laurie, T.D.	166
Maj. H. S. Green.	166
Lieut.-Col. K. J. Pearce.	166
Lieut.-Col. A. E. F. Barnes.	166
Brig. E. E. F. Baker, C.B.E., D.S.O., M.C., T.D., D.L., A.D.C.	166
Lieut.-Col. L. S. Davis, T.D.	230
Col. J. Trevor	230
328 Searchlight Battery H.Q. Staff, 1944.	230

CHAPTER ONE
EARLY DAYS

WE live at such a rapid pace in these days that very few seem to trouble about men and things of a past generation. The affairs of the past are generally ignored in the rough and tumble of everyday life. Soldiers, and others who have served in H.M. Forces, however, form a large section of the public who do not share this indifference. To them, records of events are of the deepest interest and the noble history built up by their predecessors is never forgotten.

Let us emulate this spirit by remembering that we ourselves have a history of which we may be proud.

The Train Bands of the City of London were divided into Companies and we claim descent from the "Yellow Company" who carried colours composed of a yellow background with the cross of St. George in the top left-hand corner and two five-pointed black stars placed diagonally in the lower right-hand corner of the flag.

The Train Bands, which were in reality Militia under another name, were always conspicuous for national spirit.

In 1585 its troops were sent to assist the Dutch in their War of Independence. At this time "My Lady Greensleeves" was played by the Train Bands in slow time. This same piece of music, played in quick time, became the march of the Regiment during its active service, 1914-18. Thus, after a lapse of over three hundred years, "My Lady Greensleeves" was again played in Flanders by troops raised in the City of London.

In 1589, one thousand of the Train Bands helped to seat Henry of Navarre on the throne of France ; and in 1596 the Lord Mayor twice raised one thousand men, completely armed, in less than twelve hours to help the French against the Spaniards.

It is well known how nobly the City answered the appeal to its patriotism when Spain sent her formidable Armada to, as she thought, crush England.

The City Train Bands took part in the Great Civil War and were in action on the side of Parliament at the Battle of Edgehill, 1642.

In the year 1798, when the Regiment became known as The Loyal London and also the Temple Bar and St. Paul's Association, colours were presented on the steps of St. Paul's by Mrs. Sylvester, wife of the Common Sergeant, and these were consecrated by the Rev. Thomas Bowin, Chaplain to the Association.

Under the Command of Lieut.-Col. Jasper Atkinson, in the presence of H.M. George III, the Regiment attended a ceremonial parade at Hyde Park in 1799. Turning out over four hundred strong they must have looked very impressive in their scarlet tunics with crossbelts and white buckskin breeches. The helmet was very high, trimmed back and halfway down the front with fur, on the left side a large brush of red feathers, and it is recorded that the Regimental badge, a crown and garter, was worn on the right side. All buttons were marked T.B. and S.P.

The Regiment was probably disbanded in 1802 at the time of the Peace of Amiens, but came to life again in 1803 as the Third Regiment of Loyal London Volunteers with Headquarters in Bridewell.

An ensign in the Temple Bar and St. Paul's Association, gazetted in 1799, was Henry Bates Smith who later became a lieutenant in the 3rd Loyal London Volunteers. One hundred years later his grandson, the Rev. Cooper Smith, D.D., was acting chaplain to the 3rd London. It is entirely due to this family that the Corps owes the preservation of the Regimental Colours which at present rest at headquarters.

History tells us that the 3rd London, in common with other Volunteer Corps of this period, was ultimately compelled to cease all military training owing to the policy of the Government of the day.

About 1859 a call came for a further revival of the Volunteer Movement and the following is an extract from the " Leader and Saturday Analyst " of May 12th, 1860 :

> " After taking a prominent part in public agitation on the importance of taking up arms, Mr. A. B. Richards called a meeting at St. Martin's Hall at which Sir Charles Napier presided. Subsequently Mr. Richards became Colonel, and it would appear that to him should go the honour of being the originator of the Volunteer Movement in 1859."

With the revival of the Volunteer Movement, the name of the Regiment became the 3rd City of London Rifle Volunteers with Headquarters at 79, Farringdon Street and the chosen motto of " LABOR OMNIA VINCIT." Due to its past history and associations, the Regiment was extremely proud to be one of the very few allowed the honour of marching through the City of London with fixed bayonets, drums beating and Colours flying. In the Army list of June 1861, in addition to the name of the above mentioned Mr. A. B. Richards as major, are twelve captains including the name of Capt. R. P. Laurie, nine lieutenants, three ensigns and one surgeon. All commissions dated April 26th, 1861.

The Regiment was the first "Working Men's" Corps to be started and the wisdom of allowing the men to keep their arms in their own homes was severely questioned.

Major, subsequently Col. A. B. Richards, commanded the 3rd London from 1861–67.

In 1866, some 2,000 London Volunteers took part in a combined march through London ; and the 3rd London, in their scarlet tunics, received favourable comment. In the same year, Col. Richards described the Regiment as a hardy plant which had undergone many hardships owing to the lack of a drill hall. He spoke of the Regiment being self-supporting except for the amounts received during the previous six years of £100 from the City and £10 from the Skinners' Company. That these remarks laid a good foundation is witnessed by the fact that three years later, prizes, in addition to those given by the officers of the Regiment, were provided by the Ward of Farringdon, The Skinners', Merchant Taylors' and Scriveners' Companies, and these were presented at the Guildhall by Lord Napier. Later, in 1894, additional prizes came from the Grocers', Mercers', Saddlers', Fishmongers' and Salters' Companies ; these Companies continued their support to the Regiment up to the time of the Great War and in 1937 the Regiment was "adopted" by the Saddlers' Company.

The customary toast at all functions in those days was : " Prosperity and Long Life to the 3rd City of London Rifle Volunteers."

The loss, by retirement, of Col. Bates Richards, cast a temporary gloom over the Regiment, which he had helped to revive and which benefited largely by his hard work and untiring energy.

It was proposed that he should hold an honorary colonelcy, but this he declined on the grounds that a man of rank and wealth should fill this position. He was succeeded in the command by Major R. P. Laurie in 1867, and later Col. Bates Richards was presented with an inkstand of kettle drums mounted on a tripod of rifles in miniature.

The uniform at this time was scarlet with buff facings, as worn by the old Train Bands. In memory of this and of Queen Victoria appointing H.R.H. The Duke of Clarence and Avondale as Hon. Colonel of the 3rd London, the Officers of the Regiment were permitted to wear scarlet lanyards, an honour which is still observed.

Later, H.M. King George V presented to the Regiment a portrait of H.R.H. the late Duke of Clarence and Avondale, K.G., K.P., A.D.C., Hon. Colonel of the 3rd London, 1890–1892.

According to Col. Crossman, V.D., late 3rd London, the head-dress consisted of a bearskin with a red plume as part of the uniform in 1863. In undress, the kepi, scarlet with a white band, was worn by all ranks.

with a gilt grenade in front. The bearskin was relinquished in 1864 and the kepi was worn on all parades until the shako was adopted. Later, in 1881, a black glengarry with streamers was worn, on the left side a rosette with a silver grenade with the figure 3 in the centre. Two smaller grenades were worn on the collar.

1861   1911

3rd LONDON RIFLES   7th (City of London) Battalion
THE LONDON REGIMENT

Lord Napier became Hon. Colonel of the Regiment in 1868 and remained as such until 1890. He took part in the Indian Mutiny and joined the expedition to China.

The rapid and complete success of his expedition to Abyssinia, in which he stormed Magdala, raised him to the peerage as Lord Napier of Magdala. For a time he was Commander-in-Chief in India (1870–76) and was also Governor of Gibraltar.

While in India he sent home to the Regiment a Challenge Cup to be shot for. From Gibraltar he returned home to lead the 3rd London past the Queen upon the occasion of the Royal Review at Windsor in 1881.

In 1883 he was promoted a Field-Marshal and in 1889, when Constable of the Tower, he presented a petition personally to the Corporation of the City of London with a view to obtaining new Headquarters for the Regiment. This was his last public appearance.

Field-Marshal Lord Napier of Magdala, G.C.B., G.C.S.I., passed away in 1890, and the 3rd London lined the street when he was carried to his grave in St. Paul's Cathedral.

Later a statue of Lord Napier of Magdala in Waterloo Place was unveiled by H.R.H. the Prince of Wales, while recently, in honour of his memory, the new Regimental Headquarters at Grove Park were named after him.

Major, subsequently Col., R. P. Laurie, C.B., V.D., who succeeded Col. Bates Richards in 1867, was educated at Tonbridge and connected with the banking business. In 1859 he joined the ranks of the Victoria Rifles. He was given command of a 3rd London company in 1861 and obtained his majority in 1864. In 1887 he received the Companionship of the Bath, and at Aldershot in 1899 rode at the head of the battalion past the late Emperor Frederick of Germany at the Grand Review.

In consequence of prolonged ill-health he had to vacate active command after nearly a quarter of a century and was immediately made Hon. Colonel (1892) in succession to H.R.H. the late Duke of Clarence. He remained Hon. Colonel until 1904, and a year later passed peacefully away at Canterbury.

Col. R. P. Laurie, C.B., M.P., was one of the first to receive the Volunteer Officers Decoration. He sat in Parliament for Canterbury (1879–1886) and for Bath until 1892. In civil capacity he was a J.P. for Kent and for one year (1887) was Master of the Saddlers' Company.

In 1883 a detachment visited Mystole Park, Canterbury, on the invitation of Col. Laurie, C.B., to keep the ground for the inspection of the East Kent Regiment; in 1887 he presented a silver cigarette box to the Officers' Mess to commemorate his completion of twenty years' service.

Lieut. R. M. Laurie, his son, held a commission in the Regiment; later he transferred to the Royal East Kent Mounted Rifles (East Kent Yeomanry) and subsequently commanded the 2nd East Anglian Brigade, R.F.A. After the 1914–18 War he became their Hon. Colonel—he gained the D.S.O. at Gaza. Capt. K. S. Laurie, a cousin of the late Col. R. P. Laurie, C.B., V.D., was in command of " K " Company of the 3rd London at Hammersmith, having joined the Regiment in 1887. He was the recipient of the V.D. and subsequently commanded the East India Railway Volunteers.

His brother, Maj. Allan D. Laurie, T.D., joined the 3rd just prior to the death of Queen Victoria, and although his commission was made out in her name, H.M. King Edward VII signed it. He commanded " A " Company of the 3rd London and went overseas with the Regiment in 1915 in command of " B " Company ; he served until 1918 when he was retired owing to wounds received at the Battle of Loos, and in that year received the Territorial Decoration.

Two cousins of Maj. A. D. Laurie, T.D., were subalterns in the Regiment, Mr. R. A. Laurie and Mr. P. R. Laurie ; the latter transferred to the Scots Greys in 1902 and served during the Great War, being mentioned six times in dispatches ; subsequently he became Maj.-Gen. Sir P. R. Laurie, K.C.V.O., C.B.E., D.S.O., and was for twenty years Assistant-Commissioner of the Metropolitan Police at Scotland Yard, and later Provost Marshal of Great Britain. All the above-mentioned members of the Laurie family have held office as Master of the Saddlers' Company. From the foregoing it will be appreciated that the Laurie family have served both the 3rd and 7th London and the country with distinction. Particularly, the late Col. R. P. Laurie should be remembered for the great part he played in founding the first Working Men's Corps, the old 3rd London. The Regiment were again at Canterbury in 1887 enjoying an Easter Camp, while in 1890 and 1891, Easter Camps were at Eastbourne and Shorncliffe, respectively—Aldershot was the venue in 1892.

Col. C. E. Boyle, who succeeded Col. R. P. Laurie, C.B., V.D., in 1892, remained in command for three years. Company dinners, smoking concerts and church parades at St. Bride's Church, Fleet Street, took place regularly in these and subsequent years as part of the life of the Regiment, as well as parades for drills at Regent's Park, the Tower Ditch and Gray's Inn Square. Prize distributions and half-yearly inspections took place at the Guildhall. Annual inspections were held at the Horse Guards Parade.

During 1893 many interesting events are recorded, and it would appear that the Regiment had a busy time. Most important of these events was the first issue of the Volunteer Officers Decoration, which was conferred upon the following officers for long and meritorious service:

The Hon. Col. R. P. Laurie, C.B.
Lieut.-Col. and Hon. Col. Mortimer Hancock.
Maj. and Hon. Lieut.-Col. D. Pollock.
Captain and Hon. Maj. R. Doll.
Captain and Hon. Maj. J. Hepworth.
Lieut.-Col. W. Venn (retired).
Lieut.-Col. and Hon. Col. A. Boyce (retired).
Maj. and Hon. Lieut.-Col. A. Crossman (retired).
Maj. and Hon. Lieut.-Col. J. Cawston (retired).
Surgeon and Hon. Surgeon Maj. C. Bennett, M.D. (retired).

This decoration, worn with 1½-inch green ribbon, consisted of laurels, oval shape, with the letters " V.R." in centre surmounted by a crown, in silver gilt.

At this time Parliament were discussing " badges for non-commissioned officers and men for over twenty years' service "; it is on record that the Regiment possessed forty-seven members, exclusive of officers, with over twenty years' service.

With the Queen's seventy-sixth birthday honours list came the announcement that the new Volunteer Medal would be bestowed upon all N.C.O.'s and men of the forces who had accomplished twenty years' service.

The 3rd London had the proud distinction of creating a record for the Metropolis, when over sixty past and present members received this decoration.

So flourishing were the affairs of the Regiment that a Regimental Gazette made its appearance and ran for two years with a monthly issue. Every credit for this production is due to the appointed Committee of Management who were :

Editor	Capt. Willoughby
Sub-Editor	2nd Lieut. W. Mudford
Treasurer	Capt. Wilson Fox
Secretary	Capt. C. W. Berkeley
Publisher	Capt. E. Faux
Advertising	2nd Lieut. Eliot

The marriage of the Duke of York to Princess May of Teck took place on July 6th, 1893, and the Regiment provided a guard of honour of three officers, four sergeants and one hundred rank and file ; the officers on parade were Capt. T. C. Ekin, Capt. C. W. Berkeley, and 2nd Lieut. Eliot. Another guard of honour was provided upon the occasion of the foundation stone at St. Bride's Institute being laid by H.R.H. the Prince of Wales.

Prizes were as usual distributed at the Guildhall upon this occasion in the presence of Brig.-Col. J. Trotter and Staff of the East London Infantry Brigade. At the annual inspection by Maj.-Gen. Lord Methuen, the total strength on parade was 711.

Easter Camp was at Chatham and the following year (1894) at Winchester.

Upon the visit of H.R.H. Princess Christian to Soho in 1894, a guard of honour was provided, and in the same year a team was entered for the first time for The Daily Telegraph Cup under the command of Capt. C. W. Berkeley; the team under adverse conditions put up a creditable show. At the Royal Military Tournament five sergeants and 60 rank and file gave a display under the command of Capt. C. W. Berkeley.

Col. Boyle in 1895 was promoted to command of the Western Counties Brigade, and Col. Mortimer Hancock, V.D., took command of the Regiment.

Col. Mortimer Hancock had been connected with the 3rd London from its earliest days; gazetted to the corps in 1869 he became captain in 1872 and a major in 1888.

Another officer of this period who merits special mention is Col. A. W. Boyce, V.D. Joining the 34th Foot, he saw service in the Crimea and was in possession of five medals and several clasps. In 1868 he was appointed adjutant to the 3rd London in succession to Capt. Furnivall and for many years was most popular in the Regiment. After 17 years he was appointed in 1885 second in command, in which capacity he served for six years.

The Regiment being affiliated to the K.R.R.'s (60th Rifles) drew upon this famous Corps for its adjutant and permanent staff; Maj. H. D. Banks, who succeeded Col. A. W. Boyce as adjutant, had seen service in the Afghan War of 1878, and he in turn was followed in 1894 by Capt. E. W. Thistlethwayte of the 2nd Batt. K.R.R.'s, then stationed at Gibraltar. In 1900 Capt. L. C. D. Jenner became adjutant, followed by Capt. W. J. Long and Capt. G. F. B. Hankey. The association with the K.R.R.'s was broken in 1911, when Capt. Foster of the Sherwood Foresters (Notts and Derby Regiment) became adjutant.

Upon the occasion of the Jubilee Parade in 1897 the Regiment provided officers and 100 rank and file.

Sheerness was visited in 1896 for camp and in 1899 Colchester at Easter. During the latter year the 3rd London carried off two tug-o'-war events at the Royal Military Tournament, the 110 stone and the catch weights. Also during this year three officers and 100 other ranks were attached to the 2nd Royal Highlanders (Black Watch) for training at Aldershot.

During the South African War the Regiment sent several officers and men to the serving Company of the King's Royal Rifle Corps at the front; subsequently the Regiment received from H.M. King Edward VII the right to bear the honour " South Africa 1900-1902." A contingent of the Regiment under the command of Capt. C. W. Berkeley also served in the City Imperial Volunteers (C.I.V.'s).

Capt. C. W. Berkeley was wounded in the mouth at Doornkeep, and this untimely wound prevented him taking part in the scrap at Diamond Hill.

The following is an extract from a letter written home from Pretoria : " The 3rd London men stuck it like bricks, and Capt. Berkeley said how proud he was of them."

Recuperating from his wound at Johannesburg, Capt. Berkeley was attended by his servant, Pte. Boustead, who wrote the following description of Johannesburg : " Take a few blocks of buildings from Fenchurch Street, let loose the population of Whitechapel into it, with the Mohawk Minstrels walking about in very naughty dresses."

The Regiment were on duty in Fleet Street on the occasion of the official welcome to the C.I.V.'s on their return from the South African War, keeping back the huge and disorderly crowd of too enthusiastic citizens, some of whom were killed in the crush.

During the period 1893 to 1905 great attention was paid to shooting, the number of marksmen in the Regiment increased from 82 in 1895 to an average of nearly 400 in the years 1901–5. Among the distinguished shots then were Sergt. Stevens and L/Cpl. G. Jones, each being the best shot of the Regiment four and three years respectively, thus earning the coveted crossed rifles and crown in silver. Among the best company shots of this period appear the names of Colour-Sergt. Luck, Sergts. Fryer, Patrickson, Joel and Middleton, all earning crossed rifles and star in silver. In addition to the above, the names of Drummer Eyers, Sergt. H. Price, Cpl. Lee and Pte. W. Jordan appear frequently among the prizewinners. The latter subsequently attained the rank of sergeant, and, in recent years, after fourteen years (1922–1936) as a Member of Parliament in New Zealand, resigned to take up the duties of High Commissioner for that Dominion, in London, a position he still holds. The Officers Challenge Cup was won four times by Capt. and Hon. Maj. Doll and three times by Lieut. F. S. Grimston.

Among the officers of this period who gave long and faithful service and served the Regiment with distinction was Capt. C. W. Berkeley, who joined the 3rd London in 1889 and became O.C. of " E " Company. He served in the South African War and received the Queen's Medal and three clasps, and the Coronation Medal in 1902. In the year 1908 he was the recipient of the Territorial Decoration and granted the rank of Lieut.-Colonel.

When the Great War broke out he was still serving in the Regiment and he commanded the Second Battalion of the 7th London in 1914. He was still in command when the Regiment proceeded overseas in January, 1917, but had to relinquish command the following April owing to an adverse medical board. After a short while in England he returned to France and was employed as Town Major in Winnizele. He served the Old Comrades as a trustee until his death, which occurred in 1923.

The Regiment lost the services of a very fine officer when Maj. R. S. Doll, V.D., passed away in 1925 after 56 years' connection with the Regiment. Maj. W. Mudford, T.D. (Instructor of Musketry) of "C" Company, after 36 years with the Regiment, also passed away in 1925.

Maj. C. D. Enoch was another stalwart. Educated at Clifton, he saw long service with the 3rd and 7th London. He had a neat sense of humour, and his songs were always popular, particularly his rendering of the late Maj. Mudford's "Regimental Song." Maj. Enoch served throughout 1914–18 and for part of this time was Town Major of Bruay. Despite his age he served again in the Second World War as Public Relations Officer and had the distinction of being the oldest officer serving in France.

The well known Australian war correspondent, Mr. Eric Baume, in his book, "I Lived These Years," thus refers to him: "There was Enoch—Lt. Enoch wearing the badges of a long dead regiment and with rows of ribbons on his tunic—saluted even by younger Lt.-Cols. who persisted in calling him 'Sir.'"

He was a very popular President of the Old Comrades' Association, but his activities were suddenly cut short when he was killed on duty in an accident shortly after his return from France in 1940. He was succeded as President of the Association by Maj. H. D. Barnes, O.B.E., T.D., D.L., who for many years has been a trustee and life member and is the oldest surviving officer of the Regiment.

Col. M. Hancock, V.D., was succeeded in 1900 by Col. E. C. Stevenson, V.D., who in 1904 himself retired after 27 years' service. He originally belonged to the 7th Lancashire R.V.'s, being transferred to the 3rd in 1876 and promoted captain in 1881. In 1896 he became second in command with the rank of colonel. Immediately upon his retirement he became Hon. Colonel and remained as such until 1921. He was also Patron of the Old Comrades' Association and Chairman of the Prisoners of War Ladies' Committee.

An important event took place in 1903 when new Headquarters at Sun Street, E.C., were taken over; these premises were more spacious and provided better facilities for everyone. Great credit for this event must go to Col. E. C. Stevenson, V.D., as it was due to his energy that a large sum of money was raised for this object.

Capt. L. C. D. Jenner, during his period as adjutant, introduced "Field Training" in the true sense of the term, and the Regiment began to prepare itself to become a modern fighting unit. Under his successor, Capt. W. J. Long, training in night operations on Hampstead Heath and elsewhere took place. A staff ride for officers was held at Bungay,

Suffolk, and courses of winter training for officers and N.C.O.'s were held at Linford, Essex, during the week ends.

During the early years of the twentieth century it is no exaggeration to say that the Regiment realised the true object of its existence; despite the scoffs and jeers of pacifists and official apathy, at times approaching antipathy, they did all in their power to prepare themselves for what they regarded as inevitable, that was, war with Germany, and praise and credit must be given to all those Old Comrades, unknown to fame, the fruits of whose early labours can now be seen in the Battle Honours on our Colours.

In 1902 Field-Marshal Lord Roberts inspected the Regiment at Aldershot. The Regiment took a share in lining the route for the Coronation of King Edward VII and in 1903 took part in a military parade, held to bring London Volunteers to the notice of the public.

Newhaven and Seaford were among the places visited about this time for camp, and exercises were held at Chingford, Tadworth and Linford.

Col. T. C. Ekin took command in 1904 and was the recipient in that year of the Volunteer Long Service Medal.

On the social side company dinners, dances and concerts were held at Headquarters and various City licensed premises ; at one time functions were held as far afield as The Horns, Kennington, and the Horse Shoe Hotel, Tottenham Court Road.

Under Lord Haldane's scheme of reorganisation in 1908 far reaching changes took place in the Volunteer movement.

The title of the Regiment was changed to the 7th (City of London) Battalion The London Regiment. Col. T. C. Ekin remained in command during the change-over and retired in 1912 upon completion of his service and was succeeded by Maj. The Viscount Hood, late of the Grenadier Guards. During this period red sashes for sergeants were introduced.

With the renaming of the Regiment and in honour of its past record, coupled with its strength, H.M. King Edward VII presented new colours to the Regiment at Windsor Castle in June, 1909.

Between 1909 and the Great War the Regiment went to Salisbury Plain, Borden, Camberley, West Lulworth and Eastbourne for summer camp, the average attendance being 600. During the years 1912, 1913 and 1914 Easter Camps were at the Royal Marine Artillery Barracks at Eastney, near Portsmouth.

To line the route at the funeral of H.M. King Edward VII the Regiment provided ten officers and 115 other ranks, and the Regiment were represented at the Royal Review in 1913 and also in the Lord Mayor's show of that year as in previous years.

CHAPTER TWO

August, 1914—March, 1915
MOBILIZATION

MANY of those whom this History concerns were killed in action, others returned to " Blighty " to die at a later date ; they were buried in the accepted style, and it is worth noting that the great majority of these burials were attended by their former comrades, who were present at the graveside to pay their last respects.

These men had behind them the splendid tradition of the Regiment ; many were men who in time of peace had prepared for War and had seen service with the Regiment in the days of the 3rd London.

It was their privilege to grumble and grouse. Nevertheless, they were justly proud of their nickname " Shiny Seventh " and even in the midst of battle duties would " Spit and Shine."

They fought at Festubert, Loos, Vimy, and High Wood ; many passed beyond recall at the Butte de Warlencourt in a fruitless attack against a position which, although attacked in turn by several divisions, was never captured in combat. Many, fortunate to survive together with those wounded in early days, returned and fought again at Ypres and Cambrai.

These men were about to enjoy on August 2nd, 1914 the pleasures of a Summer Camp at Eastbourne, where the battalion arrived at 4 p.m. and were back again at London Bridge by midnight, dismissed to their homes with orders to " stand by."

Mobilization came on August 5th, 1914, the men were accommodated in Curtain Road and Scrutton Street Schools, transport in Broad Street goods yard, and the officers at Armfields Hotel. The battalion at this time formed part of the 2nd London Infantry Brigade of the First London Division.

A week later, after Col. E. Faux, V.D., and the adjutant had addressed the battalion, Viscount Hood asked if the 7th would volunteer for service abroad " as a Battalion " ; practically the whole of the battalion volunteered.

It was August 20th when the battalion moved off from Sun Street at 8.30 a.m. for Bisley, which was reached after three days' marching via Wimbledon and Weybridge, where halts were made for the night.

At Bisley, on the last day of August, Gen. Sir Ian Hamilton inspected the battalion. Col. E. Faux, V.D., assumed command of the Regiment on September 7th in place of Lieut.-Col. Lord Hood, who, owing to an adverse medical board decision as to his health and fitness, relinquished command.

Saying goodbye to Bisley on September 8th, the battalion moved off to East Grinstead, where they arrived two days later after spending one night at Great Bookham and another at Reigate.

After a short stay, a move was made on the 16th to Crowborough where the battalion was under canvas ; heavy rains coupled with high winds made the first night anything but pleasant.

It was not until November 5th that the battalion left the tents behind them and entrained at Crowborough for billets at Watford which were reached at 2.30 p.m.

Now part of the 4th London Infantry Brigade of the 2nd London Division, commanded by Maj.-Gen. Sir C. St. L. Barter, K.C.B., C.V.O., the battalion was destined to stay in the Watford area for the next four months, which after the many recent changes proved quite a relief, and many happy days ensued here which will not be forgotten in a hurry.

The " Shiny Seventh " became extremely popular and many lifelong friendships were made ; to this day reunions are frequent. Several " Shinies " returned after the War to make their home in the Watford area.

One break occurred in the Watford training when, at the end of November, 26 officers and 750 men went to Braintree for a spell of trench digging.

On Boxing Day all ranks were anticipating various festivities but they received a nasty shock—at 4.30 a.m. a delayed message came through. " Alarm, Emergency Move." Ammunition was issued to the first 500 on parade, and this detachment moved off at 7.30 a.m. under the command of Maj. H. D. Barnes, and took part in what became known as the famous forced march to Berkhampsted and back. Cold rain and sleet did not improve matters and it was 4 p.m. before this detachment returned, angry that their efforts had been wasted on a fruitless excursion.

The remainder of the battalion was more fortunate ; they marched to Watford, performed the operation of entraining, and returned to billets at noon.

There were many false alarms of departure for France and many fond farewells were taken. " Surprise Movement Stunts " provided both amusement and annoyance.

New Year's Day, 1915, started with an inspection at Cassiobury Park of the battalion by Brig.-Gen. G. J. Cuthbert, C.B., C.M.G., Scots Guards. Rain poured down for the three hours that mattered ; however, the appearance of the battalion met with general approval.

About this time the Platoon system was inaugurated, the number of companies reduced from eight to four ; the four senior Colour-Sergeants were made Company Sergeant-Majors and the other four became C.Q.M.S.'s. Colour-Sergt. Hardy, of the Sherwood Foresters, was appointed Regimental Sergeant-Major to fill the position vacated by R.S.M. H. E. Lydiart who had been promoted Captain.

"H" and "E" Coy's became "A" Coy. under Capt. W. Casson.
"A" and "F" ,,   ,,   "B" ,,   ,, Capt. A. D. Laurie.
"G" and "D" ,,   ,,   "C" ,,   ,, Capt. C. J. Salkeld Green.
"C" and "B" ,,   ,,   "D" ,,   ,, Maj. H. D. Barnes.

The whole division took part in a "Concentration March" on January 4th, and were inspected on the road near St. Albans by Gen. Sir Ian Hamilton.

Five days later the battalion were again at Cassiobury Park for inspection, on this occasion by the Divisional Commander, Maj.-Gen. Sir C. St. L. Barter, K.C.B., C.V.O.

February opened with another "Divisional Concentration March." This entailed a march of about 25 miles, with an inspection by Gen. Codrington at Redbourne.

Regt. Sergt.-Maj. H. E. Lydiart had been gazetted captain in January, and on the evening of February 12th at the "Rose and Crown" he was the guest at a dinner held by the sergeants, at which he was presented with a gold watch. The dinner was given by the sergeants to members of the Watford Conservative Club in appreciation of their allowing N.C.O.'s the use of the club as Hon. Members and the club was presented with an illuminated roll of all N.C.O.'s of the battalion.

From now on everyone was being fitted out with all the necessaries which troops proceeding overseas would need ; the battalion had a medical inspection, night digging exercises, and attended a demonstration of bomb throwing at Radlett.

At last the great day arrived, no rumour this time ; this was the real departure parade. The 7th fell in by half-battalions at 9 p.m. and at midnight on March 16th, 1915, proceeded from Watford to Southampton, where the first half arrived at 7 a.m. and the second half, under Maj. C. D. Enoch, arrived at 8.30 a.m. on St. Patrick's Day, March 17th; the day was spent by the troops in the sheds. Lieut. G. D. Roche was detailed as Q.M. of the transport the "Empress Queen," which took on board at 7 p.m. 30 officers and 1,065 other ranks of the battalion. By a strange coincidence one of the embarkation officers was Maj. E. W. Thistlewayte, of the K.R.R. Corps, who had formerly been an adjutant of the 3rd London : he came on board to wish the battalion good luck and to have a chat with those officers who had served with him during his adjutancy. It was 10 p.m. when the ship cast off, the night clear and the sea calm.

The transport (men, horses and vehicles) crossed over in the S.S. "Blackwell," under the care of Lieut. T. Rushworth.

ROLL OF OFFICERS
Who went to France with the 1st Battalion, March 17th, 1915

*Col. E. Faux, V.D.	Returned to England Sept., 1916.	Commanding Officer. Mentioned in Dispatches. Awarded C.M.G. 14.1.16.
*Maj. C. D. Enoch, T.D.	... ...	Appointed Town Major of Bruay. Awarded French Legion of Honour.
*Maj. H. D. Barnes	Seriously W. at Festubert 16.5.15.	O.C. "D" Company.
Capt. R. T. Foster	... ...	Adjutant (Sherwood Foresters). Mentioned in Dispatches. Subsequently awarded D.S.O.
*Capt. W. Casson	K. at Loos 25.9.15.	O.C. "A" Company. Mentioned in Dispatches.
*Capt. A. D. Laurie	Seriously W. at Loos 25.9.15.	O.C. "B" Company. Mentioned in Dispatches.
Capt. C. J. Salkeld Green	... ...	O.C. "C" Company. Subsequently Commanding Officer. Awarded M.C. 3.6.16; D.S.O. 4.6.17. Croix de Guerre (Belgian) 2.2.18. Mentioned in Dispatches 1.1.16, 25.5.17, 24.12.17 and 25.5.18.
Capt. C. E. King-Church	D. of W's Loos 25.9.15.	"D" Company.
Capt. J. G. H. Budd	Twice W., 9.5.15 and Aug., 1918.	After Festubert appointed to a Staff position and returned to Battalion Aug., 1916. Also served with 2/7th.
Lieut. J. H. B. Fletcher	D. of W's at Festubert 13.5.15.	Founder of the "Fletcher Fund." "D" Company.
Lieut. F. M. Davis	W. 13.2.16. P. of W. Vimy 21.5.16.	"D" Company.
Lieut. R. D. Maret-Tims	To Hospital, May, 1915.	"A" Company
Capt. H. G. Head	To Hospital, April 1915.	In 1917-18 served in France with 5th Field Survey Coy. R.E.
Lieut. D. E. Ward	... ...	Machine-Gun Officer. Transferred to R.F.C.

* Signifies officers who served with the Regiment in the days of the 3rd London.
W.= Wounded. K.= Killed. D. of W's.= Died of Wounds. P. of W.= Prisoner of War.

Roll of Officers who went to France with the 1st Battalion, March 17th, 1915—*continued*

Lieut. H. M. Rushworth	W. April, 1915, and at Loos 25.9.15.	" A " Company. Transferred to R.F.C. W. again and taken P. of W.
Lieut. T. Rushworth ...	W. at Vimy 21.5.16. K. at High Wood 16.9.16.	Transport Officer. Appointed O.C. " A " Company 16.4.16. Mentioned in Dispatches.
2nd Lieut. J. L. Head...	W. 14.2.16 ...	Transferred 1916 to R.F.C. as Pilot. After the War to Royal Sussex Regt.
2nd Lieut. A. A. Ferguson	W. at Festubert 16.5.15. D. of W's Loos 25.9.15.	" A " Company.
2nd Lieut. A. J. Smith	K. at Loos 25.9.15	" B " Company.
2nd Lieut. W. Smith ...	Left prior to Loos	To Indian Army.
Capt. H. E. Lydiart ...	... ...	" B " Company. Left Battalion April, 1916, and became Area Commandant.
Capt. E. Ball	Invalided home March, 1915.	" A " Company.
2nd Lieut. L. E. Rundell	W. at Vermelles 5.6.15. W. at Vimy 21.5.16. W. at High Wood 16.9.16. D. of W's at Cambrai 10.12.17	" C " Company. Awarded M.C. 24.2.16, and Bar 8.6.16. First Officer in the Division to receive Bar to M.C.
2nd Lieut. B. R. P. Brian Wood	K. 2.7.15 ... Bombing Accident.	" D " Company.
2nd Lieut. L. C. H. Squire	D. of W's at Festubert 13.5.15.	" C " Company.
2nd Lieut. J. S. Prince	K. at Loos 25.9.15	" A " Company.
2nd Lieut. W N. Culverwell	... ...	" D " Company. Divisional Trench Mortar Battery.
2nd Lieut. H. O. B. Roberts	D. of W's from Loos 18.11.15.	" A " Company. Awarded M.C. 21.10.15. First officer of the Battalion to be decorated. Mentioned in Dispatches.
2nd Lieut. A. R. K. Aitkens	Seriously W. at Festubert. D. of W's 31.5.15.	" B " Company.
2nd Lieut. L. A. L. Flower	D. of W's at the Butte-de-Warlencourt 7.10.16.	" D " Company.
Lieut. G. D. Roche ...	Taken ill on leave Nov., 1916. Eventually served with Res. Battn.	Quartermaster. Mentioned in Dispatches.
Capt. A. H. Bell, R.A.M.C. ...	... ...	Medical Officer.
M. Maurice A. Izambard		Interpreter (Joined at Le Havre).

CHAPTER THREE

March—May, 1915

ARRIVAL IN FRANCE AND INITIATION TO WARFARE

AT 6 a.m., on March 18th, 1915, a never-to-be-forgotten date, the battalion set foot on French soil at the great port of Le Havre, and marched through the docks to No. 6 Rest Camp. Here the troops were under canvas, the weather was bitterly cold and the wind threatened to lift the tents skyhigh at any moment.

It is recorded that at the dockside, one named Thomas tried out his French at a mobile canteen, only to be told by the lady in charge : " If you spoke English I should understand you much better ! "

The following day, without any regrets, the battalion left this " Rest Camp " and made their first acquaintance with wagons marked " *Huit Chevaux. Quarante Hommes.*"

It was nearly noon when the battalion, less two platoons of " D " Company who proceeded by a later train, entrained and travelling via Rouen, St. Omer and Hazebrouck, reached Berguette at 8 a.m. on the 20th.

Two days' supplies had been drawn, together with an iron ration, plus a grocery ration for the journey. The latter was " mislaid" en route. Nevertheless, at each stop the engine driver had a queue for hot water—so evidently the " boys " obtained some tea from somewhere.

At Berguette, after being complimented by the staff on their orderly detrainment, the battalion breakfasted in a field near the station and at 10 a.m. moved off via Lillers to Auchel which was reached at 4 p.m.

Auchel, almost devoid of shops, was a small bedraggled mining town with two large fosses near by, The battalion came to look upon Auchel for a time as " home from home " to which they returned at frequent intervals to enjoy the amenities of a bath at the coalmine. The troops were billeted in barns and miners' houses. A letter written home at the time by Pte. H. Hunt says : " The inhabitants are very kind to us, and give us delicious coffee in the morning for which they refuse payment."

It is interesting to note that apart from a small reinforcing draft in charge of 2nd Lieut. L. Flower, left behind at Le Havre, the strength of the battalion was 29 officers, 996 other ranks, and one interpreter (M. Izambard, better known as " Zambuk "), 66 horses and two machine-guns.

On March 22nd, the battalion paraded with the division and were inspected by Field-Marshal Sir John French. Gen. Sir L. Barter drew his attention to our transport, which he said was the best in the division.

On March 24th the battalion marched to Bethune; it was a long march in the mud and the weather was very cold. The destination was reached at 6 p.m. and the troops were quartered in the Montmorencie Caserne, the officers being in billets near the barracks. Officers' Mess and Headquarters were at No. 14, Avenue Rouget de Lisle.

The battalion was now at long last in touch with "the real thing," as at this time each company in turn spent a night on a working party in the Festubert area which was followed by a period of twenty-four hours in the line.

"A" Company, on March 26th, was the first of the Regiment to enter the line for duty; "B" Company did the first working party. "A" Company went up in two parties: Nos. 1 and 2 Platoons under Capt. W. Casson, Nos. 3 and 4 Platoons under Capt. E. Ball. They went in under the care of the 3rd Worcester Regiment, the Oxford and Bucks Light Infantry, and the Inniskilling Fusiliers. Men of these Regiments instructed "ours" in the gentle art of trench warfare—and real good chaps did our men find them. After twenty-four hours, " C " Company relieved " A "; and " D " relieved " B " Company working party. Then on the 28th, " B " Company went in the line and " A " went on working parties; by this method each company had one day in the line and one on working parties.

The first journey up the line will be remembered by most; particularly the "no smoking or talking order" which was put into operation at Gorre, about two miles in rear of the front line.

The following description is applicable to most of the Seventh. Traversing the Yellow Road, entirely devoid of cover—or so it felt to most—and crossing a field, one arrived at the breastworks, if fortunate without mishap, and all would be nice and quiet.

Upon an enemy digging or wiring party being observed, five rounds rapid fire would be ordered; in this way many of the Seventh fired their first shots of the war against the enemy. An early-morning strafe by the enemy gave the men their christening of shell fire. Generally speaking, the line was quiet except for sniping and a few bursts of gunfire.

"B" Company, under the command of Capt. A. D. Laurie, sustained the first casualty of the battalion when, on March 29th, Pte. E. Haddy, in an exposed position, became the victim of a sniper. He was buried in Gorre Wood, the Bishop of Khartoum officiating.

Each night, from now on, the battalion suffered one or two casualties. Pte. F. J. Becknell, " D " Company, was wounded while returning from the trenches, and Ptes. Snook and Taylor were wounded while on a working party.

It would be as well here to mention the names of a few landmarks which may recall memories ; in addition to " Brewery Post " there were " Dead Cow Farm," " Welsh Chapel," " The Keep " and " Tuning Fork " : most famous of all were probably Quinque Rue (to the troops " Kinky Roo ") and the " Orchard."

Life in Bethune was good, the shops were excellent. The Café du Globe was discovered and a concert was arranged at the theatre in the Rue Victor Hugo ; all troops in the town were invited and Lieut.-Q.M. G. D. Roche contributed three items ; later on he performed at the Opera House at a concert organised by the Divisional Chaplain.

At the end of March, " C " Company suffered casualties, Pte. S. W. Bowles being killed, and Sergt. A. A. Bodkin and Pte. C. A. Johnson wounded ; nevertheless, following the example set by Capt. C. J. S. Green, " C " Company in the trenches kept very cheerful. Ptes. Parker and T. Wade were both wounded on April 2nd, the latter dying of his wounds the following day. On Good Friday, the Bishop of London, Dr. Winnington Ingram, preached to the troops in Bethune.

The O.C. of the Inniskilling's expressed his opinion that " the men of the 7th behaved like veterans."

" D " Company, occupying a new breastwork without a parados, suffered further casualties as a result of a shell burst. Pte. F. N. Bosher was killed, and the following wounded during subsequent shelling : Ptes. J. K. Allan (afterwards died of wounds), J. I. F. Clark, J. Hart, S. B. Atkinson, F. Coulson, W. J. Roberts, J. D. Dalley, E. R. Dwelly, and E. W. Carew (subsequently died of his wounds and buried in Lillers Cemetery). During heavy enemy shelling on another part of the line held by " D " Company under Maj. H. D. Barnes, 2nd Lieut. B. R. Wood and Sergt. Rayner carried out some very good work and by their personal courage set a fine example to the men ; the stretcher bearers also did good work on this occasion under Pte. Burgess. Two days later Lieut. H. M. Rushworth received a gunshot wound in the left forearm and became the first officer casualty.

On April 7th the battalion left Bethune at 7 a.m., and marching via Chocques (" Chocs " to the troops) returned to Auchel for a " rest period " ; everyone was pleased to see the boys again.

The battalion enjoyed the pleasures of baths at the mine ; route marches, drill and training filled in the week, at the end of which it was inspected by Gen. Sir Douglas Haig, and on the following day, the 14th, the battalion paraded at 2.15 p.m. and moved off to Allouagne where they remained in billets for a week, before returning to Bethune to occupy the schools in Rue Richelet.

The tradition of the "Shiny Seventh" was being maintained, and at this time a popular concert turn was Sergt. E. Mudge with his "Spit and Shine," sung to the air of "Sweet and Low," the words of which were as follows :

THE PSALM OF THE "SHINY SEVENTH"

Spit and shine, spit and shine, early every morning ;
Shine, shine, spit and shine, e'er we have finished yawning.
See how our buttons gleam in the sun,
That is the way the war will be won,
What does the Brigadier say ?
Spit and shine, my lads ; spit and shine, my lads ; shine.

Spit and shine, spit and shine, just as the day is breaking ;
Shine, shine, spit and shine, what though our bones are aching !
Tommy needs bathing but once in six weeks,
His neck may be dirty, his clothes full of leaks,
But orders are every day,
Spit and shine, my lads ; spit and shine, my lads ; shine.

Spit and shine, spit and shine, by go the weary hours ;
Shine, shine, spit and shine, in sunlight or in showers.
And when the order comes : "Over the Top,"
One thing is certain, they'll want us to stop,
Take out our "Soldiers' Friend"
And spit and shine, my lads ; spit and shine, my lads ; shine.

On April 20th Col. E. Faux and Headquarters Staff visited the trenches in the area then occupied by the 6th London with a view to taking over for a period, but this was cancelled. Two days later, Maj. C. D. Enoch, Capts. W. Casson and C. J. S. Green visited the same area and actually "ours" did take over for one day only and then marched back through Bethune and Chocques into billets at Lapugnoy.

Headquarters and Officers' Mess were here situated at the Mill House, which was very pleasantly surrounded by extensive woods. It is interesting to note here that these same quarters were reputed to have been occupied by British troops just after the Battle of Mont St. Jean (Waterloo) close upon one hundred years previously.

While here the battalion took the opportunity to enjoy a hot bath at the Auchel coalmine. Route marching and practice trench attacks filled in the time. Items of interest which occurred were as follows : Pte. Stroman went to hospital suffering with meningitis, Capt. H. G. Head was evacuated from hospital to base, and the machine-gun section became temporarily attached to the 6th London Infantry Brigade at Bethune.

CHAPTER FOUR

May, 1915

FESTUBERT

It was May 2nd when, after church parade, the C.O., adjutant and company commanders paid a visit to the trenches occupied by the London Irish. The following day the battalion moved off early and marched via Annezin and Bethune to the villages of Essars and Gorre where the troops went into billets.

On the night of the 4th the battalion moved into the line and relieved the London Irish in trenches near Meadow Farm. B.H.Q. was at Smelly Farm.

The following morning, at "stand to," Cpl. F. J. Odd was killed by a sniper and subsequently buried at Smelly Farm, Pte. Boecker was mortally wounded and L/Cpl. Hutton wounded.

Two days later further casualties were suffered when Pte. A. D. Eady of " C " Company was killed while on duty by a direct hit by the enemy on a breastwork. Sergt. R. Kiddle and Ptes. W. S. Stevens, C. R. Stanton, and R. Brill were wounded.

The battalion at this time appears to have been hungry for food and ammunition, to say nothing of work, as there appears to have been an " extra biscuit ration " and 84,000 rounds of S.A.A. sent up to the line, also 2,000 sandbags. Poor old carrying parties! Things were warming up, artillery was getting more active and L/Cpl J. B. Wakelin, " A " Company, was mortally wounded. The trenches were visited in the morning by the C.O. and a brigadier.

While on a patrol with a sergeant, Pte. Crossingham discovered the hide-out of a German sniper. Later on Maj. H. D. Barnes sniped a sniper and claimed a hit.

The 7th and 8th of May were busy days, all posts were strengthened; at night German transport could be heard rumbling along, and the shelling of our lines became much heavier.

On the 9th an attack on Aubers Ridge on our left opened, local shelling commenced at 4.45 a.m., followed by a heavy bombardment by our guns at 5 a.m., and at 5.40 a.m. all mortars in the area opened up, " B " Company experiencing some of our own shells falling short.

Capt. Budd spotted Germans crossing our front from right to left. One of our lads had his hand blown off and walked all the way to the dressing station.

The bombardment was the heaviest heard so far, although in volume and duration it was quite insignificant to that which followed later on. Our front came in for a good deal of enemy shelling, and back at Gorre where transport was packed ready to move at a moment's notice, shells were falling in and around the village. The field ambulance began to get busy when the wounded arrived. A ten-year-old French girl said to one of our officers : " My heart is wounded for the poor soldiers " ; she was kindly led away from the grim sights of the village.

H.R.H. The Prince of Wales, accompanied by two Staff Officers, climbed the church tower to observe the battle ; he also chatted to the wounded and passed his cigarettes around. A few days later many men of the battalion had the pleasure of seeing him on the march with the Guards.

Another 32,000 rounds of S.A.A. went up the line on the 10th ; the front line companies had been keeping up heavy rifle fire during the night to prevent the enemy repairing his wiring which had been cut by our artillery.

Lieuts. Maret-Tims and J. S. Prince, with a corporal and three men, had been out on patrol for two hours and all returned unhurt ; they brought in information of a stream of considerable width, the existence of which was unknown to us.

During the last few days the battalion suffered several casualties. Sergt. Graham was badly wounded, Ptes. A. Payne and S. Weeks were killed, and the following were wounded : Ptes. H. Thorpe, L. Emery, S. Palmer, H. Rige, W. Tidman, J. Childs, A. Scott, G. Burroughs, A. Z. Couk, P. Rose, Books, Brown and Parrington, also Corpls. W. Pallant and D. Long.

On May 11th the name 2nd London Division, which had already been changed to London Division, was again changed to the 47th (London) Division, and on this night the 8th London relieved " ours," who moved into Brigade Reserve at the Tuning Fork, when working parties became the " order of the night."

Snipers were for ever busy and casualties occurred, many on the road up from Festubert and in the open portion between the front and support lines. Between the latter it was decided to cut a communication trench and this work fell to the 7th and another regiment on the night of the 12th. The portion dug by " ours " was approved by the R.E. officer in charge and the party were about to start on their way back to Gorre when they were recalled to improve the other half of the trench which the other regiment had been working on. The troops were not too pleased at having, as they thought, this extra work pushed on to them, particularly as daylight was approaching. However, they put their backs into it and to encourage them Lieut. J. H. B. Fletcher and Lieut. L. C. H. Squire walked up and down on top saying, " The sooner the job is completed the sooner you will be back in billets." This extra work proved to be very unlucky for the 7th as, with the first streak of dawn, the enemy opened up with a machine-gun and both officers received wounds from which they died shortly after. The loss of these two officers, the first officers of the regiment to forfeit their lives, was a severe blow. Lieut. Fletcher was transport officer during early days of mobilization, being a hunting man and knowing a good deal about horses. Both were buried the following day in the Town Cemetery of Bethune, Major C. D. Enoch, Lieut. and Q.M. Roche and Lieut. T. Rushworth being among those able to be present to pay their last respects. Other casualties from this working party were Pte. G. Jay, died of wounds, L/Cpl. A. Allen and Pte. G. Offen who were both wounded.

In accordance with a First Army Order dated May 13th, the 47th and 1st Divisions were temporarily united and were known as " Barter's Force " under the command of Maj.-Gen. C. St. L. Barter, G.O.C. of the 47th Division, responsible for the defence of the line from Festubert across the canal to the Vermelles-Loos Road. This force ceased to exist at 9 a.m. on May 20th.*

During the next few days artillery bombardments were very frequent, and on the 16th the First Army made a big attack north of Festubert on the immediate left of our division. On this day the battalion came under the orders of the 22nd Brigade of the 7th Division, and in the early hours of the morning moved up to occupy the intermediate line, each man carrying full pack and two hundred extra rounds of ammunition.

To the 7th London fell this day the honour of being the first battalion of the division to go into action against the enemy and obtaining awards for gallantry.

A great bombardment opened at 3 a.m., and five hours later the battalion moved forward to occupy what had been the German front line, and immediately set to work reversing the parapets of the breastwork. Many " souvenirs " were collected, but the majority had to be dumped later on.

In moving forward, some companies experienced great difficulty in crossing the dykes owing to the weight of the equipment carried by the men and the heavy shelling that they encountered. " B " Company, under Capt. A. D. Laurie, found the trench they were to occupy was a ditch full of water.

Among the early casualties was Maj. H. D. Barnes. He suffered a very serious chest wound which was dressed on the spot by Drummer A. Danny Steele, and he was taken down to the dressing station at Smelly Farm, where the M.O., Capt. A. Bell, was being kept very busy.

---
* British Official History.

Sergt. F. Rich, of the machine-gun section, and Sergt. Joel were also wounded. Later on, Lieut. A. A. Ferguson came down wounded and was sent off in an ambulance. The wound received by Maj. Barnes proved serious enough to prevent the battalion in France having the benefit of this keen and efficient officer and no one regretted it more than he that he never became fit enough to return to the unit on active service.

Capt. C. J. S. Green, with two platoons of " C " Company, had moved forward to the captured German support line which was occupied by the Bedfords, many of whom were wounded.

The attack was being held up by a strong enemy position in an orchard. Having drawn from " D " Company an extra 50 rounds of S.A.A. per man, Capt. Green proceeded forward via the Quinque Rue, and, after a consultation with the O.C. Royal Welch Fusiliers, he reconnoitred the orchard position and returned to lead his men, together with a party of ten Royal Welch bombers, to attack, continuing on through a long communication trench and into the open over a ditch waist deep which led into the orchard; the men took up prone positions in extended order and dug in with the aid of their entrenching tools.

The whole party now came under heavy machine-gun and snipers' fire from a barn and a haystack. This fire was returned but, even so, it was impossible to entrench properly and several of our men received wounds.

After three-quarters of an hour, Capt. Green decided that the present position, so far in advance and unsupported, was dangerous, and having ascertained that the troops in the rear had returned to the original German front line, he gave orders to regain the communication trench.

This trench was found to be empty of troops for a distance of over a thousand yards, so Capt. Green led his men back to the old German front line. Throughout the whole of this action Lieut. L. A. L. Flower rendered valuable assistance as also did Sergt. G. Hayward. L/Cpl. A. E. Keeling, whose name is recorded among others of the 7th at Le Touret Cemetery, was reported missing after this action. He was last seen diving through a hedge, calling out " Come on, boys ! I can see them!"

The battalion returned to the 140th Brigade the following day, but remained in the line, in support, for the next three days under heavy and nerve-racking shell fire, and suffered many casualties.

A loss to the battalion was Lieut. A. R. K. Aitkens, of " B " Company, who was mortally wounded. Recommended by Maj. Allan D. Laurie for a commission, Lieut. Aitkens had joined the 7th at Watford. He was an excellent officer and quickly became popular with all ranks.

During these three days in the line, many deeds of heroism were performed. Capt. H. E. Lydiart and C.S.M. Hill, by their coolness and quiet courage, inspired the men under very trying circumstances. Reconnaissances under fire were carried out by Lieuts. H. O. B. Roberts and J. S. Prince; each returned with valuable information. Sergt. Kipling did good work all through in a platoon short of N.C.O.'s, and performed a valuable job in building a parapet under fire, in which work he was assisted by Ptes. Bowerley, Garrod and Colton.

Sergt. Rolls, wounded while on patrol, was brought to safety by Ptes. Peat and Smith. Pte. Wyld got stuck in a ditch while on patrol, and Pte. A. Day went back by himself and rescued him.

Excellent work in carrying messages under shell fire was performed by Pte. Bacon, and while a wounded officer of the Bedfords was being attended to by Pte. King, he himself was wounded and owed his safety to Pte. Tidman. Pte. Chicken worked continuously in attending the wounded. Pte. F. Jobson was badly wounded and eventually lost the sight of one eye.

The following is from an account written a few days after the event by L/Cpl. H. Bond:

> "My section made a grand charge under heavy shell fire. Half-way over we came to a brook about six feet wide; we leapt it but got stuck in the mud; we went on over another brook about the same as before and got safely to a German trench. After bombing the German trench, it was a hard job to get back owing to rifle and machine-gun fire, three chaps got hit and one got stuck in the mud."

As a result of the attack on the orchard, the first awards of the D.C.M. to members of the battalion were made. To Sergt. T. E. G. Hayward:

> "For conspicuous gallantry on May 16th, 1915, at Festubert; Sergt. Hayward continued to lead his platoon under a heavy fire after he had been wounded during an attack. He displayed great coolness and bravery and set a fine example to the men with him of devotion to duty."

And to Pte. A. E. Day:

> "For gallant conduct on May 16th, 1915, at Festubert. During an attack on German trenches, he rescued a man who was unable to extricate himself from a water course, and succeeded in bringing him into safety under a heavy shell fire."

In connection with Capt. C. J. S. Green's action, of which a brief and modest description has been given, the following is reprinted from "The Fighting Territorials," by Sir Percy Hurd (*Country Life*):

> "The Seventh were badly shelled in the reserve trenches, and were then used to support two regular line units, and finally they

occupied the German trenches. Capt. Green, with a half-company, went still further forward."

Another extract from a letter of a member of the Regiment, written on May 18th, reads as follows:

" Captain Green took two positions across a stream, which was up to their necks, attacked the Germans in flank, and had a hand-to-hand fight in an orchard. He shot three Germans with his revolver, and but that he was not supported and had to fall back, would have done a great deal more."

The following Brigade order was issued by Brig.-Gen. G. J. Cuthbert:

" The Brigadier has been much pleased and gratified on receiving a report from the Brigadier-General Commanding the 22nd Infantry Brigade at the good work done by the 7th London Regiment while attached to his command, and more especially by Capt. Green's company when employed in the direction of M.1. on May 16th. He further mentions specially the Adjutant, Capt. Foster, as having been of the greatest assistance in keeping him informed as to the situation.

" (Signed) R. TEMPEST, Major, Bde. Major 140th Inf. Bde."

The Seventh had been tried and tested and had not failed; they performed well that which was required of them and earned the praise of all. The cost to the Regiment in casualties was 23 killed and 128 wounded.

On the 19th, the battalion were relieved by the Canadians and moved back through the dark to Le Quesnoy; it was a very dog-tired and mud-stained crowd of troops that straggled in at all hours throughout the night, platoon by platoon. The following day, and for one day only, the battalion enjoyed a well deserved rest. A telegram was received from the Sergeants' Mess R.M.A., Eastney Barracks, congratulating the " Shiny Seventh " on their action at Festubert.

On May 21st, the battalion marched to Bethune and occupied a tobacco factory; four days later they were back at Gorre where they arrived at 4.30 p.m. and bivouacked in a dark, dirty and damp wood. Here, while acting as brigade reserve, working parties were carried out nightly until the end of the month when the battalion said " goodbye " to Festubert and all that it meant to them.

Over twenty years later, a party of Old Comrades visited the Battle-fields and arrived at the famous Festubert cross-roads; no fewer than 12 of the party then present were with the Regiment at Festubert in 1915. In addition to Lieut.-Col. C. J. S. Green and Lieut. Head, there were present the following: G. Gardner, W. Robertson, F. Rich, J. Shepherd, E. Collinge, G. Addison, A. Steel, A. Setford, W. Horley, and G. Hill.

CHAPTER FIVE

June–August, 1915

THREE "CUSHY" MONTHS

JUNE 1ST, 1915, found the battalion resting in a field near Beuvry. After the issue of rations a move was made to the trenches of Vermelles where the Coldstream Guards were relieved. After the breastworks of Festubert these trenches cut out of the chalk were very comfortable.

" B " and " C " Companies occupied the front line with " A " and " D " in support ; B.H.Q. was comfortably situated in the cellars of Le Rutoire Farm. Dug-outs were a pattern of comfort and elegance and the enemy were about a thousand yards away ; Vermelles itself was a heap of red brick ruins. Inter-company relief took place during the stay in this sector and shrapnel and whizz-bangs were the greatest trouble, Pte. C. Todemore being wounded by the former.

The enemy landed a whizz-bang right outside a dug-out in the support line, killing L/Cpl. L. Crossingham (age 17) and Dmr. B. Boast (age 18), and so seriously wounding C.S.M. Wally Howes that he died on the way to the dressing station. The latter's loss to the Regiment was a nasty shock as he was a fine soldier in every sense, popular with all, and the proud possessor of an Army number consisting of two ones. Other casualties at this time were 2nd Lieut. L. E. Rundell, Sergt. Haxell (returned to duty) and Ptes. W. Harris, A. Mannock, P. W. Messenger and Wannell —all wounded. L/Cpl. Crossingham and Dmr. Boast lie buried next to each other in Dud Corner Cemetery, Loos. C.S.M. W. Howes is also buried in the same cemetery.

2nd Lieuts. J. Hartley and D. Sutton joined the Regiment here, having arrived from the 2nd Battalion.

It turned out to be a real hot day on the 7th when " ours " were relieved by the K.R.R's and marched to Mazingarbe, where they arrived dirty, dusty and thirsty at 3.30 a.m. to operate as Divisional Reserve.

A general clean up and baths at Fosse 20 put the troops in good order for the nightly working parties. Lieut. R. N. de D. Fearnside-Speed, from the 2nd Battalion, arrived here and Lieut. A. A. Ferguson (wounded at Festubert) returned for duty.

The battalion, on June 12th, relieved the 17th London Regt. in the line west of Loos, that is to say in front of Maroc.

During this tour, Pte. E. Lynch, who was on sentry duty with Pte. R. Ashley, became the victim of a sniper and Lieut. Flower went out to locate the sniper, but only found the spot where he had fired from. L/Cpl.

Bosher, Ptes. Talridge, G. Glover, I. Cornish, A. Farley and H. Bardwell were wounded. The trenches in this area were a revelation, so well were they constructed. L/Cpl. T. Bubb about this time was accidentally killed on a bombing course.

A move was made on June 21st to billets in the Philosophe and Mazingarbe area, the battalion being relieved by the 15th London and going to brigade reserve and subsequently into divisional reserve. About this time, smoke helmets were issued as an official effort to cope with Hun poison gas.

Early in July the battalion suffered, as a result of an accident at the brigade bombing school where he was instructing, the loss of Lieut. B. R. P. Wood. Known affectionately as " Splinter," he was one of the brightest and most popular officers. At Watford he was a sergeant and, while there, obtained his commission. He was buried in Mazingarbe Cemetery. The " War Illustrated " dated August 21st, 1915, published his photo in their Roll of Honour.

On July 6th " ours " relieved the 20th London in the front line in a position then furthest south of the British Army. After four very quiet days the 7th were relieved by the 8th London and went into brigade reserve at South Maroc; this recently evacuated garden city was to become another " home from home," and the furnishing of the respective villas became a matter of inter-company competition.

C.Q.M.S. H. Hughes recalls the " sight that had to be seen to be believed " of the cooks coming down the main road dressed in frock coats, black trousers and wearing top hats. Pte. F. E. Trigg recalls Albert Cook careering round in feminine attire.

An extract from a letter written home at the time by Pte. Ted Horley ran as follows :

> " The village where we are billeted has only recently been evacuated by the inhabitants and consequently we are fairly comfy, having mattresses to sleep on and table and chairs in the room, not to speak of table covers and cloths, china plates galore, vases with fresh picked flowers and my—do we see life ! Yesterday for tea we had lettuce, sardines, bread and butter and marmalade, and what do you think we had for dinner today : Green peas, young carrots, new potatoes, cauliflower and boiled beef. For afters, we had apples and, of course, the inevitable cigarette. All the vegetables we get from the gardens, and there is a fairly good supply."

The troops were cheered here with the news that leave to Blighty was a possibility. Everyone was perfectly happy. True, working parties remained, but the battalion carried these out free of casualties.

The 8th London occupied the front line and were relieved by the 7th on the 18th. Two companies of the 10th Gordons were attached to "ours" for instructions in trench warfare during this tour, which lasted four days, when the 21st London Regiment relieved the battalion, which returned to occupy comfortable billets in South Maroc.

Col. E. Faux took temporary command of the 140th Brigade during the absence on leave of the brigadier, and Maj. C. D. Enoch assumed command of the battalion.

At the end of July the battalion were relieved by the 17th London and went into brigade reserve at Philosophe, and after four days were relieved by the 13th Argyll and Sutherlands and moved into corps reserve at Lapugnoy.

It is quite evident that, although out of the line, the troops were kept well occupied, as the following extract from a letter written at this time shows:

> "It may seem peculiar to say so, but while we are on this rest we have less time to ourselves than we do when we are in the trenches. Monday, for instance, I did this 7–7.30 a.m. Physical Drill. 9–11 a.m. Drill. Then at 12.45 p.m. we marched, in full marching order, to have a bath, arriving back at our billets at 7.30 p.m. The weather was awfully hot, especially on Monday, when I think a thunderstorm was threatening, so you can guess what good a bath did us—especially when I tell you that they did not even give us a clean shirt."

The troops are happy as long as they can have a "grouse," and the 7th were in good spirits: away from the line and leave was on—only a few at a time—still, everyone was hoping that the percentage would be increased, and that his turn would be next.

Another move was made on August 7th. Headquarters, machine-gunners, and "C" Company going to La Beuvriere and the other companies to Fouquereuil and Gosnay.

Brig-Gen. G. J. Cuthbert, commanding 140th Brigade, inspected the battalion on the 11th and expressed satisfaction with the turn out, remarking that he thought our transport the best in the Army. The following day, the battalion moved back again to Lapugnoy, and two days later to billets at Les Brebis. From here the battalion supplied working parties on the Grenay Line until the 21st, when they marched into La Beuvriere at midnight.

As a result of the battalion's work on the Grenay Line, the following message was received from Brigade:

"In forwarding this report, the Brig.-Gen. Commg. directs me to express the gratification he has felt at the approbation earned by the unit under your command for the manner in which all ranks have carried out their duties whilst working under O.C. 25th Army Troops Company R.E.
"(Signed) J. H. WESTLEY, Capt.,
"B.M. 140th Inf. Brigade."

The report read as follows :

"I wish to bring to your notice the good work done by the 7th Batt. London Regt. on the Grenay Line defences. The men all worked well and the officers gave much assistance. The carpenters of the battalion did much useful work in roofing dug-outs.
"(Signed) J. C. E. CRASTER, Maj. R.E.,
"O.C. 25th A.T. Comp. R.E."

Company drill and musketry were the order of the day during the battalion's stay at La Beuvriere. A draft of 35 other ranks joined here from the 2nd Battalion and 2nd Lieuts. J. E. Tiplady and A. D. Light, of the 5th Middlesex, were attached for duty.

On August 25th the 47th Divisional Sports took place in brilliant weather before a large assembly. The bands of the 21st London Regt. and the 6th London Field Ambulance performed throughout the afternoon, while a camp-fire concert on the edge of the wood, where the performers were in a convenient hollow in full view of everybody, happily rounded off a "top hole" show.

The next day the battalion, marching via Houchin, returned to their former billets in South Maroc, the battalion being in brigade reserve, and working parties were resumed.

On the night of the 29th the battalion relieved the 8th London in the old trenches ; the weather was atrocious, as can be imagined from the following description written home at the time by Pte. W. Horley :

"Our section was in a sap for two days and it rained hard both these days. There is no cover at all in a sap, and we could not go out, except for absolute necessities. We got awfully wet ; this was especially the case on the Friday. We had our overcoats and waterproof capes on, but the rain was driving in our faces best part of the time, and one could hardly see through the periscope. There we were in a trench deep in soft chalky mud, rain pelting down, and all the prospects were a drop of tea and a relief sometime during the night. So we contented ourselves with singing, and kept it up till tea-time, to cheer ourselves up ; we are never in the dumps."

CHAPTER SIX

September, 1915

LOOS

SEPTEMBER found the 7th still in the front line at **Maroc**; artillery activity proved livelier than upon previous visits of the battalion to this sector.

In the pouring rain on the 3rd, the 21st London relieved "ours," and the boys tramped back to billets at **Les Brebis**, turning out again the same night for working parties.

This last tour of the line had been an unfortunate one for the battalion as the following, Ptes. E. Sporle, D. K. Judd, A. N. Lewis, F. Durrant, E. Colton, F. Burr, G. Clifford, E. Green, A. Sanders, T. Gibson, B. Dibbs and G. Carnell, were all wounded.

The transport section had found the nightly journey up through Nouex-les-Mines and Les Brebis very tiring, added to the fact that their bivouacs were swamped out.

After two days at Les Brebis the battalion were moved back to Haillicourt by London motor buses; this was the first occasion that the troops had enjoyed the pleasure of this type of transport in France.

For the next five days the boys enjoyed a well earned rest and change of scenery; during this time Lieut. H. Rushworth returned for duty, having recovered from his wounds.

The buses took the boys back to Les Brebis on the 11th; working parties were resumed and the battalion suffered further casualties from enemy shelling, when L/Cpl. F. V. A. Taylor and Pte. J. G. Chapman were killed, Pte. G. Myers mortally wounded, and L/Cpl. Hearson wounded.

The stay at Les Brebis was only of two days' duration, and the 13th found the boys back again at Haillicourt.

Training became more intense, particularly over the flagged battle course laid out to resemble the actual ground over which the 7th were to attack; the pioneer section had made over 500 flags for use on this battle course. The weather was gloriously fine, though, if anything, too hot, as the troops found out during the practice attacks; the remainder of the time was occupied with physical drill, bayonet-fighting, skirmishing and bombing practice, with cricket matches to round off the day.

The great news of the coming attack was made known: the troops received the " Secret Orders for the Assault of the Double Crassier," and all were fully aware of the confidence placed in them to do their best.

The following, from a letter written home at the time by one of the men, sums up the situation neatly :

"The boys of the battalion are all looking forward to the coming trial, not with excitement or with dread, but with quiet determination to do their duty whatever happens, and to gain their objective ; and if anyone can win through you can bet the 'Shiny Seventh' can, and I am sure that London will have no cause to be ashamed of her 7th London."

The stay at Haillicourt had served as a real tonic to the troops, and all had that peculiar feeling before the show, as to whether they would survive or not, and it is interesting to record that while resting here one of " C " Company officers expressed the opinion " that he had a feeling that he would survive the show " ; the other officers of that company present were all in agreement with the opinion stated. Happily, in this case, the premonition proved perfectly correct.

On September 23rd the battalion left Haillicourt, leaving behind them in reserve several 2nd Lieutenants under Maj. C. D. Enoch, and spent the night at Les Brebis.

On the night of the 24th they prepared and left for the line ; the spirit of the men as they went up was grand. Although small kit and greatcoats had been dumped, each had plenty to carry—double rations, extra ammunition, distinguishing artillery discs, three sandbags carried across the chest, and every sixth man had a pick or a shovel in addition to rifles ; for headgear, the smoke helmets were worn rolled up around the forehead ready for use if necessary.

The battalion took over assembly trenches in W.2 sector and most of the men snatched a few hours' sleep before the "stand to" early on the morning of September 25th. The outstanding feature of the landscape in front of " ours " was the Double Crassier, as these two immense slag heaps were known.

The capture of the Crassier and the trenches at the west end of the Crassier, together with 800 yards of the German second line north of its junction with the Crassier, were the immediate objectives of the battalion.

For the past four days our artillery had been pounding away at the enemy's positions and our planes had been up continuously. On the 25th, at 5.50 a.m., gas was discharged from the forward saps ; our artillery was going it hammer and tongs, throwing over shells of all sizes. Forty minutes after the discharge of gas our boys went " over the top," and from the enemy trenches, red, white and green rockets went up as a signal for artillery support.

Led by Maj. W. Casson, " A " Company had the difficult task of capturing the Double Crassier, and this formidable obstacle was attacked by them in four waves, platoon after platoon.

" B " Company in line, under the command of Maj. Allan D. Laurie, attacked and captured its objective—the German front line trenches to the left of the Crassier.

" C " Company, also in line, led by Capt. C. J. Salkeld Green, followed up " B " Company and, passing straight through them, attacked and captured the enemy's second line of trenches some 400 yards further on. This position subsequently became the British front line.

" D " Company, commanded by Capt. C. E. King-Church, also in line, followed up " C " Company to the German front line in support of " B " Company.

The whole attack on all fronts met with heavy enemy artillery and machine-gun fire. Maj. A. D. Laurie, who was seriously wounded early on, lay in front of the German front line and wrote reports to Col Faux on the progress of the action, which were of great assistance.

Many officers, N.C.O.'s and men fell, either killed or wounded, between our line and the enemy's wire.

The survivors pressed on in spite of determined resistance, particularly at the Crassier, and overcame all opposition the enemy, who fought to the last moment, gave in at the sight of cold steel their dug-outs yielded many prisoners : and those who would not come out of them were bombed out.

Although the German wire had been in places severely dealt with by our artillery, many of our men were mown down against uncut wire, and those who went through the gaps also suffered heavily. In addition, our gas hung about and rolled back on our own lines, causing much confusion.

The Regiment suffered heavy losses, the percentage among the officers and N.C.O.'s being very high, and very great credit is due to those who survived for the fact that all companies of the battalion reached their objectives in good time and according to plan as had been carried out in practice.

Work of consolidation on the captured positions was at once commenced, but was interrupted on " A " Company's front by an early vigorous and determined enemy counter-attack at the west end of the Crassier.

Maj. W. Casson, with great courage and entire disregard for his own safety, personally conducted the defence of his front in full view of not only his own men but those of the enemy. Although this gallant company was literally cut to pieces, Maj. Casson by a very fine piece of soldiering, held the German counter-attack until reinforcements arrived. In the midst of success this fearless officer was unfortunately killed. Beyond all doubt, the splendid example set, the encouragement to the men given by this officer, and his magnificent behaviour in the face of the enemy, was worthy of a Victoria Cross ; his loss was a severe blow to the battalion. Such was the tragic and dramatic end of this officer who, a few months previously at Watford, had been serenaded by men of his company. Upon the occasion of his marriage, they sang " For he's a jolly good fellow " outside his billet, and were " admonished " the following morning on parade by him, when he " thanked them for their unseemly conduct of the previous night outside his billet." His photograph appeared under the heading of " Britain's Roll of Honoured Dead " in " The War Illustrated " dated November, 1915.

Maj. W. Casson was born in 1873, son of Maj. Thomas Casson, J.P., of Denbigh. In civil life he was an electrical engineer of repute and was responsible for carrying out important works on the Continent and in New York. Originally he served in the ranks of the 2nd South Middlesex V.R.C., 1891–96, and was commissioned a Lieutenant in the Northumberland Fusiliers (Newcastle-on-Tyne Volunteer Battalion) before coming to the 3rd London.

A brother officer writes of him as follows :

> " Bill Casson's only thought was for the Regiment and for the well-being of his men. He was a perfect type of Regimental Officer, absolutely selfless, untiring, utterly loyal and completely fearless in battle ; withal an acute sense of humour and enjoyment of the simple things of life which made him the vast number of friends who felt that his death left a gap impossible to fill."

Many deeds of valour were performed by all ranks of the battalion in this action ; unfortunately the majority were never recorded owing to the witnesses being killed.

The splendid discipline of the men was proved over and over again, as, for instance, those of " D " Company, with Capt. C. E. King-Church and all other officers casualties, and of " B " Company, with Maj. Allan D. Laurie and four other officers all casualties. The men of these companies carried on and captured their objective, occupying the enemy's line under the orders and guidance of Sergt. Salmon, who was a pre-war 7th man, and deserved very great credit for his action on this day.

The stretcher bearers performed wonders ; they were everywhere, attending to the wounded and dying, exposing themselves without fear, and suffered many casualties among their numbers.

Lieut. F. M. Davis was battalion bombing officer; he delighted in bombs, and was very active on the right flank performing most excellent work.

It is recorded that L/Cpl. J. Condon, the boxer, who was wounded, went over with his gloves strapped to the back of his kit, as though he intended setting up a school of instruction in the German lines.

Nightfall on September 25th found the strength of the company officers as follows: " A " Company entirely without officers, as, in addition to Maj. W. Casson, Lieut. J. S. Prince had also been killed, and Lieuts. J. H. Jackson, A. A. Ferguson and H. O. B. Roberts wounded, the two latter so seriously that they both died.

In " B " Company, Lieuts. A. J. Smith, J. E. Tiplady and A. K. Sanderson had been killed, and Maj. A. D. Laurie and Lieut. G. B. Slater wounded. Lieut. F. M. Davis, of " B " Company, was a survivor, although upon this occasion he was bombing officer; the only other surviving officer of " B " Company was Capt. H. E. Lydiart.

To " C " Company, under the skilful leadership of Capt. C. J. Salkeld Green, went the distinction of being the only company to go through the attack without suffering any casualties among the officers, who were Lieut. L. A. L. Flower and 2nd Lieuts. J. D. Hartley and D. Sutton. This was remarkable, because " C " Company went over between " B " and " D " Companies, and had some 400 yards further to go.

In " D " Company all officers became casualties. Lieut. R. N. de D. Fearnside-Speed had been killed, and Lieut. H. M. Rushworth and Capt. C. E. King-Church both wounded, the latter so seriously that he died as a result of his wounds.

With greatly depleted forces the battalion held on to its hard-won positions. Throughout the night they " stood to " continuously, ready to repel threatened counter-attacks; this night proved very trying, as the rain teemed down and the trenches became ankle-deep in mud. The men, being in fighting order, without greatcoats, were quickly soaked to the skin.

Dawn broke on the 26th and found the 7th consolidating their gains and endeavouring to make the trenches more comfortable; the two machine-guns captured in the attack were sent down the line as trophies.

Fortunately, enemy shelling on the battalion front was not too heavy, although the rear areas received the enemy's attention, particularly Maroc.

On the 27th the 8th London relieved " ours," who returned to the old British front line, where they remained for the next three days, when they were relieved by troops of the 152nd French Division.

During the past few days our transport had had a very difficult time, and they deserve great praise for delivering the goods despite enemy shelling and congested roads.

On the day of the attack all roads in the rear were blocked, the square at Nouex-les-Mines was full of wounded, the steps of the Mairie (which was in use as a Field Ambulance) were crowded with wounded, and more wounded were sitting or lying on each side of the main street.

All the way through Mazingarbe and up to Les Brebis was one long line of motor ambulances, G.S. wagons and country carts, the latter (driven by civilians) all full of wounded.

On the night of the 30th, following relief by troops of the French Division, the battalion, greatly reduced in strength, marched into reserve at Quality Street, Philosophe, and thence on in the rain and bitter cold by a circuitous route of 12 miles to Verquin, which was reached at 7 a.m. on October 1st.

The troops, weary and sad at heart, dead beat, plastered from head to foot with mud and chalk, entered their billets and very quickly got down to a much needed rest and sleep. Later in the day a roll call was taken, and a memorial service was held for those who fell in the recent action; 13 officers and 292 other ranks were killed, wounded or missing in this action.

Under the shelter of the Crassier a long trench was dug and here were buried many of the 7th dead; officers were placed on the right, then N.C.O.'s, with the men next. Many men at first reported "missing" were subsequently found to have been wounded.

Among those wounded were C.S.M. R. Hill, Sergt. H. Harper, Cpls. F. Barlow, W. Gander, and C. Brown; L/Cpl. H. Layen, Dvr. Bennett, Ptes. G. Balding, C. Britton, E. Bullis, A. Gough, W. Frosdyke, E. Hammon, A. Hogarth, A. Hutchinson, G. Parsons, F. Snell, and G. Palmer. C.Q.M.S. H. Hughes and Pte. Johanson both received serious wounds, which in each case necessitated the amputation of an arm.

Col. E. Faux, V.D., was greatly upset at the severe losses sustained by the battalion, and subsequently when he was made a Companion of the Order of St. Michael and St. George, he stated on a battalion parade that he was proud to wear the honour on behalf of the magnificent work performed in action by all ranks of the battalion in the Battle of Loos.

To Lieut. H. O. B. Roberts went the proud distinction of being the first 7th London officer to be decorated. He was awarded the M.C. for his gallant conduct in action on the Crassier; unfortunately this brave and resolute officer did not live long to enjoy the honour bestowed upon him.

For his gallant conduct on the Crassier, Sergt. A. J. Taylor was awarded the D.C.M. and the French Croix de Guerre, the latter being pinned on his breast by General Sir Douglas Haig at a special parade.

"A" Company, with all officers casualties, were in a precarious position when C.S.M. George Hill took charge and rallied the remnants of the company. For his excellent work on this and previous occasions he was awarded the D.C.M. Shortly after Loos, C.S.M. G. Hill gained a commission in the Tank Corps, and for his exploits at Passchendaele in his Tank " Fray Bentos " was awarded the M.C.

Sergt. T. H. Gilder, who did such good work at Festubert, again performed his task of attending to and clearing the wounded. For his splendid work in this action he was awarded the D.C.M.

Signallers of the battalion performed wonders, instituting and maintaining communications throughout. For gallant conduct in this connection, Sergt. H. J. H. Powell received the D.C.M. Within five minutes of zero hour a message was signalled back to Headquarters giving information that the Crassier attack had been successful. The reply from Col. Faux read, " Well done ' A ' Company ".

Another D.C.M. went to Pte. F. M. Allan for gallantry in action.

Subsequently, the following officers had the honour of being mentioned in dispatches :

    Col. E. Faux, V.D., Commanding Officer.
    Capt. R. T. Foster, Adjutant.
    Maj. Allan D. Laurie, " B " Company.
    Maj. W. Casson, " A " Company.
    Capt. C. J. Salkeld Green, " C " Company.
    Lieut. H. O. B. Roberts, M.C., " A " Company.

Again the " Shiny Seventh " had proved its efficiency and upheld the traditions of the Regiment and the Territorial Army. They had carried out their task, withstood enemy counter-attacks and handed over the advanced positions intact.

All this, but at a cost of many valued and treasured lives.

1st BATTALION ROLL OF OFFICERS AT LOOS

Col. E. Faux, V.D.   Maj. C. D. Enoch, T.D.
Capt. R. T. Foster, Adj.

" A " Company	" B " Company
Maj. W. Casson, K.	Maj. Allan D. Laurie, W.
Lieut. A. A. Ferguson, D. of W's.	Capt. H. E. Lydiart.
Lieut. H. O. B. Roberts, D. of W's.	Lieut. F. M. Davis (Bombing
2nd Lieut. J. S. Prince, K.	Officer).

1st Battalion Roll of Officers at Loos—*continued*

2nd Lieut. J. H. Jackson, W.
†*2nd Lieut. Houghton

Lieut. A. J. Smith, K.
†Lieut. J. E. Tiplady, K.
2nd Lieut. G. B. Slater, W.
†2nd Lieut. A. K. Sanderson, K.
*†2nd Lieut. Hazel.

" C " *Company*
Capt. C. J. Salkeld Green
Lieut. L. A. L. Flower
2nd Lieut. D. Sutton
2nd Lieut. J. D. Hartley
†*2nd Lieut. J. H. Thorne

" D " *Company*
Capt. C. E. King-Church, D. of W's
Lieut. H. M. Rushworth, W.
Lieut. R. N. de D. Fearnside-Speed, K.
†*2nd Lieut. A. D. Light.

Lieut. W. N. Culverwell, Trench-Mortars
Lieut. T. Rushworth, Transport Officer.
Lieut. G. D. Roche, Quartermaster.
Capt. A. H. Bell, R.A.M.C., Medical Officer.

Well deserved congratulations on the operations of the battalion came from all quarters. The Advanced First Army sent the following :

" At sunset on the first day of the great battle we have now commenced the Field-Marshal Commanding in Chief desires me to convey to the First Army his hearty congratulations and warmest thanks for the splendid work accomplished. He feels confident that the fine courage and magnificent spirit which animates all ranks will ensure a speedy victory over the enemy."

From the G.O.C. of the division came the following wire :

" Well done. Warmest congratulations to all ranks. Corps Commander has just been personally to congratulate the 47th Division and the troops attached to it on the success of today's attack. He stated that the division has most satisfactorily accomplished all that had been asked of it. The G.O.C. has greatest pleasure in conveying this appreciation to all ranks."

The following came from the Fourth Corps :

" The Corps Commander desires you to convey to all ranks his admiration of the gallant manner in which your Division captured all the objectives given to it, and of the skill with which they have maintained the captured positions."

Col. E. Faux, V.D., issued the following in Battalion Routine Orders on October 1st :

" The Commanding Officer wishes to place on record his pride

---
† Denotes Officers attached from Middlesex Regiment.
* Denotes Officers who remained on reserve with Maj. C. D. Enoch at Houchin.
K.= Killed.   D. of W's= .Died of Wounds.   W.= Wounded.

7TH LONDON OFFICERS AT WATFORD, 1914

7TH LONDON SERGEANTS AT EASTNEY, 1914

Facing page 39

7TH LONDON OFFICERS AT WATFORD, 1914

(Back Row)
2nd Lieuts. A. R. K. AITKENS, L. E. RUNDELL, J. S. PRINCE, A. J. SMITH, W. SMITH, H. O. B. ROBERTS.

(Middle Row)
2nd Lieut. J. L. HEAD, Lieuts. F. M. DAVIS, H. M. RUSHWORTH, 2nd Lieuts. B. R. P. WOOD and BOYD, Lieut. D. E. WARD, 2nd Lieut. L. A. L. FLOWER, Lieut. R. D. MARET-TIMS, Lieut. J. H. B. FLETCHER, 2nd Lieut. A. A. FERGUSON, 2nd Lieut. W. N. CULVERWELL, Capt. A. H. BELL (R.A.M.C.), Capt. E. BALL, Lieut. and Q.M. G. D. ROCHE, Lieut. T. RUSHWORTH.

(Front Row)
Capts. H. G. HEAD, C. E. KING-CHURCH, A. D. LAURIE, R. T. FOSTER (Adjt.), Maj. C. D. ENOCH, T.D., Col. E. FAUX, V.D., Maj. H. D. BARNES, Capts. W. CASSON, C. J. S. GREEN, J. G. H. BUDD, H. E. LYDIART.

7TH LONDON SERGEANTS AT EASTNEY, 1914

(Back Row)
Sergt. S. LEE, L/Sergt. G. MARR, Sergts. J. ANGUS, J. ROBERTS, W. PENNINGTON, A. NORTON, C/Sergt. J. J. PATRICKSON, Sergts. A. ATKINS, W. WOOD, G. SHEPHERD, F. POWELL.

(Middle Row)
Sergt. Inst. F. PAYNE, Sergts. T. MIDDLETON, H. COLLINS, C/Sergt. R. JOEL, C/Sergt. W. WHEELER, L/Sergt. A. SPIRES, C/Sergt. G. HILL, Sergts. A. WOODWARD, J. SHEPHARD, W. BONFIELD, R. HILL, L/Sergt. HOSKINS, C/Sergt. H. HUGHES, Sergt. Inst. E. CRUWYS.

(Front Row)
Sergt. J. MERLINI, C/Sergt. T. MORE, Sergt. F. NUBBERT, Q.M.S. J. GRIFFEN, Capt. R. T. FOSTER, Col. E. FAUX, V.D., Lieut. and Q.M. G. D. ROCHE, Lieut. A. GIBSON (R.M.A.) Sergt.-Maj. H. E. LYDIART, Q.M.S. J. DUFFY, Sergt.-Dr. J. DENISON.

at the achievement of the battalion in the recent action at the Double Crassier. The battalion has been congratulated by the G.O.C. 47th Division, the G.O.C. 140th Brigade, and the C.O. takes this opportunity of thanking all ranks for their gallant conduct, which has added greatly to the good name already earned by the battalion in the field."

The great story of the gallant and successful attack by the " Shiny Seventh " reached London a week or so later, and the London daily papers published the story for the world to read at large.

Newspaper captions read " Great British Charge," " The Glorious ' Shiny Seventh,' " " The Slag Heap Victory," " Undying Fame for the ' Shiny Seventh. ' "

An extract says :

"London must be amazingly proud of its ' Shiny Seventh.' Their part in the last British advance will live in history as much for the sporting and cheerful manner in which they went to the assault of the German positions as for the heroism with which they stormed and won and held the notorious ' slag heaps.' " *

Lieut. J. H. Jackson, who was wounded, wrote home and the following are extracts from his letter :

" I am only repeating the expressed opinion of the Corps, Brigade and Divisional Commanders when I say that no finer battalion ' went up and over ' than the 7th Battalion The London Regiment. Staggered as we are at the loss of so many dear friends, magnificent officers and men, a loss we have not fully realised yet, the knowledge that the battalion so well maintained the good name it had already earned on the field goes a long way to solacing us." *

Lieut. A. A. Ferguson, who died of wounds, lies buried in the cemetery at Nouex-les-Mines. He had crossed over to France with the battalion in March, 1915, and had proved himself an efficient officer ; his photograph appeared in " The War Illustrated " dated April, 1916.

Lieut. H. O. B. Roberts, who was awarded the M.C., did splendid work, and was as cool as a cucumber until he was seriously wounded. This popular officer some time later died as a result of his wounds.

2nd Lieut. J. S. Prince, who came out to France with the battalion in March, 1915, and was killed in this action, was a good and popular officer without fear, and only twenty-three years old. Always interested in science, he had, only a few days prior to his death during a night-

---

* News of the World

working party, given a lecture on the stars to a group of officers in No-man's land.

Maj. Allan D. Laurie, O.C. of " B " Company, became a serious casualty early on, but managed to see his company's success in capturing the enemy's front line ; he eventually became a patient at No. 2 Red Cross Hospital, Rouen, before being evacuated to " Blighty."

While in hospital, Lord French spoke to him in high praise of the part the 7th London had played at Loos ; it occupied, he said, " a most important position as the right flank of the attack, and everything depended on it, and it fully justified the confidence reposed in it."

Lieut. A. J. Smith, who also came out with the battalion in March, 1915, although wounded remained at duty, and even made a tour of the front line, selecting the best positions for the machine-guns prior to being killed.

Lieut. J. E. Tiplady, who was so seriously wounded that he subsequently died of his wounds, had recently joined the battalion from the Middlesex Regiment. He was a keen soldier and had spent a good deal of his time in Russia before the War ; his experiences at the old Russian Court were very interesting.

2nd Lieut. G. B. Slater, another painstaking and efficient officer, unfortunately became an early casualty.

Capt. C. King-Church, thirty-six years of age, was a pre-war 7th officer ; he was seriously wounded and died on his way down in an ambulance. Capt. King-Church was gazetted in 1911, and promoted Captain in 1914 ; he was a scholar of Bradfield and Oriel College, Oxford.

Lieut. R. N. de D. Fearnside-Speed, who was also killed, was twenty-six years of age, and survived by a brother serving in the 2nd Battalion. Col. Faux thought highly of this officer, who had such a quiet and lovable character. By his death many felt that they had lost a great friend.

In this attack alone the battalion lost seven of the officers who accompanied the battalion across the water in March, 1915.

2nd Lieut. A. K. Sanderson, who was unfortunately killed, had only recently been attached to the 7th from the Middlesex Regiment.

Capt. A. H. Bell, R.A.M.C., despite the handicap of suffering from gas, had a very busy time at his aid post, and afterwards came up and dressed the men on the field of action.

The following are extracts from a letter written just after the action by Capt. H. E. Lydiart :

> " Everyone is paying us the highest congratulations, but we have paid dearly for it ; our casualties are nine officers dead and four wounded ; the number of N.C.O.'s and men are 292, and include a great number of our old battalion men.

"Among the N.C.O.'s and men of 'B' Company killed are Sergts. Moxon, Johnson, Kiddle and Tyson, Cpl. Greenyer, L/Cpls. A. Godfrey and E. C. Godfrey. Bell came over and dressed our wounded. Green's name has gone in for dispatches, also Roberts. Casson will probably be awarded the V.C., for he did magnificently."

Pte. W. E. Horley wrote home as follows :

"We went over the top into a perfect hail of machine-gun bullets—they let us have it properly; still, we kept on and soon reached the German trenches. Most Germans turned tail and bolted, and we had some fine sport fetching them down. About four of us in five minutes turned about 20 out, 11 of them out of one dug-out. Another four, who held their arms above their heads suddenly turned and bolted up the trench, so we let fly at them."

Pte. H. Hunt wrote home as follows :

"It was magnificent the way our chaps went across and gained their objectives, and hung on like glue despite three counter-attacks from the Huns, the first of which came within fifteen minutes of our occupation. Our fellows did splendid. I am proud to be one of the 'Shiny Seventh,' and I console myself with the knowledge that my humble efforts helped on that glorious day. The regiment we were up against was a resolute enemy; we left our trade mark on them, and I bet they won't forget us in a hurry. Some of the prisoners thought our chaps were Guards the way they went in at them; they put up their hands and cried 'Mercy Kamerads.' One prisoner looked at the shoulder plates of one of our fellows, and then exclaimed 'What! London Territorials!' I am sorry to have to tell you I have lost two good chums—one is Wally Brooks and the other is Sydney Thompson. Wally was killed outright, and Thompson is missing."

The following are extracts from a letter written home by H. Norton to his brother in the 3rd Battalion :

"You know by this time that the 'Shiny Seventh' have been in a proper scrap, and I might say we have earned a good name for the 47th Division.

"We left our billets last Friday week and marched to the trenches. It was pouring with rain, so by the time we got there we were wet through to the skin. We proceeded to the first line, arriving there at 2.30 a.m. Saturday.

"We laid down to have a sleep, being awakened at 5 o'clock. The artillery started the ball rolling. Hell was let loose for twenty minutes. Suddenly, from our position, we could see that our first line were mounting the parapet.

"We went over and across that Valley of Death, not giving a thought to danger, but simply of having our revenge for fallen comrades who were dropping on all sides of us.

"Almost immediately a 'coal box' landed in the trench a few yards from me; the concussion of the air almost bowled me over. I was not there five minutes when the Huns made a counter-attack, so I was just in time to take part in the fun. I took up bomb throwing; then something happened—the store of bombs ran out and the Huns began to gain ground. They bombed us at fifty yards. I can tell you things looked pretty black for us until we were reinforced. Gradually we got the better of the argument, and put many of the Huns to sleep for good and all.

"It was terrible slaughter, but we were rewarded by driving them out of it altogether. The victory was ours. You should have heard the cheers that went up; they were deafening, they had had a lesson to last a lifetime. I cannot say how I got through without a scratch, but it was done.

"Poor old Bill Ellis was wounded in the leg, and my pal Ted Taylor is missing." *

L/Cpl. H. Bond's description of September 25th in diary form is brief and very much to the point.

"Raining all night. Rum 5.30 a.m. Over the top 6.30 a.m. sharp, gas helmets on. First line got Double Crassier, first in trench, shot German at gun—took six prisoners."

At a memorial service for officers, N.C.O.'s and men of the 7th held at St. Botolph's, Bishopsgate, at which the Bishop of London officiated, a letter from Col. Faux was read in which he said:

"They have done their job, and done it well; but I fear I have lost three hundred."

Sergt. Donaldson who died as a result of gas poisoning, had, unknown to himself, been gazetted a day or so previously as a lieutenant. He was only nineteen years of age and is buried under that rank in Loos British Cemetery, where also are buried Maj. W. Casson and Lieut. A. J. Smith.

In the same cemetery are the graves of about forty 7th London men "Known unto God."

At Loos Dud Corner Cemetery is a panel containing about ninety names of 7th London missing.

---
* Territorial Service Gazette.

CHAPTER SEVEN

October, 1915—January, 1916

WET DAYS

THE early days of October found the battalion minus many familiar faces, but enjoying a well deserved and much needed rest at Verquin. These days were spent in cleaning up and making good deficiencies of kit, and officers acting as censors on the men's letters had a busy time, as everyone was writing to let their relatives know of their recent experiences and of their safety.

A welcome addition to the strength, in the shape of a draft of 59 other ranks, arrived on the 6th, when a move was made to Nouex-les-Mines.

Lieut. J. L. Head rejoined the battalion here, as also did Lieut. L. E. Rundell who had recovered from the wound he received at Vermelles. From the 3rd Battalion the following officers, Lieuts. V. H. Jordan, E. B. Brewer and J. Chatterton arrived in time to accompany the battalion to Mazingarbe on the 8th, where the battalion operated as reserve for the battle of Hulloch and carried out many working parties.

During the early hours of the 14th, " ours " moved up into support, occupying the old British front line opposite Hulloch.

After four days in this position, " ours " took over the front line from the 8th London near Hohenzollern Redoubt. Continual rain waterlogged the trenches, and the men suffered considerable discomfort.

Our lines received a good deal of attention from the enemy's artillery, and the battalion suffered the loss of the following N.C.O.'s and men: Cpls. N. M. Nisbett, C. W. Bosher, R. F. Bosher, L/Cpl. F. H. Eastoe, Ptes. W. Bowers, H. F. Buckingham, A. Jacobs, H. Stubbs and H. J. Walden, all killed by shell fire during this spell in the line.

The general condition of the line is perhaps best related by the following extracts from a letter by Pte. H. Hunt, of the machine-gunners:

> " We have had a deuce of a time lately. We are in a village just behind the line, having had twelve days of the hottest part it has been our privilege to hold, and this after the terrible time we had at Loos.
>
> " We went into the trenches and spent six days in the supports and four in the front line.
>
> " For nine days our duty consisted in taking rations up to the gun teams in the line. We used the road for quickness, and this came in for the usual ' strafing '—in fact, we were followed down the road by a dozen shrapnel shells.

"I found the front line a very warm quarter—70 yards from the Germans, who 'strafed' us all day long and handed out a particularly heavy ration of hate at breakfast, dinner and tea in the form of bombs, trench mortars and aerial torpedoes. Excellent shooting by our artillery put the 'tin-hat' on the trench mortar guns. The Germans got more than they bargained for ; our guns played ' Old Harry ' with their trenches and made a fine mess of them."

The 8th London came up on the 21st and relieved the battalion, which returned to the support lines for one day, when it was relieved by the 21st London, and moved back into the old British front line.

The following night the battalion was relieved again, this time by the 15th London, and marched back to Mazingarbe, arriving at midnight.

About this time Maj. C. D. Enoch took up an appointment as 4th Corps Claims' Commissioner at La Buissiere.

Col. E. Faux, V.D., went on leave from Mazingarbe and, upon his return from England, took command of the brigade during the temporary absence of Brig.-Gen. G. Cuthbert. The battalion came under the temporary command of Capt. C. J. Salkeld Green and returned to the front line on the 30th, to relieve the 20th London in a nasty bit of the line, which was a pronounced salient left of Loos and the Quarry, and suffered several casualties on the way in.

After two days, during which time it rained continuously, the battalion was relieved by the 15th London and moved into the support trenches in the Loos Alley and Gun Alley area.

Ninety-six N.C.O.'s and men, many from the 3rd Battalion, and others who had been wounded at Festubert and Loos, arrived at transport lines and were sent on to join the battalion in the line ; they had a rough journey in the pouring rain and were shelled twice en route.

The battalion had a most uncomfortable time ; the weather was atrocious and the enemy shelled daily, fortunately only causing slight casualties, Ptes. W. H. Hayes and J. Fisher being killed.

A move was made to the old German front line on November 8th, where the battalion was in reserve ; 2nd Lieut. A. R. Wallis joined the battalion here.

" Ours " relieved the 6th London in the front line on the 11th and found the trenches in a terrible state ; heavy rains had caused the sides to fall in and all trenches were ankle-deep in water, Posen Alley being particularly bad.

Rain fell continuously until the 14th, when fine weather prevailed with a hard frost at night, and on this date " ours " were relieved by the 8th Battalion Berkshire Regiment and marched into billets in the Abattoir at Mazingarbe.

The following day the battalion moved to Nouex-les-Mines, and while on the march official photographers took cinematograph pictures of them. At 2.20 p.m. the troops entrained and arrived at Lillers at 3.15 p.m., where very comfortable billets were occupied.

The battalion, now in Corps Reserve, remained here until December 14th, and the change of scenery was much enjoyed.

For two nights running—November 25th and 26th—a grand concert was held at St. Cecilia's Hall in the Grand Place and, on each occasion, before a packed house, L/Cpl. F. Redway gave an amusing performance. With the aid of a dark-skinned member dressed in a sheepskin coat and carrying on a silver salver " a head with a lemon in its mouth and complete with a German helmet," L/Cpl. Redway, dressed as " Salome," danced to the tune " In the Shadows," played by Pte. Butt on the violin.

On December 1st and 2nd Divisional exercises were carried out, reveille being at 5 a.m., and the battalion moving off two hours later for a trek to Glemenghem. The following day the battalion moved off at 7.30 a.m. and, marching via Estree Blanche and Auchy-au-Bois, arrived back at Lillers at 4 p.m.

The sergeants held their annual dinner at the Estaminet Lion d'Or ; R.S.M. Hardy was in the chair. The principal guests were Col. E. Faux, Capts. R. T. Foster, C. J. S. Green, H. E. Lydiart, and G. D. Roche. This proved a very successful function, marked by an eloquent speech from Col. Faux.

Entertainment was provided by R.Q.M.S. Cruttenden, Sgts. Whale and Mudge, also Pte. Butt.

All good things come to an end and what became known as the " first Lillers " ended, when orders were issued to roll blankets in bundles of ten— a sure order meaning departure.

The battalion bade farewell to Lillers on December 15th, travelling by train to Nouex-les-Mines, from where they marched to billets at Verquin ; they remained at the latter place in divisional reserve for four days.

On the 19th the battalion, marching via Verquigneul, Labourse and Sailly Labourse, arrived at the support lines south of the quarries in front of Vermelles and relieved the 18th London Regiment, the relief being completed by 12.50 a.m.

The battalion, situated in Chapel Alley and Devon Alley support area, spent a great deal of their time in cleaning up the trenches.

The 15th London were holding a nasty piece of the line, known as the Hairpin, the name given to this part of the line being the result of a previous attack by the British, which was only partially successful.

About 50 yards of the German front line on the ridge was captured, and from each end of this strip a trench was dug back to the British front line, thus forming the famous Hairpin.

The enemy attacked this part of the front and the 15th London Regiment lost heavily in two counter-attacks.

2nd Lieut. J. Chatterton of the 7th, and his bombers, were ordered up to form a block. This officer, wounded early on in the forehead, remained at his post, together with eight other ranks of the 7th London, and maintained the position throughout.

A report on the exploit of 2nd Lieut. J. Chatterton was sent in to the higher authorities, and at a later date the following letter from Brig.-Gen. G. J. Cuthbert, Commanding the 140th Infantry Brigade, was read out on a parade of bombers by the Commanding Officer:

> " I think that he, and all under him, acted with great gallantry and judgment, and I have much pleasure in so informing the Major-General Commanding the Division."

Our area came in for a good deal of shelling from the enemy, and Chapel Alley suffered a miniature landslide.

Any hopes that may have been entertained of spending Christmas out of the line were dashed to the ground when, at 4.30 a.m. on the 23rd, the battalion moved up into the front line and relieved the 6th London.

With the battalion during this tour of the line were a party of officers and N.C.O.'s of the 7th Leinsters attached for instruction ; the communication trenches were about two feet deep in water and, although the runner taking the party up the line had waders on, the visitors were not so fortunate and their first experience of the trenches was decidedly unpleasant.

Their first experience of shelling came in the afternoon when our artillery put up a test concentration on the Quarries.

On Christmas Eve, at 6 a.m., the support battalion was moved forward to the old British front line and the reserve battalion occupied Curly Crescent and trenches east of Vermelles water tower, to reinforce the line in case of attack.

That these moves were well founded was proved at 7.20 a.m., when we exploded a mine opposite Hohenzollern Redoubt.

Our lines were heavily shelled and the battalion was fortunate to escape with the loss only of three other ranks wounded.

Christmas Day turned out nice and bright ; early on one of our officers shot one of an enemy patrol. Later on in the day the G.O.C. of the division, accompanied by the brigadier, paid a visit to the trenches and found the men spending their time endeavouring to clear the trenches of mud and water with the aid of scoops and pumps. The trenches were like canals, knee-deep, and it was as well that the men had been served with waders. Nevertheless, the men were never dry ; apart from the wet trenches, the dug-outs were also wet.

The diary of Cpl. H. Bond records the following for Christmas Day :

"Stood to 6 a.m. for half an hour ; Cpl. Clark and myself singing, and all the boys very jolly. Post up at 7 a.m., then breakfast ; I cooked some bacon on a tin of dubbin. Clark had a parcel and we had a fine feed that day. At 2 o'clock on working party, clearing water from trenches. Germans about 100 yards away and also in a sap 35 yards off—so near that we both use the same barbed wire."

On Boxing Day the enemy continued to shell our lines and the battalion lost L/Cpl. F. Woods and Pte. G. H. Gladwin, both being killed.

The 24th London Regiment came up on the 27th and relieved " ours," who moved to billets at Verquin, arriving at 2 p.m. smothered in mud, and in a dead-beat condition, after eight days of wallowing in trenches of mud and water. The condition of the line during this tour resulted in nearly 100 men being sent to hospital with trench feet. The following day at Labourse the men were able to enjoy one of those rare occasions when baths were available.

On the last day of the year the battalion moved off at 8 a.m. into Brigade Reserve at Sailly Labourse.

Several moves were made in the first few days of the New Year ; commencing on January 2nd, the battalion took over a part of the line south of Hohenzollern Redoubt from the 6th London Regiment.

The following day " ours " were relieved by the 1st Dismounted Battalion, who had been temporarily formed from cavalry regiments, and marched back to Verquin. On the way back along the road to Nouex-les-Mines the enemy shelled persistently, but the battalion suffered only two casualties, both other ranks, slightly wounded.

On the 4th the battalion moved off again and took over billets at Les Brebis, where at this time 2nd Lieut. E. W. C. Lonnen joined for duty from the 3rd Battalion.

On the following day a move was made at 5 p.m. towards the line, where the battalion relieved the 32nd Regiment, 18th Division of the French Infantry, in the Maroc sector. It proved quite a change to take over some decent trenches.

The higher authorities had launched a salvage campaign, the collection of which was being arranged for by a special staff appointed to deal with this matter. Some members of our transport, led by Sergt. Whale, decoyed the salvage staff from their hut and, during their absence, decorated the hut externally with a few painted signs, such as : " Best prices given for old iron," " Rifles exchanged for rum," " Salvage oeufs grown in our own bomb factory," and a few others. These notices created a good deal of attention ; fortunately for the practical jokers the salvage officers took it all in good part.

On the 8th " ours " were relieved by the 22nd London Regiment, and " C " and " D " Companies went to Maroc, and " A " and " B " Companies to Les Brebis ; after a couple of days an inter-company relief took place.

Another very welcome gift from the 3rd Battalion arrived in the shape of more socks and 20,000 cigarettes, which were distributed among the troops, and the battalion also received a parcel of comforts, mouth organs, etc., from the Sports Fund of the " Daily Express."

On January 12th the battalion took over the support lines in the Loos sector, with H.Q. in the old German front line near the Lens-Bethune Road. " A " and " B " Companies were in the cellars of Loos, and " C " and " D " occupied the cellars in Maroc ; 2nd Lieut. M. Juriss joined here for duty from the 3rd Battalion.

Col. E. Faux took over temporary command of the 140th Brigade, and the battalion under the command of Capt. C. J. Salkeld Green moved up into the front line on the 15th in the right section of the Loos sector. The right company held the front line from Lens-Bethune Road to Copse Lane, and the left company from Copse Lane to Loos-Fosse 12 Road.

Enemy mines were suspected in this area and preparations were made in case of an attack for the local reserve and bombers to assemble in Enclosure Avenue. The support company were prepared for four parties of ten men, each under an N.C.O. and complete with a group of bombers, to take up positions at Regent Street and South Street, Wood Street, Copse Lane, and Scrub Lane.

Each man was to carry four sandbags; a supply of picks, shovels, wire, S.A.A., and bombs were to be available for each party.

However, despite the careful arrangements, nothing more exciting happened on this turn in the line than the dispersal of a German working party by rifle and machine-gun fire just before the break of dawn one day.

The enemy working party were observed and a machine-gun was trained on them with the aid of a Very light fired by an officer ; within twenty seconds of the light extinguishing itself, the machine-gunner let off a good burst. It is recorded that the bodies of eight of the enemy were counted when daylight broke.

Meanwhile, back at transport lines, things were happening. Daily the enemy shelled, and transport H.Q. had several narrow escapes ; it was suspected that an enemy observation plane had mistaken a large refuse pit and the four cookers for a gun position and R.F.A. limbers. On this " information " over came the shells, and one man of the transport received a slight wound on the chin ; the only other effect was that the " Drums," who had been practising vigorously on the first floor, " ceased practice " and beat a hasty retreat to the cellar in double quick time.

Pte. F. J. Pitt, who had been attached to the salvage company, died suddenly in Les Brebis, and was buried in Mazingarbe Cemetery, the salvage company supplied the bearers and four of our buglers sounded " The Last Post."

The " London Gazette " of January 14th confirmed the award of the C.M.G. to Col. E. Faux, V.D., and the D.C.M. to Sergts. H. Powell and T. Gilder and L/Cpl. F. Allan ; the three latter decorations were presented on the 23rd, prior to a church parade, when Gen. Sir Charles Barter pinned the ribbon on the tunic of each in turn.

The 23rd London relieved the 7th on the 20th, and the battalion moved back into billets at Bracquemont near Nouex-les-Mines, the last of the troops arriving in at 3 a.m.

The battalion only had four days' " rest " when they were on the move again. It was on the 24th that the 17th London were relieved, and on the following day " ours " were relieved by the 8th London and moved into support at North and South Maroc. On January 25th Pte. R. Ashley, while serving as a brigade sniper, was wounded in the head.

While the battalion was in support at Maroc a party of 83 other ranks arrived at transport lines ; this number included 25 old timers under Sergt. Burden, who had returned from hospital ; they went up the same night, with the rations, to join the battalion.

From the 3rd Battalion came a batch of 2nd Lieutenants, which included R. N. Eve, R. E. Taylor (N.S.W.), H. D. Long (formerly a corporal of the battalion), J. M. Stirling (late London Scottish), Cecil Rack (Cape Town), F. B. Wade (Maritzburg), and C. A. H. Hoole (Aliwal North). These officers also went up with the rations to join the battalion in the line.

On the first day of February the 23rd London relieved the battalion, which marched into billets at Les Brebis.

It was on this day, at 11 a.m., that a Taube nearly wiped out the quartermaster's stores ; four bombs were dropped, causing 15 casualties.

Col. E. Faux, C.M.G., V.D., went on leave to England, and Capt. C. J. Salkeld Green continued in temporary command of the battalion.

While at Les Brebis an enemy shell landed between two of our cookers and wounded five men, two of them seriously. All told there were 50 casualties in the village on this day.

CHAPTER EIGHT

February—March, 1916

THE AFFAIR AT THE COPSE

ON February 5th the battalion returned to the line in the Loos sector and relieved the 17th London Regiment. The following day a large working party of the 7th were employed under Royal Engineers, making a trench to the left and in rear of Harrison's crater. The enemy shelled our lines with mortars and rifle grenades for over an hour and a half in the morning, and our T.M.B.'s retaliated; we suffered casualties, L/Sergt. A. E. Parker and L/Cpl. A. R. Jennings being killed. Both were subsequently buried in St. Patrick's Cemetery, Loos; one other rank was wounded.

Considerable damage was done to our trenches on the 7th, and the following day was spent on repairs.

A very useful item of equipment was at this time delivered to the battalion in the shape of eight metal food containers; these operated on the Thermos principle, and enabled hot food to be sent from the rear up to those occupying the front and support lines.

Hot food in the front line was greatly appreciated by the men, as the chief mainstay of those in the line up till now had been " Fray Bentos," with an occasional " drum up " when and where circumstances permitted with the aid of a " Tommy " cooker.

The containers were elliptical on plan and about two feet deep, the top plate or cover being bolted down, and the whole carried on the back with the aid of straps, in a similar manner to the pack. With a fully-loaded container the carrier knew all about it, particularly if the cover was a bad fit or insecurely bolted, and he stepped on the loose end of a duckboard and pitched forward, the immediate result being that a good splash of hot stew would strike the carrier in the nape of the neck, soaking his tunic and slowly streaming down his back.

A journey up the line carrying a food container was not exactly a picnic, particularly if you desired suddenly to go to earth on the approach of a whizz-bang. Nevertheless, these food containers proved a blessing to the men in the forward areas, and their arrival in the line was always heralded with a shout and a rattling of mess tins. Enemy shelling continued to be on the heavy side, and kept our men busy repairing the damaged trenches. Early in the morning of February 9th our men in the front line were withdrawn to safety as a mine of ours was due to be exploded; this went off at 4 a.m. near the sunken road on the left of the copse, about 50 feet away from the trench. Work was started immediately to clear the trench, consolidate and wire the German side of th crater. The enemy shelled the crater during the day, wounding three of our men.

By the following morning a bombing post had been established on the near mound of the new crater, with a sap leading to it from our trench. Work on a sap on the right of Hart's crater was carried on with, and a patrol of ours went out at 7 p.m. and encountered a German working party. The battalion had three more men wounded on the 12th, and the day following Ptes. W. G. Middleton and T. Rust were killed and Lieut. F. M. Davis wounded, fortunately only slightly, but enough to put him in hospital for two weeks ; he returned to the battalion on the 27th. A practice gas attack was held at midday on the 13th, and it would appear the troops were slow to tuck the ends of the helmet under the collar.

The battalion was due for relief, but many exciting happenings and casualties occurred before this took place.

Most unexpectedly to the majority the enemy exploded a mine at the Copse at 7 a.m. on February 14th ; unfortunately some of our men went up with it.

As usual when the unexpected happens there is always someone about who manages to size up the situation promptly and act accordingly. In this instance, L/Cpl. J. Hodge, who was on the spot when the mine went up, had his Lewis gun working before the debris had finished falling ; of the German party who endeavoured to rush the crater only one got back to his lines alive. The enemy were sending over whizz-bangs, rifle grenades, and trench mortars, and while L/Cpl. J. Hodge was busy with his gun L/Cpl. J. Crisford led a bombing group up the opposite side of the crater ; actually he was the first man up on that side. L/Cpl. S. Warner, with two men, in full view of the enemy, occupied a position overlooking the crater which prevented the enemy from approaching unobserved. Although wounded, L/Cpl. S. Warner remained in his position, under fire, throughout the day.

Two of our officers—2nd Lieut. J. Chatterton, battalion bombing officer, and 2nd Lieut. and temporary Capt. L. E. Rundell—displayed great initiative and gallantry. A double block was made 15 yards from the enemy, and the consolidation of the crater was supervised by them under heavy fire.

That evening the 2nd Munster Fusiliers and the 1st Battalion of the Gloucesters relieved the battalion, which marched to their old billets at Bracquemont.

The explosion of the enemy mine caused the following casualties : Ptes. J. Bull, T. C. Chizlett, J. J. David, H. J. Daykin, H. A. J. Feast,

F. Harris, H. C. Matthews, E. Purdon, E. S. Tanner, H. E. Wass and H. H. Wood, all being killed. Lieut. J. L. Head was wounded, as also were 17 other ranks.

The following is an extract of a letter published in the " Clapham Observer," dated March 24th, 1916, written by Pte. H. Hunt:

" The last morning brought us a most unpleasant surprise, for at 7 a.m. the Germans blew a mine up underneath our front line, fortunately with very few casualties, as it was during ' stand to ' and no one was asleep in the dug-out.

" It was quite light when this happened and we were utterly taken by surprise, and for a few minutes confusion reigned. However, the captain of the company to which I am attached handled the situation in a splendid manner, and one of our gun teams caught the German storming party and wiped them out. They numbered 50 or more."

From the brigadier came the following :

" The brigadier congratulates you and all concerned in the very effective, prompt and gallant way in which the very difficult situation at the Copse has been dealt with. He wishes to have the names of any officers and other ranks whom you may consider deserving of immediate reward submitted to him as soon as possible."

As a result of the good work performed at the Copse two M.C.'s and three D.C.M.'s were awarded ; the following being the citations for these awards :

2nd Lieut. J. Chatterton, M.C.

For conspicuous gallantry and ability on February 14th, 1916, at the Copse, where the Germans exploded a mine unexpectedly. This officer was battalion grenadier officer. After double blocking a damaged trench 15 yards from the German line, he was of great assistance to 2nd Lieut. (T.-Capt.) L. E. Rundell in the task of consolidating the crater. This officer on a previous occasion behaved in a very gallant manner in a bombing attack near the Hairpin on December 20th, 1915.

2nd Lieut. and Temp. Capt. L. E. Rundell, M.C.

For conspicuous gallantry and ability on February 14th, 1916, at the Copse, where the Germans exploded a mine unexpectedly. This officer's instant grasp of the situation and prompt initiative enabled him to repulse the German attempt to rush the crater, and he superintended the consolidation of the near edge under a heavy fire. This personal gallantry and indifference to danger encouraged the company under his command to accomplish their difficult and dangerous trial.

L/Cpl. S. Warner, D.C.M.

For conspicuous gallantry and ability on February 14th, at the Copse where the Germans exploded a mine unexpectedly. This N.C.O. and two other men, at about 7 a.m. directly after the mine exploded, advanced under fire and occupied the ledge overlooking the crater which was in full view of the Germans in Snipers House. Although this N.C.O. was wounded early in the day he remained there under fire until 5.30 p.m., when he returned. He was able to overlook the crater and his presence there kept the Germans away who otherwise might have got over there unperceived.

L/Cpl. J. Hodge, D.C.M.

For conspicuous ability and presence of mind on February 14th, 1916, at the Copse, where the Germans exploded a mine unexpectedly. He was on duty with a Lewis machine-gun when the mine exploded, but got his gun into action before the debris had finished falling, and by this means prevented a German " rushing party " from reaching the crater. Only one German out of the rushing party was seen to return.

L/Cpl. J. Crisford, D.C.M.

For gallantry on February 14th, 1916, at the Copse, where the Germans exploded a mine unexpectedly. He led a grenadier group up on to the crater under fire very soon after the mine exploded, and was the first man up on that side of the crater.

The above awards were presented by Gen. Sir Charles Monro, K.C.B., G.O.C. 1st Army at divisional H.Q. at Bruay on March 13th, 1916.

With the action at the Copse, the battalion said goodbye to the Loos sector. For once in a way rumour came true and everyone was in good heart when the news spread that the battalion were off to Lillers.

Lillers, with its ancient market place and comfortable billets, appealed to all.

The mention of the name itself put a different aspect on life. English beers were obtainable in Lillers and a decent meal could be had for a couple of francs.

Many of the 7th had previously enjoyed the hospitality of Lillers, and these, together with those who had joined the battalion since the " first Lillers " (less a party of 25 N.C.O.'s and men who left to join as a working party the 173rd Tunnelling Company) paraded on the 15th along the main Nouex-les-Mines road by the corner of Rue General Chanzy and moved by rail to reserve at Lillers, where they arrived at 1 p.m. and remained until the end of the month.

Most of the time was spent in company inspections, rifle exercises, platoon drill, baths and route marches. Gen. Sir C. Monro, K.C.B., commanding 1st Army, inspected the brigade in the Grand Place.

2nd Lieuts. F. M. Withers and J. M. Lee joined the battalion here, as also did a draft of 36 other ranks.

Many route marches had taken place, and when the battalion fell in on February 29th, several N.C.O.'s and men were under the impression that they were due for another route march and many marched off with packs " specially packed " to resemble full packs. Unfortunately for these " dodgers " the presumed route march turned out to be a divisional trek.

The battalion paraded at 8.40 a.m. in the Rue de Bethune, facing the Grand Place, and marched via St. Hilaire, Rely, Estree Blanche and Basse Boulogne to the First Army training area at Enguinegatte, where they arrived at 2.30 p.m.

It now dawned on the " dodgers " that Lillers had been left behind for good, and the least that can be said is that a week later the quartermaster came to their assistance and arrived with two lorry loads of men's effects, etc.

Brigade exercises were carried out daily until March 4th when the battalion moved to Therouanne, arriving at noon.

The weather turned bitterly cold and sleet and snow fell continuously. The roads became very bad, and several men were detailed to assist transport with the aid of drag ropes.

Probably owing to the weather the men were not overworked; the inhabitants were hospitable, and the billets very comfortable.

On the 9th a move was made to fresh billets at Fontaine les Hermans for one night only, as on the following day another move was made to Beugin where billets were occupied about 4.45 p.m.

Excitement was provided that night by a fire which occurred in one of " D " Company billets.

Snow was still about and nothing beyond inspections, church parade and baths at Calonne-Ricouart took place until the 16th when a move was made towards the line via Houdain and Fresnicourt to Villers-au-Bois, near Souchez, where huts were occupied at midday. That same night a party of two officers and 50 other ranks performed work for the R.E.'s at Cabaret Rouge.

St. Patrick's Day, March 17th, the first anniversary of the battalion's departure for France, was the occasion of many celebrations. All officers who came out with the battalion were invited to H.Q. Mess by the special desire of the commanding officer.

The following sat down to dinner: Col. E. Faux, C.M.G., V.D., Capts. C. J. Salkeld Green, H. E. Lydiart, F. M. Davis, L. E. Rundell, M.C., Lieut. T. Rushworth, and Lieut.-Q.M. G. D. Roche. These were the only officers present with the battalion of those who originally came out a year ago. Also present at the dinner were Capts. Ferguson, R.A.M.C. (M.O.), J. Hartley and Lieut. D. Sutton (adjutant). Following toasts to " The King " and " The Regiment " came the toast of " Those who came out with us but are no longer with us." On the following day the transport section held their " anniversary concert " in a barn, the Padre's gramophone was used, and the talent available put up a creditable show.

"*I've got it—give us your pliers*" *Signallers: 7th London*

CHAPTER NINE

March—May, 1916
CARENCY AND SOUCHEZ

THE start of the battalion's second year on active service found them in huts at Villers-au-Bois, where they remained until March 20th, when they paraded at 11.30 p.m., and moved up to what was to them a new area to relieve the 17th London in the Carency sector near a sugar refinery.

Headquarters here were situated in a hole in the side of a quarry and the relief was completed at 2.50 a.m. on the 21st. The part taken over was not exactly ideal, consisting as it did of a series of very poor trenches, and dug-outs were noticeable by their absence.

" A," " B " and " D " Companies each did a day in the line, while " C " Company sent up 30 men each night to strengthen the company in the line.

Work was immediately started upon repairing the trenches, much time being spent improving Boyeau Pelletier, laying trench boards in Chemin Creux, and wiring the front.

The 21st London relieved the battalion on the night of the 26th, and they arrived back in billets at Villers-au-Bois about 2.30 a.m. the following morning. 2nd Lieut. H. S. P. Symonds rejoined the battalion here from Le Havre, where he had been acting as an instructor. During the recent turn in the line the battalion suffered the loss of Ptes. A. Mince and H. Pope, both killed, and 15 other ranks wounded; one of the latter remained at duty throughout.

Shortly after the troops arrived at Villers-au-Bois they were served out with hot tea and rum; breakfast was at 11 a.m., and two hours later the battalion moved off to Verdrel, where they arrived at 3 p.m. The battalion remained in this area for the next five days, during which time large working parties of five officers and 250 other ranks paraded each day and reported to Gouy for work under R.E.'s. One such party were fortunate enough to be carried by buses to Ablain. Those who missed the working parties had physical drill, company inspections, etc.; at various times the battalion had baths at Fresnicourt.

Capt. G. D. Roche had arranged rather comfortable H.Q. for himself; in fact, it was rather " a posh rear H.Q.," with a neat bordered path to the garden. A plate affixed to the gate proclaimed " No hawkers or circulars," and another stated, " Huns, horses and cycles not admitted "; the house itself was named " Roche's Retreat," which some wit altered to " Rogue's Retreat."

At the end of the month Brig.-Gen. Cuthbert went on leave. His place on brigade was filled by Col. E. Faux, C.M.G., V.D., and Capt. C. J. Salkeld Green assumed temporary command of the battalion.

An outbreak of measles occurred in the area and Lieut. H. D. Long with 37 other ranks were isolated in the Ablain St. Nazaire end of the wood.

The battalion moved on the morning of April 1st to huts in Bouvigny, and relieved the 19th London Regiment.

The weather was lovely and bright, and transport in moving up went astray and came out on to a ridge in full view of the Hun. Transport immediately opened up to 200 yards between vehicles, and a great sigh of relief went up when the last limber got clear and under cover of the wood.

Church parade was held on the morning of the following day, and in the evening the battalion proceeded to the Lorette trenches and relieved the London Irish, H.Q. being situate among the ruins of Ablain St. Nazaire.

The battalion occupied the trenches until the 7th, when they were relieved by the 23rd London Regiment. " A " and " B " Companies going back to Villers-au-Bois, " C " and " D " to Carency.

The battalion had been hard at work repairing the trenches, and had remained free of casualties during this last tour, but unfortunately Capt. H. E. Lydiart was sent away by ambulance to hospital at Lillers with rheumatic fever.

No doubt the strain of war and the bad weather had their effect on Capt. Lydiart, as he was not a young man, having in his earlier days gone through the siege of Ladysmith. He was always convinced that he would survive the war, and in this he was correct. He came to the 7th in 1909 from the K.R.R.C. In December, 1914, he retired from the Regular Army and was commissioned as captain with the 7th London in January, 1915, and came overseas with the battalion. This officer performed most valuable work both at Festubert and Loos ; he left the battalion with the sympathy of all, and took with him many good wishes for his speedy recovery. When he recovered, he was unfit for active service, and after a short spell with the 3rd Battalion he returned to France in September, 1916, as adjutant of the 4th Corps School at St. Riquer. In March, 1917, he was appointed town major of Bapaume, later becoming area commandant, Willeman area, being finally demobilized in 1920. His son served with the 2nd Battalion, being awarded the M.M. in 1917.

On April 13th, the 22nd London relieved " ours " which moved off into billets at Estree Cauchie (Extra Cushy to most troops !) and while here supplied large working parties to the R.E.'s at Gouy Servins. About this time 2nd Lieut. Symonds was appointed town major of this place. Lieut. T. Rushworth, who had been transport officer since August, 1914, now took over "A" Company and Lieut. F. B. Wade was appointed transport officer.

The G.O.C. of the division, Gen. Sir C. Barter, inspected the battalion on the 19th in the rear of Ohlain Chateau and on the following day the battalion paraded at midday and moved to Gouy Servins where it remained for the next six days, supplying working parties by day and night.

Capt. J. G. Budd returned and 124 other ranks joined the battalion here ; Lieut. L. A. L. Flower rejoined from England.

On April 25th, officers of the battalion visited trenches in the Carency area ; on the following day "ours" was relieved by the 24th, and at 1 p.m. moved to Villers-au-Bois and relieved the 17th London Regiment. At 6 p.m., the 21st relieved "ours" which, at 7 p.m., was ready to move off up the line, but owing to heavy shelling of its intended route by the enemy it was not until two and a half hours later that a move was made.

Eventually the battalion, which had moved up the line without packs—not at all a healthy sign—relieved the London Irish during the early hours of the 27th in the right sub-section of the Carency sector, the relief being completed by 2.20 a.m.

The line had been fairly peaceful in this area for some considerable time and no doubt the quietness served to mask the great activity going on underground. That the battalion were extremely fortunate during this tour of the line is beyond all doubt ; they had hardly got settled in the line, which was all fresh to them, when the enemy shelled Zouave Valley with shrapnel. Later on in the morning the front line was shelled for two and a half hours with heavy trench mortars and rifle grenades ; our artillery retaliated then and quiet reigned until 4.30 p.m. when the enemy shelled again until 7 p.m.

On the following day, April 28th, the enemy shelled our front and support lines in the morning. The afternoon remained quiet—the lull before the storm—as at 7.30 p.m. the Hun touched off a mine on our right front which was held by the 74th Brigade of the 25th Division. Our artillery opened up, as also did that of the enemy, and Zouave Valley received thirty minutes of intense shelling.

At 4.30 a.m., on the 29th, the R.E.'s blew a camouflet on our left ; this touched off an enemy mine and so formed what became known as the Broadbridge crater. Zouave Valley was pounded with 4·2's ; fortunately we only sustained one casualty, slightly wounded.

More excitement came on the last day of the month. The morning opened quietly and our guns set the ball rolling ; the enemy retaliated and heavy shells passed overhead, travelling in each direction for one and a half hours. Our support line came in for heavy shelling and at 6.50 p.m. the enemy blew two mines on our left, almost under the front line and slightly left of a mine blown before the battalion came in the line. A severe enemy bombardment accompanied the blowing up of these mines, especially on Zouave Valley, particularly at the Souchez end.

May opened quietly, the enemy making a small bombing attack on one of our saps which was repulsed without loss.

On May 2nd, at 11.40 p.m., the 21st arrived and relieved the battalion which marched out via the Cabaret Rouge road, Duck Walk and Villers-au-Bois to Maisnil Bouche, where it arrived at 4 a.m. all ready to occupy the billets awaiting them.

Despite the mines and the heavy shelling, the total casualties suffered by the battalion were one other rank killed, 2nd Lieut. E. W. C. Lonnen and 20 other ranks wounded. The battalion remained at Maisnil Bouche for the next five days and the weather was nice and fine. Company training took place in the mornings and firing on the ranges occupied the afternoons. One company per day were inoculated and a visit was made to Fresnicourt for much-needed baths.

Working parties were not omitted as four officers and 200 men may recall by the work they did on the Maistre line at Carency under the R.W.F.'s.

On May 8th, at 8 p.m., the battalion moved to Villers-au-Bois and relieved the 20th. The next ten days were spent here and the time was occupied with company training, inspections and working parties. Large parties were provided for the tunnelling company and also carrying parties for the T.M.B.'s.

On May 11th, Maj. C. J. Salkeld Green assumed command of the battalion in the absence of Col. E. Faux, C.M.G., V.D.

An inspection of the battalion was carried out at Maisnil Bouche by the G.O.C. of the division, Gen. Sir C. Barter. Afterwards the battalion marched past in column and returned in close column with the drums playing " Greensleeves."

It was about this time that the regiment became affiliated to the Middlesex Regiment. Meanwhile, transport had been inspected by Col. Blythe, C.M.G., O.C. divisional train. The weather turned very wet and the usual church service was held in a hut.

May 17th saw the birth of the Quarante Se(p)t, the Divisional Follies, when they gave their first performance and from which they never looked back.

CHAPTER TEN

May 21st, 1916
VIMY

THE name of Vimy, usually associated with the Canadians, is a name which, to those who were with the battalion in May, 1916, conjures up visions of an occasion when the enemy were prevented by the bravery, endurance and pluck of the battalion from completely wiping out the 7th London as then constituted.

Those who came to the battalion after Vimy always listened with awe and respect to the "old soldier" fighting this battle over again.

The battalion were enjoying the benefit of comfortable billets and the scenery of Villers-au-Bois when on May 18th orders came for them to take over the Berthonval sector of Vimy Ridge. It was at 9 p.m. when the battalion commenced to relieve the 13th Cheshires, two companies being at Cabaret Rouge and the other two companies being with H.Q. and details in Zouave Valley.

On the following day, again at 9 p.m., the battalion began to relieve the Royal Irish Rifles in the right sub-section. This relief was completed at 1.40 a.m. on the 20th. Meanwhile, transport had been moved forward to Camblain L'Abbe.

On our left the 20th London were holding the right of the 141st Brigade and joining the 140th Brigade at Ersatz Alley. The 10th Cheshires were on our right.

An advanced post on our left front was manned by one platoon of " D " Company and one Lewis gun, under Lieut. H. D. Long, while the centre advanced post was occupied by an N.C.O. and party with one Lewis gun, under Lieut. A. R. Wallis.

The front line on the left was occupied by the remainder of " D " Company under Capt. F. M. Davis; two platoons of " C " Company under Lieut. M. Juriss were in the centre front, while on the right were two platoons of " B " Company and one Lewis gun under 2nd Lieut. V. W. Mileman and Lieut. H. Hampton; the latter also being in charge of the Lewis guns.

In the support line were the remaining two platoons of " B " Company with one L.G. under Capt. J. D. Hartley, while Capt. L. E. Rundell, M.C., with the remainder of " C " Company, occupied Old Boot Street. " A " Company under Lieut. T. Rushworth, the support company, were in a quarry on the side of the hill. 2nd Lieut. R. E. Taylor was in charge of the bombers who manned a post on the right.

It quickly became apparent that "ours" had entered a decidedly warm sector. Owing to heavy enemy shelling during recent days there had been little or no work carried out by our predecessors; overhead phone wires gave the troops a lot of trouble on their way in, the trenches were in a very bad condition and the front was not wired. The troops had hardly settled down when they were subjected to three-quarters of an hour bombardment of H.E. and shrapnel.

During the first night "A" Company were employed wiring and they performed a good job as they wired practically the whole of our front.

At dawn a party of the enemy were seen in front of their line; subsequent events indicated that they were cutting their wire.

Throughout this day, the 21st, particularly in the afternoon, the enemy maintained heavy trench mortar fire; exceptionally heavy shelling on our front and support lines was experienced, causing casualties and interruptions of the signalling communication services.

The enemy shelling increased its intensity, minenwerfers came over and "D" Company men in the detached post were practically wiped out; Lieut. H. D. Long was killed and only four survivors managed to get back to our front line. On the right, the platoon under Lieut. H. Hampton was twice shelled out of the front trench to the support line. This particular section of the front was almost knocked flat and became untenable. L/Cpl. Lucas displayed great coolness in staying behind, during one of these temporary evacuations, to dig out his gun which had been buried. The signallers performed many acts of bravery in exposing themselves in order to mend broken wires and re-establish communications.

The company in the neighbourhood of White Hart Street was also heavily shelled.

At 3.40 p.m. the intensity of the shelling increased still further and Zouave Valley was bombarded with heavies and tear gas; the shelling was incessant and concentrated on our front and support lines.

Communication up International Trench became impossible, and telephonic communications between B.H.Q. and the left company ceased at 3.40 p.m.

This terrific barrage, with which tear gas was mixed, and the like of which had never before been known, lasted until 7.55 p.m. when the enemy advanced close upon his own barrage. The attack came right across the whole of our front; the left company were completely cut off as was also the detached post at the top of Old Boot Street and Central Avenue. Rifles and bombs of the few dazed and unwounded survivors were either not fit for use or had been buried by the intense shelling.

During the period of this attack, " A " Company had taken up a position along the ridge above the Duck Walk between Central Avenue and International Trench.

Directly the news that the enemy had captured our front and support line reached Maj. C. J. S. Green, then commanding the battalion in the absence of Col. E. Faux, who was acting brigadier, he at once with great foresight, ordered, at 8.40 p.m., two platoons of " A " Company, under Capt. T. Rushworth, to counter-attack and drive the enemy out of our centre front. Sergt. H. Duck put in a considerable amount of good work encouraging the men under heavy fire during this counter-attack.

Owing to the small numbers the attack was not successful, but it certainly shook the enemy, causing him to waver and hesitate. The survivors of this attack returned to join the other two platoons on the ridge who, under 2nd Lieut. V. F. Kelly, had been giving supporting fire.

The position on our left which, as previously stated, had been cut off, was precarious, and at 8.55 p.m. the 6th London were asked to send reinforcements. 2nd Lieut. R. E. Taylor took out a patrol on the right and returned with valuable information, and the bombers under his command formed a block in Central Avenue. The enemy were in part of International Trench and forming a double block. At 9.20 p.m. a company of the 6th London, with two Lewis guns, proceeded up International Trench which they held facing south, and they also sent another company to line the ridge on our left.

Owing to the difficulties of communication, no personal interview between Maj. Green and the C.O. of the 6th London was possible, but at 9.45 p.m. a verbal message was received that the 6th were counter-attacking on our left. By way of co-operation orders were given for our support company to counter-attack on the right and for the bombers to advance up Central Avenue.

All available men of " A " Company and the bombers under 2nd Lieut. R. E. Taylor moved forward, but owing to the very heavy enemy machine-gun fire they were prevented from making progress.

It was after 10 p.m. when the enemy shelling eased down that advantage was taken of the lull to consolidate our positions and to replenish the supply of bombs and ammunition in the forward area.

" B " Company H.Q. had been blown in, the signaller on the telephone was killed, and 2nd Lieut. J. M. Stirling, slightly wounded and badly shaken, was sent to the rear by the M.O.

About 12.40 a.m. on the 22nd, Maj. Green was informed by the brigadier that the 7th Brigade on our right were counter-attacking at 1 a.m. and asking for co-operation. Maj. Green requested that this attack should be postponed until 2 a.m. owing to the difficulties of arranging details in so short a time.

Nevertheless, the 7th Brigade made their counter-attack at 1.10 a.m.; far too soon for the co-operation requested to be arranged.

Between 1 a.m. and 3 a.m. the enemy again put up a very heavy barrage. At 3.30 a.m. a company of the 6th London, in charge of Capt. Neely, was placed under the command of Maj. Green.

As the Boche guns quietened, our work of consolidation went on, and the 7th then held a line from the double block made by Capt. L. E. Rundell in Old Boot Street, down Central Avenue facing north, and a line along the ridge up to about halfway between Central Avenue and International Trench where we joined the 6th London; the attached company of the 6th were in support along the Duck Walk.

During the early hours of the morning Maj. Green, together with Maj. Whitehead of the 6th London, made a personal reconnaissance of the ground and decided to advance the positions then held by about 250 yards. This decision was put into effect at 7 p.m., when the 7th advanced to a line in front of our previous position on the ridge above the Duck Walk, an old French trench being dug out and occupied.

Another line was dug into a bank about 100 yards in front of the first ridge and 150 yards behind the previous trench. This was occupied as a support line.

In these movements the 6th London co-operated, and when the 1st Royal Berkshires relieved the 7th on the night of the 22nd, they were handed over four lines, one 250 yards in front of the Duck Walk ridge, a second 100 yards in front of the latter ridge, a third along the ridge, and one along Central Avenue and up to the double block in Old Boot Street. The battalion returned to Camblain L'Abbe, being met on the road and served out with hot tea and rum.

Such in brief is the story of the " Shiny Seventh " at Vimy.

Countless deeds of heroism in this action have to be omitted owing to the scarcity of details; many of the 7th risked their lives to bring in wounded men. Hardly any of those saved could tell who it was that carried them to safety. Signallers again, and likewise stretcher bearers and runners, performed yeoman service as they did at Festubert and Loos.

Quite early on many men in the front line were killed, others were wounded; and when the attack came a great number of the latter were made prisoners. L/Cpl. H. Lovelock, from an advanced post, gave early information of the attack, afterwards assisting to man the double block.

Lieut. H. Hampton performed his duties in an exemplary manner until he became a casualty. His arm was broken by a gunshot wound soon after the attack started, and his servant, Pte. A. Reader, was killed while taking him to the dressing station.

Capt. L. E. Rundell, in forming a double block, showed great presence of mind in handling a difficult situation and undoubtedly prevented the enemy from obtaining further gains. In connection with this action he was recommended for a D.S.O., but was awarded a bar to his M.C.

The prompt counter-attack ordered by Maj. C. J. Salkeld Green and put into effect by two platoons of "A" Company under Capt. T. Rushworth, had a considerable effect on the German attack; at no other part of the front was the enemy counter-attacked so promptly.

Had it been possible for greater numbers to have been used in this counter-attack there is little doubt that the lost positions would have been regained.

The decision to make this attack and, later, the personal reconnaissance of Maj. C. J. Salkeld Green, when he selected the positions to which the 7th advanced and handed over to the relieving battalion, stamped him as an officer of outstanding ability and greatly added to the reputation he had made for himself previously in the actions at Festubert and Loos.

A few lines on the happenings in the rear during the attack will not be out of place here.

Great excitement prevailed in all rear areas; slides were flashed on the 25th Divisional cinema screen recalling immediately various men to their units, and concerts were similarly interrupted.

The 142nd Brigade was hastily collected and sent up to reinforce the battalions on our left.

Mont St. Eloi, the railhead for the area, was heavily shelled and received a good "dubbing" of gas shells.

The ration train was prepared and casualties among the transport and personnel occurred; the light railway leading up the line was blown up in several places.

The only two officers killed in this action were Lieuts. A. L. Hancock and H. D. Long; the latter originally came out with the battalion as a corporal. N.C.O.'s and other ranks killed numbered about 40.

Capt. F. M. Davis and Lieut. W. V. Brooks, who had been wounded, were taken prisoners, as also was Lieut. M. Juriss, who had stayed behind to look after some wounded men of his company; his name had only that day appeared in Divisional Orders as having been awarded the M.C. Lieuts. V. W. Mileman and J. Chatterton were both wounded.

Capt. T. Rushworth during the counter-attack received about 70 small wounds in the leg and back from a German bomb, his uniform being torn to shreds.

Capt. L. E. Rundell, M.C., 2nd Lieuts. W. E. Miller, A. R. Wallis, R. E. Taylor and H. C. Ridgway were all slightly wounded.

The following are the citations and awards to officers and N.C.O.'s of the " Shiny Seventh " for their actions at Vimy.

Capt. L. E. Rundell, M.C.,had the honour of being the first officer in the division to obtain the distinction of being awarded a bar to his M.C.

2nd Lieut. R. E. Taylor. Awarded M.C.

This officer showed conspicuous ability and gallantry during the period May 21st–22nd at Vimy Ridge.

This officer was battalion bombing officer, and his personal example and able handling of the bombers assisted the defence greatly. At a time when information as to the battalion's right flank was urgently needed, he took out a bombing patrol and brought back valuable information.

His cheerfulness and devotion to duty under most trying conditions were a fine example to others.

2nd Lieut. (Temp. Capt.) L. E. Rundell. Awarded Bar to M.C.

This officer showed great ability on May 21st–22nd at Vimy Ridge in dealing with the situation after the support line was captured. He secured the blocking of Old Boot Street and Central Avenue and continued to occupy these communication trenches although for a considerable time both flanks were exposed.

The resolute dealing with the situation resulted in the retention of this important communication trench and the formation of a defensive flank.

No. 1101 Sergt. G. W. Steele. Awarded D.C.M.

At Vimy Ridge on May 21st–22nd. This N.C.O. was in charge of a bombing section. He showed at all times a fearlessness and coolness which were a valuable example to all. On one occasion he volunteered to get in a wounded man who lay about 100 yards in front of our block when the exact position of the enemy was unknown, although it was known to be near the wounded man. He was successful in getting our man in.

2nd Lieut. R. E. Taylor and Capt. L. E. Rundell with whose company he was working, speak in the highest terms about this N.C.O.

No. 2435 Sergt. H. Duck. Awarded M.M.

In the counter-attack on the night of May 21st–22nd at Vimy Ridge. This N.C.O. rallied the men when they were shaken by M.G. fire and steadied them under shrapnel fire. Later, after the counter-attack had failed and the company were occupying a position which afforded very little cover, he steadied the men by walking about in the open. He set an excellent example to all under him and gave great assistance to his officers.

No. 1698 L/Cpl. H. J. Sumner. Awarded M.M.

Acted as battalion runner on May 21st–22nd at Vimy Ridge. This N.C.O. repeatedly went through the heaviest fire to carry messages and showed judgment and resource in carrying out his duties.

He was always the first to volunteer for any dangerous message.

No. 2418 L/Cpl. H. Lovelock. Awarded M.M.

On May 21st–22nd at Vimy Ridge. This N.C.O. was in charge of an advanced bombing post during the bombardment and gave early information of the enemy's attack.

He assisted in building a double block and remained in charge of this block until the battalion was relieved. Also under a heavy fire he went back and brought in a man who was seriously wounded.

No. 2993 L/Cpl. R. Newton. Awarded M.M.

This N.C.O. went out on very many occasions on May 21st–22nd at Vimy Ridge under very heavy shell fire to mend the signal wires, and on several occasions communications were only re-established by his indifference to danger.

L/Cpl. B. T. Ferris, who was at this time attached to the T.M.B., also gained the M.M. for his gallant conduct.

Others of the battalion to be awarded the M.M. were Sergts. W. A. Claydon, W. P. V. Coles and G. Marr, L/Cpl. W. Shepherd, and Ptes. G. Barclay and A. Steele.

The following are extracts from a description written at the time by Lieut. H. Hampton.

> " When the bombardment commenced, bad as it appeared to be, it was nothing to what we got later. The enemy kept up a nerve-racking bombardment with heavy trench mortars seasoned with 'beaucoup' rifle grenades. The casualties on the first day were not heavy, but these H.E. shells had a worrying effect upon the men; it was impossible to get any sleep in the front and support lines.
>
> " The T.M. business became very hot indeed: the front line was practically blown to pieces and the men were simply moving up and down dodging the T.M.'s which came over in salvoes.

"The Lewis guns were buried and dug out again, as were most of the men, not once but many times. With the trench levelled, I retired with the remnants of the two platoons down the centre communication trench, where I was joined shortly afterwards by Lieut. Mileman and a few more men.

"Later we re-occupied the front line and then came the most intense bombardment that had, ever since the war started, been concentrated upon British troops in such a small area.

"We were almost blinded by fumes, and the men lay down in the bottom of the trenches, most of them with smoke helmets on. It looked as if the whole battalion would be wiped out, and the noise was terrific.

"The barrage completely isolated the ridge from all outside help and seemed to gain in intensity every hour. When the attack came the enemy succeeded in cutting off 'D' Company, where no semblance of a trench remained. The advanced posts were wiped out, fighting to the last.

"Things looked black, the front and support lines gone, and the last line of defence as regards the ridge itself, was 'up agin it.' The gallant counter-attack made by Capt. T. Rushworth enabled Capt. Rundell to establish a double block, and this the Huns never succeeded in passing.

"This certainly was the biggest thing the battalion was ever in, and well the boys stood up to it, greatly outnumbered and pasted by shells of every calibre which simply turned the ground over and over again.

"Part of H.Q. dug-out was blown in. Several wounded officers lying in there at the time were dragged into an adjoining dug-out. A batman was killed, and two others wounded.

"The battalion had many casualties, but it was a proud day for the 'Shiny Seventh,' who had acquitted themselves so well, and also for Maj. C. J. Salkeld Green, who commanded the battalion in action for the first time."

From a letter written by L/Cpl. S. Phelan the following are extracts :

"On the Sunday we got into closer touch with the Huns than usual. They bombarded us for four hours with the heaviest stuff they had, and then came over.

"They eventually captured two of our lines.

"We had news of our gun team. During the bombardment they were quite safe; since then we have heard nothing more as the Germans got into the line and took prisoners.

"As far as I can make out, nobody came back from that part of the line."

Pte. Frank Meader wrote to one of his former comrades who had been wounded as follows:

"We came out two nights ago, having been up to our necks in it, but it's really marvellous what one can do in a few hours towards cleaning up. The boys are still in great spirits and it is fine to be with them marching back to billets."

Extracts from a letter written by Sergt. F. Redway:

"I am comparatively safe after the most awful onslaught the British have had in the war. We relieved a regular battalion and had three companies in the line with 'A' as reserve in a quarry.

"Casualties occurred during the first twenty-four hours; the enemy evidently got wind of our artillery being changed, for they acted at this very period.

"In the afternoon started the most awful bombardment of the war; the air simply rained great 5.9's.

"It was the work of a genius. They put up a barrier of shells across the valley, preventing supports and reserves coming up; every trench of importance was marked, observation posts, etc., and our batteries were badly punished.

"The gas affected our eyes and I ordered the boys to put their gas helmets on, fix bayonets, and be prepared for anything.

"A man was seen moving about in front and S.M. Collins rushed out and got him in. He was a bomber wounded in two places.

"Upon the instructions of Lieut. A. R. Wallis I had to examine a trench, find the position of the enemy, and report back to him.

"With a bomber for company we crawled 80 yards and upon turning a corner we rushed into two of them.

"One was promptly put out of action, and as we only had to report the presence of the enemy, we ran back like hell.

"Words fail to describe the hours up to when we were relieved, and then came a six-mile march back, absolutely done to the wide.

"This morning we had a roll call. It was awful."

L/Cpl. W. Robertson writes the following interesting account:

"Proceeding along the communication trench from the valley to the front line, our guide appeared lost. Very lights gave a fitful glare and there was that peculiar odour of recent explosion with a growing sense that nasty things had happened recently. Eventually a private of the Royal Irish Rifles whom we met, put us right.

"He also volunteered information about a short disused length of trench slightly in rear of our post. He said, ' If I were you, and Jerry plants anything near the post, I would occupy this trench; it seems to miss all the muck.'

"Except for the sentry post, we made our home in this piece of trench and eventually spent a considerable time hugging the side, watching the earth go up and down around us, and the great fountains of water as stuff of all sizes fell into the waterlogged shell-holes.

"Our trench did indeed bear a charmed life, and our informant was correct when he said ' it seems to miss all the muck.' Even so, we were not sorry when another section of the bombers came up to relieve us that night.

"In the late afternoon of the following day the whole valley was full of smoke, tear gas and shell bursts when Lieut. Taylor came along and said ' we were going to find out where Jerry was.' It was now getting dark, and as we moved up the communication trench it was decided to form a pukka bombing party. This we did, and advanced in true text-book style. At one spot, what we thought to be a Jerry turned out to be one of our own chaps badly wounded. It was lucky for him that a Jerry flare went up as we were about to lob over a Mills bomb.

"We pushed farther on and made a block in the trench where we remained until relieved."

Herewith the story of C.Q.M.S. Addison :

"On May 21st the ration limbers left Camblain L'Abbe about 5 p.m. for Mont St. Eloi; as we moved off along the Arras road the enemy were throwing over some heavy stuff, including tear gas.

"We arrived safely at our destination, and despite continued shelling, rations were loaded on the trucks of the light railway.

"Continued enemy shelling and tear gas had caused the ' Gas Alert ' to be sounded, and everyone donned P.H. helmets, the flannel bag and mouthpiece affair. Then it was found that the rails had been blown up at several places.

"The brigade T.O. ordered the trucks to be unloaded and dispatched me with a message to Capt. G. Roche ' to send up all the men he could for a carrying party.' This meant a journey of three miles for me. After a good run I got a lift on a gun limber and had my inside shaken out.

"Returning with two limbers and about 20 men, rations were loaded and, travelling via Villers-au-Bois, we reached a point near Carency, unloaded and sorted out essential rations.

"From this point a party of the 4th Royal Welch Fusiliers became the carrying party. Sergt. Taylor, A/C.Q.M.S. of 'A' Company and myself of 'B,' were detailed to go with this party. We proceeded towards the line which we reached as dawn was breaking. All communication trenches in Zouave Valley were obliterated and in small parties the men were instructed to run down the forward slope and dump the rations in a heap. One point stands out : in one sandbag was a bottle of Scotch for 'B' Company Sergeants. This I planted near a Y.M.C.A. soup canteen. On the return journey I made for this spot, but found that some 'rats' had been there."

An extract of an article written on Vimy by Pte. H. Preston is included as it affords another viewpoint and is based on a biblical text.

" ' Though I walk through the Valley of the Shadow of Death.' We have often repeated this well-known verse of the Psalmist, but to how many has it been brought home to witness the living truth of these words?

"Today the best and bravest of us in France have the full sense of these words engraved on our minds, never to be forgotten.

"It seems as if nature herself had almost allied herself with the human slaughter and sacrifice that goes on continuously. The Valley is haunted, a most uncanny feeling comes over us."

Beyond all doubt those who survived this turn in the line experienced shell fire such as up to this time had not been known. It is recorded that 70,000 shells were fired by the enemy, while our own divisional artillery fired 32,000 rounds between May 21st–24th.

Never before had such a terrific artillery scheme been put into operation—heavy trench mortars, shrapnel and high velocity shells, together with tear gas shells rained down upon the front line and supports.

Our own artillery, caught in the midst of a relief, had four guns knocked out in less time than it takes to write.

This was the first occasion when what became known as the "box barrage" was used. How anyone in the area survived the shelling it is difficult to understand. Men and guns were buried and dug out, men were wounded and fought on, untold acts of bravery were performed by all ranks. Runners carrying messages had miraculous escapes, and after hours of continuous shelling the enemy attacked, the main weight falling upon the "Shiny Seventh." The enemy reached our last line of defence where he was finally held.

That the enemy was checked was due to the great bravery of the 7th, who, after the initial shock, rallied, and by skilful leadership aided by the prompt counter-attack made within forty-five minutes of the enemy's attack, succeeded in holding and finally advancing their positions.

CHAPTER ELEVEN

May—July, 1916

SOUCHEZ AGAIN

IT was 1.20 a.m. on May 23rd when the relief from Vimy was completed, and three hours later the battalion arrived at Camblain L'Abbe where it remained for three days, moving off at 8.20 a.m. on the 25th for Bruay, arriving shortly after noon.

For the next nineteen days the battalion remained in Bruay and enjoyed a well-earned rest and change of scenery. Drafts totalling 67 men arrived making a welcome addition to the strength, and the following officers also joined: 2nd Lieuts. L. A. Bam, W. Ryall, H. U. T. Bowley, J. W. Pym, A. E. Hope, W. G. Thurnell, G. R. Jury, A. S. Thomson, and H. T. Johnstone.

The honours list published on June 4th contained the well-merited and highly-deserved award of the M.C. to Maj. C. J. Salkeld Green.

Replenishment of kit, baths, company training, classes for N.C.O.'s, battalion drill, range firing, etc., an inspection by the 1st Army commander, Gen. Sir C. Monro, C.B., at Calonne Ricouart, and a presentation of honours and awards took place during this stay at Bruay, which culminated with a visit to the battalion on June 11th of the Lord Mayor of London, Sir Charles Wakefield,

In the afternoon the battalion sports started at 2 p.m., music being provided by the band of the 6th London Field Ambulance. Unfortunately just after the third event had been completed a violent thunderstorm washed everyone off the ground.

On the 12th the battalion paraded at 9 a.m. and moved off through Hersin to Bouvigny-Boyeffles, and on the following day another move was made to Bois de Noulette where the 11th West Yorks were relieved in the reserve position at Souchez; from here working parties operated.

On the next evening "ours" relieved the Civil Service Rifles and the companies occupied the line in the following order: "A" centre, "B" left, "D" right, while "C" were in reserve.

Except for one and a half hours trench mortar activity, which caused an officer and one other rank to be wounded, this turn in the line was quiet, only marred by one incident—an enemy sniper killed 2nd Lieut. J. G. Ralph.

One company of the Howe Battalion of the Royal Naval Division were attached to us for instruction during this visit to the line.

In Sir D. Haig's dispatches of April 30th, published about this time in the press, the following names were "mentioned": Lieut. T.

Rushworth, Lieut.-Q.M. G. D. Roche, and C.S.M. (acting R.S.M.) H. Collins.

On June 20th the 7th were relieved, and it was 5 a.m. the following morning when the last company arrived at Hersin, where the stay only permitted of a short rest and clean up.

The battalion relieved the 8th London on the 22nd in Souchez 1 sector. This relief was delayed by bad weather, and the trenches being full of water, it was 1 a.m. before the companies settled down to the following positions in the line : " A " left, " C " right, " B " reserve, and " D " in support.

During this time a control post was retained at Boyeffles of 14 drummers and half a dozen men of " B " and " C " Companies, under 2nd Lieuts. W. G. Thurnell and E. W. Pearse.

Capt. Budd and 2nd Lieut. Cribb also kept their permanent working party.

After a couple of quiet days in the line, the 21st London came up and relieved the battalion, who moved into billets at Fosse 10 on the 26th.

The following day a parade for baths was held at Hersin, followed by the usual clean up, inspections and company training.

On the 29th the enemy shelled the mine and neighbouring houses without causing any casualties to " ours."

On the following day the battalion moved off at 8 p.m. to relieve the 23rd London on the Lorette Spur, " A," " B " and " C " occupying the right, centre and left positions respectively.

The battalion had only been in the line about half an hour when the division on the right made a raid ; consequently the 7th suffered in the retaliation this raid provoked.

The battalion in the line had enjoyed another quiet spell, and on July 4th they moved and relieved the 15th London in the Souchez 1 sector. While here two other ranks were wounded, and on the 7th, 2nd Lieut. J. W. Pym, who had only joined the battalion at the end of May, was unfortunately killed by a sniper in the early part of the morning.

On the same day the services of another officer were lost to the battalion when Lieut. J. L. Head departed for the Royal Flying Corps.

The battalion were relieved by the London Irish, and at 2 a.m. on the 8th were back again in old billets at Fosse 10.

While here lectures were attended by officers and N.C.O.'s and the battalion paid a visit to the baths at the brewery of Sains en Gohelle.

Night working parties provided by " ours " for the 142nd Brigade cost the battalion two other ranks killed and two wounded.

On the 12th, Brig.-Gen. G. J. Cuthbert, C.B., C.M.G., vacated the command of the 140th Brigade to become G.O.C. of the 39th Division. He was succeeded by Brig.-Gen. Viscount Hampden, C.M.G.

A special Order of the Day was issued:

> "In bidding goodbye to the 140th Infantry Brigade the brigadier wishes to thank all ranks for their most loyal co-operation and help during the period that he has been in command. He greatly regrets that he is unable to say goodbye personally to units, but he wishes them to understand how fully he appreciated all they have done, their unfailing gallantry in action, and their smartness, cleanliness, efficiency and unvarying good conduct in billets. It has made his period of command one of continuous pride and pleasure.
>
> He wishes them all good luck in the future, and his best wishes and remembrances will always go with them.
>
> "(Signed) G. J. CUTHBERT,
> "Brig.-General.
> "Commanding 140th Infantry Brigade."

A move was made on July 13th to Coupigny, and on this date the Corps Commander made a presentation of medal ribbons, at which the 7th supplied three officers and 100 men to represent the brigade.

On the 15th the battalion relieved the 1st Royal Berks at Camblain L'Abbe, and on the following day, Sunday, attended a church parade held in a near-by wood.

Company training was carried out during the next few days, and while here 2nd Lieut. H. E. Howlett joined for duty.

On July 17th the battalion lost the services of 2nd Lieut. W. E. Miller, who died of wounds as the result of an unfortunate accident at the Bomb School, Hersin.

The new brigadier, Viscount Hampden, C.M.G., carried out an inspection of the battalion on the 21st, and on the evening of the day following the battalion paraded at 8.45 p.m. and relieved the 15th London in the notorious trenches of the Berthonval sector, the scene of the battalion's recent famous action.

Upon this occasion all four companies were in the line; reading from left to right, they occupied the line in the following order: "D," "B," "A," "C." This was a quiet tour of duty and altogether different from the famous May 21st period.

CHAPTER TWELVE

July—September, 1916
THE TREK TO THE SOMME

THE 4th Middlesex Regiment relieved " ours " on the night of July 26th, and the battalion bade farewell to Vimy and Souchez and moved out via the Duck Walk and Villers-au-Bois to Maisnil Bouche, where they occupied billets for a short while and moved off again at 1.30 p.m. to Beugin, where billets were only occupied for one night.

Transport, while on the march to Beugin, was inspected in turn by the corps commander, divisional general and our new brigadier.

At 9.10 a.m. on the 27th the battalion paraded facing La Comte and marched to La Thieuloye, where the usual training and inspections were carried out.

South African troops were in this area and some of our officers who came from South Africa met several of their old friends, and many celebrations followed.

On July 30th the battalion paraded at 11 a.m. and marched in very hot and dusty weather to Haute Cloque, where a halt was made for lunch, and then on to Blangermont, which was reached at 6 p.m. after a march of nearly 16 miles.

A great number of the men dropped out on the march owing to exhaustion from heat and trouble with their feet, and this led to a foot inspection on the day following. 2nd Lieut. L. A. Bam and Sig./Sergt. Powell were taken so seriously ill that they had to be evacuated to the Field Ambulance at St. Pol.

The first day of August found the battalion in billets at Villers L'Hopital ; while here bathing in the river was enjoyed, bathing parades being held between 6 p.m. and 7 p.m., after returning from a route march.

A supply of coloured ribbons arrived and were issued to all, to be sewn on the sleeves, each company being distinguished by different colours : " A " blue, " B " green, " C " red, and " D " yellow. The way the colours were sewn on did not meet with approval and had to be altered —much to the disgust of the men, who were not good with the needle.

Headquarters staff played a cricket match against transport, and Maj. Green led his staff to victory.

On the 4th a move was made at 4.30 a.m. through Hiermont to Yvrencheux, which was reached about 10 a.m. The weather was exceedingly hot and company training took place during the cool of the evening. On the following morning another move was made to Le Plessiel, which was reached at 10 a.m. after marching through the villages of Oneux and Millencourt.

On August 6th Col. E. Faux, C.M.G., V.D., rejoined and resumed command of the battalion which for two weeks remained in the lovely village of Le Plessiel, a short distance from Abbeville.

This was the Third Army training area and a great variety of work was performed, several field days, attacks on a system of trenches were carried out and also night operations.

The days spent here were happy, billets were good, the inhabitants friendly and the weather excellent. There was plenty of opportunity for everyone to get fit and for all ranks to get to know each other well.

A draft of 55 other ranks helped to bring up the strength of the battalion, and on the 13th the sports previously cancelled owing to bad weather, were carried out and quite fittingly completed with races for the children of the village.

On the 16th the battalion marched to the famous Foret de Crecy, and took part in wood fighting before returning to Le Plessiel.

The battalion paraded early on the morning of the 20th and marching through Caours and Villers-sous-Ailly reached L'Etoile; en route a divisional outpost scheme was practised and it was 5 p.m. before billets were reached; these were very good, and it was regretted by many that the stay was for one night only.

Another early start was made on the following morning in order to miss the heat of the day, and the battalion proceeded via Vignacourt to the long straggling village of Naours.

Reveille on the following morning, August 22nd, was at 4.45 a.m., and at 6.30 a.m. the battalion were on the road again to Mirvaux; the next day a further move was made via Beaucourt to Franvillers.

The battalion remained in Franvillers for nearly three weeks, during which time they carried out practice brigade attacks, night schemes, musketry and bayonet fighting.

One day an attack on Farm St. Laurette was carried out, and on another day a divisional exercise took place, the battalion parading at 3.15 a.m. for this event.

The battalion practised the coming attack over a flagged course, all ranks were well trained and prepared for the task which lay before them. Everyone was well versed in the part he had to play, and the greatest secret of the war, the use for the first time of tanks, from which so much was expected, had been made known to the troops.

Capt. T. Rushworth rejoined the battalion, having recovered from his wounds, and upon the occasion of a transport section dinner he was presented with a silver cigarette case by A/Q.M.S. Norton.

CHAPTER THIRTEEN

September 15th, 1916
HIGH WOOD

ON September 12th a move was made to Albert, where the battalion occupied billets near the Grand Place; at this time the whole area around Albert was alive with camps, troops, stores and guns. Everyone was in good spirits, and all were keen and fit for the forthcoming attack.

Enemy shells fell near the billets on the first day without causing casualties, but two days later six other ranks were wounded, one of whom was Cook/Sergt. C. Burgin, who unfortunately died as a result of his wounds.

At 1.15 p.m. on the 14th the battalion paraded in fighting order, all being well loaded with reserve rations, extra ammunition and bombs.

All the way up the line were to be seen preparations for the coming show as the battalion moved forward, platoon by platoon, to Bazentin le Grand, and on up through Elgin Avenue, to take over the trenches from a battalion of the 142nd Brigade, in front of High Wood. It proved a long journey up, and all were glad when the destination was reached.

Considering the magnitude of the coming attack and the tremendous number of men and great amount of material in the area, the 7th managed the journey to the line very well, but suffered early casualties shortly after completion of relief.

Capt. and Adjt. D. Sutton was wounded soon after arrival at B.H.Q. in Seaforth trench, and 2nd Lieut. C. R. Jury was unfortunately killed. 2nd Lieut. A. S. Thompson later was badly wounded and died as a result of his wounds.

Several officers had been left behind at transport lines outside Albert as reserves and a runner was sent back for Lieut. A. E. Hope to come up to act as liaison officer, while 2nd Lieut. H. T. Johnstone took over the duties of adjutant.

2nd Lieut. F. C. Pettigrew acted as liaison officer between the battalion and the New Zealanders, who were on our right; on our immediate left were the Civil Service Rifles.

Another early casualty was Pioneer L/Cpl. G. Michelmore, who was killed, and two other pioneers were wounded by the same shell.

The attack about to be made had three objects: First, a line clear of High Wood; second, a position known as the Starfish line; third, the strong Flers line.

The "Shiny Seventh" and 15th London were to open the advance for the 8th London to pass through them and capture the Starfish line, and in turn the 6th London were to pass through them to the Flers line.

The 7th were to attack in four waves, the order of the companies from left to right being " D," " A," " B " and " C." These waves were to advance with 50 yards distance between them, over a 400-yard front, behind a barrage ; each wave had its objective, which was to be consolidated immediately upon capture.

After the first two waves had left the front line, two minutes before zero, the third and fourth were to move forward and occupy the vacated trenches. The objective of the latter waves was a line known as the Switch line, and after its capture they were to dig in a line of posts 50 yards in front of it.

Two tanks and bombers were to protect the left flank of the battalion.

Advance troops were to signal their positions to the contact plane by lighting red flares when the plane fired out a white Very light, each platoon carrying 15 flares.

Such, in brief outline, was the part the " Shiny Seventh " had to play.

At 4 a.m. on September 15th the companies moved forward to the assembly trenches.

No attempt will be made here to describe the waiting period before zero, except to say that it was quiet, and that a rum issue was made to the waiting troops.

Promptly at 6.20 a.m., zero hour, a terrific barrage crashed down on the enemy's lines 150 yards in front of the 7th, who immediately advanced as arranged and took the first line in their stride ; the barrage moved forward at 50 yards per minute to the second objective which the 7th successfully carried. A tank moved forward along the eastern edge of the wood and then moved in front of our line where it stopped, drawing heavy fire upon our trenches.

Heavy enemy machine-gun fire was heard on our left early on, and it appears that the 15th in moving forward to their assembly trenches had been spotted ; they suffered severe casualties and consequently were not up with the 7th whose left flank thus became exposed. Contact was made at 8 a.m. with the New Zealanders on our right and it was 9.30 a.m. before news was received that " A " Company of the 15th had reached the Switch line ; by 12 noon the whole of the wood was reported clear of the enemy.

The rapid advance of the " Shiny Seventh " was not without casualties. All companies suffered, " C " and " D " reported heavy losses and the other two companies slight. Many who had escaped death at Festubert, Loos, and Vimy found a final resting-place at High Wood ; likewise, many of those who had recently joined the 7th in the several drafts the battalion had received. A great number were wounded, and those who were able to make their own way back were indeed fortunate.

The first batch of prisoners sent back totalled 104, including three officers, and their services were utilised by stretcher bearers as carrying-parties for our own more seriously wounded.

All companies came in for persistent enemy shelling, and this considerably interfered with the work of consolidation.

Communication between companies and B.H.Q. was extremely difficult; the telephone was impossible, as lines were cut to pieces as soon as they were laid.

Messages were carried by runners, and this proved to be the only means of communication. Several casualties occurred among the runners, but they succeeded in carrying out a very difficult task.

At 3 p.m. the companies were reorganised and a new position 100 yards in front of the Switch line was dug.

Carrying parties made the most difficult journey up to renew supplies of ammunition, bombs and water, while stretcher bearers moved about in the open tending the wounded; they appeared to bear charmed lives and defied enemy bullets and shells.

A machine-gun captured by 2nd Lieut. A. H. Hoole was sent back, but two minenwerfers also captured were too heavy, and had to be left.

Those left behind at transport lines had been sent for to come up to replace casualties.

The battalion suffered a great loss on the 16th when a shell killed Capts. T. Rushworth and H. Petley while they were on their way from B.H.Q. to their companies.

Capt. Rushworth, a pre-war 7th officer, came out with the battalion in March, 1915, as transport officer. He was appointed to command "A" Company in April, 1916. Previously mentioned in dispatches he had been wounded at Vimy. Having proved himself thoroughly capable and efficient he was popular with all ranks. His loss was severely felt by all.

Two other officers were slightly wounded, Capt. J. D. Hartley and 2nd Lieut. W. Ryall.

The positions held by the 7th were still being heavily shelled by the enemy, all companies suffered further casualties, and 2nd Lieut. W. G. Thurnell was seriously wounded and died shortly after he arrived at the dressing station.

"Ours" now held two lines, the front and a support line with reserve bombers in Worcester trench. There were many alarms of an enemy counter-attack and the troops "stood to" several times, but the night passed quietly except for intermittent shelling of High Wood and the Switch line.

On September 17th at 7.30 p.m. Maj. C. J. Salkeld Green, M.C., took over command of the battalion. B.H.Q. was moved to Bazentin le Grand in dug-outs, 2nd Lieut. A. E. Hope became acting adjutant, and transport came forward to occupy a position in Bottom Wood near Mametz Wood.

A message received from brigade read as follows :

> " Corps commandant wishes to convey heartiest congratulations to all ranks on performances of yesterday."

During the evening of this day, the 17th, the 20th London relieved " ours " who moved back to the old British front line.

Dealing with the lighter side of war, much amusement was caused as the tale spread through the battalion, of the following remark by one of our officers during a particularly gruesome period at High Wood : " I wonder what ' Mr. High ' would say if he saw what a mess we have made of his —— Wood ? "

B.H.Q. again moved, this time to a position at the junction of High Alley and Black Watch trench.

In the early hours on the morning of the 18th the battalion moved forward to relieve the 8th London in the Starfish line east of a redoubt bearing the same name. Extremely bad weather had set in, and this, coupled with heavy shelling and lack of guides prevented the battalion from reaching its objective, the 8th having moved forward to carry out a minor operation before the arrival of the 7th.

At 12 noon the enemy commenced to bomb down the position held by the 7th in Starfish trench towards the redoubt, so the bombers and all available bombs were sent forward and the enemy were beaten back.

Maj. C. J. Salkeld Green, M.C., came to see for himself the forward positions ; he also saw the C.O.'s of the 6th and 8th London and made a report on the whole situation to the brigadier.

Early on the following day, September 19th, a party of stragglers who had been mixed up with other regiments in the advance, were gathered together and moved forward into the Starfish line where the whole battalion was now concentrated.

At 9 a.m. this line was bombarded by enemy heavy howitzers, as also were our battery positions, several casualties occurring in the front line.

The weather improved slightly, and at night the battalion were relieved, but this proved to be very slow owing to the heavy shelling.

2nd Lieut. H. E. Howlett and 36 other ranks were the first to arrive at Bottom Wood ; they arrived at 3 a.m. It was 6.30 a.m. on September

20th before the last remnants of the sadly depleted " Shiny Seventh " reached transport lines. Here the conditions were very bad ; the weather had now worsened and there was no shelter for the men, who had to remain in the open.

The battalion, which a few days previously had gone into the line so fit and strong, straggled in by instalments, wet to the skin and covered in mud from head to foot. All were welcomed with hot tea and rum, and throughout the night hot stew was kept going by the cooks who worked like trojans under Cpl. Abbott.

Later, at 4.30 p.m., the wet and weary battalion moved back into billets at Albert, where they arrived at 8 p.m.

No praise is too high for those who took part in this action ; the men went into battle magnificently, wave by wave, just as at the last rehearsal. To the stretcher bearers the greatest praise is due, many of the wounded owing their survival to the courage and tenacity of the " S.B.'s " who worked throughout, carrying, from the advanced front to the Aid Post situate near B.H.Q.

As a result of this action, 2nd Lieut. C. R. D'A. Wigney was awarded the M.C. and the following were awarded the Military Medal :

    C.S.M. S. Burden   Pte. H. V. Gill
    L/Cpl. C. W. C. Bacon   Pte. P. Warren
    L/Cpl. G. R. Dickens   Pte. W. M. Baker
    L/Cpl. H. Hendry   Pte. E. T. Griffen
    Pte. P. H. Coles   Pte. C. Newton
    Pte. W. Edwards

With proud regret the battalion record, due to this action, that 17 officers and over 300 N.C.O.'s and other ranks were killed or wounded.

In addition to those officers already mentioned, Lieut. H. F. Stapleton was killed and the following wounded :

Capt. L. E. Rundell, M.C. ; Lieut. H. P. Symonds ; 2nd Lieuts. V. F. Kelly, J. M. Lee, E. Vaus, R. E. Taylor, M.C., J. H. Jackson, and W. F. Carruthers.

From G.H.Q. came a telegram from H.M. the King, which read as follows :

> " Congratulate you and my brave troops on the brilliant success just achieved. I have never doubted that complete victory will ultimately crown our efforts and the splendid results of the fighting yesterday, 15th, confirms this view.
> "GEORGE R.I."

L./Cpl. W. Robertson writes as follows of the attack:

"On the way up we saw two tanks or landships as they were then called; they looked like a box squashed diagonally, with a track running round on each side.

"My position with the bombers was on the left of the battalion; we went over with the second wave and skirted the edge of High Wood. Lieut. R. E. Taylor, M.C., was in charge of the first wave and he, together with Sergt. G. Steele, D.C.M., went after an enemy machine-gun post which they silenced, but were both wounded in the effort.

"The ground we attacked over was just fine powder; shells did not so much as make shell holes but merely moved them; of the German trenches there was no trace.

"We subsequently moved to the right where we took up a position in the Starfish; Capt. L. E. Rundell was wounded during this move. Then came the rain and also several enemy barrages which we survived; unfortunately, Sgt. J. W. Angus was killed. In the early hours of the morning we were relieved and made our way back."

"These men, thy friends"
Stretcher bearers: 7th London

CHAPTER FOURTEEN

September—October, 1916

BUTTE DE WARLENCOURT

ON September 21st the battalion moved to Henencourt Wood where they stayed for a week in huts, during which, after a good clean up, the time was spent in the usual company parades, musketry, and bayonet fighting.

The strength of the battalion was helped by the arrival here of a draft of 194 other ranks, mostly of the East Surrey Regiment, but including 37 old 7th men who had been wounded in earlier actions. This welcome draft arrived under the charge of 2nd Lieut. W. Hutton.

Other officers to join the battalion here were 2nd Lieuts. V. F. Hosken, G. B. Slater, E. W. Pearse. Sergt. W. P. V. Coles, who had been awarded the M.M. at Vimy, rejoined the battalion here as a 2nd Lieutenant.

September 25th, the anniversary of the Battle of Loos, was the day that Col. E. Faux, C.M.G., V.D., returned to England. He was much affected at leaving the battalion he had brought out to France; it was a severe test to him saying farewell to the officers, particularly to those who came out with the battalion in the first instance. Maj. C. J. Salkeld Green, M.C., retained command of the battalion.

Col. Edward Faux was an old Volunteer officer who had seen very long service with the 3rd London. For several years he was O.C. of " H " Company. In 1902, he received the Volunteer Decoration. He subsequently became Hon. Colonel of the Regiment and President and Trustee of the Old Comrades' Association; these positions he held until his death in 1937, which occurred after a long illness.

On September 28th, Maj.-Gen. Sir Charles St. L. Barter, K.C.B., C.V.O., left the division which he had commanded since the early training days in the Watford area. He was succeeded by Maj.-Gen. Sir George F. Gorringe, K.C.B., C.M.G., D.S.O.

A move was made by the battalion on the 29th to Becourt Wood where work was immediately commenced on improving the bivouacs and cleaning camp.

On October 1st, a move forward was made to the north edge of Mametz Wood; extra ammunition and bombs had been issued to all ranks, and at 11 p.m. that night a further move forward was made to Chester Street, Bazentin; B.H.Q. was situate in Mill Street.

Rain fell continuously throughout the following day, making the ground very muddy and slippery.

2nd Lieut. S. Edgar and 15 other ranks joined the battalion here from base; they were dog-tired after a long journey.

On the evening of the 5th, the battalion moved forward again to occupy the old British front line near Eaucourt L'Abbaye. Progress was very slow, the night being pitch black, and the going exceedingly heavy; coupled with these difficulties the guides lost their way and the battalion was shelled.

It was nearly 2.30 a.m. on the 6th when the battalion, thoroughly tired out, were settled in their new surroundings. The journey up had cost the battalion one officer (2nd Lieut. T. G. V. Parker) wounded, two other ranks killed, and ten wounded.

Early in the morning the enemy heavily shelled our positions, and also the sunken road by B.H.Q. The day which followed passed fairly quietly with some shelling of rear areas.

Transport was having a very difficult time; mud was so thick that limbers required extra horses, and these were at times up to their girths in mud. Carrying parties made up of reserve signallers, cooks, etc., were not having a very happy time carrying heavy loads in the thick slippery mud. Six men, just returned from hospital, were put to assist the carrying parties, and of these Pte. T. G. Such was unfortunately killed.

Very few of the men in the line had any idea of the forthcoming attack; the dumping of packs and the issue of extra bombs, etc., had caused quite a few to realise there was " something doing," and this was confirmed when the order came that all greatcoats were to be dumped in an old German gun pit.

At 9 p.m., on the evening of October 6th, guides were picked up at a spot where the sunken road crossed the Flers Switch and the battalion moved forward and occupied the jumping-off trenches of the Flers line, the order of companies reading from right to left being " C," " D," " A," " B."

A few comments on the battalion and the coming attack will not be out of place here.

The area taken over by the 7th was entirely fresh, and as it was almost a case of straight in the line and over the top, no one had much opportunity to gather the lie of the land.

The battalion were far from being at full strength as the losses of High Wood had not been fully made up.

The coming attack differed in many respects from that on High Wood; no previous practice attacks had taken place, and neither had there been any rehearsals over a flagged course.

Newcomers to the ranks of the battalion since High Wood hardly had time to get to know the old hands, and the several officers who had recently joined the battalion hardly had time to get acquainted with the platoons to which they were posted.

Apparently the original scheme and time of the attack were altered at the last minute owing to the discovery by an aeroplane reconnaissance of certain fresh enemy trenches.

Under cover of a creeping barrage the "Shiny Seventh" were to attack through the Post Office Rifles in four waves, each wave consisting of a platoon of each company in line.

The final objective of the 7th was a mound, about 70 feet high, known as the Butte de Warlencourt, and a trench running away to one side, over 2,000 yards distant.

On our right were the 15th London, while on our left were the 23rd Division, the dividing line between the latter and the 7th being the Martinpuich—Warlencourt road.

Bombers of "B" and "C" Companies were to go over with their companies, while those of "A" and "D" under the battalion bombing officer were to establish a double block. Lewis gunners went forward with their companies.

Now for the attack itself. Zero hour was finally 1.45 p.m. on October 7th. At the outset all went exceedingly well, the men going over in great spirits and keeping splendid lines behind the creeping barrage. Enemy shrapnel bursting over our jumping-off trenches was very heavy; this burst high and the troops, who were all moving forward, were not greatly troubled by it.

In the course of the first 100 yards occurred one of those events which may be described as the light side of war, and herewith the story of Sergt. F. Moon as told in the London "Evening News":

"A Charlie touch in No-man's-land.

"On Saturday we went over the top and had rather a hot time. Soon after we started a sergeant friend of mine was hit, and shortly afterwards a good sized piece of shrapnel struck my haversack and set fire to some Very lights and ground flares which I was carrying. My equipment was soon in flames and I was dancing about like Charlie Chaplin with his coat tail on fire in 'Charlie the Tramp.'

"It wasn't very comical to me, I can assure you, as I had a Mills bomb in each side pocket; the haversack was on my back, of course, and, fortunately for me, I was carrying a spade *pushed* down between my equipment and my back, so that the actual shovel part protected my neck from being burnt.

"Every time a Very light or ground flare ignited I felt a bump. I discarded my equipment as soon as I could get it off, but this was no easy job, with spare bandoliers, gas mask and box respirator to be taken off first.

"One of my platoon who came up to help me was shot at my side and wounded rather badly, I am sorry to say. Soon we were all caught in such concentrated machine-gun fire that we had to take cover and dig ourselves in as best we could."

The last paragraph in that story in a few words tells of the tragic happenings to the 7th.

Casualties for the first 300 yards were extremely light; shortly after this a sunken road was crossed and the ascent of the rise on the opposite side commenced.

It was when advancing beyond the crest of this hill that the trouble commenced. As the 7th reached the sky-line they all came under a most intense enfilading machine-gun fire from a trench about 200 yards away on the left, and also from other well sited enemy guns. Almost immediately Capt. V. H. Jordan was hit, a sergeant close by was killed, and 2nd Lieut. V. M. Mileman was wounded.

This murderous machine-gun fire completely wiped out our leading waves, and in succession the waves following, who were so gallantly led on by their officers.

The crest of the hill was quickly covered with killed and wounded. Some of the men were on their knees in the ready position just as they had dropped. Shell holes were a haven of safety for any who could crawl into them.

The continuous line of the fallen bore silent testimony to the unflinching bravery with which the 7th had advanced upon their objective.

The enemy now started shelling the area with 5.9's, and his snipers were picking off anyone who dared move, and so those of the battalion who remained alive had to stay put until it became dark.

At dusk Lieut. V. W. Mileman took up a position slightly in rear of the crest of the hill; from the surrounding area about 50 fit men were collected.

These men were organised and set to work digging to connect up the shell holes to form a T-shaped trench; most of the digging was performed with entrenching tools. A Lewis gun was placed at each end of the T which, when completed, was about 80 yards long and the stem about 40 yards. Several wounded men reached this trench, which soon became overcrowded.

It would almost appear that all the survivors of the battalion found this trench, if such it could be rightly called, as it was only about three feet deep.

Until 9 p.m. there was no direct communication between Lieut. V. W. Mileman's party and B.H.Q. Immediately following the attack signallers had pushed forward and laid lines to establish touch with advance companies, but heavy shelling broke all the lines and it was only by the use of runners that early communications were established.

About two hours after zero, Ptes. W. E. Horley and R. E. Bond were dispatched from B.H.Q. to go forward, search for, and find the position of the battalion and report back.

These two, after a search of about two hours, found Lieut. V. W. Mileman and his party, and returned safely to B.H.Q. Their journey up had been made mostly across the open under heavy fire, to say nothing of sniping and in daylight; the information they brought back was most valuable. Both these runners made several trips between the line and B.H.Q. Pte. R. E. Bond guided a party of R.A.M.C. men up, which resulted in saving about 40 of 7th wounded. Ptes. W. E. Horley and R. E. Bond were both awarded the M.M.

The collection of wounded was very difficult; the cries of " stretcher bearers " from the wounded was heartrending. Hard as the stretcher bearers worked, it was impossible for them to clear the vast number of wounded, particularly as casualties occurred among their numbers, one being killed and five wounded, thus reducing their effective strength.

Many valiant acts were performed in this action, as is proved by the awards. Rations, ammunition, bombs and water were got through with difficulty to the trench.

2nd Lieut. E. W. Pearse, although wounded, returned to the line with 2nd Lieut. C. Cartwright, who had just come out from England and joined the battalion in the line on the evening of the attack. His arrival was a blessing, as he proved himself a tower of strength.

A fellow officer wrote afterwards of his (2nd Lieut. Cartwright's) work upon this occasion:

" Without wishing to throw bouquets, he was splendid, and by his wonderful example and energy was largely instrumental in enabling us to do the work which we had planned."

During the night, from the T-trench, small patrols were sent out right and left to try and establish contact with units on the flanks.

These patrols were only partially successful; the nearest troops appeared to be the 6th London, in front of Eaucourt L'Abbaye, approximately 600 yards away slightly in rear of our right flank. Several more wounded were carried into the already crowded T-trench, and further digging had to be performed to make room for them.

A small party was placed out in front to give warning of any enemy approach.

Just before dawn, Lieut. H. T. Johnstone, who had been wounded, was found and carried in by Lieut. C. Cartwright.

With the arrival of daylight on October 8th, the enemy quickly spotted the T-trench and began shelling with 5.9's; this was kept up spasmodically throughout the day. Fortunately, apart from smashing in the trench in several places, no further casualties occurred.

In the rear, B.H.Q., acting on orders, moved back at noon to transport lines and instructions were given for the whole front to be divided into three areas for the purpose of relief.

At 8 p.m., Lieut. V. W. Mileman received orders for his party to join the 6th London, in front of Eaucourt L'Abbaye, where they then came under the orders of Lieut.-Col. W. F. Mildren, C.B., C.M.G., D.S.O., T.D.

An officer arrived at the T-trench soon after dusk and placed a lamp over the top of the position, showing to the rear; this, it was understood, to be in the nature of a guide for another battalion who were attacking that evening.

Unfortunately it was not possible to clear all the wounded from the T-trench, and those left behind were made as comfortable as possible.

2nd Lieut. V. W. Mileman who, despite his early wound, had carried on throughout, was relieved by 2nd Lieut. F. C. Pettigrew.

The following night, October 9th, at 11.30 p.m., the remains of the battalion returned to transport lines where hot tea and stew were kept going throughout the night.

On the 10th a move was made back to Albert where billets were occupied.

The " Shiny Seventh " had been severely hit in this action and it was only a skeleton of a battalion that came out. A great number of familiar faces were missing, but there still remained enough old " originals " to pass on to newcomers the spirit of the " Shiny Seventh."

The attack on the Butte failed—like many attacks subsequently delivered by other divisions—and the famous Butte was never captured by combat; it fell into British hands when the Germans retreated from the Somme battlefield during February, 1917.

The casualties in this action were seven officers killed and six wounded; while among other ranks 292 were killed, wounded or missing. Of these it is known that over 100 were killed; included in this number was Sergt. H. Lovelock who had been awarded the M.M. for bravery at Vimy, together with a large number of the East Surrey draft.

Of the officers killed, Capt. L. A. L. Flower was a severe loss to the battalion. He was one of the original officers who came out in March, 1915. Quiet but efficient, he always showed consideration for those who served under him. Thirty-two years of age, Capt. L. A. L. Flower gave his life gallantly leading his company in what proved a futile attack. A stone in Warlencourt Cemetery records the fact that he is "Believed to be buried in this cemetery," and the inscription on the headstone reads "Their glory shall not be blotted out."

Another severe loss was Capt. V. H. Jordan who was killed early on ; he joined the battalion about the end of 1915, and for a time was with " B " Company ; later he became captain in " D " Company. Prior to obtaining his commission he was a sergeant in the reserve battalion ; his brother also served as a sergeant in the regiment. Subsequently Capt. V. H. Jordan was " Mentioned in Dispatches." 2nd Lieut. W. J. Merchant and 2nd Lieut. H. C. Ridgway were both killed in this action.

Another sad loss to the battalion was 2nd Lieut. W. P. V. Coles, M.M., who also lies buried in Warlencourt Cemetery. As a sergeant, he came out with the battalion in 1915 and was awarded the M.M. for bravery in the action at Vimy. He had only recently rejoined the battalion at Henencourt and this was his first time in action as an officer.

Another officer killed was 2nd Lieut. Victor F. Hosken ; he had only recently joined the battalion from base. Many who knew him at home will recall how full of life and dash he was, he had shown those qualities that make for leadership and his loss was regretted by all who knew him.

2nd Lieut. Surrey Edgar who was also killed, had only joined the battalion a few days previously ; he was a quiet, unassuming type, and at home had been very popular with all ranks.

The following officers were wounded : 2nd Lieuts. V. W. Mileman, E. W. Pearse, H. T. Johnstone, G. B. Slater, W. Hutton and T. G. V. Parker.

Of the N.C.O.'s and other ranks who were killed, over 30 are buried in the near-by Warlencourt Cemetery.

The total casualties of the 7th London at High Wood and the Butte de Warlencourt were :

Officers, killed, wounded and missing	30
Other ranks ,, ,, ,,	600

For the whole division the figures are 296 officers and 7,475 other ranks, killed, wounded and missing.*

From these figures it will be seen that the 7th bore a good share of the regrettable losses of the division and it is quite fitting that the 47th Divisional Memorial should be sited at High Wood.

The losses suffered by " ours " at the Butte appear exceedingly severe when consideration is given to the fact of the High Wood losses and consequently the reduced strength of the battalion's attacking power.

For the gallant part he played in the action at the Butte de Warlencourt, 2nd Lieut. V. W. Mileman was awarded the M.C.

---

* The 47th (London) Divisional History.

The following N.C.O.'s and men were awarded the M.M.:

Sergt. H. Monck	Pte. W. Sage
L/Cpl. C. E. Fuller	Pte. H. C. Christmas
Pte. A. Brownsall	Pte. W. C. Betts
Pte. W. E. Horley	Pte. R. E. Bond

The following is a copy of a " Special Order from Brigade and Division" by Brig.-Gen. Viscount Hampden, C.M.G. :

" The brigadier wishes to place on record his pride in the splendid gallantry and fighting qualities displayed by all ranks 140th Brigade during the operations of the past four weeks.

" The capture on September 15th of High Wood, which had for many weeks held out against all British attacks, was a feat which the brigade can ever be proud of taking part in, whilst the taking of ' Cough Drop ' and ' Starfish ' on the same day, and of a portion of the Flers line in the early morning of September 18th, were successes which had a far-reaching effect on all operations in that theatre of war.

" The fine attempt on October 7th to capture the Butte de Warlencourt was unfortunately unsuccessful owing, it must be admitted, to the very effective handling of the enemy's machine-guns.

" A footing on the high ground was gained and an advance of several hundred yards made, but the attainment of the objective was impossible in the face of so heavy a fire.

" No troops could have done more ; not a man turned back.

" No praise is too high for the courage and determination shown under exceptionally trying circumstances.

" The brigadier shares with all the sorrow at the loss of gallant comrades, but the sacrifice they made and glorious example set will be remembered always."

The following is a copy of a letter received from 47th Division :

" The divisional commander has much pleasure in communicating to the division the highest appreciation expressed to him by the corps commander of the gallantry shown and of the good work done by the 47th Division during the last ten days' operation.

" The capture of Eaucourt L'Abbaye is a feat of which the division may indeed be proud. Although the Butte de Warlencourt still remains in the enemy's hands and the gallant attempt to capture it by a coup de main was not successful, good consistent progress has been made and it is this steady determined progress which cannot fail to bring the battle to a successful termination."

CHAPTER FIFTEEN

October, 1916

YPRES

THE battalion, which had moved to Albert on October 10th, was joined by 2nd Lieut. E. L. Vaus upon his return from hospital and also by 2nd Lieut. H. U. T. Bowley.

A general clean up, baths and company parades took place during the next couple of days and on the 13th the battalion entrained for Longpre, which was reached at 7 a.m. the following morning; this journey, scheduled to take six hours, lasted seventeen, owing to several halts, during which many begged hot water from the engine-driver in order to make a mess-tin of tea.

After detraining, a march of six miles removed any stiffness of joints, and it was 10.15 a.m. when the tired troops arrived at Brucamps.

Sunday, the 15th, following church parade, Brig.-Gen. Viscount Hampden, C.M.G., presented medal ribbons to those who had earned awards at High Wood, with the exception of C.S.M. S. Burden, who had succumbed to wounds received in that engagement.

On the following day, at 4 p.m., the battalion were off again, proceeding to Longpre. After an hour's wait, the train moved off at 7.21 p.m. and travelled via Abbeville, reaching Caestre at 3.30 a.m. on the 17th. From here the battalion marched through Godewaersvelde in fine weather to the Boeschepe area, where they arrived at 11 a.m.

On the 17th, Capt. K. O. Peppiatt joined the battalion, as also did 2nd Lieut. L. E. Bishop, who had recovered from his wounds. These two officers arrived with a draft of fifty-nine other ranks, which included several wounded men returning for duty. They had had a rough journey from the base; sixty-six hours in trucks, followed by an all-night march, only to find the battalion had moved, which meant another train ride and a further march.

Capt. K. O. Peppiatt was appointed adjutant pending the return of Capt. D. Sutton, M.C. Capt. B. F. Ayrton and 2nd Lieut. R. N. Eve joined from base and 2nd Lieut. R. J. Cook also rejoined the battalion.

The 7th were now in Belgium as part of the Second Army, and were destined to stay there for nearly a year.

Greeted with rain soon after arrival in Belgium, they were to see much of it during their stay in the western province of Flanders. Difficult as it may be to believe, for those who only knew Ypres during the hectic days of Hooge and Passchendaele, the battalion had come to the Salient for rest and recuperation.

After High Wood and the Butte de Warlencourt, the area of Ypres at first seemed relatively quiet, though always the height of discomfort.

The water-logged state of the ground in most places prevented the digging of trenches; those that existed were shallow and built up with sandbags; in many cases only breastworks existed and these were entirely devoid of parados.

In parts, stout deal "A" frames were used in an inverted position; the repairing of these after an enemy shoot provided many hours of labour for R.E. working parties of P.B.I. and at the same time gave the troops an opportunity to express their innermost thoughts of Jerry, which they did in no uncertain manner.

Dominion and Halifax Camps were the chief homes of the 7th when out of the line; while in reserve, Swan Chateau, Segard Chateau, dug-outs near Cafe Belge and huts at Dickebusch.

Apart from a few trips to and from Ypres by train, the battalion usually made the journey up the line via Lille Gate or Voormezeele.

A journey up the line was quite an ordeal, even in fine weather, but going up during a strafe or in the pouring rain, or alternatively, strafe and rain together, combined with the darkness, became a nightmare.

The route usually followed by the footsloggers was via Vlamertinghe, over the railway at Ypres and along by the naked walls of the old Cloth Hall—the view by moonlight being most impressive—and into Rue de Lille, passing out of the town through Lille Gate and over the old moat.

By the time Ypres was reached the battalion would be strung out in platoons about one hundred yards apart.

Beyond Lille Gate the famous Shrapnel Corner had to be negotiated. Three roads met at this junction; the enemy generally chose to shell this spot during hours of darkness and consequently transport in each direction went by at the gallop and troops had to keep well to the sides of the road and at the same time take care not to get too far over. More than one had to be pulled out of the ditch.

Once past this unhealthy spot Very lights would go up in front and on both sides, giving the impression that the enemy completely encircled the Salient.

The battalion either took the left fork up to Railway Dug-outs, Hill 60, Ravine and Strong Point Nine sectors or carried straight on, passing Woodcote Farm on the left and farther along on the same side the ruins of Bedford House, to a duckboard track which led to the Bluff and Hedge Row sectors.

On a quiet, uneventful night, such a journey might be completed in about five hours from Dominion Camp to the front line.

CHAPTER SIXTEEN

October 19th—December 26th, 1916

THE BLUFF, CRATERS AND HILL 60

ON the 19th the battalion moved off to relieve the 13th Australian Infantry in the Bluff sector. Marching via Westoutre and Reninghelst, the 7th arrived at Swan Chateau. Headquarters staff and one company remained there, the other companies picking up guides near Cafe Belge at 8 p.m. and proceeding to the Bluff Tunnels, the relief was completed about midnight with one man being slightly wounded.

For the majority work commenced right away; tired as the troops were after the long journey up the line, working parties had to be provided, but fortunately the weather was now fine although very cold.

Parties of N.C.O.'s and men were provided for the Bluff and Ravine mining shafts and to carry material from Lankhof Farm, also a ration party to push the trucks along the tramway from Bedford House. Parties also were found for work on the communication trench from crater " A " to the Wynde and on crater " B." In addition, two large parties operated under the R.E.'s.

From the foregoing it will be realised that the 7th were fully occupied; these parties continued nightly for the next four nights.

Excitement prevailed on the 22nd, when at 6 a.m. the enemy exploded a mine under a crater held by the 6th London. One company of " ours," together with two sections of bombers and two Lewis gun teams moved forward in support of the 6th and the remainder of the battalion was ready to move at a moment's notice if required. However, the 6th were able to manage without assistance.

Late in the afternoon of the 24th, the 7th commenced to relieve the 6th London; this was completed by 8.15 p.m. and so for the first time the " Shiny Seventh " took its place in the front line of the famous Salient. On the 25th 2nd Lieut. A. Elsbury joined for duty.

At this time the Divisional front was from the Comines Canal to Hill 60 with two brigades in the line. The 7th usually held the right sector of the right brigade or the right sector of the left brigade.

The trenches and craters were in a terrible state and "C" Company were the first to occupy the craters, with a platoon in each of " A " and " B " craters, one in Thames Street and another in Gordon Post.

" A " Company had one platoon in the front line, one in King Street and two in the tunnels, the latter also to act as " Crater rushing parties " if necessary. " B " Company had a platoon in the front line, one in support and two in King Street. " D " Company had one and a half platoons in the front line and a similar number in support, the remaining platoon being in International Trench and the Bean.

The battalion carried out several tours of this sector and while the companies interchanged positions, the craters and trenches in the main, apart from enemy shelling, remained static for a considerable period.

Cooks for the first time accompanied the companies and had fairly good quarters in the tunnels and were thus able, with the aid of containers, to send up hot meals to the troops in the front line.

There was also a trench wader store in the tunnels; here waders were dried and changed. Another innovation was that all ranks had to have a change of socks daily and to rub their feet with whale oil to prevent trench feet and frostbite. This led to each company appointing an N.C.O. to superintend the job, needless to say, quickly becoming known as O.C. Socks.

While the planked and strutted tunnels afforded good sleeping quarters on wire beds, with excellent protection from shells and shrapnel, the trenches around were notable for the scarcity of dug-outs and funk holes.

The time was spent much the same way upon every visit to this sector. Patrols, particularly around the craters, trench repairs and deepening of the sumps for drainage, building up and improving parapets.

The most annoying part was the way Jerry would let a party complete a job of work and with a couple of whizz-bangs scatter to the four winds the results of the hard and tedious labour of the P.B.I.

Occasionally Jerry would, by way of variety, set about levelling the Hedge Row front and King Street supports with H.V. shells, or he would, in reply to a shoot by our T.M.'s, vent all his spite on the craters. Snipers were always busy on both sides and victims were frequent, in fact, some declared that the enemy used whizz-bangs for sniping.

Generally the enemy was fairly consistent as far as his shelling periods went; his guns would open up about 2.30 p.m. and would cease upon our own artillery retaliating. Then about 4 p.m. our T.M. batteries would commence on a wire cutting operation and hardly had they completed their effort when Jerry would retaliate. At times the whole lot would go together and things got rather warm.

After five days in the line the battalion, on October 29th, were relieved by the 20th London, the companies making their way out independently to Dominion Camp. This camp was one sea of mud, over ankle deep, a single duckboard track leading round to the small wooden huts, in which it was only possible to stand up straight in the middle and which were devoid of heat and light.

Maj. J. A. Eckes of the 7th King's Liverpool Regiment, attached for duty, joined the battalion here, as also did 2nd Lieuts. C. D. Metcalf and P. Traynor.

On the 31st the battalion paraded to witness Maj. C. J. Salkeld Green, M.C., present medal ribbons to those who had distinguished themselves at the Butte de Warlencourt. Capt. J. Hartley and Lieut. C. Wigney, M.C., were about this time both sent down the line sick.

On November 1st Brig.-Gen. Viscount Hampden, C.M.G., visited the camp and witnessed the troops performing company drill in the mud.

The following day the battalion was inspected by General Plumer; owing to the heavy rain the battalion only marched by and then returned, soaked to the skin, the men to their huts with no means whatever of drying their saturated clothing.

New box respirators were distributed, company drill and N.C.O.'s classes helped to pass the " rest " period away.

On Sunday, the 5th, a church parade was held in the cinema at Scottish Camp and a brigade church parade, at which four of our officers and eighty other ranks attended, was held at Vauxhall Camp, after which medal ribbons were presented by the G.O.C., Maj.-Gen. Sir F. G. Gorringe, to the following : 2nd Lieut. V. W. Mileman, M.C., C.S.M. H. Collins, M.S.M., Sergt. A. Norton, M.S.M., and M.M.'s to Sergt. H. Monck, Cpl. C. E. Fuller, Cpl. C. Newton, Cpl. H. Bacon, Ptes. W. C. Betts, W. Horley, A. Brownsall, R. Bond, and W. Edwards.

A gas demonstration was held in one of the huts on the following day; afterwards, at a football match, 2nd Lieut. C. V. Hosken dislocated his knee and eventually went down the line, as also did Lieut. V. W. Mileman, M.C., who had some shrapnel splinters to be taken out of his hand.

The battalion left Dominion Camp at 12.50 p.m. on the 8th and moved to reserve positions for the Hill 60 sector, relieving by daylight the 23rd London at Belgian Chateau, where B.H.Q. and the Aid Post were situate.

Large working parties were again provided, this time carrying for R.E.'s from Jackson's Dump to Larch Wood, while a smaller party carried from Brisbane Dump.

On the 11th a move was made into support ; B.H.Q. and the Aid Post together with " B " Company joined " A " at Railway Dug-outs, the other companies remaining at Belgian Chateau.

One other rank was wounded but otherwise all was quiet for a couple of days, and on the 13th the battalion took over from the 8th London the right sub-section of Hill 60. B.H.Q., Aid Post and " A " Company were at Strong Point Nine, while " C " and " D " held the right and left of the front line respectively; this relief started at 5 p.m. and was completed five hours later.

On the 15th the enemy shelled Jackson's Dump at 10.30 a.m. with 4.2's and shrapnel; between 2 p.m. and 3.30 p.m. his artillery and T.M. batteries were again active and at 4 p.m. he dropped several L.H.V. shells on the front line.

Capt. K. O. Peppiatt evidently took a poor view of this trip, as his diary records " 11 degrees of frost last night—more like being with Shackleton at the Pole than with the B.E.F. in Sunny Belgium."

The South African officers with " ours " felt the cold very much and even Lieut. C. Cartwright was seen early one morning looking " thoroughly miserable," if one can imagine this officer looking miserable.

On the 18th the Post Office Rifles came up and relieved the 7th, who moved back to Halifax Camp, reaching this home of rest at 2.45 a.m. the following morning. About this time 2nd Lieuts. P. W. Roots, C. M. Goldsbury, J. K. St. Aubyn, G. C. Davenport, J. F. Preston, A. E. Gibson, C. E. Long, and G. A. Webster joined for duty.

While the battalion had been in the line, the time had come for Lieut. and Q.M. G. D. Roche to go on leave. While proceeding to base he was taken ill but managed to reach England where he was admitted to hospital and found himself in the same ward as Capt. J. Hartley. Lieut G. D. Roche, a pre-war 7th officer, crossed over to France with the battalion and after his return to England, was posted to the reserve battalion, his position with the battalion being filled by Lieut. F. B. Wade. Originally, Lieut. Roche was a sergeant in the 5th London and was gazetted to the 7th in 1909. He died in 1927 at the age of fifty-nine.

On the 20th the battalion supplied large working parties and on this day 2nd Lieut. C. J. A. Coulshaw, formerly a sergeant in the battalion, joined for duty and 2nd Lieut. P. Retief arrived from base with a very welcome draft of three hundred N.C.O.'s and men.

This draft were all from the 25th London (Cyclist) Battalion, well trained through an unusually long stay at home. Many had joined up in the early days of the war and the rawest recruit among them had nine months' service. They turned out to be one of the best drafts received by the battalion; all N.C.O.'s retained their rank and these and others proved their salt, gaining both promotion and decorations.

On the arrival of this draft, the following is from the diary of Sergt. S. Weaver :

> " The men poured out of the huts to see the ' new blokes ' and as the battalion had only come out of the line the night before they were in every stage of dress, or undress, from overcoats to pants and shirt-sleeves. By comparison we felt like show soldiers, conscious of our brand new uniforms and equipment."

Major C. J. Salkeld Green, M.C., welcomed the draft with a few brief words on the traditions of the " Shiny Seventh." From the diary of the writer the following is quoted :

> " Specialists were called for but the draft were shy, they hesitated to class themselves as specialists in the face of men with actual battle experience. Four men, Mitchell, Hitchcock, Brown and Dunham stepped forward as stretcher bearers and were handed over to Cpl. Leary of the Aid Post."

On the 23rd the battalion returned to the trenches in the Strong Point Nine area, relieving the Post Office Rifles. " A " and " B " went into the front line, " C " occupied Railway Dug-outs, while " D " remained with H.Q. at Strong Point Nine. Pte. A. Richardson was killed on this day while guiding an R.A.M.C. Colonel round the line.

The following morning the enemy carried out his usual shoot and Jackson's Dump got it rather badly for an hour with 4.2's and shrapnel. In the afternoon our trench mortars opened fire and the enemy retaliated with " rum jars " and " toffee apples " on our front line, and for a couple of hours it was decidedly unhealthy. This shelling was a regular daily occurrence and one officer records the following time-table :

> " 2.15 p.m. our trench mortars strafe. 2.30 p.m. enemy retaliates with " rum jars." 3 p.m. we retaliate with eighteen pounders. 3.30 p.m. they use L.H.V. shells. 4 p.m. we then get the heavy stuff to work. 5 p.m. all quiet."

The 20th London came up on the 28th and relieved the 7th, who returned to Dominion Camp, more of which later.

With all the daily shelling, casualties were light : Cpl. S. Cole was killed and seven men were wounded. Of these, five were of the Cyclist draft, Ptes. Chambers, Austin, Wheeler, W. Priddis, and Greedy. The last two both received " Blighty " wounds from shrapnel at Jackson's Dump. Chambers was seriously wounded and the S.B.'s had a difficult job in getting him down the line ; the trenches were too narrow for a stretcher and he had to be carried over the top through mud knee deep.

At this time many notice boards appeared, reading " Is your gas helmet in the alert position ? " Who recalls the reply of the battalion wag, written underneath in the best French conversational style, " No, but my brother is in the band " ?

This turn in the line, for the Cyclist draft, was an experience which stood them in good stead. Very few had managed to sleep and all were weary on the way back to Ypres after the battalion was relieved.

At Ypres all were amazed and delighted to find a train awaiting them to take them back ; all went well until the train stopped and orders given to detrain. It was pitch black and those first out of the carriage discovered the drop on to the permanent way a long one, into about two feet of mud. With full equipment on this was no joke for tired troops, as before the first man had risen the second man was out of the carriage and on top of him.

Then came the march up a cobbled road and across several fields and ditches to Dominion Camp ; during the last part of this journey practically every man of the draft fell over at least once owing to the darkness and the rough going. Several fell in one or other of the ditches ; Pte. F. Giles was one who got saturated. On arrival at the huts at 3.30 a.m. blankets were drawn and the troops quickly got down to rest and sleep.

The battalion remained at the rat-infested Dominion Camp until December 8th, during which time the weather was bitterly cold and wet. Parades, gas helmet drill, baths at Poperinghe, route marches and a church parade helped to fill in most of the time.

About this time the name of Maj. C. J. Salkeld Green, M.C., appeared in the Gazette as a Lieut.-Col. This was duly celebrated at H.Q., Brig.- Gen. Viscount Hampden, C.M.G., Brig.-Maj. R. T. Foster, D.S.O., and Staff-Capt. Maj. E. W. Hughes, D.S.O., M.C., being among the guests.

The promotion was well deserved, popular and fortunate for the battalion. He had long been recognised as an officer of outstanding merit, a stern disciplinarian, indefatigable and tenacious, and above all, regardless of his own personal safety.

Lieut.-Col. C. J. Salkeld Green came to the 7th London in 1910 when as a sergeant of the Inns of Court O.T.C. he was gazetted as a 2nd. lieut. and appointed to " G " Company which later he commanded ; promoted lieut. in 1911 and captain in 1912, he won, during this time, the Officers Challenge Cup three times in succession and upon two occasions took part in teams which were placed third in the Napier Cup. He was awarded the M.C. in June 1916.

On December 8th, the 7th moved up the line and relieved the 24th London in the Canal Sector ; H.Q., " A," " B " and " C " Companies proceeded to Ypres by train, while " D " Company went up by road.

The craters were taken over by " C " Company and the trenches by " D," while " A " occupied the Bluff Tunnels and " B " were in reserve at Chateau Segard.

Very careful preparations had been made for a camouflet to be blown on Monday, the 11th, to cut into the German galleries and capture any men found there. Except for Lewis gunners, bombers and a squad of stretcher bearers, " C " and " D " were withdrawn upon this occasion from the craters.

Under 2nd Lieut. W. G. Macintosh, " C " Company provided two N.C.O.'s and twelve men as a covering party, 2nd Lieut. G. C. Davenport acted as liaison officer and all working parties were cancelled. The following night Capt. C. Cartwright was in charge of the covering party.

The battalion " stood to " and at 6.34 p.m. a terrific underground explosion took place, trenches and tunnels rocking like a ship at sea in a storm. Following the explosion, the Canadian tunnellers immediately commenced digging into the galleries of the enemy. At the same time the enemy in the front line got "wind up " and sent up a great number of green and white lights, to which his artillery responded.

At 10 p.m. an enemy patrol was observed ; our covering party was withdrawn to allow our artillery to disperse the enemy, which they did in no uncertain manner.

Our tunnellers made good progress and over five hundred feet of the enemy's galleries fell into their hands, together with a large quantity of mining apparatus ; our own galleries were connected up to those captured and two dead Germans were carried down the line.

With regard to the craters, the following is an extract from the diary of Sergt. S. Weaver :

> " Breakfast was due up, but we never had it because a terrific German ' strafe ' broke out. Trench mortars, ' minnies,' ' rum jars ' and even grenades joined in the din and destruction. There was nothing we could do about it except to take what cover we could, and for a while the ' strafe ' concentrated on the crater lip and then began to drop in the crater itself. At last orders came to withdraw to the tunnel entrances and be ready to rush into position again should there be a raid, but sentries were to stay. We did this by pairs, as fast as we could. Fritz seemed to have the range exact and it was a miracle that we all got safely through."

This continual shelling resulted in an enormous amount of work having to be carried out to the trenches and the tunnel entrances, particularly in the Wynde.

Patrols, in addition to those sent out from the craters, were also sent out on the left company front and the writer, with Cpl. Padley, took part in one of these excursions into No-man's-land. Before leaving to patrol, care was taken to ensure that each post was advised that a patrol was going out. On returning, Cpl. Padley reported at H.Q. and we each got a good tot of rum and were excused working parties for the rest of that night and the following day.

The mud of the craters was dreadful and one officer suggested the appointment of a harbour master and putting up a notice board reading " Any more for the Mudlark."

In " A " crater, sentry and Lewis gun posts were perched on the crater lip in rough holes. Along the bottom of the crater were a few splinter-proof dug-outs for the use of those off duty during the day, at night everyone was outside but smoking and talking were prohibited. Crater " B " was filled with mud five or six feet deep, the sentry posts being reached by a narrow crumbling ledge just below the front edge of the crater.

Another unhealthy spot was an advance post beyond the head of the Wynde which was held at night only, by four bombers and an N.C.O.

The approach was a shallow trench thigh deep in liquid mud, those on duty could only lean against the wet, slippery and sloping sides of the trench, occasionally moving round to make a change of position.

Standing orders were, no talking, smoking or sleeping, two hours up and two down. " A " Company bombers' regular visitor was Pte. B. Lansom, who, although himself a teetotaller, thoughtfully waded out with a special issue of rum for those on this lonesome duty. Many will recall this post and also, what was then a sumptuous breakfast, after " stand down," of bacon, fried bread and hot tea in the dug-out at the top of the Wynde.

Early on the 15th the enemy started a slow bombardment of our lines, which grew in intensity and lasted till 10 a.m. A machine-gun emplacement in " A " crater received a direct hit and " A " Company had to go without breakfast owing to the orderlies having suddenly to go to earth when a couple of whizz-bangs arrived, the dixie of bacon being upset in the mud and filth under the duckboards of the trench.

A much detested working party was the carting of clay from the mining sap; sandbags being scarce did not improve matters. The miners cut with a bayonet large pieces of wringing wet blue-greyish clay which had to be carried through the tunnels for about four hundred yards in sandbags, and then, as sandbags were precious, the bag had to be untied, the contents tipped out in the open and the process repeated. In carrying the clay, the wet oozed out and soaked through your tunic and, as the weather was bitterly cold, it was not so good. After this the job of untying the bag and getting rid of the contents, shivering with cold and with frozen fingers, was no easy matter in the dark.

After 15 days in the line the battalion was relieved by the 6th on the 23rd, and went into reserve at Swan Chateau, Woodcote Farm and the Canal Bank; on the 24th, the companies at the two latter places moved back to Chateau Segard; all were glad to be back for Christmas Day.

During this turn in the line the battalion suffered the loss of several other ranks killed and 18 wounded, two or three of the latter being wounded by spent bullets at Lankhof Farm.

An amusing episode occurred during the relief. Capt. K. O. Peppiatt, while waiting for "Relief Complete" to come through, was alarmed to receive from an officer, who shall be nameless, a code message "53." This meant, according to the code in use on that day, "Have repulsed enemy attack." The officer who sent the message was congratulated the following day by the adjutant for his "very fine rearguard action down the duckboards"; what he really meant to have sent was "56," which was "Relief Complete."

The troops received a "Christmas box" in the shape of the cancellation of day working parties, but this was spoilt for most of the men by a very unseasonable dinner of bully beef and hot water stew; those who had received Christmas parcels were the lucky ones.

On Boxing Day some heavy batteries near by received attention from the enemy, who sent over some big stuff, which caused the battalion to lose Ptes. C. A. Hallworth and T. C. Ward, who died of wounds.

Cloth Hall: Ypres

CHAPTER SEVENTEEN

December 27th, 1916—April 8th, 1917
WINTER IN THE SALIENT

THE London Irish relieved the 7th on the 27th, and they moved back to Dominion Camp; while here, amends were made for the poor Christmas dinner, when on New Year's Eve roast pork and Christmas puddings were served up to the men, as also was an increased issue of rum. Platoon officers, armed with a liberal supply of cigars, visited the men in their huts. All sections at this time were celebrating; the Regimental Staff held a dinner. The 140th Brigade held a dinner for sergeants, which will be long remembered by those who attended. The stretcher bearers had a special " do," attended by Cpl. W. Leary, Cpl. B. Norford, F. Meader, C. Phillips, E. Hone, " Toby " Martin, W. Edwards, M.M., F. Dunham, B. Schartan, L/Cpl. P. Cole, M.M., " Jock " Camp, Warwick, Chrome and Gordon. The sanitary section joined in the celebrations, another bright lot of lads : G. Viles, A. Edmunds, Bateman, Pither, Wright, West and Farr. The transport section held their dinner and produced an excellent menu.

While returning in the dark to camp, after attending one of these festivities, one of our officers walked into some barbed wire and got the worst of the deal, being badly cut about the face. He suffered during the next few days a good deal of chaff, a Court of Enquiry being suggested for " self-inflicted wounds."

The weather was extremely cold throughout the " rest " period and apart from several dinners, the time was occupied by a church parade, baths, gas helmet drill, working parties and route marches.

Other interesting items were the Gazette announcement of an M.C. to Capt. D. Sutton, and the D.C.M. to C.S.M. H. Collins, M.S.M., and the arrival of a new Medical Officer, Capt. S. P. Hodgkinson (R.A.M.C.).

A battalion concert was held, which was a great success, and on January 8th the battalion entrained to Ypres and relieved the 22nd London Regiment in the Hill 60 sector ; it poured with rain the whole way up, and everyone got soaked to the skin.

" A " and " B " occupied the front, " C " were in support at Strong Point Nine, with " D " at Railway Dug-outs. Each day in the line was much as before, with all the usual " daily hates," Jackson's Dump receiving its full share.

Several blinding snowstorms occurred during this tour, and all were glad when the Post Office Rifles came up on the 13th and relieved " ours," who returned to Halifax Camp, except " C," who went to

LIEUT.-COL. C. J. SALKELD GREEN, D.S.O., M.C., T.D.

LIEUT.-COL. C. W. BERKELEY, T.D.

LIEUT.-COL. S. L. HOSKING

MAJ. H. D. BARNES, O.B.E., T.D., D.L.

Pioneer Camp; the journey back was a nightmare through a bitter snowstorm. While in the line the battalion lost four men killed.

Some of " B " Company were returning in a lorry from a working party up the line when the lorry caught fire; one of our chaps found what he thought to be an old blanket, and with this he smothered the flames. Upon closer inspection the " blanket " turned out to be the driver's " posh " coat. As the lorry was now useless, the troops started to march back, leaving the driver in a cloud of profanity, cursing the war, lorries, and particularly the infantry.

On the 18th it was snowing hard when the battalion relieved the 8th London in the Hill 60 sector. Shelling during this tour was not so intense as on previous visits, but sniping activities on both sides increased, our own snipers claiming eight victims. The 8th returned on the 22nd and relieved " ours," who moved back to occupy positions at Railway Dug-outs, Belgian Chateau and Fosse Way, as support battalion.

Everywhere at this time was frozen hard, and those from Railway Dug-outs, taking rations to the company at Fosse Way, made the journey through the frozen trenches with sandbags over their boots to prevent slipping. All the roads were like skating rinks.

Working parties were in great vogue, and of these the pick was at Hill 60 for the Australian Tunnelling Company, best remembered for the crate of large pieces of cheese placed near their H.Q. from which each member of the working party extracted a piece as he went by, and on completion of the job received a generous tot of rum.

The 19th London relieved " ours " on the 26th, who moved back to Dominion Camp.

In order to make sure of a fire for their hut, some of the boys loaded a stretcher with a couple of railway sleepers, which they carried back as a " casualty."

Following the usual clean-up, church parade at Ottawa Camp, baths, route marches, company and specialist training, respirator drill and officers' classes, the time arrived for the battalion to go in the line again.

Capt. K. O. Peppiatt, with four company commanders, on the last day of January, paid a visit to the line about to be taken over. His diary records " that two of the company commanders were under 21 and two just over. Some age. It made me (at 23) feel comparatively ancient." The officers referred to were Capts. A. R. Wallis, L. E. Rundell, M.C., L. E. Bishop, and E. L. Vaus.

The battalion relieved the 23rd London on February 3rd in the Bluff and Hedge Row sector. " C " Company again occupied the craters, " A " the centre front, " B " the left front, while " D " were in support.

Each afternoon during the stay in this sector the enemy shelled our trenches heavily, particularly the Wynde and King Street, but on most occasions the enemy's shelling ceased upon our own artillery retaliating.

On the 5th, just before the morning " stand down," a sharp crack rang out on the Hedge Row front, and the men of the post who were " standing to " in the trench ran forward to the post in an advanced sap, to find that Pte. L. G. Shepherd had been killed by a sniper. He was a popular lad with his platoon, and his loss cast a gloom over them.

That night Lieut. A. Gibson and his Fighting Patrol (commonly known as " the body-snatchers ") went out, and included in this patrol was the brother of that morning's casualty. During the day, enemy shelling cost the battalion three other ranks wounded.

About this time 2nd Lieut. V. H. Raby joined us, and Capt. H. H. King was attached to the battalion from the Post Office Rifles.

Inter-company relief took place on the 7th; " B " moved into the craters, and " D " relieved " A." " C " went back to Chateau Segard, and " A " to the Bluff tunnels. The weather was bitterly cold and, as a reminder, the code word for the relief was " Freezing."

At night, after two hours' sentry duty, one had to run up and down the duckboards to restore the blood circulation, then, wrapping one's feet in sandbags, endeavour to get some rest in a funk hole. Sleep came easily, but the bitter cold penetrated right through everything, and one woke up nearly frozen stiff, and then recommenced running up and down the duckboards. By the time one could feel a little life coming into the feet it was time to do another two hours' sentry duty.

On the 9th the battalion had two men killed, one of whom was L/Cpl. J. Gardiner of " D " Company; he was buried at Chester Farm Cemetery, and while the padre was carrying out the last rites several bullets whizzed by.

News came through that 2nd Lieut. E. W. Pearse had been awarded the French Croix de Guerre.

Early on the morning of the 10th the Fighting Patrol reported that Jerry was " standing to "; our artillery was turned on to his front line. That night the enemy threw a large number of bombs into No-man's-land; he was very nervous, and appeared to be expecting a raid.

While on top of the Spoilbank, seeing about a Lewis-gun post, Capt. B. F. Ayrton was wounded by a sniper.

Another company relief took place on the 11th, " C " taking over the craters, while " B " went into the tunnels. " A " relieved " D," who went to Chateau Segard.

On the 12th we had two men wounded, the following day two more were wounded, one being Pte. A. M. O'Hara, who will be remembered by his very fine football play ; he was seriously injured and succumbed to his wounds three days later.

On the 14th our front lines were evacuated in the morning and again in the afternoon to allow our artillery to put in some shooting practice. The front and support lines of the enemy were heavily shelled, and from what could be seen from our lines of the material going up in the air, his trenches must have suffered considerably. That night and the night following, our patrols bombed a sap opposite the craters, for the loss of one man wounded. About this time, 2nd Lieut. A. T. S. Smith, of the 7th, was posted to the 6th, and on his way to report for duty he was wounded and eventually evacuated to " blighty."

Prior to an inter-company relief on the 15th we had another man wounded. " B " relieved " C," who returned to Chateau Segard. " D " relieved " A, " who went into the tunnels. The weather agreed with the code word for relief, " Thawing," and it was at this time someone suggested that the sobriquet of " Shiny Seventh " should be altered to the " Briny Seventh." The trenches were in a bad state and, even with the specially designed bolt covers, the men had great difficulty in keeping their rifles clean and fit for action ; the craters were flooded, and when a shell arrived in it a sheet of water shot up swamping everything and anyone near it ; across the centre ran a very unstable, springy and slippery bridge of one plank, the short cut from one side to the other.

On the 16th our trench mortars shelled the enemy's line heavily and, judging by the explosions, must have scored a direct hit on a bomb store ; the enemy retaliated and we suffered three casualties, all wounded.

The following day our front lines were again cleared while Jerry's front was bombarded. Later on the enemy put up a heavy bombardment on our right, and that night the patrols found Jerry again very jumpy and nervous. We had one man wounded during the day.

On the 18th the enemy made a raid on our left front which, owing to the alertness of the sentry on duty, Pte. H. Vincent, was frustrated, the enemy leaving two of their number dead in front of our wire and two more were captured.

The raid was well planned ; enemy trench mortars opened up on our support lines and the Bluff and machine-guns poured out a hail of fire on each flank. The Germans taking part in the raid had been taught the English for " Hands up " and " Go on " and were instructed to leave behind them identity discs, pay books, correspondence and shoulder straps. At 4.30 a.m. the raid commenced, visibility being about ten yards. Pte. Vincent spotted the raiders and blazed away with his rifle, thus giving the alarm ; he then threw eight or nine bombs at them and to all intents and purposes the raid was over with the result as stated above. For his bravery in the face of the enemy he was awarded the M.M.

Later that day our front line was vacated between the hours of 11 a.m. and 4 p.m., while our artillery blazed away at the enemy's front and supports, but for once in a while there was no serious retaliation and we had only one man wounded ; however, retaliation arrived with a bonus on the following day and for over two hours in the afternoon " minnies " fell all along Hedge Row and King Street. We had one man killed and five wounded. That night the 20th London relieved us and we returned to Dominion Camp, arriving in the small hours of the 20th.

The usual programme of baths, route marches and gas helmet drill was carried out.

On the 27th we relieved the 24th and 21st London at Hill 60, " A " going to Belgian Chateau, " B " to Railway Dug-outs, " C " to Battersea Farm, and " D " to Strong Point Nine. Lieut. P. D. Evershed arrived with a draft of 70 men in time to accompany the battalion up the line.

March 1st broke fine and sunny and that night 2nd Lieut. A. E. Gibson took out his Fighting Patrol for five hours, the trench from Glasgow Post to Berry Post was thoroughly examined and found to be waist deep in water. The following night he repeated the patrol and this time came across two Germans occupying a sap. At a distance of six yards, Lieut. A. E. Gibson and the patrol opened fire and threw several bombs into the sap. No reply came ; neither were any lights put up. Later the following was received from brigade :—

> " The brigadier considers that the reconnaissance reports sent in by 2nd Lieut. A. E. Gibson reflect great credit on this officer and the patrol under his command. (Signed) W. E. Ind, Capt., A/Brig.-Maj., 140th Infantry Brigade."

On the 3rd the 7th relieved the 6th London in the left sector ; this was a fresh area to the 7th who usually took the right sub-sector. On the day following, shortly after 2 p.m. two enemy planes were sent crashing down by one of ours. One of these planes fell within our lines and from dug-outs close by there was a rush of men, no doubt bent on collecting a souvenir. Lieut. A. E. Gibson found both pilot and observer dead ; hardly had the men reached the plane when the enemy opened up his artillery and smashed the plane to pieces. In scattering to safety some new records were made by our men for the hundred yards.

That night at 7 p.m. the enemy put a mine up on our left and another on our right, causing much " wind-up." Snipers on both sides were busy ; " ours " claimed on the 6th to have hit a German officer as he came out of his dug-out. On the 8th the enemy dropped six " minnies " in Swift Street; 2nd Lieut. P. W. Roots was wounded but carried on.

Larch Wood and Zillebeke Switch received attention on the 11th from the enemy and we had two killed, one of whom was L/Cpl. J. M. Wiseman, and one wounded.

At 4 p.m. on this day the battalion moved into support and supplied large working parties. Lieut.-Col. C. J. S. Green, M.C., took over command of the brigade temporarily and during his absence the battalion was commanded by Capt. L. E. Rundell, M.C.

The enemy shelled Railway Dug-outs and Zillebeke Halt with 5·9's on the 15th and that night the 19th London relieved us and we returned to Dominion Camp being shelled on the way out with tear gas.

Following a general clean up the battalion also paid a visit to the Divisional Gas School. On the 16th it was announced that the Field-Marshal Commander-in-Chief had awarded the M.C. to Capt. E. B. Brewer, who was then commanding the 140th T.M. Battery.

On the 17th a battalion concert was held to celebrate the second anniversary of active service. Of the officers who came out in 1915, only two now remained with the battalion, Lieut.-Col. C. J. Salkeld Green, M.C., and Capt. L. E. Rundell, M.C. Of other ranks, about 200 remained; these were mostly details, transport and pioneers, etc. The programme showed a picture of "Tommy 1915" and as then, "March 17th, 1917." At the piano were 2nd Lieut. G. L. Head, Sergt. C. Whale, and Dmr. Barnes; there were 28 turns.

On the 21st, following the washing of feet and the use of much whale oil, the battalion left for the line. " A," " B," " D " by train to the Asylum, Ypres, and " C " on their " flat feet," the battalion relieving the 23rd London at the Bluff.

The weather was bright and clear and enemy balloons were up in strength. As a result all day working parties were " washed out " as also was the rifle inspection of the support company, which usually took place on the duckboards outside the tunnel entrances.

On the 23rd, at 8.30 a.m., the enemy " minnied " our line for two hours; again at 4.10 p.m. on the 24th, the enemy heavily bombarded our front line, supports and the craters for three hours, and at 7.10 p.m. an S O S went up on our right as the enemy were observed crossing No-man's-land. Our artillery immediately replied and our Lewis guns opened up. Nevertheless, a party of Germans entered " A " crater and blew up the tunnel entrances. This party was driven out by men of the 7th who, operating in two parties, under Capt. L. E. Rundell, M.C., worked over-ground and regained occupation of the crater.

Lieut.-Col. C. J. Salkeld Green, M.C., who had been temporarily commanding the brigade, returned to the battalion during the bombardment; excitement always seemed to wait until he was with the battalion.

In the preliminary shelling prior to the attack, Pte. N. Moses was killed and three others wounded and, as a result of the actual attack, we had two killed and 11 wounded. Lieut. A. E. Gibson suffered badly from concussion, as also did three other ranks.

Two officers, 2nd Lieuts. S. Blackhurst and D. B. Clarke, joined the battalion from base on the 24th.

The following day fine weather prevailed; balloons were up behind both fronts and artillery of each side was busy bombarding back areas. We had two killed and three wounded, including Capt. E. L. Vaus.

The 6th London arrived on the night of the 29th and relieved the battalion, who returned to the huts at Dickebusch. The men of Nos. 1 and 2 platoons, after baths at Halifax Camp, were fortunate, as they stopped on the way back at a farmhouse to find hot coffee and biscuits awaiting them, this treat being provided for them by the respective platoon officers, 2nd Lieuts. P. D. Evershed and J. Preston, and was a gesture greatly appreciated by the men.

The medical officer, Capt. S. P. Hodgkinson, gave the drummers a series of first aid lectures, and initiated a competition in first aid among the S.B.'s. The last six had a final test, which resulted in P. Hitchcock winning, with Pte. F. Dunham second and Pte. Hone third.

One of the events of this stay at Dickebusch was a boxing tournament. Lieut. G. R. Peel and two other officers acted as judges, Sergt. J. King was the referee, and the M.C. was C.S.M. S. Jeffries.

The Lille Gate: Ypres

CHAPTER EIGHTEEN

April 9th—May 11th, 1917
THE SPOILBANK

THE time soon arrived for the battalion to return to the trenches, and on April 9th the usual order came out in connection with the feet and whale oil.

The battalion was to take over what was for them a new sector, known as Spoilbank, south of the Ypres–Comines Canal, and immediately on the right of our usual sector. Capt. K. O. Peppiatt reconnoitred the line, and his report " that Jerry could see your bootlaces as you came up the communication trench," was not very encouraging.

On the night of the 9th we relieved the Royal West Kents, " A " and " B " occupying the front line, with " C " and " D " in support, the relief being delayed by the enemy sending over " tear gas " shells.

This new sector adjoined the canal and the craters, these being on our left, while on our right was a gap known as the Mudpatch, of about 350 yards between us and the neighbouring troops.

The first day in the line the battalion had the bad luck to lose Pte. W. Bezley, who was accidentally killed just after stand down. His death was due to that unhappy but necessary habit of having " one up the spout," coupled with the cold weather. Lieut. G. C. Davenport, at this time battalion sniping officer, was himself sniped, and 2nd Lieut. D. B. Clarke was wounded.

More snow fell, and although it made the surrounding country look pretty, when the thaw came it made the trenches very wet and muddy.

A notice board was put up for Jerry; it read " Vimy Ridge and 11,000 prisoners taken. Your turn next."

On the 12th the enemy sent over some very heavy shells, scoring hits on the Bluff, Norfolk House and Estaminet Lane, while Old Kent Road was pelted with rifle grenades; the following day he sent over 4.2's on Dickebusch and Ypres. In the early part of the evening an enemy working party was observed, and our snipers claimed two hits.

On the 14th Pte. P. Balaam was killed and Pte. Anning wounded while on a working party. On this night a patrol of "ours" went out in charge of Sergt. H. Monck, M.M. Eventually eight men returned, leaving Sergt. H. Monck and Pte. J. Luton unaccounted for.

The 8th London came up on the 15th, and relieved " ours," who returned to Dickebusch, via Convent Lane, that long, never-ending communication trench which reached to near Voormezele, and in which so many men got wedged when in full pack and someone else tried to pass in the opposite direction. While this relief was in progress, news came through that Sergt. Monck and Pte. Luton had returned. These two, having arranged for the remainder of the patrol to act as a covering party, went forward and found a party of Germans at work in a trench. They threw six bombs among this party, and then made for the area of the Mudpatch, where they observed a party of 11 Germans about to go out on patrol. While following this patrol, a German working party of about 20 men were encountered, and in avoiding this party they lost sight of their own patrol. Sergt. Monck and Pte. Luton had changed direction so many times that it was not at all surprising that they got lost and entered a German trench in mistake for one of our own. In an endeavour to get back to our lines another trench was approached where a working party was operating ; these turned out to be Germans, and Sergt. Monck and Pte. Luton had to take cover in a shell hole, as it was now beginning to get light. This shell hole proved to be about 35 yards from the German front line, and Sergt. Monck and Pte. Luton had to occupy this position in the pouring rain for 16 hours, until it was dark enough for them to gain our lines. Sergt. Monck, who already possessed the M.M. for gallantry at the Butte de Warlencourt, was awarded the D.C.M. in connection with this patrol and the information he returned with, and Pte. J. Luton the M.M.

While at Dickebusch the men had a medical inspection for scabies, baths at Halifax Camp, range firing and bomb practice. Capt. D. Rooney took over command of " D, " and 2nd Lieut. C. D. Metcalf was appointed intelligence officer.

The boxing competitions were resumed, but apparently Jerry objected, as he shelled the area and we had one man wounded.

A church service was held in a barn, and at a battalion parade M.M. ribbons were presented to L/Sergt. C. Bowers and Pte. C. Gadd, both of " C " Company.

On the 24th the battalion moved, " A " and " B " to Swan Chateau, " C " to Segard Chateau, while " D " was split between Strong Points 7 and 8.

The whole of the battalion carried out working parties nightly at Brisbane Dump, Woodcote Farm, Lankhof Farm, Petticoat Lane, Bedford House, and Spoilbank for the next eight nights. These jobs were not without casualties, and the battalion lost Pte. H. Vincent, M.M., and two other men killed and eight wounded.

On May 1st the following officers joined the battalion : 2nd Lieuts. B. N. Cryer, A. G. Coulson, F. L. Morgan, and C. R. Featherstone.

The enemy shelled Swan Chateau on the 2nd with 5·9's, and on this day 2nd Lieut. A. Hope left us to join a T.M. battery.

The battalion moved on the 3rd back to the Spoilbank sector, and relieved the 6th London, " A " occupying Old Kent Road and Old French Trench, " B " in West Terrace and the Lock House, while " C " and " D " were in support at Arundel House and Old Grenade Trench.

The enemy remained fairly quiet ; nevertheless we had two men wounded on the 5th, and on the following day 2nd Lieut. W. H. Daish was wounded, and also one other rank.

On the 7th our artillery gave it to the enemy really strong in the morning and repeated the dose in the afternoon ; by way of retaliation the Bluff received a good peppering—-our casualties were one killed and four wounded. The enemy on the 9th heavily shelled the whole of our front, wounding two of our men, and then switched to back areas.

Again on the 10th the enemy shelled our front, if anything, heavier than on the previous day when he had raided the Hill 60 area. The shelling commenced just prior to dawn, with a barrage on the front and at the same time a 9·2 narrowly missed Arundel House ; had this been a direct hit it would have made a nice mess of " A " Company. As it was it only served as an alarm, for within two seconds the men were out and dispersed along Old French Trench, in time to see the S O S's going up.

In the interval between the S O S and our artillery replying, all the brigade machine-guns on the Bluff opened up and the rat-tat-tat of these guns was terrific until the reply of our guns drowned the noise they made. The shelling of both sides lasted quite a considerable time, apparently Jerry had again endeavoured to raid the Hill 60 area.

CHAPTER NINETEEN

May 12th—June 5th, 1917

TREK AND TRAINING

FOLLOWING relief by the London Irish the battalion returned to Dickebusch huts and the men spent the day cleaning up, and all had baths at Halifax Camp. During the afternoon enemy artillery, searching for our battery positions, landed a heavy shell which took away part of a hut used by R.S.M. Wright; the R.S.M. was out at the time or else there might have been a different story to tell.

On May 13th the battalion started out early in the morning and joining up with the 15th London, formed the " C " column, under the command of Lieut.-Col. C. J. Salkeld Green, M.C., and marched to Watou via Ouderdom, Reninghelst and Boeschepe.

On the following day the march was resumed, an early start being made in order to miss the heat of the day; the battalion fell in at 4.40 a.m. and passing through Caestre reached Wallon Cappel where a halt was made for the night.

The battalion were off again early on the 15th and marching via Ebblinghem, through country unspoilt by war, reached Zudausques about four miles outside St. Omer.

Everyone here had comfortable billets and the stay, which lasted two weeks during fine and glorious weather, proved beneficial to all.

Parades started early and were finished by midday, the remainder of the day being spent in visits to St. Omer, inter-platoon football match competitions, with a trip to the local estaminets in the evenings.

It was about this time that Brig.-Gen. Viscount Hampden, C.M.G., * returned to England and command of the 140th Brigade was assumed by Brig.-Gen. H. P. B. L. Kennedy, D.S.O., who retained command until the end of the war.

The major part of the work carried out by the troops consisted of practice attacks on a taped-out course, over ploughed fields, with flag bearers on the flanks representing the barrage.

A drum-head church service was held, after which Maj.-Gen. Sir G. F. Gorringe, K.C.B., C.M.G., D.S.O., presented medal ribbons to a number of 7th N.C.O.'s and men.

The medical officer, Capt. S. P. Hodgkinson, gave a "spread" to the stretcher bearers and sanitary section, which was greatly appreciated by them all.

---

* See Appendix F.

The London Gazette dated May 25th, 1917, announced the following names of the 7th as being Mentioned in Dispatches:

Lt.-Col. C. J. S. Green, M.C.; 2nd Lieut. E. W. Pearse; 2nd Lieut. F. C. Pettigrew; Cpl. W. F. Norford and Cpl. R. Kettle.

The adjutant was exceptionally busy and 2nd Lieut. V. H. Raby was appointed assistant adjutant. 2nd Lieut. L. W. Winterflood joined the battalion here.

The time spent at Zudausques was very happy and before leaving most companies had platoon photographs taken. The M.O. was taken with a group of his stretcher bearers and sanitary section and it is interesting to record that of 31 who formed the group, six went through to the end without a scratch; eight were killed, eight were made prisoners and the remainder were wounded.

The rest came to an end all too soon and on May 30th the battalion, fighting fit, entrained at St. Omer for Poperinghe, whence it marched to tents at Patricia Camp, and while here all the men had baths and numerous kit inspections. A cricket match was played against the 6th London Field Ambulance and the inter-platoon football competitions were completed.

A working party of three officers and 180 men, carrying T.M. ammunition, was a sharp reminder that we were back in the war area.

Lieut.-Col. Green, M.C., addressed the battalion and spoke of the coming attack and the traditions of the " Shiny Seventh," and on June 3rd the battalion moved forward to Dickebusch village and occupied the cellars of half-ruined houses.

At night the road was crowded with transport, while at the rear of the cottages pack mules loaded with 18-pounder ammunition went by in a steady procession.

On June 4th the award of the D.S.O. was announced to Lieut.-Col C. J. Salkeld Green, M.C. This gave cause for much rejoicing throughout the battalion as it was an award thoroughly deserved and, if anything, long overdue.

On the 5th, the battalion moved forward and occupied the tunnels at the Spoilbank; the journey up was very slow owing to the congestion caused by the large number of troops all making their way forward.

The men were kept inside the tunnels by day in order to prevent their presence being observed by the enemy. An air of expectancy prevailed as none knew the actual time and date of the attack, but all were quietly confident that the preparations, of which they had heard and seen so much, were of such magnitude that nothing could stop the attack from being successful.

CHAPTER TWENTY

June 6th—September 7th, 1917
MESSINES, WHITE CHATEAU AND FORET FARM

THE 47th Division formed part of the 10th Corps of the Second Army, and this Corps was deputed to capture about 6,000 yards of front to a depth of about 1,500 yards, which included positions known as the Damstrasse on the right, the White Chateau, both banks of the Ypres–Comines Canal, Hill 60, and Battle Wood on the left.*

The attack of the 140th Brigade was to be carried out on the south side of the canal, the final scheme for the 7th being as follows : " D " and " B " Companies, from our front line at the Spoilbank, were to attack and capture the enemy's front line and support trenches. " A " Company, passing through, were to bear half right and capture the White Chateau. " C " Company were to capture another strong point. The men of each company, for purposes of easy identification, wore a strip of coloured cloth, in addition to the battalion colour, which was a yellow diamond, and moppers-up wore a white armlet. Orders were issued for all surplus kit and overcoats to be left behind, and officers were dressed and equipped as the men. A contact plane, bearing three broad bands of white on the fuselage, was to operate with the attackers for the purpose of reporting upon advance positions. " B " Company were ordered to detail " moppers-up " for the canal bank up to and including the Iron Bridge.

The 6th and 15th London Regiments were to pass through the 7th to objectives farther on, tanks were to co-operate, but, as it turned out, one broke down and another reached the White Chateau after it had been captured.

Such was the scheme of attack, and now for the part as played by the " Shiny Seventh."

On the night of June 6th, 2nd Lieut. C. D. Metcalf, Sergt. H. Monck, D.C.M., M.M. and 18 other ranks, went out on a wire-cutting expedition, and the news spread that the attack would be at dawn on the following morning.

At 11 p.m. that night, the 7th moved forward, " D " and " B " Companies to occupy the front line, and " A " and " C " the newly dug assembly trenches in the rear of the front line, a slow journey owing to the congested state of the trenches.

---
* The 47th (London) Divisional History.

The night had been fine and fairly quiet, but about 2.30 a.m. the enemy sent over a few rifle grenades, which resulted in Ptes. Smith, Lansom and Pennell being wounded.

Promptly at 3.10 a.m. on June 7th, the great attack commenced: 19 mines were fired, and the artillery in the area opened up along the whole of the front simultaneously.

Over went the 7th amidst the greatest din ever heard; our artillery kept up a rapid rate of fire, some creating a creeping barrage and others silencing enemy batteries. The front line and immediate supports were captured with the greatest ease; those of the enemy found still alive were quite dazed and only too willing to be taken prisoner, but here and there a few stubborn defenders were speedily dealt with.

In the half light of breaking dawn and the storm clouds of dust created by the shelling it was difficult to retain a sense of direction, and not all immediately made the half-right change for the attack on the White Chateau. "A" Company "moppers-up" dealt very faithfully early on with the small dug-outs which lined the Damstrasse.

Early on, less than 12 men of "A" Company had reached the area of the Chateau, which loomed up like a large mound about 30 feet high.

From the angle of this mound a sniper caught several of our men, and at one time over a dozen casualties were laid out, at various intervals on a line from the angle of the Chateau back to the Damstrasse.

Capt. A. R. Wallis of "A" was seriously wounded on his way over, and took no further part in the attack. Lieut. J. Preston arrived at the Chateau, and led a frontal attack, some of our men throwing bombs from the top of the mound down on the other side, while the enemy were returning stick grenades. In addition to the sniper, the enemy had a machine-gun post to one side, and although the initial attack was carried out with great dash, our numbers were insufficient to capture the Chateau.

The 7th dug in in front of the Chateau in three or four groups, and from these positions "A" Company bombers fired Mills bombs from their rifles so that they dropped on the far side of the mound.

The contact plane roared over at a very low altitude, and signalled for the troops to give their positions, flares were lit and the plane circled the Chateau and raced away; in less than two minutes, our artillery opened up, obtaining many direct hits on the Chateau.

A platoon of the 6th London, led by Capt. Collins, arrived, and with the 7th made a brave but unsuccessful attack to scale the mound, and the 6th then moved off to make a wide detour to the right.

By now many more of the 7th had arrived, and Lieut. J. Preston organised an attack at each side, finally rushing in from the rear, covering all exits from the Chateau and killing all the enemy outside. Smoke bombs were thrown inside one of the entrances, and with this the White Chateau was captured, and out came the occupants with their hands up—80 of them.

Lieut.-Col. C. J. S. Green, D.S.O., M.C., who was on his way up to organise an attack on the Chateau, arrived as the Germans surrendered.

The men were ordered to dig in and a shell landed about thirty feet ahead causing casualties, including the writer, who received a small piece of shrapnel just to the side of the right eye.

The 7th dug in and consolidated their positions, and during the day the battalion area of the battlefield was cleared of casualties.

On the following morning, from 8.40 to 9.30 a.m. artillery of both sides went at each other wholesale. A counter-attack on our right was beaten off, and " D " Company moved forward to the new front line between Oak Avenue and South Oak Alley and, while here, beat off two determined counter-attacks.

For the next two days the battalion was very heavily shelled, particularly between 9.30 p.m. and midnight.

On the 11th the P.O.R.'s relieved " ours," who moved back to support lines, and on the following day, the 12th, were relieved by the 12th Battalion East Surrey Regiment, and moved farther back to Alberta Camp at Reninghelst.

How delighted were the survivors to get back; again the " Shiny Seventh " had successfully carried out its task.

The casualties incurred were : one officer, Lieut. P. W. Roots, killed, and 12 wounded, 63 N.C.O.'s and men killed and 13 reported missing; the wounded numbered 263. Pte. D. Mitchener, seriously wounded by a sniper, died of his wounds in hospital; he is described in a letter as being " one of the finest chaps that ever breathed."

Among the officers wounded, in addition to Capt. A. R. Wallis, were Lieuts. C. Cartwright, C. Bowers, A. E. Murray, P. Traynor, J. M. D. Phillip, R. J. Cook and 2nd Lieut. S. Blackhurst.

For his bravery in the face of the enemy, 2nd Lieut. J. Preston was awarded the M.C. 2nd Lieut. S. Blackhurst, who although wounded and marked " severe " at the aid post, returned to the line and insisted on remaining at duty, was also awarded an M.C. Other recipients of the M.C. were 2nd Lieuts. R. N. Eve and R. J. Cook. Capt. K. O. Peppiatt was subsequently " Mentioned in Dispatches."

Sergts. C. W. C. Bacon, C. C. Bowers and J. King each received the D.C.M. Pte. W. M. Baker received a bar to his M.M., and the following N.C.O.'s and men each received the M.M. :

Pte. J. C. Huntley, Cpl. W. H. Davey, Pte. G. Halls, Pte. P. Huggins, L/Cpl. G. Marson, Cpl. W. Norford, L/Cpl. A. Baker, Pte. W. Dilley,

Pte. J. Harris, Pte. H. Hyder, Pte. F. Meader, Cpl. M. C. Rasberry, Pte. F. Chalk, Pte. E. J. Gordon, Pte. H. Honig, L/Cpl. S. McCullum, L/Cpl. J. Nodder, L/Cpl. G. Shepherd.

On the exploit of 2nd Lieut. J. Preston, the following is quoted from the 47th Divisional History:

> "But our men were not to be denied, and at the third attempt, in which Lieut. J. Preston, 7th Battalion, especially distinguished himself, the last of a determined party of the enemy were at last forced to surrender."

Never before had such a concentration of artillery been used; approximately 20,000 tons of shells were launched at the German positions, including 537,747 rounds from 18-pounders. During the first 24 hours of the battle, 7,200 prisoners, 67 guns, 94 trench mortars and 294 machine guns were taken. Up to date this attack proved to be the most successful carried out by the British Army.

From the diary of Pte. F. Dunham, stretcher bearer of "A" Company, are the following extracts:

> "Toby (Martin) and I were just wishing each other good luck when we heard a mighty rumble and a roar; to our left and right we could see flames and smoke from the mines.
>
> "The attack was in full swing; prisoners taken looked scared and fatigued. We came across a few of our chaps slightly wounded and all had attended to their wounds with their field dressings
>
> "Hostile shelling was now severe and casualties began to increase. We bandaged several; one poor chap had a smashed leg, so we used a piece of wood from a trench as a splint and made him comfortable.
>
> "I then came across Capt. Wallis with a shrapnel wound in the thigh. He had roughly dressed it but I made a proper job of it and left him to await the arrival of a carrying party.
>
> "We came next to Cpl. Short, unfortunately he was beyond our aid.
>
> "Using a door from the Chateau as a stretcher, and with the aid of two officers' servants, we collected several casualties and put them under cover of the Chateau. This was very tiring work owing to the rough ground and the door being awkward to carry. The poor chaps had a job to keep on it when it tilted; no doubt it was an uncomfortable journey for them, but they did not complain.

The battalion remained at Alberta Camp for three days and on June 15th marched to Caestre, and on the following day moved on to Lynde, where the next twelve days were spent.

Lynde provided a fine change for the troops, the weather perfect and the billets comfortable; parades were over by midday and the afternoon gave way to sports, cricket matches and swimming. A brigade church parade was held each Sunday at Ebblinghem while the battalion were here, and the 7th played a cricket match against the 21st London, whose band was in attendance, rounding off the evening with a concert. The programme, labelled " The White Chateau," showed a sketch of that place on one side and on the reverse a picture of a church with the caption " Another Rest Spot." A great number of items were got through; there was a galaxy of talent about at this time, and among those of the 7th who performed were Sergt. C. Bacon, Ptes. Conway, Bending, Allen, Wallis and Daniels.

Most successful of the entertainments was a swimming gala and carnival held in the canal at Blaringhem, followed in the evening by a torchlight tattoo by massed bands of the division.

At a special parade medal ribbons were presented to those who had received awards for the recent White Chateau attack.

June 28th found the battalion on its way to the war again, marching through the pouring rain to Meteren, and on the following day to bivouacs at Ridge Wood.

From here large working parties of six officers and nearly four hundred men were supplied every night for road repair work and cable-laying near the old Iron Bridge, and during the first two nights the battalion suffered casualties, four other ranks being killed and three wounded.

In the forenoon of July 4th H.M. The King visited the area. The troops lined the route unceremoniously and cheered most heartily as he passed by. In the evening the 18th London relieved " ours," who moved back to Alberta Camp, while here the troops had baths at Chippewa Camp and gift parcels from Queen Alexandra were distributed. Capt. K. O. Peppiatt, who had been acting as adjutant for the previous nine months, took over command of " A " Company on the return from England of the adjutant, Capt. D. Sutton, M.C.

On July 8th the battalion relieved the 22nd London in a line south of Hollebeke Road in the area of Optic Avenue, the support companies occupying some large German concrete dug-outs, and the relief was completed during the early hours of July 9th. The first calamity occurred when the enemy obtained a hit on a shelter occupied by the drummers, eight of whom were wounded and of these two died shortly afterwards.

At 9 p.m. on July 9th a party of twenty-five N.C.O.'s and other ranks, under 2nd Lieut. C. M. Goldsbury, made a raid on a strong point known as Foret Farm. The attacking party was met by strong rifle and machine-gun fire, and the enemy put down a box barrage around the farm. Nevertheless, a well-placed rifle grenade landed in the entrance to the strong point, enabling 2nd Lieut. Goldsbury and his party to rush up and throw some Mills bombs inside, and out came nine of the enemy. These prisoners were sent back under escort but only five arrived; presumably the remainder were killed by their own shellfire.

2nd Lieut. Goldsbury was wounded, and on his way back was wounded again when near our line. Lieut. J. Preston sent out two stretcher bearers, who brought in the wounded officer to the safety of our lines.

The raid had proved quite successful, despite the casualties which were suffered; one other rank was killed, five missing and 15 wounded, and as a result of the shelling of our lines 2nd Lieut. W. G. Macintosh was also wounded.

The following messages were received at H.Q.:

"Congratulations from Divisional Commander on the success of last night's raid," and "Army Commander wishes to congratulate all concerned on the success of the operation on night of July 9th–10th."

For the part he took in the action 2nd Lieut. C. M. Goldsbury was awarded the M.C. Sergt. F. Moon received the D.C.M. and M.M.'s were awarded Cpl. H. Baker and Pte. J. A. Cook.

On July 11th an enemy plane shot down three of our balloons; their artillery was very active and the 7th had three men wounded.

2nd Lieut. S. Blackhurst, M.C., having recovered from his wounds, rejoined the battalion and 2nd Lieut. W. J. Johnstone arrived from base.

The 15th London relieved "ours" on July 16th, who moved back to Bois Confluent and Bus House; during this relief the enemy put down a barrage of gas shells and later on this night one company on a working party was caught by enemy artillery and suffered one killed and four other ranks wounded. In addition to these casualties the battalion, during the past three days had lost one man killed and five wounded.

A comparison of the German dug-out and ours is recorded in the diary of one of our officers and reads as follows:

"Remarkable—in Boche lines we had dug-out with 6 ft. of concrete on top; in British lines we have a dug-out covered with a sheet of corrugated iron and sandbags."

The men were not too comfortable in this area; by day they suffered enemy shells searching for battery positions and at night they had to put up with gas shells when on working parties.

About this time 2nd Lieuts. E. A. Clarke, A. M. Thompson and F. Glenton joined from base.

Dealing with working parties, which were operated nightly, the following are extracts from the diary of Pte. F. Dunham. After describing the difficulties of the journeys up and back through the gas shelling and over the rough tracks, the diary continues :

"Capt. K. O. Peppiatt was in charge of the party. He was a fine soldier and not afraid to take his share in risky jobs. He gave us orders to keep gas masks on till he told us to take them off and we had to hold each others ' tails ' to keep in touch. Progress was slow, but K.O. kept going and the further forward we got the worse seemed the shelling, shells were dropping everywhere around us. It was a nerve-racking experience. We met the R.E. officer, who said we had better return. K.O. was a sport and set a good pace for ' home.' All were glad eventually to get their masks off. It was remarkable that our long file of human beings came through all this shelling without a casualty."

The battalion during the last few days lost the services of 2nd Lieut. W. J. Johnstone and six men, all wounded.

Back at support lines the enemy continued to shell and our artillery replied ; it is recorded that the new officers had difficulty in distinguishing " departures " from " arrivals."

On July 24th the 7th were relieved by the 15th Battalion Hants Regiment and moved back to Kenora Camp. On this day, Capt. K. O. Peppiatt's diary records :

"Some camp. Tents for officers, bivvies for the men. Heavy thunderstorm, all men soaked. I managed to sneak a barn for my men and am now awaiting a visit from the Maire."

The battalion stayed here for fifteen days, the first day being spent by the men in getting almost three weeks' dirt and grime off their clothing and bodies. The usual parades, company drill and baths, etc. kept the men occupied and at a battalion parade the Divisional Commander presented medal ribbons to recipients of awards.

The following officers, 2nd Lieuts. W. R. Wallis, A. C. Robinson and T. Peters, joined the battalion here from base and 2nd Lieut. J. K. St. Aubyn returned from hospital.

Rain had set in and the camp soon became very muddy. Cards were being played by most of the men who were not letter-writing and apparently cards were also being played by the officers according to the diary of one who records the following amusing note. "Played against the C.O. and 2nd-in-command at bridge. Got them 1,600 down. Somewhat tactless but quite profitable."

On the evening of August 6th the Drums gave a concert. Drummer C. J. Ling opened the show with the whole party singing " The Shiny Boys," Drummers D. Steel and Dupen gave McNamara's Band,

Drummers Lamin and Allen gave "The would-be Actors." The concert was concluded by a sketch "Doctor Killem-Kemist" in which Sergt. Drummer G. Gardener took the part of the Doctor and Drummer Lamin his assistant.

On August 8th the battalion moved up to Ridge Wood and relieved the London Irish; it rained hard all the way up and the men arrived soaked to the skin.

Sergt. Brabham, who had been severely wounded on a working party, was visited in hospital by Sergts. S. Weaver and Fuller, who, while realising his case was pretty hopeless, did their best to cheer him up. Sergt. Brabham died on Aug. 20th.

From Ridge Wood the 7th performed many working parties and most uncomfortable they proved to be. Mostly in the area of Hill 60 and the White Chateau, the parties had to run the gauntlet of heavy enemy shell fire upon each occasion.

Eventually on August 13th the 7th was relieved and returned to Kenora Camp, from where, two days later, it marched to Abeele and entrained for St. Omer, which was reached at 7 p.m. Longuenesse proved to be the destination of the 7th and this village was reached about 10 p.m.; billets were good and the weather was gloriously fine.

A brigade church parade was held at the Chateau de la Croix, the service being taken by the Bishop of Khartoum, and on August 22nd the Follies gave a four-hour show of old and new numbers in an R.F.C. hangar. The rest was suddenly interrupted by orders for a return to war and on the 24th the 7th embussed, arriving at Halifax Camp at 7 p.m.

Rumours of an impending attack were rife and these were substantiated by lectures, several jokes being about good swimmers only being required. Owing to enemy bombing of back areas at night-time, the men were set to work building sandbags around the huts. At the same time the battalion was supplying working parties of over four hundred men, one party spending the best part of a day carrying bombs from Hell Fire Corner to the front line; they had a rough time, shelled with gas while working and with high velocity missiles on their way back.

On August 28th five officers and thirty-seven other ranks were dispatched to Corps reinforcement camp at Oudezeele, in view of the impending attack. But a few days later news came that the proposed attack was washed out.

September arrived with fine hot weather, but the nights were spoilt for the men by enemy bombing and the days by long-distance high velocity shells. A church parade was held at Vancouver Palace; this, for many, was their last with the battalion, as shortly afterwards the 7th moved up the line and suffered one of its worst periods.

CHAPTER TWENTY-ONE

September 8th—September 16th, 1917
GLENCORSE WOOD AND CRYER FARM

ON September 8th the battalion moved by companies to Segard Chateau, where the 10th Battalion of the Cheshire Regiment was relieved; here, the troops dumped their packs and greatcoats and on the following day relieved the 8th Battalion Border Regiment in the Glencorse Wood sector. The division on this day came under the orders of the 1st Anzac Corps.

It was extremely hot and sunny, and the relief carried out in daylight in full view of the enemy observation balloons. Late in the afternoon, after a long and tiring cross country journey, " A " and " C " Companies reached the Hooge Craters. From the end of the craters nearest to Zouave Wood, a brushwood track ran about a half mile long, which led to a junction with the famous Menin Road. The track, known as Therandbaxi Track, ended at the Menin Road at a point known as Clapham Junction, so called as being a junction of the track, the tunnels under the Menin Road which were used as B.H.Q., and the trenches on the far side of Menin Road.

" A " Company crossed the track in parties of fives, the first of which had nearly reached the cover afforded by the bank of the Menin Road, when the enemy sent over a series of shells, which caught the rear party, wounding Sergt. Maybury and Cpl. Wharton and killing L/Cpl. Cunningham; the latter's loss was keenly felt in his company, as he was one of the bright lads, always so happy and cheerful.

Proceeding through Clapham Junction to Justa Trench on the other side of the Menin Road (the trench was well named because it was only " just a " trench and no more), " A " Company took over the left front, while " C " occupied the right front. " B " were in support at Half Way House, and " D " remained in reserve behind Clapham Junction.

Lieut. A. Thompson, two N.C.O.'s and ten men per company, acted as a permanent ration party and were accommodated in Wing House. A job on a ration party was generally considered to be a snip, but this party had a very bad time of it, as those supplying the forward companies had to make several journeys, there and back, across the Therandbaxi Track. As this track was under observation by the enemy, and any movement on it resulted in enemy shelling, more than one man of the carrying party would have welcomed a return to his company.

The left of the front line skirted Glencorse Wood, inside of which one platoon manned a large crater for a 24-hour stretch. All men were on duty after dusk for the whole night, and by daylight had to push his head and shoulders into a funk hole level with the ground, and cover his feet with a ground sheet to prevent being observed by any enemy plane that might fly over. This post was very uncanny, as it was surrounded by hundreds of tree stumps which by night all appeared to move.

Out in the open lay several of our tanks, which had been bogged in earlier attacks; one or two of these were used as advance posts.

The only decent dug-out in the front line was a German pillbox, used as a company H.Q. Some of the men dug funk holes in the side of the trench, but these could not be made very large owing to the sandy nature of the soil. Many just sheltered under a piece of corrugated iron laid across the top of the trench and covered with a layer of sand-bags.

Back at transport that night a tragedy occurred; a long-range gun scored a direct hit, killing three men and wounding 20 others.

During the first night and throughout the following day, the enemy heavily shelled the front line, Clapham Junction and the track, in fact, the latter was shelled continuously throughout the whole of the time the battalion was in this sector. During the first day in the line " ours " lost two men killed and six wounded.

Each night patrols went out at different parts of the line; these were uncomfortable patrols owing to the large number of enemy dead which still lay about unburied.

On September 12th the whole area occupied by the 7th was heavily shelled with mustard gas for two and a half hours, and Zouave Wood for two hours.

During this spell in the line 2nd Lieut. J. Preston, M.C., carried out many patrols, invariably making a round of calls from our front line to the several advanced posts.

The 7th had a fresh experience in the way of shell fire by our own artillery, which, at various times during the day, put down a practice barrage on the rear lines of the enemy. Sometimes these would consist of brigade machine-guns, 18 and 60-pounders, at other times it would be 4.7's and a heavy type of " dug-out smasher "; occasionally the whole lot would go together. While these practice barrages took place, those in the front line received orders to fix bayonets and take as much cover as possible by flattening themselves into the parapet. The din was terrific, nothing like it had been heard before. When these barrages switched to the left of the sector held by the 7th, it was possible to watch the results in comfort, and from the resultant clouds of red-tinged dust which arose as the shells exploded, one imagined they were falling on the remnants of a village.

Retaliation followed most of these barrages, and the 7th suffered accordingly. During one period of exceptionally heavy enemy shelling, one of our officers, looking at a newspaper one of the men was reading, drew attention to the headlines which read " Germans short of scrap iron," and passed the following terse comment : " I wonder what it would be like if they had plenty ? "

One of our men wanted for gas guard appeared to be missing from the line, when it was recalled that a shell had landed near a little earlier on just after he had passed by. A search revealed his body, which had been flung on top of the parapet ; he was only identified by the crisscross manner in which he did up his putties.

Outside " A " Company's H.Q. two sentries did duty, and precisely at the hour of midnight L/Cpl. Craven, having carried out relief of one sentry, stopped by the other sentry, Pte. Staines, and said : " I'll get your relief in a minute." At that moment the enemy scored a direct hit on the parapet, killing both L/Cpl. Craven and Pte. G. Staines ; the other sentry, the writer, had a narrow escape. Before dawn Cpl. Craven and Pte. Staines were buried together in a deep shell hole.

On the morning of September 14th a party of about fifty of the enemy were observed marching towards our lines on the left front, carrying two or three white flags. Orders were received to halt and search them before passing them down the line, but as the orders were received the party vanished behind Westhoek Ridge.

Lieut. J. Preston, M.C., and six other ranks went out on patrol for two hours, and returned with documents taken off a dead German.

A brief and breezy description of this turn in the line is recorded in the diary of one of our officers, and the following are extracts :

> " Moved up the line, Boche shelled us with vigour. Very interesting bit of the line, more like battle outposts than trench holding. Stormy night (this refers to shells, as the weather was gloriously fine). Boche strafed with great vigour at 1.30 a.m., normal till 4.30 a.m., when he performed again.
>
> " For variation Fritz treated us to some gas shells during the night. Two humorous efforts at ' Stand to ' ; message asks for ' Number of blankets required to protect from gas all dug-outs in my area.' Not very difficult, as we have exactly one dug-out. Second effort asked for name of a ' suitable man for a cinematograph operator.' "

After referring to the events of September 15th, the diary continues :

> " Stood to 5 a.m. Our people did an hour's practice barrage, repeated at 10 a.m. Boche did a little back chat.

"About the stormiest time most of us remember ever having spent in the line."

In order to advance our position ready to obtain a better jumping-off position for the forthcoming attack, 30 men from each of "B" and "D" Companies, under Lieut.-Col. C. J. Salkeld Green, D.S.O., M.C., accompanied by the adjutant and 2nd Lieuts. B. N. Cryer and A. C. Robinson, on September 13th went down the line to carry out practice attacks.

During previous attacks on this particular post by the 2nd Corps, it had held out strongly and had resisted all attempts to capture it.* Our party put in a lot of hard work, performing twice over the flagged course in the morning and four times during the afternoon. On September 15th they returned by motor bus to Ypres and proceeded along the Menin Road on foot. Between Hooge and Clapham Junction they were heavily shelled, but fortunately got through without casualties; this journey from Ypres to Clapham Junction took three and a half hours.

Once in the tunnels each man was served out with 170 rounds of S.A.A., three sandbags, Mills bombs, picks and shovels, wire-cutters, etc.

The party moved into position and were served out with a rum ration; at 4.10 p.m., zero hour, our barrage crashed down on the objective and "over the top" went the attackers in daylight, in two waves, accompanied by signallers, runners, stretcher bearers, and four pigeons for messages.

2nd Lieut. A. C. Robinson became an early casualty and in rushing the strong point, 2nd Lieut. B. N. Cryer was killed. The opposition was speedily overcome and the strong point and surrounding trenches were ours. In memory of 2nd Lieut. B. N. Cryer, who so gallantly laid down his life, the position was named "Cryer Farm."

A new pattern light machine-gun was captured and as there was plenty of ammunition, this gun was put to good use against the enemy during his counter-attacks; the total number of prisoners captured was 36.

Our men quickly got to work under the direction of their N.C.O.'s; all communication trenches were double blocked and the trenches put in a state of defence ready for counter-attacks which the enemy were expected to make. Our runners had a very hectic time. Pte. R. Bond, M.M., returned to B.H.Q. with information on the position a quarter of an hour after zero. The Battalion Intelligence Officer from our front line gave a running commentary to B.H.Q. simultaneously with the operation:

> Lieut.-Col. C. J. S. Green records that "an Australian V.C. stood on the top of the Menin Road with me while the attack was made. He congratulated me on the way the men went over and then casually strolled off through the German counter-barrage back to

* The 47th (London) Divisional History.

his battalion in the rear." He had come up to discuss the relief which was to take place the next day.

When dusk fell, Capt. L. E. Bishop and 45 other ranks, guided by Pte. R. Bond, M.M., went over as reinforcements, taking with them a supply of S.A.A. and hot food. Throughout the night two carrying parties operated and all the wounded were evacuated.

Three times the enemy attempted to regain his lost ground and each time he was driven back ; the first of these attacks was at 1 a.m. followed by a more determined effort at 2 a.m. and again at 5 a.m. Upon this occasion his attack commenced just as our guns started a practice barrage. Heavy losses were inflicted on the enemy, who retired in disorder, presenting some very fine targets for our Lewis gunners.

Our total casualties in this attack, apart from the officers already mentioned, were two men killed and four wounded, which was a light price considering the importance of the captured position.

Daylight afforded relief to the garrison of "Cryer Farm" and to the troops in the line. About 5 p.m. in the afternoon of September 16th, the battalion was relieved by the 1st Australian Infantry Battalion.

This was an unusual relief, as from Clapham Junction orders were given to leave six at a time and to make their own way back to Segard Chateau ; the track was shelled throughout the incoming relief, but when the battalion moved out the artillery of the enemy was less active.

On the way out, Lieut. V. W. Mileman, M.C., was killed by a direct hit. The battalion lost two officers killed, 2nd Lieut. B. N. Cryer and Lieut. V. W. Mileman, M.C., and two wounded, 2nd Lieuts. A. C. Robinson and J. K. St. Aubyn. Ten other ranks were killed and 60 wounded. Of 2nd Lieut. B. N. Cryer, a brother officer writes :

> "He was a very charming personality ; he was very quiet and concealed under a somewhat diffident manner, competence and, I think, power of leadership."

Many mourned the loss of Lieut. V. W. Mileman who had distinguished himself at the Butte de Warlencourt and had been popular with all.

Everyone was glad to be out of it and thanked their lucky stars they were still alive ; the tour had been one of the stickiest of line duty the battalion had experienced.

For the part they had played in the attack on Cryer Farm, Capt. L.E. Bishop was awarded an M.C., Sergt. A. Baker and Pte. A. E. Newnham were each awarded the D.C.M., Pte. R. Bond, M.M., was awarded a bar to his M.M., and the following were each awarded the M.M. : Cpl. F. G. Brooks, Ptes. C. C. Foster, G. Pettitt, H. Wilcox, E. T. J. Vivian, and P. Jones.

The following is the citation of Pte. A. E. Newnham:

> "For conspicuous gallantry and devotion to duty as one of an attacking party. On reaching the objective he patrolled down a trench single handed and came across several of the enemy, whom he fired on, killing two and bringing back four as prisoners."

Once again the "Shiny Seventh" had carried all before them, having attacked and captured a German strong point in daylight, repulsed three determined counter-attacks and handed over to its relief a valuable forward post which gave fine observation over enemy positions and proved of great assistance as a jumping-off position.

The following are extracts from a version of the attack by Cpl. F. G. Brooks, who was upon this occasion the recipient of a Military Medal:

> "Cryer Farm, situate in front of Clapham Junction and to the north of Inverness Copse, which we attacked, was named after 2nd Lieut. B. N. Cryer who was killed instantly almost at the entrance to the pillbox. The attack took place on a Saturday afternoon in glorious sunshine (real cricket weather), at 4.10 p.m. 2nd Lieut. Robinson was wounded as he left our trench. The enemy did not put up much of a fight and we took 36 prisoners. About a dozen of the enemy were killed. In the counter-attacks the enemy penetrated quite close, particularly on the right flank, even to our rear. After a stiff fight he was driven off."

There was a certain amount of relief when news passed round that the battalion was about to leave the Salient for good.

Messages of appreciation were received from Gen. Sir Herbert C. O. Plumer, G.C.M.G., G.C.V.O., K.C.B., A.D.C., and Lieut.-Gen. Sir W. R. Birdwood, K.C.B., K.C.S.I., K.C.M.G. C.E.I., D.S.O.

Eleven months had been spent by the "Shiny Seventh" in the Ypres area, and the cemeteries and the magnificent Menin Gate Memorial record the names of many of our comrades who made the great sacrifice there.

CHAPTER TWENTY-TWO

September—November 26th, 1917
ARRAS

SEPTEMBER 17th was spent by the men at Segard Chateau cleaning up, and the following day a move was made to the area of Steenvoorde, three hundred by bus and the remainder on foot. On the 20th the battalion moved again, this time to the Eecke area, on the next day it entrained at Caestre for Aubigny, thence to Acq, which was reached at 8 p.m., three companies being in huts and one in billets.

On September 24th the battalion moved to Anzin St. Aubyn, and relieved the 21st London Regiment. On the following day we were on the move again, marching via Roclincourt to Roundhay Camp, where the Nelson Battalion of the 63rd Naval Division was relieved.

Working parties commenced straight away and continued for a week in the area of Bailleul Post, Ditch Post and Towy Alley.

While at Roundhay Camp 2nd Lieut. H. H. Harman joined from base, and on October 3rd the battalion was relieved by the 20th London Regiment and moved back to Anzin St. Aubyn, where the men were quartered in huts and empty houses. 2nd Lieut. R. G. Miller joined the battalion here from base.

The battalion moved off on October 10th in fighting order, travelling by light railway to Ashford Junction, and subsequently relieved the 23rd London Regiment. " A " Company, in support, were to supply rations and water to the other companies. " B " occupied the centre front of Chambers Alley and Railway Trench. " C " were on the left front at Bradford Post and Cadorna Trench, with " D " Company on the right in Blandford and Marine Trench. The cookers did not accompany the companies in the line and raw food was served out to the men, who had to make the best job they could of cooking.

On October 11th our people discharged gas on our left on Oppy village and Crucifix Trench, and men of all our companies had to wear their gas masks until the code word " Greensleeves " was passed along. After dusk Lieut. H. H. Harman, Sergt. H. Monck and four men went out on patrol seeking advanced enemy positions, but found nothing fresh.

A notice board was erected in No-man's-land and on it in Polish was an invitation to " Come over to us and you will be well treated."

The front line was shelled with pineapple bombs and Pte. W. C. Noad was killed and three other men wounded. On October 17th the enemy heavily shelled our lines for over two hours ; over five hundred shells fell during this period.

The battalion was relieved on October 18th by the Civil Service Rifles and moved into the chalk trenches of the Red Line area.

An " A " Company working party was heavily shelled for over an hour with 5·9's ; fortunately they were able to move into some deep trenches near by and escaped casualties, although many shells fell very close. At this time 2nd Lieuts. R. W. Thomas, C. T. Watson and R. J. Hayres joined the battalion from base.

The 7th were relieved by the London Irish on October 26th and moved to St. Aubyn, where the men had baths and a general clean up.

The last day of October found " ours " acting as battalion in reserve, having relieved the Civil Service Rifles at Roundhay Camp, and from here the men performed many working parties on the railway cutting.

On November 9th the battalion moved up the line and relieved the Civil Service Rifles in the right sub-section, " A " being in Willie Trench on the right, with " D " on the left in Chico Trench. " B " and " C " Companies were both in support. After four days we were relieved by the 24th London Regiment on November 13th, and moved out via Towy Alley and Roclincourt to Aubrey Camp.

On November 14th the men had baths at Roclincourt and spent the day cleaning up ; company training and range firing were resumed. The 7th, on the 18th, were relieved by the 10th East Yorkshire Regiment and moved into Corps Reserve at Bray.

It began to dawn on many that we had finished with the Arras area and most of the men were sorry, as after Ypres the last two months had been fairly comfortable. Many rumours were about that the battalion was off to Italy, jokes about ice-cream and fighting with knives were abundant. On November 21st a move was made to Habarcq, and on the following day to the Wanquetin area of Simencourt.

News of the great Cambrai attack was being discussed and it became apparent that the 7th were making for that region, when on November 24th they moved via Ransart, Adinfer and Ayette to Courcelles-le-Comte. On the following day the battalion marched through Bapaume to Beaulencourt, where bivouacs were occupied.

German prisoners were seen being marched back to the cages, and those of the Regiment who said we " were for it " were not far wrong.

CHAPTER TWENTY-THREE

November 27th, 1917—February, 1918
BOURLON WOOD

AFTER a cold and snowy night the weather broke gloriously fine on the morning of November 27th, and the men were warned to be prepared for a move. The 47th Division on this day became part of the Vth Corps (Third Army), and the battalion was about to take part in its last major engagement, although this was unknown at the time.

Buses carried the men up to Beaumetz over freshly captured ground, and at dusk the 7th completed their journey on foot, arriving at Doignes, where bivouacs were occupied.

During the night, which was cold and wet, and early in the morning the enemy artillery shelled our area searching for battery positions.

The battalion moved forward in pitch darkness on the 28th and occupied some trenches of the Hindenburg line; a further move forward was made on the 29th to the Hindenburg support line and having crossed the Canal du Nord, the 7th occupied Kangaroo Trench.

All dug-outs were full of troops of the 2nd Division and we remained out in the open trench. However, the weather was kind, and after a fairly quiet night the early morning of November 30th broke fine and sunny.

All this area was fresh to the 7th, the trench overlooked the village of Graincourt, which appeared intact. In front was the Bapaume-Cambrai road beyond which was Bourlon Wood, situated on a ridge rising above the Bapaume-Cambrai Road, the whole filled with a thick undergrowth.

The 7th were on this day lent to the 2nd Division, but were withdrawn from them before nightfall.

All seemed nice and peaceful on the morning of November 30th, when at 8.30 a.m. the enemy guns opened up with terrific force. Shells simply rained down on Graincourt, and Bourlon Wood was treated to an intense gas-shell bombardment. Simultaneously the enemy launched a determined attack against the haunches of the salient. Our artillery replied and both sides carried on the duel until about 10 a.m., when the enemy was seen from the support position held by the 7th, with the naked eye, advancing in extended order over the ridge beyond the Bapaume-Cambrai Road and on the left of Bourlon Wood. At the same time low-flying enemy planes roared over the trenches and machine-gunned the men of the 7th who were standing in the trench without cover. How the men escaped being hit was a miracle, and these enemy planes were the cause of much " wind up " as at times they just skimmed over the top of the trench and the occupants could be plainly seen.

Every moment the men expected the order to move forward in support of the front line. The battalion suffered several casualties, and Pte. Ward of " A " Company was killed.

All along the line in our area the front held, but at 2 p.m., after another heavy bombardment the enemy attacked and drove a wedge in between the left of the 6th London and the right flank of the 2nd Division. A gap formed between the 6th and 15th London Regiments, but a prompt counter-attack by the 6th London restored the line. The 8th London also made a counter-attack at 5 p.m.

The 141st Brigade front held firm against all attacks of the enemy, but the 19th London suffered many casualties from gas, their strength being ultimately reduced to nine officers and sixty-one other ranks.*

Meanwhile, the enemy made a considerable advance to the south and captured the village of Gouzeaucourt.

The day had been hard for the 47th Division and for London troops in particular, and in thanking the Division for the magnificent defence of the important position entrusted to them Sir Douglas Haig wrote:

> " Though exposed throughout the day to the repeated assaults of superior forces, they beat off all attacks with the heaviest losses to the enemy, and by their gallant and steady conduct contributed very largely to the security of the divisions engaged on the whole front of attack."*

Pte. W. G. Browning, a runner, volunteered to take a message back, an errand he successfully completed despite the heavy shell fire and for which exploit he was awarded a Military Medal.

Meanwhile, on the front of the 56th Division one of " ours," Cpl. W. J. Lucas, who had left us at Ypres to take a Commission, was upholding 7th traditions. As a 2nd Lieut. on this day he won a Military Cross, the citation for which reads as follows:

> " During an enemy attack he organised the main line of defence, and got forward continuous supplies of bombs and ammunition. He set his men a splendid example and the successful resistance of the line against determined enemy attacks was largely due to his courage, coolness and skill."

To return to the battalion who were still in Kangaroo Trench. 2nd Lieut. Morgan and six of our men had been wounded and one man killed. The M.O. ordered Pte. Cavers, who had been badly wounded, to be evacuated and the job of carrying him down the line fell to S.B.'s

---

* The 47th (London) Divisional History.

Ptes. Dunham and Phillips, who were assisted by two sanitary men, Ptes. Viles and Edmunds. When this party returned, they found the 7th gone. The battalion had received orders to dump packs and greatcoats (incidentally, this was the last they saw of them) and in fighting order had moved off. When the S.B.'s returned they buried Pte. Ward and then set about finding the 7th. The country was new to them and even back at Brigade H.Q., where Capt. L. E. Rundell, M.C., was interviewed, they could not obtain the position of the battalion and they wandered all over the place for a couple of days before rejoining.

At midnight, by a circuitous route, the 7th moved round the village of Anneux and crossed to the other side of the Bapaume-Cambrai Road and halted in a sunken road. The position of the front line was uncertain, and after a short wait " A " and " B " Companies moved on in single file, up a sunken road leading towards Bourlon Wood. Conditions up this sunken road were horrifying; dead and wounded were lying all over the road and had to be stepped over. Funk holes in the side of the banks each had its occupant; all were dead, and by the light of a rising moon the effect was ghastly. The groans of wounded and appeals for help assailed the men of the 7th as they ascended this road.

Near the top the men were led off to the right and told to dig in before daylight. Being equipped with only entrenching tools, this was a tall order, but for their own safety everyone got to work.

Shortly after 3 a.m. on December 1st, a message was passed along " All 7th men to cross to the left of the sunken road." The men had been intermixed with the 15th London. In executing this order the men were silhouetted by the moonlight and observed by the enemy, who opened up with machine-guns and inflicted several casualties on our men.

Again the men started to dig in and by daylight had managed to get a series of slit trenches, which that night were connected up with each other and a continuous line made, but only about three feet deep.

Rations were scarce and water scarcer. Sandbags containing rations for five arrived; these included tea, sugar and tins of cocoa, all of which were useless, as the men had no means of cooking, and even if they had, the water ration was only a mugful each. The tins of condensed milk proved very welcome.

The enemy continued to shell at odd times and the battalion had four men killed and six wounded.

In the front line the men were expecting to be relieved and were greatly surprised when later on the men of " C " and " D " Companies arrived to say they were " going over the top."

The enemy at dusk appeared to be very nervous and shelled our front line with pineapple bombs; a party of the enemy were observed in No-man's-land and our machine-guns opened up and were quickly followed by rifle fire all along the line. Apparently this was a party of the enemy going out to occupy a forward post.

The men of all companies were mixed up in the front line and many obtained an additional rum issue when a mess tin of rum came along with a message, " ' C ' Company men only," followed shortly afterwards by another for " A " Company men only, and so on.

At 8.10 p.m. a battery of our guns opened up and over went " C " and " D," accompanied by several of " A " Company, and two companies of the 8th London went over on our right. B.H.Q. was situate in a German gunpit and Lieut.-Col. C. J. S. Green recalls the occasion as being " The only time I fought a battle in comfort." Within two minutes prisoners were entering our lines as also were our own wounded; the opposition was not very severe and the attack resulted in fifty-two prisoners and eighteen machine-guns being captured and the line advanced between three and four hundred yards. At 9.35 p.m. a platoon of " A " Company was ordered forward to fill in a gap. Out of 10 officers who took part in this attack only two came out unscathed and both subsequently were decorated. Lieut. R. W. Thomas was awarded an M.C., and 2nd Lieut. C. R. Palmer a bar to his M.C.

In connection with this attack, the following is an extract from the 47th (London) Divisional History :

> " Officially described as a ' minor operation,' colloquially dismissed as a ' good show,' it was in reality an effort at a time when troops were tired, which reflected great credit and produced valuable results."

The " Shiny Seventh " took part in three phases of the Battle of Cambrai, defence, attack and withdrawal. In forwarding the Commander-in-Chief's congratulations to units of the division, the Divisional Commander added: " England, and London especially, may well be proud of you."

The following message was sent by the Army Commander :

> " Will you please convey to the G.O.C. 47th Division my very best congratulations on their excellent achievement last night.
>
> " This operation was of the greatest value to the situation and reflects the greatest credit on those who carried it out.—J. BYNG (General)."*

In " The Times " of November 12th, 1921, the Military Correspondent, writing of the 47th Division, records : " Their finest achievement—and

---

* The 47th (London) Divisional History.

SOUTH AFRICAN OFFICERS
3/7th (City of London) Battalion The London Regiment
Sutton Mandeville, July 1916

(*Back Row.*)
2nd Lieuts. K. G. ANDERSON, W. W. HUTTON, A. BEHRN, D. PHILLIP, T. W. SCLATER, A. F. MURRAY, G. D. JOHNSTONE, C. D. METCALF, T. G. V. PARKER, G. A. WEBSTER, A. ELSBURY.

(*Third Row.*)
2nd Lieuts. W. A. C. TAYLOR, E. D. BOURKE-MACAULEY, S. EDGAR, W. G. MACINTOSH, C. E. LONG, C. CARTWRIGHT, W. URQUHART, J. DUMINY, R. MICHELL. F. CHURCHILL. A. G. McLEOD, R. ECKSTEEN, H. WHITBY.

(*Second Row, sitting.*)
2nd Lieuts. V. F. HOSKIN, A. E. GIBSON, L. MICHELL, Maj. J. NICOL, V.D., Lieut.-Col. Sir P. Van B. STEWART-BAM, 2nd Lieuts. R. G. MILLER, F. B. BARLING, W. J. JOHNSTONE C. V. HOSKIN.

(*Front Row.*)
2nd Lieuts. R. STEVENSON, E. S. C. REES, H. SHILLITO, N. L. HINES

OFFICERS WITH THE RESERVE BATTALION
3/7th (City of London) The London Regiment

(*Back Row.*)
2nd Lieuts. G. C. DAVENPORT, W. W. HUTTON, C. D. METCALF, F. H. E. WOOLLETT, J. P. SCOTHORNE, P. D. EVERSHED, W. J. JOHNSTONE, R. EKSTEEN, E. J. SAFFERY H. D. B. DRUMMOND, W. W. HOSKEN, E. M. BOURKE-MACAULEY.

(*Fifth Row.*)
2nd Lieuts. W. A. C. TAYLOR, P. W. ROOTS, C. T. WATSON, C. E. LONG, G. D. JOHNSTONE, A. E. GIBSON, R. MICHELL, T. G. V. PARKER, F. B. BARLING, F. C. LUXTON, N. L. HINES.

(*Fourth Row.*)
2nd Lieuts. A. G. McLEOD, C. G. SCUDAMORE, S. EDGAR, P. TRAYNOR, P. J. RETIEF, R. E. STEVENSON, W. J. MACKINTOSH, C. M. GOLDSBURY, S. F. FORBES, C. V. HOSKEN, C. CARTWRIGHT, H. R. M. CHAMBERLAIN, H. C. PLATTS, K. G. ANDERSON, E. S. C. REED.

(*Third Row*).
2nd Lieuts. I. D. MONTGOMERY, G. W. M. HARE, L. MICHELL, R. W. THOMAS, L. E. JAMES, A. ELSBURY, A. T. S. SMITH, A. J. E. BEHREN, J. D. M. PHILLIP, A. F. MURRAY, H. B. SMITH, J. F. PRESTON, S. SCUDAMORE, W. URQUHART, H. A. SALTER, G. A. WEBSTER.

(*Sitting*.)
Lieut. W. N. CULVERWELL, Capt. R. C. A. F. MOLYNEUX, Capt. B. F. AYRTON, Capt. D. E. WARD, Capt. H. E. LYDIART, Maj. L. P. MANSFIELD JONES, Maj. W. MUDFORD, T.D., Lieut.-Col. Sir PIETER C. VAN B. STEWART-BAM, Capt. L. E. PEPPIATT (Adjt.), Maj. J. NICOL, V.D., Capt. T. RUSHWORTH, Capt. K. O. PEPPIATT, Rev. EVERARD DIGBY, C.F.. Capt. M. BRIDGEMAN, R.A.M.C., Lieut. and Q.M. H. M. RYLAND.

(*Sitting on Ground.*)
Lieut. H. A. BROWN, Lieut. F. S. MARSH, Lieut. D. GRAHAM, 2nd Lieut. R. G. MILLER, Lieut. W. H. KIRBY, Lieut. D. ROONEY, Lieut. P. LUDBROOK, 2nd Lieuts. L. MILLER, R. J. HUNT.

SOUTH AFRICAN OFFICERS WITH THE RESERVE BATTALION
AT SUTTON MANDEVILLE, JULY 1916

OFFICERS WITH THE RESERVE BATTALION

Facing page 134

one may perhaps say the finest in the military history of any London formation—was its defence of Bourlon Wood."

The battalion was relieved by the 23rd London and the troops thought they might be going right back; they were soon disillusioned when they occupied some trenches in the area of Hughes Switch.

The casualties of the 7th during these two days were: 2nd Lieut. H. B. Lewis killed, 35 other ranks missing and 14 killed, while 121 men were wounded. Among the officers wounded were 2nd Lieuts. R. H. Rogers, G. C. Davenport, G. V. Parker, C. T. Watson, C. E. Hopkins, and D. B. Clarke. Capt. W. J. Johnstone was so seriously wounded that he died ten days later.

Among the N.C.O.'s who were killed in this action were some popular men, such as Sergt. C. C. Bowers, D.C.M., M.M., Pte. W. Edwards, M.M., affectionately known as "Dad," a stretcher bearer, killed while trying to bring in a wounded man, Sergt. J. H. Seddon, M.M., L/Cpl. A. J. Elms, L/Cpl. R. Lord and Sergt. P. P. Maguire. Pte. P. Lord was wounded for the third time. Pte. W. Sage, known to all as "Tich," was severely wounded, one of his legs being completely shattered.

Pte. J. C. Huntley was awarded a bar to his M.M., and the following were awarded the M.M.: Pte. W. G. Browning, Pte. A. Cornell, L/Cpl. G. L. Crudgington, Pte. G. H. Downs, Sergt. G. E. Edwards, Pte. C. Fairman, Pte. A. Knight, Cpl. A. Missions, Sergt. E. C. Pilley, Pte. F. G. Taylor, L/Cpl. J. A. Wilson, Cpl. E. Winter, Pte. W. Winter.

Cpl. F. G. Brooks, M.M., upon this occasion was awarded the D.C.M., and the following is an extract from the "London Gazette":

"350366, Cpl. F. G. Brooks, M.M., 1/7th Battalion, London Regiment. For conspicuous gallantry and devotion to duty during an attack. At a critical stage of the operation he carried an important message from his company commander to battalion headquarters under heavy machine-gun and shell fire. Subsequently he carried several messages forward under heavy fire and brought back important information. He showed splendid initiative and determination."

The following is from the pen of Cpl. F. G. Brooks, D.C.M., M.M.:

"On the night of November 30th we moved up to a new position, north of the Bapaume-Cambrai Road and in close proximity to Bourlon Wood. At this time we were all feeling the strain of the last few days—water had been short and on the night of December 2nd we learnt that two of our companies with two companies of the 8th on our right were to attack up the slope of Bourlon Wood.

"Our orders were to take the German front line, advance one hundred yards and dig in. There was little time for preparation but the Mills grenades arrived and the S.R.D., and at 8.10 p.m. the attack started. Capt. J. G. H. Budd was in charge of forward H.Q.

"The Germans met our attack with heavy machine-gun fire and at first it appeared that the attack would fail. Fighting took place in the shallow trenches which the Germans had obviously dug in great haste. The opposition was soon overcome."

The men had to spend the night in the open trenches of Hughes Switch, as all the dug-outs were crowded out. The weather was bitterly cold, and it was a great relief when daylight came, bringing with it a hot breakfast, the first the men had tasted for some days. This was followed by a wash and shave, also the first for several days as water had been more precious than victuals.

On December 4th a move back to the Hindenburg Line was made.

The battalion made a further move on December 7th, relieving the Post Office Rifles at Flesquieres. "A" and "C" Companies took over the left and centre of the front respectively, with "B" and "D" in support, the relief was completed by 9.45 p.m.

This turn in the line proved fairly quiet as the enemy was some distance away, and apart from early morning displays of hate by his artillery on our front line and the sunken road, we were not troubled too much. Patrols of an N.C.O. and six men went out nightly and returned without mishap. Our only casualty was Pte. Lacy, who was wounded, and the S.B.'s had a long and difficult carry in the mud and rain in getting him back to the dressing station.

The battalion received a nasty blow on December 10th when it learned that Capt. L. E. Rundell, M.C., who had been serving at Brigade H.Q., on this day died of wounds received from a shell burst. Capt. Rundell had crossed over with the battalion in 1915, and had been three times wounded—at Vermelles, Vimy and High Wood; for his gallantry in action he had been awarded an M.C. and Bar, being the first officer in the Division to accomplish this double.

With the post which arrived on December 10th, came several parcels, and many were for men who in the recent fighting had become casualties. After extracting personal items, which were returned to the senders, the perishable goods were divided among the platoons and, in view of the meagre rations at this time, proved a welcome addition.

Most of the men were in a worn condition, and on the night of December 11th, the 19th London Regiment took over and the battalion moved back by platoons, via Havrincourt and Hermies to Ruyalcourt.

Once clear of the line the men set off to the rear, but it was a straggling crowd which was met on the road by the cookers and were served out with rum and cocoa. Thus fortified, the men fell in and carried on in proper marching order; further on officers and men who had come up from Transport lines met the remnants of the battalion.

The 7th, it must be remembered, had not been back to a camp since the end of November, when they had left Beaulencourt for Doignes, and much had happened in the meantime. Therefore, it was a great pleasure to the survivors to be met and welcomed on their way back by those who had been fortunate enough for one reason or another to miss this very sticky turn in the line.

Ruyalcourt was reached at 4 a.m., and everyone was glad to get down to rest and sleep.

The next few days were spent in cleaning up, baths, etc., and replenishment of kit. After a short rest the " Shiny Seventh " moved off to the war again, when on December 15th the line west of Flesquieres was taken over, a composite battalion of the 141st Brigade and the 21st London Regiment being relieved.

The first morning in the line proved misty; on the next day, December 17th, the village of Flesquieres was shelled, and the 7th had one man killed.

It was a fairly quiet turn in the line for the 7th, and throughout the weather remained misty and visibility bad. A unit of the 17th Division relieved " ours " on December 21st, and we moved back to tents in the area of Bertincourt. On the following day the battalion paraded at 8.30 a.m., and moved by train from Etricourt to Mericourt, whence a march to billets at Ribemont, which was reached at 6.15 p.m.

The battalion was out for a well-deserved rest, and the men appreciated being among civilians again; the Follies were close by at Mericourt and were attended at some time or another by most of the battalion.

After a good clean-up, preparations were made for Christmas; the battalion produced a Christmas card, designed by one of the Pioneers, Pte. A. Cresswell, which depicted two drummers, one in the style of dress then worn and the other in attire of days gone by; the top left corner showed St. Paul's in the distance, and the opposite corner a sketch of " Tower Bridge " at Loos, with the 7th badge in the centre.

On Boxing Day a battalion dinner was held in a shed near the railway station; the men were waited on by the N.C.O.'s and afterwards the brigadier-general paid a visit and made a short speech.

The weather turned extremely cold, snow fell and the temperature dropped to below freezing point. In order to keep warm the men scrounged firewood wherever they could, and from a wood near by many trees were cut down, so many, in fact, that strict orders were issued to stop this practice. Night excursions were made into the wood by parties of men armed with a cross-cut saw, and the noise made was enough to waken the dead; trees were cut down into reasonable lengths and drawn home on a sledge. One party returning home with their spoil in the dark were suddenly pounced upon by someone with a torch. Knowing they were for the "high jump," if caught, the party of woodcutters fled, leaving the loaded sledge to be drawn home by men of another company, who, by the simple expedient of shining a torch, had "won" the results of a night's labour of half-a-dozen men.

January 10th, 1918, saw the end of this holiday from the line; the men were rested and all fit and well. The battalion was loaded into small open railway trucks at Mericourt and left at 10.30 a.m., for what proved to be the last home of the 1st Battalion in France; after a long ride across desolate country they detrained and marched to Lechelle, where Nissen huts were occupied.

Two days later, on the 12th, the battalion moved off to relieve the 22nd London Regiment in the line at Premy Salient; the journey up was a long one, cookers accompanied the battalion and hot tea was provided. "A" and "C" Companies took over the left and left centre, with "B" and "D" on the right and right centre of the right sub-sector. From the support trenches to the front the journey was slow and very difficult, owing to the muddy and waterlogged state of the trenches, most being more than three feet deep in thick liquid mud.

On January 14th it was decided that the front line should be evacuated and all posts were withdrawn, except one per company. R.E.'s came up, prepared all the dug-outs for demolition, and these gun-cotton charges were set off at midnight when the remaining men were withdrawn.

On the way out the men had to dump their packs and fill in trenches, work which annoyed some of them, who expressed the opinion that Jerry was welcome to the trenches for what use they were. It was about 1 a.m. when the old trenches were filled in and the new line at Kaiser Support was reached, the code words for completion being "Beer, Rum, Whisky," and it can be safely recorded that the men welcomed their share of the code words on completion, which, of course, was rum. The password for the trench-filling operation, which was completed without a casualty, was "Shiny."

The weather was extremely wet and miserable, and the men had to carry out working parties with rations not too plentiful and, taking things all round, nobody was particularly happy. From the diary of Pte. F. Dunham, the following deals with the period under review:

"We had a working party on the 15th at 5 p.m. The job was wiring in No-man's-land, and the journey to and fro took us about six hours all told. We progressed through the mud at the rate of about one hundred yards in fifteen minutes, and in the trench just outside B.H.Q., where the mud was thigh deep, chaps were sticking in it, unable to move until pulled out. Some even had to leave their waders stuck in the mud and wriggle their legs free, to finish the journey in stockinged feet.

"We all got out of the trench once (this in itself was a feat, as the sides were so slippery), thinking it would be better going along the top, but the surface was like glass, and chaps were slipping over in the dark every minute, so we slid back into the trench again. The boys did very little work, and it was a wet and muddy crowd that returned to their dug-out about 2 a.m."

Rain continued and nightly patrols were sent forward to the evacuated line from where they fired a few Very lights and some rounds of rifle fire in an endeavour to make the enemy believe the trenches were occupied.

The 6th London Regiment arrived on the night of January 22nd and relieved "ours," who moved back into support at Ribecourt where the troops occupied the cellars of the half-ruined houses.

It was here that the men were able to welcome Capt. L. E. Peppiatt, who a few days previously had joined the battalion. Many were known to Capt. Peppiatt and it was a pleasure to them when he accompanied Lieut. P. D. Evershed on a tour round the village to greet old faces; even those men who had not known him at home were pleased to greet him as the brother of one known affectionately to the troops as "K.O."

During the afternoon of January 24th, the whole of the village of Ribecourt was heavily shelled and at the same time the enemy laid down a complete box barrage around the village; the battalion had three other ranks wounded. Later that night we were relieved by the 17th London Regiment and moved back through Trescault and by train to the Canteen Sidings at Ytres to Divisional Reserve at Lechelle.

The weather turned misty and cold on the Sunday when a brigade church parade was held, at which the Bishop of Khartoum preached, and later on medal ribbons were presented by the Division Commander, Maj.-Gen. Sir G. F. Gorringe, to the following officers and men of the "Shiny Seventh": Capt. L. E. Bishop, M.C., 2nd Lieut. C. R. Palmer, M.C. (Bar). Sergt. E. Edwards, Cpl. W. Leary, Pte. T. Mills, Pte. C. Foster and Pte. W. G. Browning each received the M.M.

On January 27th, unknown to the men at the time, confirmation was received that the " Shiny Seventh " were to be broken up. Due to the reorganisation of brigades on a three-battalion basis instead of four, the 1/6th, 1/7th and 1/8th Battalions of the 47th Division were to be disbanded and their personnel drafted, partly to their 2nd Battalions in the 58th Division and partly to other battalions of the 47th Division, and some to the 1/7th Middlesex Regiment.

Lieut.-Col. C. J. Salkeld Green, D.S.O., M.C., who was away on leave, knew nothing of the tragic end of the battalion ; he was recalled and that night the officers held a meeting.

On the 29th, the battalion paraded for the last time and was addressed by Lieut.-Col. Green, who explained the position which, despite the rumours, came as a bombshell to the men and was a great blow to all those who had been privileged to serve in the " Shiny Seventh," and particularly to those who landed in France with the battalion and had served in it prior to that date. Lieut.-Col. Green, to whom the break-up of the battalion came as a great blow, asked the men " to do their utmost wherever they were sent and to maintain the reputation they had gained, and never forget that at one time you were a soldier in the ' Shiny Seventh ' and as such are second to none in France."

The acting adjutant, Capt. V. H. Raby and the clerks at B.H.Q. had been working overtime preparing the necessary nominal rolls. These were completed by 9 a.m. on the morning of January 29th. In the words of Capt. Raby " it was altogether a horrible business carrying through the dispersal of those then serving with the battalion."

The break-up of the battalion was effected in the following manner : 14 officers and 375 men (" A," " B " and " D " companies) were to join the 19th London Regiment, five officers and 140 men (" C " company) were to join the 1/7th Middlesex Regiment. Headquarters with personnel and 200 other ranks were to go to the 2/7th Battalion 58th Division. In arriving at who went to the 2/7th, pre-war Territorials and men who had served with gallantry longest with the battalion were selected. All W.O.'s other than R.S.M. and R.Q.M. Sergt. proceeded to Reinforcement Camp, together with surplus officers.

The mess cart was sent back to search far and wide to provide food for a final dinner for the men, which the officers provided.

A mock funeral of the " Shiny Seventh " was held ; a grave was dug and a cross erected, which was suitably inscribed with all particulars ; this ceremony was attended by a large number of men and the ritual of a funeral service was performed with all seriousness.

The first party to leave was that destined for the 19th London Regiment, and they paraded under Capt. L. E. Peppiatt in the afternoon of

January 29th ; the drums played them to the station, where last farewells were taken and as the train moved off the band played " Auld Lang Syne." Among the officers who accompanied Capt. L. E. Peppiatt were Lieuts. P. D. Evershed, E. A. Clarke, G. L. Head, C. R. Palmer, M.C., L. W. Winterflood, and 2nd Lieuts. A. G. Feaveryear, G. A. Webster, E. J. Pryer, W. R. Wallis and J. B. White. Of these officers, Lieut. P. D. Evershed and 2nd Lieut. A. G. Feaveryear were killed. Capt. L. E. Peppiatt, Lieut. J. B. White and Lieut. L. W. Winterflood were each awarded the Military Cross and Capt. Peppiatt a Bar to his M.C. Lieut. R. W. Thomas, M.C., also joined the 19th and during the German attack in March was gassed and evacuated to " Blighty."

At a later date, Capt. P. Ludbrook joined the 19th and subsequently served as adjutant under Lieut.-Col. C. J. Salkeld Green, D.S.O., M.C., when he commanded the 1/19th after the Armistice.

2nd Lieut. A. G. Feaveryear, who fell in September 1918, was a young officer who had speedily endeared himself to those under him.

Lieut. P. D. Evershed, who fell in August 1918, gallantly leading his men, had proved himself popular with all ranks ; always generous and with kindly thoughts for those in his charge, he will long be remembered by men of " A " company for his interest in the bombers' section, and inter-platoon sports which he did so much to encourage.

The officers, N.C.O.'s and men of the 7th received a very cordial welcome from the 19th and rapidly became absorbed in the unit to which they were attached. It is hoped that it is not unduly presumptuous to believe that the efficiency of the 19th was not impaired by the addition of the newcomers. Since the war, 7th London officers and other ranks have always found a warm welcome awaiting them at 19th London functions.

On January 30th, the party detailed to join the 1/7th Middlesex embussed at Bertincourt under 2nd Lieut. A. M. Thompson.

These were very sad days for Lieut.-Col. Green, the only officer left serving with the battalion out of the original officers who had crossed over to France in March 1915. His earlier career has been outlined in a previous chapter, and to this must be added the honour of being awarded the D.S.O. and four times " Mentioned in Dispatches." The following month he was awarded the Belgian Croix de Guerre, which was followed by the Territorial Decoration. Lieut.-Col. Green for a time assumed Command of the 22nd London Regiment. After the Armistice he commanded the 1st Battalion of the 19th London Regiment, and following this he commanded the cadre of the 47th Division when it returned home for demobilization. Later he became a trustee and life member of our Old Comrades' Association and has always taken the keenest interest in the affairs of the organisation, which has upon many occasions benefited by his knowledge and guidance.

Transport of the battalion under 2nd Lieut. S. Blackhurst, M.C., remained intact and served for a time with an American division, surplus men being transferred to other battalions.

On February 2nd, Pte. H. Brooks and Sergt. R. Coleman were awarded the Belgian Croix de Guerre and Sergt. C. C. Bowers the Belgian Decoration Militaire.

On this day B.H.Q. and personnel proceeded to join the 2nd Battalion. Parading at 7.30 a.m. they marched to Bertincourt headed by the band who had arrived out from England about three months previously but whose instruments had only recently come to hand. The Divisional Commander, Brig.-Gen. and most of the Division and Brigade Staff officers together with the bands of the 15th and 21st London were waiting at Bertincourt to see them off.

Among the officers who either accompanied Lieut.-Col C. J. S. Green and this party to, or subsequently joined the 2/7th Battalion were Capts. V. H. Raby, K. O. Peppiatt, H. S. F. Symonds, J. G. H. Budd, Lieut. C. D. Metcalf and 2nd Lieuts. H. H. Harman and B. C. Davis; the latter officer subsequently went to the 22nd London Regiment with whom he was seriously wounded, and after being taken back to the rear in a tank died of his wounds on the way down. His brother, Capt. F. M. Davis, had been wounded and made a prisoner of war at Vimy.

The buses carrying the 1/7th officers and men reached Berteaucourt from where the men marched to Domart, which was reached at 2.30 p.m., and were met by Lieut.-Col. S. L. Hosking—the band played them to their new home, where they were all well received and quickly settled down. Lieut.-Col. Green said good-bye to the 7th on February 6th. Many old acquaintances were renewed and it was not long before everyone had put aside the friendly rivalry which existed between the two battalions and all joined together to bring fresh honour and glory to the " Shiny Seventh," remembering the old saying " Once a Seventh always a Seventh."

CHAPTER TWENTY-FOUR
2/7th Battalion The London Regiment
1914—January, 1917
FORMATION AND TRAINING

THE Great War was only a few weeks old when the Authorities decided that second line units of the Territorial Army should be formed.

The 7th London were well to the fore with preparations at their Headquarters in Sun Street, Finsbury Square. Maj. W. Mudford, who subsequently became second-in-command of the second battalion, was already at Headquarters, where recruits flowed in at a steady rate, and he performed valuable work in organising the Companies as formed and directed their early training, which was carried out mainly at Regent's Park and at Victoria Park.

Capt. A. Prince assisted in enlisting recruits and Capt. C. J. S. Green returned from the 1st Battalion for a period to assist in the new formation which was placed under the command of Lieut.-Col. C. W. Berkeley, T.D.

Sergt. F. Payne (Grenadier Guards) who was with the 1st Battalion, became R.S.M. of the 2nd Battalion and performed trojan work throughout. Under his guidance civilian volunteers became soldiers with a high standard of efficiency. Sergts. T. Lee and T. Middleton also returned to Sun Street to render assistance.

On 19th November, 1914, the battalion paraded on the Embankment under the Command of Lieut-Col. C. W. Berkeley, T.D., and moved off to their first war station at Burgess Hill.

The battalion had been formed on the eight company system which shortly after arrival at Burgess Hill was reduced to four. Maj. S. L. Hosking and Capt. H. S. Green arrived from the 1st Battalion, the former to take command of " A " Company and the latter to become adjutant.

Soon after reaching Burgess Hill the issue of uniforms was completed, but rifles were scarce for a time and had to be passed from one section to another for training.

Most of the troops were in billets; some of the houses they occupied had been empty for years, and in some cases had leaky roofs. The winter of that year was about as bad as it could be, and considerable hardship was caused in the empty houses and shops by lack of fuel for drying sodden clothing. Those lucky enough to be placed in private billets were fortunate indeed, as the inhabitants rose to the occasion and did all in their power to make everyone comfortable.

Meals were taken in the refreshment hut at Victoria Park. The Q.M., Lieut. E. Gallagher, with inadequate appliances did his utmost to turn chaos into some semblance of order, but there were few cooks with any experience at all and the others had to learn as they went along. Consequently, one day the cooking would be good and the next day—well, not so good.

Sunday afternoons were enlivened both for the romantically minded and for the more humorously minded members of the battalion, by the arrival of the "Sweethearts' Train," a special from London bearing a full cargo of the "Girls whom the battalion had left behind them." The entertainment value of this weekly event lay in the spontaneous application of a rule that each reunited couple were required to run the gauntlet of their cheering companions formed into a lengthy double rank, before escaping to freedom.

On the whole Burgess Hill was a pleasant spot, the training being made more interesting by musketry instruction *à la* Bisley and Hythe under Lieut. L. E. Peppiatt and Sergts. Scothorne and Williams. In fact Sergt. Scothorne had returned from Bisley early in the year marked "Distinguished."

The battalion made three moves during 1915, the first being to Crowborough and the second in April to Norwich where the troops were situated first in the Old Catton end of the town; the third move was made on June 19th, 1915, to Ipswich.

Volunteers for the Machine Gun Corps were called for, and resulted in the departure from the battalion of Sergt. W. Kerr and twenty men. Final orders to this party, given by R.S.M. F. Payne, were: " Don't forget the Regiment you have come from; you are going amongst a lot of others, hold yourselves up so that we can be proud of you. You will now proceed to . . . . etc. Right turn, quick march." This party did not let the 7th down; one third of their number were killed and Sergt. W. Kerr was awarded the M.M. for events at Ypres on July 28th and 29th, 1917.

In July, 2nd Lieuts. Halley-Jones, E. J. Simons, E. W. Player and A. A. Shearman joined the battalion for duty. All four came from the Inns of Court O.T.C., the two former via the 10th Battalion East Surrey Regiment and the two latter via the North Staffordshire Regiment. 2nd Lieut. E. J. Simons subsequently transferred to the A.S.C. and at Villers Bretonneux was instrumental in providing dixies for the battalion to replace those affected by gas—a very timely opportunity of serving his old friends.

The division formed part of the First Army, Central Force (Home Defence), and while at Ipswich the first anniversary of the formation of the battalion was celebrated by a sports meeting. The following list gives the names of the winners of most of the events. 100 yards Full

Equipment, Sergt. Polge ; Sack Race, Pte. Hardington ; Pillow Fight, L/Cpl. Redway ; Wrestling on Ponies, Pte. Norton ; 100 yards Officers Race, Capt. M. W. Godson ; Bun Race, L/Cpl. Bennet ; Tug-of-War, " D " Company under S.M., J. Archdeacon and Sergt. L. Williams ; 100 yards Open, Sergt. Hooper. The major event, the marching contest of over 6 miles in the Belstead and Washbrook area, was won by " B " Company in one hour and thirty-five minutes, by a team under 2nd Lieut. E. J. Simons and consisting of S.M. Elvy, Cpl. Shaw and sixteen other ranks. Prizes were presented by Brig.-Gen. C. McGrigor at a concert the same evening, held at the Suffolk Cyclists Drill Hall.

The battalion remained at Ipswich for thirteen months and up to and during this time over 800 N.C.O.'s and men were sent to the 1st Battalion and recruits trained to keep up the strength. The battalion trained in earnest, all ranks completed a musketry course and officers and N.C.O.'s paraded in Gippeswyk Park for arms drill under R.S.M. F. Payne, before breakfast—memory of cold fingers.

Many concerts were enjoyed by the troops. " D " Company put on an excellent show with a sketch " The Gazekas Pearl," written and produced by Lieut. J. E. G. McConnel. The orchestra of eight performed well. Cpl. Mardorf had a busy night ; apart from giving a turn he performed in the sketch, acted as stage manager and took part in " Tally Ho." Others who provided entertainment were Cpl. Ridgway, Sergt. Richards and Pte. Stiffen.

Sergt. E. A. James gave the " Marching Song of the Shiny Seventh " which had been written by Major Danford Thomas and ran as follows :

> Come, Comrades, come to sound of drum,
>   In swinging song uniting ;
> Who one and all obeyed the call,
>   A wrong to be arighting ;
> Battalions three, four thousand free
>   Men, volunteers for fighting,

Repeated in Chorus :
> One magic thrall unites us all,
> The name of " Shiny Seventh."

> Forgotten cheers are in our ears,
>   For drafts when they were leaving :
> We will not prate, but emulate
>   The fame the First's achieving :
> Give us our chance when we're in France,
>   Our web of glory weaving ;

Repeated in Chorus :
> Again the Hun must quickly run
> Before the " Second Seventh."

> Tonight we praise the strenuous days,
> In patriotic chorus ;
> Of comrades slain mid toil and pain
> Who've gone to France before us ;
> God grant us now to keep our vow,
> To serve the land that bore us.

Repeated in Chorus :
> And may we give some names that live
> From England's " Shiny Seventh."

In connection with the various concerts the battalion were fortunate to have the services of Lieut. J. E. G. McConnel who, besides being an experienced and inspiring producer, possessed the gift of being able to turn out topical verse and dialogue till further orders. " In the Trenches," " Scrubbing Fatigue," and " The night when the old cow died," these and other items were packed with satirically topical references which delighted the troops and were enjoyed even by the victims.

On May 4th, 1916, the battalion moved to Foxhall Heath, four miles outside Ipswich, and experienced the " joys and pleasures " of sleeping under canvas. Whilst here a divisional trek under active service conditions was undertaken. Leaving camp on a day of sunshine and showers the battalion marched 17 miles (during which time the showers turned into a steady downpour) and bivouacked in the open.

While at Foxhall Heath the battalion were inspected by Sir John French.

No account of Ipswich days would be complete without mention of the church parades which became a popular spectacle with the townsfolk, who were generosity itself. The long column swinging along through the narrow streets, led by the band, Lieut.-Col. Berkeley taking the salute and each platoon and company " chucking a chest " and putting all they knew into the march past, while being mentally conscious of the all-seeing eyes of Capt. H. Green and R.S.M. F. Payne, on the alert for any blemish on the performance.

The next move was on July 13th, 1916, to Sutton Veny and great strides were made in completing the training of the battalion ready for active service, as in December 1916 the War Office notified G.H.Q. France that the 58th Division would embark in January, 1917.

The battalion formed part of the 174th (2nd/2nd London) Infantry Brigade of the 58th (2nd/1st London) Division. Brig.-Gen. C. McGrigor, late Scots Guards, commanded the 174th Brigade and the division was commanded by Major-Gen. H. D. Fanshawe, late Royal Artillery, who had just taken over from Brig.-Gen. E. J. Cooper, late Royal Fusiliers.

Two years of training had resulted in a battalion of high efficiency; officers and men were keen to get going and all were anxious for the day to arrive to go overseas. It was about this time that Lieut. E. C. Stringer departed from the battalion to join the R.F.C.

The battalion marched to Yarnbury Castle, where they carried out trench warfare. To make the occasion more realistic it rained " cats and dogs " the whole time and the troops, facing the downpour behind inadequate protection, reached a speedy conclusion that " trench warfare " was a much overrated amusement.

Christmas 1916 came and went. Rumours of a move at any moment were rife, but the New Year found the battalion still in occupation at No. 9 Camp, Sutton Veny, near Warminster, in Wiltshire, everyone in fine fettle and the " esprit de corps " of all ranks splendid.

During the first two weeks of January 1917 alarms of a move overseas were frequent and many days were mentioned as the day of departure, but as time proceeded these days came and went.

Slowly but steadily the men were gradually fitted out with all the necessities of a soldier proceeding on active service and when ammunition was drawn the excitement increased.

Several parades were held in " embarkation order " but without tin helmets and these generally finished up with battalion drill. The weather was bitterly cold, under foot it was muddy and slippery and quite a few failed to appreciate drilling under these conditions with full pack.

On Wednesday, January 24th, the battalion went on a route march in full embarkation order. On the following day they were inspected and after this came a medical inspection and the issue of rations for twenty-four hours.

On Friday the 26th, the battalion paraded at 6.30 a.m. and marched to Warminster Station. This was the real thing at last; all ranks were delighted that the tension had ended and that they were at last on their way. Many fine men marched with the battalion that day; unfortunately, for many their last march in England, but the memory of those who failed to return does not fade.

The battalion entrained for Southampton, which was reached after a two hours' journey and the remainder of the day was spent waiting in the sheds at the docks.

Eventually the troops and transport embarked on the Huntscraft and Mona's Queen—the latter formerly an Isle of Man paddle steamer. After waiting a couple of hours these boats moved off and with their human cargoes made the crossing of the Channel during the hours of darkness. This journey for many of the 7th was extremely trying, the sea was very rough and some cases of rifles placed on the deck as general cargo, and fortunately not belonging to the battalion, were washed overboard. The weather was bitterly cold and the men were packed like sardines, very little space being available for kit and rifles.

The Huntscraft, a captured German cattle boat, was used to convey regimental transport. Down below where the mules were lodged in two long double rows of stalls, the stench beggars description. Matters were not improved when the lights were extinguished and the ship started to zig-zag; a green sea was taken on board and poured straight down the hold on frightened mules and seasick troops indifferently.

When the Huntscraft and the Mona's Queen finally docked the situation was neatly summed up by one member of the battalion as follows: " Leave, catch me ! I'm staying till they build the b . . . . . tunnel."

There were many cases of " mal-de-mer " ; and all were heartily glad when Havre was reached at about 4 a.m. on January 27th, 1917. The date is given in full as this is a memorable day for the 2/7th.

ROLL OF OFFICERS
WHO WENT TO FRANCE WITH THE 2/7TH BATTALION THE LONDON REGIMENT, January 27th, 1917.

Lieut.-Col. C. W. Berkeley, T.D.	Commanding Officer	Remained in Command until April 1917, then Area Commandant, Winnezele.
Major S. L. Hosking ..	Second-in-Command. Subsequently Commanding Officer, September 1917	Gassed April 1918 at Villers Bretonneux.
Capt. L. B. Freeston ..	Adjutant	Invalided home March 1918
Lieut. J. E. G. McConnel ..	Signals Officer ..	To R.E.s' Signals June 1917.
Lieut. A. Mantle	Intelligence Officer	K. Bullecourt May 23, 1917.
Lieut. & Q.M. E. Gallagher..	Quartermaster ..	
Lieut. H. Whitby	Transport Officer..	With battalion throughout.
Capt. H. J. B. Fry.. .. (R.A.M.C.)	Medical Officer ..	Left battalion October 1917.
Capt. The Rev. L. H. Lang, C.F.	Chaplain	W. Bullecourt June 1917.
Major H. Salkeld Green ..	O.C. " A " Company	K. at Wurst Farm, Ypres September 20, 1917.
Capt. C. L. Faux	2nd i/c " A " Company	Became Divisional Musketry Officer June 1917.
Capt. D. G. W. W. Fearnside-Speed	O.C. " B " Company	W. at Bullecourt May 1917.

Capt. R. F. Potter ..	2nd i/c " B " Company, later O.C. Co.	For a period Lewis Gun Instructor, Le Touquet.
Capt. M. W. Godson	O.C. " C " Company	Became Divisional Entertainments Officer in March 1917.
Capt. W. D. Coleridge	2nd i/c " C " Company	Subsequently O.C., then Adjutant, October 1918.
Capt. R. F. J. Danford Thomas	O.C. " D " Company	In March 1917 Railway Disbursing Officer. Afterwards organised Corps Reinforcements Camps.
Lieut. P. B. Berliner	Subsequently O.C. " D " Company and then Adjutant	W. and awarded M.C. at Malard Wood August 8, 1918.
Lieut. P. Halley-Jones ..	" A " Company	Awarded M.C. 1917. K. Malard Wood August 8, 1918.
Lieut. R. R. Walker	" A " Company	K. March 23, 1918.
Lieut. L. Michell ..	" A " Company	At Bullecourt first 2/7th Officer to be decorated. Awarded M.C. and transferred to R.F.C.
Lieut. A. Ecksteen	" A " Company	W. at Bullecourt May 1917.
Lieut. G. H. Symondson ..	" B " Company	Left battalion March 1917.
Lieut. G. G. Jackson	O.C. " C " Company April 1918	W. at Malard Wood Aug. 1918.
Lieut. H. J. Player..	" C " Company	
Lieut. G. H. S. Montagu ..	" C " Company	
Lieut. A. A. Shearman	" C " Company	D. of W. at Cagny April 20, 1918.
Lieut. G. W. M. Hare	" D " Company	
Lieut. E. H. Ireland	" D " Company	Left battalion December 1917.
2nd Lieut. S. Shannon	" B " Company	Awarded M.C. W. April 1918.
2nd Lieut. E. C. Halsey	" B " Company	K. at Cherisy June 19, 1917.
2nd Lieut. W. E. Gregory ..	" B " Company	
2nd Lieut. R. E. Stevenson	" B " Company	Gassed at Villers Bretonneux April 1918.
2nd Lieut. M. W. Hooker..	" B " Company	Assistant Adjutant June 1917.
2nd Lieut. M. Sharp	" B " Company	Awarded M.C.
2nd Lieut. G. Shillito	" D " Company	Transferred to R.F.C. 1917.

WARRANT OFFICERS AND SENIOR N.C.O.'s.

R.S.M. F. Payne ..		W. Awarded M.C.
R.Q.M.S. F. J. Smith		
C.S.M. H. Johns	" A " Company	Evacuated March 1917.
C.Q.M.S. L. Williams	" A " Company	Awarded D.C.M.
C.S.M. A. Elvy	" B " Company	W.
C.Q.M.S. F. Scothorne	" B " Company	Awarded French Médaille d'Honneur.
C.S.M. G. Frost	" C " Company	K. October 20, 1917.
C.Q.M.S. F. J. Heale	" C " Company	Awarded M.S.M.
C.S.M. J. Archdeacon	" D " Company	W. Awarded D.C.M.
C.Q.M.S. W. M. C. Norie ..	" D " Company	W.

NOTE.—K.= Killed.   W.= Wounded.   D. of W.= Died of Wounds   All ranks are those held at the date of embarkation.

Every effort has been made to ensure the accuracy of this list and any corrections, omissions or additions would be welcomed for record purposes.

CHAPTER TWENTY-FIVE

January 27th—May, 1917
TRENCHES AND WORKING PARTIES

THE battalion, gradually regaining their shore legs, proceeded to No. 1 Rest Camp, which lay alongside Rue Kitchener; the march, not likely to be forgotten in a hurry, was about six miles. The camp proved to be one of tents, and twenty-two men were packed in each, which was just as well because the weather was still extremely cold; the ground was frozen and a high wind was blowing. Nevertheless, the rough weather did not prevent a somewhat weary and tired battalion getting down to sleep. The rough crossing and the long march up the hill to the camp with the temperature well below freezing was enough to sap the vitality of any man.

Capt. Fearnside-Speed went into the town and managed to purchase four bottles of brandy, such as it was, and distributed this to the worst cases. It was not to be wondered at that these " cases " increased considerably as the news went round.

The remainder of that day and best part of the Sunday were spent cleaning up; food was not too plentiful and the men were not sorry when they paraded at 4.15 p.m. and marched to Havre from where, that night, they entrained at the Gare des Merchandises for a destination then unknown to the majority.

Most of the men were travelling in the usual trucks; those who thought they were only going for a short journey and neglected to make use of their blankets soon realised their mistake, as this train journey lasted until the early hours of Tuesday with the usual halts and shunting for which these journeys up the line were so famous. Writing of this almost interminable snowbound railway journey, C.Q.M.S. F. Scothorne records :

" Some of the more innocent members of the 7th were easily persuaded that they were passing through Russia. Incidentally, on one of the many halts, two of the men left the train and failed to return when it started.

" They were reported missing but were nevertheless present at Abbeville, having had a free dinner at a farmhouse and caught up with the train by walking along the track."

Eventually the battalion detrained at Aux-le-Chateau and marched three miles over snow-covered hilly roads to Vacquerie-le-Boucq. Here barns were occupied and the men enjoyed a comfortable sleep prior to partaking of their first hot meal since leaving Havre; incidentally, the

OFFICERS OF THE 2/7TH BATTALION THE LONDON REGIMENT

(Back Row. Left to right) Lieut. De LAVISON, Lieut. A. MANTLE, Lieut. G. H. SYMONDSON, Lieut. E. C. STRINGER, Lieut. E. J. SIMONS, Lieut. G. McCONNEL, Lieut. P. B. BERLINER, Lieut. A. K. WICKHAM.
(Front Row. Left to right) Lieut. C. F. BAILEY, Capt. R. F. POTTER, Capt. L. B. FREESTON, Capt. D. G. FEARNSIDE-SPEED, Capt. R. F. DANFORD THOMAS, Maj. W. MUDFORD, Lieut.-Col. C. W. BERKELEY, T.D., Maj. S. L. HOSKING, Maj. H. S. GREEN, Capt. M. W. GODSON, Capt. C. L. FAUX, Capt. and Q.M. E. GALLACHER, Lieut. G. H. S. MONTAGU, Lieut. G. S. JACKSON.

Facing page 150

sergeants of " B " had to clean the muck out of a pig-sty before they could occupy it.

The following day, the last one of January, the battalion went for a route march, which relieved any stiffness that may have remained in the joints as a result of the train journey; in the afternoon came the first pay parade abroad.

Apparently the bread issue was not too good or else the air had increased the appetite, as Cpl. H. Lydiart's diary records " bought some French bread which is ripping tack, their coffee is great, but the French fags are vile."

The battalion stayed here until February 5th, the time being spent in route marches, lectures and kit inspections; many paid a visit to Frevent which was about three miles away and possessed a decent canteen.

No. 13 Platoon went off for a week to Pas and were employed making fascines.

On the 5th the battalion moved to Beaurepaire, a distance of about 15 miles; the majority found this hard going owing to the frozen state of the roads, coupled with the carrying of ammunition and full packs. Dinner was taken on the roadside and on arrival at their destination one company at least was unlucky for hot food owing to the cooker being held up at one of the hills.

February 8th proved a red-letter day for the battalion, as it was on this day that they first went into the trenches, parading about 1 p.m. and travelling in lorries for about 12 miles, then marching three miles to the village of Berles; here packs were stacked under the guard of another regiment and several men lost their small kit, their first experience of real scrounging by old soldiers, a habit they soon acquired. Guides were picked up, and passing through a ruined house into a communication trench the battalion went straight into the line at Monchy-au-Bois and Ransart; this part of the line, just south of Arras, was at this time considered to be quiet.

The battalion went into the line under the guidance of the 1/5th and 1/6th South Staffords (T.F.), 46th Division, and thus received their baptism of rifle and shell fire.

The 7th took to line duties like old-timers and after two days the S. Staffords paid them the compliment of moving out and leaving them to carry on. The weather during the early part of this tour of the line was very severe; the ground was frozen and there was plenty of snow about. On the 12th it commenced to thaw and then there was plenty of slush.

The first line duty was marred by an incident which later was all too frequent, when an enemy shell wrecked a dug-out, killing a corporal of the S. Staffords and Pte. C. Higley of "ours." Thus the battalion sustained its first casualty.

The 7th were relieved on February 13th and moved back in lorries to Halloy, about two miles away from the previous billets. Huts were at first occupied, but on the following day some barns were taken over as billets.

During the four days here the men had baths, drill and kit inspection, also an inspection of the battalion in full marching order.

While here "A" Company received a visit from Lieut. C. F. Bailey, who it may be recalled was Transport Officer of the 7th at Ipswich and Sutton Veny. Lieut. Bailey was now serving in the R.F.C. and Capt. C. L. Faux, after his visit, accompanied him along the Arras-Doullens Road. Capt. Faux was the last of the battalion to say good-bye to Lieut. Bailey ; a few days afterwards his plane crashed in flames and he was killed.

A move was made on the 19th to Humbercamps where the 7th stayed for one night and then moved back into the line on the left of Berles.

This part was fairly quiet, the enemy being some considerable distance off. Earlier on the front lines had been much nearer to each other down in the valley until they were flooded out, when both sides retired up the slopes.

While here the battalion suffered its second casualty when Pte. H. E. Aldred was killed. The trenches were knee-deep in mud and water and after the majority of the men were soaked through, trench waders were issued. An inter-company relief took place on February 22nd, and two days later " ours " were relieved and moved back to Bailleulmont, a few miles to the rear. During the few days here a church parade was held, inspections and gas instruction filled in the time until the last day of February, when the battalion returned to the line and occupied trenches in the area of Lincoln Lane. An extract from the diary of Cpl. R. Richards reads as follows : " Took over left Sector from 2/5th London. Got stuck in the mud on the way. Front line mostly mud and water."

The battalion returned from the line to Humbercamps on March 4th. The billets here were old barns fitted up with wire bunks, three tiers high, and those who occupied the top bunks caused the usual annoyance to those on the bunks below, quite apart from the frolics of the rats.

The rest period ended on March 6th when " ours " moved back into the line in front of the ruins of Monchy. A Boche machine-gun and a few snipers helped to keep alive the fact that there was a war on.

A sunken road, which crossed No-man's-land diagonally, was held at our end by half a dozen bombers, and on the right of the line was a gap which was a waste of shell holes, between " ours " and the neighbouring regiment; in the centre was another gap between the two company frontages and these gaps were regularly patrolled. Sergt. Lawson on one patrol found all the mud that was going. Upon another occasion when Cpl. H. Lydiart and Pte. Bond started out on patrol they walked on and found the adjoining front-line troops had been withdrawn, so they carried on until they came to the position held by the L.R.B.'s, a distance of some 600 yards.

In this part of the line No-man's-land varied between 80 and 150 yards, and one moonlight night a German working party was spotted, one of whom, standing on the parapet clearly outlined in the moonlight, was presumed to be the officer in charge. Sergt. " Puck " Hewitt took careful aim and the Boche fell back in the trench. It is recorded that " he was either hit or had a devil of a fright."

The enemy gave our front a good deal of trouble with rifle grenades. Pte. Dulwich was slightly wounded, and by way of retaliation our trench mortars let fly.

On March 9th the battalion had two more men wounded and on the 11th the enemy shelled the village of Berles, sending over about 300 shells which fell in and around the village.

The companies in support were kept very busy on carrying parties, and plenty of time was spent on the irksome duty of gas guard. An inter-company relief took place on the 12th, the weather at this time being very severe and everything frozen.

The Post Office Rifles relieved " ours " on March 17th and the battalion returned to Bailleulmont; from here the men were employed on working parties, and the news came through that Jerry had cleared out of Ransart and Monchy.

At dawn on the 17th it had been noticed that the enemy dropped an occasional shell on his own front line at Monchy.

The 58th Division pushed forward and on the 18th occupied a line at Hendecourt and along the northern edge of Adinfer Wood, while patrols penetrated four miles in advance of the old front line at Ransart.*

To return to the 7th, on March 19th " A " Company came to La Herliere where they were billeted in huts. Later they were joined by the remainder of the battalion. The men were kept very busy on working and carrying parties, and on the 23rd there was an extra large party engaged on repairing roads near Monchy. These parties carried on until the 29th when the battalion marched about ten miles to Grouches. This march along the Arras-Doullens Road was not at all bad, but once the road was left the battalion struck very muddy conditions.

* British Official History.

April 1st found the 7th on the move again, marching about 14 miles to our first billets at Vacquerie-le-Boucq. The next day after a rather longer march than the previous day, the battalion arrived at Regnauville where billets were occupied. Everyone had just got settled when down came the snow.

Some rather humorous situations arose here in several billets; the men waking up the following morning to find that the snow had penetrated the roofs and that their blankets and kit were covered in snow. The situation was not so good when the thaw started and water dripped everywhere; these were really and truly fine weather billets.

On the 4th reveille was early and the battalion, parading at 6.50 a.m., marched about five miles to an embussing point at Quoeux, and travelling in buses and lorries throughout the day via Doullens, Mailly-Maillet was reached and the troops were billeted in empty houses, mostly devoid of windows and in many cases without roofs. The battalion's promenade towards the coast was over. England was apparently again safe from invasion.

"Ours" stayed here until April 15th, during which time much hard work was carried out salvaging and the men had many opportunities of exploring the battlefield. The old trenches, littered with British and German equipment, were examined with great interest, as also were the two abandoned tanks marked H.M.L.S. "Cheerful" and "Camille."

The battalion attended a short open-air service on Good Friday, and on the following day, the 6th, reveille was at 4 a.m., breakfast of bully, biscuits, and tea at 4.45 a.m., and at 5.15 a.m. the men moved off to the old trenches, where they spent the day salvaging bombs and ammunition from the Beaumont-Hamel battlefield; hard and tedious work.

Owing to an unfortunate accident the battalion lost Sergt. A. Bicknell, L/Cpl. C. W. J. Robertson, L/Cpl. A. Carter, L/Cpl. J. H. Mitcham, L/Cpl. R. G. Sealy, Ptes A. A. Rhodes, T. Clarke, and R. Erwin, killed, and 2nd Lieut. R. E. Stevenson, L/Sergt. Hales, and Pte. Garraway were wounded. This accident was most regrettable; a 2-inch T.M. bomb carried by Pte. T. Clarke exploded as he dropped it at the dump, killing him instantly and those gathered around. The dump caught fire, Very lights were exploding and boxes of Mills bombs commenced to burn. Lieut. Shillito and Cpl. R. Richards succeeded in extinguishing the flames with shell-hole water. The burial in a communal grave took place on Easter Sunday, the Rev. L. H. Lang officiating. He records: "It was a day of warm sunshine, suggesting of resurrection and a life beyond." Sergt. Bicknell had served in the South African war; he was a good soldier in every sense.

Salvage work continued until April 13th, when the men had the unpleasant task of burying dead. It was a ghastly job, some hundreds of bodies covered with only a few inches of earth had to be unearthed, identified if possible, and then buried properly.

The battalion was not sorry when a move was made on the 16th to Bihucourt. Here the men bivouacked, and as usual on these occasions, down came the rain and the camp quickly became a glorious mass of mud. The diary of Cpl. R. Richards records: "The only day that beats Yarnbury."

Certain changes in command took place on the 22nd, Brig.-Gen. C. G. Higgins, C.B., D.S.O., taking over the command of the 174th Brigade from Brig-Gen. C. McGrigor, under whom the brigade had trained for over two years.

A battalion stalwart, Maj. R. F. J. Danford Thomas, left on the 28th to become Railway Disbursing Officer, and subsequently to organise what afterwards became the Corps Reinforcement Reception Camps. Capt. M. W. Godson also left about this time to become Divisional Entertainments Officer. Capt. W. D. Coleridge assumed command of "C" Company, and Lieut. P. B. Berliner took command of "D."

Throughout the remainder of April the 7th carried out many road-mending working parties—in fact, they became quite experts at the work.

Early in May the battalion was providing large parties carrying trench mortar ammunition up the line. Our artillery had been giving it to the enemy hot and strong for some time now, and on the night of May 2nd-3rd one of the carrying parties, while our guns were shelling the enemy in preparation for the great attack on Bullecourt, found themselves mixed up with men of the 62nd Division just as the enemy opened up his artillery in support of his front line S.O.S.'s. L/Cpl. A. Taylor and Sergt. Edwards got safely through the barrage, as also did several of the men, but many had to lie low for five hours before they could get back. Unfortunately, Pte. F. Welch was killed and Pte. "Darky" Jennings and three other men wounded.

The weather had now changed for the better and glorious sunshine was enjoyed by day. Sergt. T. Goodhall, Cpl. H. Lydiart, L/Cpl. Brewer and several others took the opportunity of having a look round Bapaume, which they found completely in ruins.

The battalion now turned its attention to serious training, and on May 5th practice attacks were made and a brigade gas demonstration was attended.

At the latter, the battalion was moved into position along with the remainder of the brigade, all placed facing the wind. After a long wait orders were given to don gas respirators and after these had been adjusted the gas cylinders were turned on and released a dense cloud of gas.

At the crucial moment, the wind changed, sweeping the gas cloud right clear of the waiting troops, who were greatly amused at the incident; apparently no further supplies of gas were at hand as the experiment was not repeated.

That night, the 5th, a storm broke and everyone was put to it to keep their bivouac dry. For the first two weeks of May the battalion trained hard, musketry and practice attacks for " over the top " were carried out.

The battalion also provided large parties around Ecoust St.-Mein and Bullecourt, taking a large share in the construction of Bullecourt Avenue, the main communication trench from Longatte to the eastern end of Bullecourt.

Part of the work carried out by the battalion was the forming of a large dump of eighteen-pounder ammunition at the back of Ecoust village. For three days this was built and witnessed by the Boche both from the air and observation balloon, and then they decided to shell the dump and the whole lot went up. On May 10th Lieut.-Col. C. W. Berkeley, T.D., returned to England, having been in command of the battalion since its formation; about a week later Lieut.-Col. E. N. French, of the Lincolns, assumed command of the battalion.

On the 15th the 7th moved about three miles nearer the line and occupied tents and shelters in and around the village of Mory.

CHAPTER TWENTY-SIX

May–June, 1917

BULLECOURT

BULLECOURT—a name long to be remembered by the battalion—was its first big show and it came through with flying colours.

It may be recalled here that the first attack on Bullecourt had opened on April 11th and had proved a failure. However, since the failure, the Fifth Army Staff had been busy preparing schemes for further action and among other divisions the 58th and 62nd who had both arrived in France about the same time, were moved into the area.

The British Official History records that the 62nd Division went into action in connection with the fresh attack on Bullecourt which opened on May 3rd and that on the night of the 12th the 173rd Brigade relieved the 15th Australian Brigade. Three days later, at 4 a.m. on the 15th the Germans launched a counter-attack and thus the 173rd Brigade fought its first action.

On the night of the 15th the 174th Brigade relieved the 91st Brigade of the 7th Division who had been engaged for twelve days and were exhausted, the 2/5th and 2/8th London Regiments took over the front line and " ours " moved forward in accordance with the brigade relief.

Orders had been issued for the capture of the west half of Bullecourt by the 174th Brigade, and again quoting the British Official History, " at 2 a.m. on May 17th, from a line in front of the railway the attack was launched by the 2/5th following a hurricane bombardment of two minutes." As a result of this assault 23 prisoners and five machine-guns were captured.

The following night, the 18th, the 7th moved forward in battle order, each man carrying two days' rations. "A" Company occupied a line which appeared to be the bank of a railway cutting, there were no trenches, and funk holes in the side of the bank provided the only shelter. The remaining companies were in the cellars at Ecoust village.

The front had been taken over by the 6th London on the night of the 18th at which time the enemy was holding as his front line what was formerly a support line of the Hindenburg trench system, and known to us as Bovis trench.

The 6th London was to make a two company frontal attack on Bovis trench. In connection with this attack their support companies, of whom some were taking part in the attack, moved forward on the night of the 20th. In addition to the two 6th companies making the frontal attack, platoons from their other companies were to attack, one along the

Bullecourt Factory Road and another was to work along the Riencourt Road.*

The 7th moved up on the night of the 20th and occupied the positions vacated by the 6th support companies, which was the original Hindenburg front line; H.Q. was a deep German dug-out.

At 4 a.m. on the 21st the 6th made their attack, which turned out for various reasons to be unsuccessful, and their wounded and survivors returned to our lines and remained throughout the day with the 7th. That night " ours " relieved the 6th, " A " Company moved into the right of the line under Lieut. L. Michell and " D " Company under Lieut. P. B. Berliner took over the front on the left of " A." " B " Company, under Capt. D. G. W. W. Fearnside-Speed, and " C " Company, under Capt. W. D. Coleridge, were in support on the right and left respectively. The relief was completed in the early hours of the morning, the artillery of both sides shelling continually throughout the change over.

The German trenches taken over had been almost completely obliterated; their dug-outs were as usual very deep and had stood up well to the shelling of both sides and they came in very useful for the left support company, but there were none in the right place for anyone else, unfortunately.

Lieut. H. Lazenby, who had only recently joined the battalion at Mailly-Maillet, was wounded early on, as also was Lieut. A. Ecksteen, a South African who had seen service in France prior to joining the 7th at Sutton Veny.

Sergt. Hardwick and Pte. Pask carried out a patrol to the adjoining brigade front on the right of " A " Company; on a similar patrol, Cpl. F. Jordan was badly wounded by a sniper, most of this journey being a shell hole to shell hole trip. Pte. Hart was also wounded.

Early on the morning of the 22nd and throughout the day the enemy shelled our lines very heavily, one shell wrecking a shelter and burying L/Cpl. Brewer, Ptes. Collier and Lutgen.

At Brigade H.Q. it was apparently thought that the enemy was holding his front line lightly, but our front line reports indicated that this was not so; nevertheless, Lieut.-Col. E. N. French received instructions to capture Bovis trench.

It was decided to use a bombing party to kill or capture those manning the machine-gun post on the right and then bomb along the trench to where a dead tree marked the end of the trench. If this position was reached, then the raiders were to put up a signal and " A " Company were then to advance over the top and hold the trench.

Such was the scheme to be put into effect on the night of the 22nd at

* 6th London History.

7 p.m. when Cpl. H. Lydiart, in charge of the bombing party consisting of L/Cpl. A. Taylor and 11 men, made a detour in No-man's-land and entered Bovis trench, which they found to be held in strength. The raiders bombed along the trench for about 40 yards, bombing two dug-outs and inflicting casualties on the enemy.

An enemy support company came up a communication trench and their superior numbers forced our party to retire. For some time bullets and grenades were flying about in No-man's-land, machine-guns were blazing away and the artillery of both sides chipped in.

Shortly afterwards the enemy launched a counter-attack on "A" Company's front, and Lieut. L. Michell, the officer in charge of the attacked portion of the front, speedily organised the defence of the line. Our men used their rifles to good effect, and the bombers and Lewis gunners also came into the picture.

Just before dawn " B " Company were ordered forward to reinforce " A " and advanced across the open to the front line. The attack was repelled with loss to the enemy, but not without loss to ourselves.

Capt. D. G. W. W. Fearnside-Speed, while leading his company over the top, became a casualty and was brought in by C.S.M. Elvy and a party of men. Sergt. Harmer was also wounded.

All companies came in for heavy shelling and consequently suffered casualties. Pte. Jolly and some others helped to bring in Pte. Tapsell, who was wounded, as also was Cpl. Bradfield.

Lieut. R. R. Walker instructed Cpl. Lydiart to report to B.H.Q., and on the way he met Lieut. A. Mantle the Battalion Intelligence Officer, on his way up to find out what was happening in the line. Cpl. Lydiart explained the position on " A " Company's front, and Lieut. Mantle then proceeded to another part of the front, and it was while on this journey that he was killed by shell fire.

The loss of this officer, the first of the battalion to forfeit his life, was a severe blow. Lieut. Mantle had crossed over with the battalion and had proved himself popular with all ranks.

In paying tribute to Lieut. A. Mantle, a brother officer records:

" Alec was still a schoolboy, full of high spirits and ready for fun, but keen and serious about his job. No one so full of the spirit of youth came to fill the gap he left."

In the early part of the night the battalion was relieved by the 2/9th London Regiment, and it was a thoroughly weary and depleted battalion that reached Mory at dawn on the 23rd.

This action at Bullecourt had been a costly affair to the 7th. All told, the battalion had lost one hundred and twenty killed or wounded.

The battalion had every reason to be proud of its performance, for without a doubt they had proved steady in defence and ready in attack.

For his splendid and exemplary leadership and bravery in this action Lieut. L. Michell, a South African of " A " Company, was awarded the M.C., thus he became the first officer of the 2/7th to be decorated.

Cpl. H. Lydiart, for his gallant conduct, was awarded the M.M., and so he became the first N.C.O. to be decorated. The award was well deserved, and Cpl. Lydiart received the congratulations of the Commanding Officer.

Capt. H. J. B. Fry, the Medical Officer, was kept extremely busy throughout. He was a man of great distinction in his profession and gave just as much care to doing a simple field dressing as he would to an important surgical operation. Entirely without thought of his own safety and comfort, his life ended some years after the war as a result of infection contracted in an experiment of research.

During this turn in the line the shelling had been terrific, Capt. P. B. Berliner records :

" Enemy shell fire was heavy and concentrated with practically no intermission during the time the battalion held the line. At no other time was anything like such a heavy enemy artillery concentration experienced by the battalion."

The following are extracts from the British Official History of Bullecourt :

" At Bullecourt a fierce and bloody struggle, in which on the British side from first to last six divisions were engaged upon a few acres of ground, raged for a full fortnight. By the end the dead on both sides lay in clumps all over the battlefield and in the bottom or under the parapets of the trenches, many hundreds had been hastily covered with a little earth. Losses of ours totalled over a thousand a day for the fortnight. ' Second Bullecourt ' had the reputation of a killing match, typifying trench warfare at its most murderous, its only redeeming feature being the courage shown on both sides.

" The losses of the 58th Division in this action were 32 officers and 680 other ranks, not including the 175 Brigade."

Capt. Fearnside-Speed records an amusing incident which took place when the company commanders went up on a preliminary visit to the line. They met a party of fifty prisoners being marched down by an N.C.O. of the Highlanders. All the men had their hands in their trousers pockets. On being halted for an inquiry as to why they took no notice of a British officer, the N.C.O. replied that they had to go along like that, otherwise their trousers would have fallen down. It transpired that he had cut off all their buttons so that they could not run away.

The weather was extremely good when "ours" moved up and relieved the 2/10th London Regiment on May 28th. "A" Company occupied the L'Homme Mort trench, generally having the benefit of good accommodation in German dug-outs; the support companies remained under cover by day and at night were all out on normal trench routine, improving trenches, salvaging and burying the dead of both sides—not at all a pleasant job, particularly in dealing with those bodies which had been lying out in the open, exposed to the heat of the day.

Shelling was pretty heavy during this tour, and Pte. S. Cownden, a stretcher bearer, was killed and Pte. Bridgeman wounded.

Inter-company relief took place and finally, on June 3rd, the battalion was relieved by the 2/10th and returned to its old camp for a few days, after which it had another short spell in the line between the 9th and 14th, during which Cpl. P. G. Endall was killed.

". . . . 7th Battalion will provide a working party"

CHAPTER TWENTY-SEVEN

June 16th—August 24th, 1917
CROISILLES, CHERISY AND METZ

ON June 16th "ours" moved to St. Leger and on up to a part of the sector to the left of a village in the Hindenburg Line, opposite Fontaine-les-Croisilles and Cherisy.

While here the battalion held part of the recently captured Hindenburg Line, which still included several old German strong points made of reinforced concrete with trenches leading from one to the other.

Lieut. S. Shannon, Sergt. H. Lydiart, "Tommy" Goodall, and six or seven men, got pretty close up to one of these strong points held by the enemy, in an endeavour to capture prisoners.

The enemy withdrew via a trench to the next strong point, and while our party was examining the vacated strong point the enemy returned in greater strength and our party were forced to make a strategic retreat.

The artillery fire here was fairly heavy but could not be compared with Bullecourt, snipers and the pineapple type of rifle grenade being the principal nuisances. While here the battalion suffered the loss of 2nd Lieut. E. C. Halsey, who, while in the act of getting a Lewis gun into position, unfortunately fell a victim to an enemy sniper. Pte. F. H. Staines was wounded by a sniper, and while being brought in by the stretcher bearers was hit again, this time fatally.

One of our stretcher bearers was seriously wounded in the stomach, and the urgency of the case necessitated a carry "over the top." Capt. the Rev. L. H. Lang, his servant, Pte. H. Smith, and a stretcher bearer, made the effort, and while doing so the Padre was wounded. Incidentally, Pte. H. Smith, who was looked upon as a faithful friend by the Rev. Lang, died of influenza during the occupation of Cologne.

The 1st Staffordshires relieved the 7th on the night of June 23rd, and while on the way out a shell caught the rear of No. 4 platoon, killing Ptes. F. T. F. Fuller and A. C. West, and wounding Sergts. A. Hardwick, H. Lydiart and Pte. Luke. Both the sergeants had their wounds dressed at Ecoust; Sergt. Lydiart was marked "slight wound—return to unit," while Sergt. Hardwick was sent to base hospital.

At the end of June the battalion was at Courcelles-le-Comte, and during the first week of July some hard training was carried out. On the 6th the battalion moved via Bapaume to Bancourt, and on to Metz-en-Couture near Havrincourt.

About this time Lieut. H. C. Woolner joined for duty and was posted to "C" Company.

Here the 7th tooR over a line on July 9th, which was situate some 800 yards from the enemy, and a start was made immediately to dig a new line considerably closer.

About 100 yards in front of the sector was a copse known as Boar Copse, about 90 yards long. At dawn on the first morning in the line, the enemy sent over some shells on our line and, under cover of Boar Copse, advanced and endeavoured to raid the front occupied by No. 1 platoon. Unfortunately for the enemy, he failed to catch the men napping; in fact, he found them very much on the alert, and it is to the credit of No. 1 platoon that the enemy was repulsed, leaving eight of their number, all killed, behind them.

Sergt. W. Neben, who was in charge of the platoon, got most of his men out of the trench, lined the parados as the Germans started to throw bombs into the trench, and opened fire.

Sergt. W. Neben, who was wounded but remained at duty, and L/Cpl. Brooks, who also performed well, had, by their coolness and courage in the face of the enemy, set a fine example to the men, and each was the recipient of the M.M.

The battalion had several casualties. "A" Company lost six men wounded and Pte. E. Ashley killed, one of the wounded being Pte. Harmon.

After this attempted raid it was decided to have a fighting patrol around Boar Copse. All went well on the first two patrols, but on the third night the Boche ambushed our patrol, which on this night was provided by "B" Company under Capt. R. F. Potter, a skirmish ensued in which one of the enemy was killed, his body being found by a patrol the following night, when a trip wire was being put out in front of the copse. The battalion also established a snipers' post in the copse.

"Ours" were relieved on July 18th, and moved back to Metz-en-Couture. All were very glad to get back out of the mud, everybody being pretty well caked up with it.

All the houses in the village being destroyed, the men occupied reserve trenches just in front; these were comfortable, shelters were pretty good, and from the orchards near by plenty of fruit could be collected.

On the 28th "ours" marched to Bertincourt and occupied tents. On the following day lorries took them to Bapaume, where they entrained to Beaumetz-les-Loges, from where they marched to huts at Simencourt, arriving in the small hours of the 30th.

The journey by rail had been made in carriages instead of the usual trucks, but 12 in a compartment with full marching order, spoilt any idea of comfort the men might have had when they first boarded the train.

Simencourt and the time spent there is well described in the following, from the pen of Sergt. H. Lydiart, M.M.:

> "Simencourt, a village six miles south-east of Arras, was similar to hundreds of other villages in northern France, just the usual straggling place, but the war had not reached it.
>
> "To men who spent four months in the devastated areas without seeing a civilian, who had sheltered in bivouacs, wrecked houses, and anything but a real house, it was good.
>
> "Clean huts in the orchards, baths at Berneville, and sometimes in the evening the 'Goods' divisional concert party instead of orderly sergeants shouting 'Fall in blank company working party,' made a welcome break.
>
> "The battalion had changed since its arrival in France, then it was well trained but raw. There was a tendency to look upon themselves as well-meaning amateurs, who would never equal the feats of the 1/7th at Festubert, Loos, Vimy and the Somme. Bullecourt had altered all that by proving the battalion to be good all round, well trained and disciplined. The men felt that they had met the Boche in a real tough scrap and beaten him, and were consequently full of beans.
>
> "The tail end of the worst winter for years, and a wretched spring had taken toll of some of the older and less fit men, a number of whom had gone to hospital, thence to base or 'Blighty.'
>
> "In addition men had to be found for out-of-the-line jobs—brigade, division, A.S.C. loading parties, and the like. The battalion naturally detailed the less fit men, so that the men who were left were the toughest.
>
> "Some good men had been lost since arrival, and the few small drafts to reach the battalion did not make up the wastage.
>
> "The fighting strength (as distinct from the nominal strength, which included everyone, wherever employed) was now about five hundred.
>
> "Training at Simencourt was hard, with plenty of field work, route marches and night digging.
>
> "On several occasions the battalion marched to the old trenches at Wailly for training with tanks; this was good fun, but the average infantryman paid more attention to the tanks than training, until the novelty wore off.
>
> "Taken on the whole, the stay at Simencourt was pleasant and enjoyed by all."

CHAPTER TWENTY-EIGHT

August 24th, 1917—January 31st, 1918
YPRES, POELCAPPELLE, PASSCHENDAELE

ALL good things come to an end, and on August 24th the battalion left Simencourt and marched to Arras, where three companies entrained, " A " remaining behind to perform a job of loading limbers, pontoons and ambulances, etc., on to trucks.

The battalion detrained at Godeswaersvelde and marched via Poperinghe to Brownlow Camp near Vlamertinghe. On the march a number of motor transport columns hurtled by, half choking the troops with petrol fumes, and the men cursed them fluently from a now extensive vocabulary.

" A " Company, at Arras, spent the day sightseeing, but at night really found out what hard work was. Once a train was loaded the men were free to rest until the next train was ready for loading. Most of the men gave up all idea of sleep after sweating at the loading; the stones of Arras station were far too cold. This company rejoined the battalion on the following day.

Many of the 1st Battalion, who were in camp near by, visited the 2/7th and were greeted by old friends, and there were many happy reunions.

On August 27th the " Shiny Seventh " moved forward to occupy dug-outs along the banks of the Yser Canal, near the famous Essex Farm. A notice-board on the side of the footpath leading to the duck-boarded towpath of the canal read " Eyesore Canal." Seen through the dark and rain, with its rows of dug-out entrances and its muddy denizens, it looked like some prehistoric town of cave dwellers.

The men were comfortable in these dug-outs. On the forward bank of the canal a row of dug-outs opened off the tow-path and shafts ran into the bank at intervals which linked a lateral tunnel running inside the bank, electrically illuminated, and from which openings had been made on both sides, the forward slope being loop-holed to cover the flat ground in front of the bank.

There was even a pollard willow growing on the bank which on closer inspection proved to be a steel O.P. with bark and branches wired on.

The rear bank was also dug-outed, but not to the same extent, while behind was a collection of Nissen huts and shelters of various shapes and sizes.

The XVIIIth Corps (Lieut.-Gen. Sir Ivor Maxse), to which the 58th Division now belonged, were in the vicinity of St. Julien, the sector being a two-division front.

Following the established practice of the Army, battle surplus of each battalion were sent back to act as a cadre in case the battalion met with disaster or, alternatively, to act as replacements for casualties, and to conform with this practice the 7th sent a party to Houtkerke.

On the night of August 28th, " ours " moved forward from the canal bank, past Oblong Farm and Kitchener Wood on the left and two hundred yards further on to the mebus* known as Alberta, which was destined to be B.H.Q. Proceeding along the track the line of low mebuses on the right, known as the Bund, were passed and then the Steenbeek was reached. These were landmarks which later on were to become very well-known to one and all of the battalion.

The part taken over had recently been captured by the 48th Division, and the trenches were no more than a series of shell holes situate on the left of what remained of the village of St. Julien, to a position known as Triangle Farm, where the Langemarcke-Zonnebeke Road crossed the Poelcappelle Road and formed part of the Blunt Salient. The supports were shell holes a hundred yards or so in the rear of the road and the Steenbeek mebuses housed the reserves.

The main route into this sector of the front was over a track known as Bath track, which started at Goldfish Chateau near Vlamertinghe, and ran to Reigersberg Camp and over the canal bank. The track, although constantly shelled, was kept in a good state of repair by a Labour Corps. In the rear areas the track was carried over large craters on piles but nearer the line the track zig-zagged all over the place to avoid the craters. From the end of this track a taped line led to Maison du Hibou mebus and then on to the road, some three hundred yards of really bad mud.

From the Steenbeek to the German positions of Hubner trench was a rise of about five yards, not much, but a lot in that low-lying country, sufficient to give the enemy good observation and our troops the wettest part of the land.

St. Julien was just an island of rubble in a sea of mud ; the map showed the Steenbeek as being ten feet wide, eight feet deep, with banks five feet high, but heavy shelling by both sides had pulverised it out of all semblance of a stream. On the far side the bank had completely gone and the stream flowed anywhere to make worse the ground already waterlogged by heavy rain.

The troops went into the line in battle order, carrying haversacks in lieu of packs and were all well loaded with rations, mills bombs, extra S.A.A. and sandbags. Tommy cookers were issued and proved a real blessing to the men in the shell holes. Extra water was taken up in

---

* A contraction of the German name for "maschineneisenbetonunterstellung," or concrete machine-gun emplacement, otherwise called " pillboxes."

MAJ. ALLAN D. LAURIE, T.D.

MAJ. H. S. GREEN

MAJ. SIR. K. O. PEPPIATT, K.B.E., M.C.

LIEUT.-COL. A. E. F. BARNES

LIEUT.-COL. K. J. PEARCE

BRIG. E. E. F. BAKER, C.B.E., D.S.O., M.C., T.D., D.L., A.D.C.

petrol cans and slung cavalry water bottles, picks, spades and trench stores all helped to complete the individual load of the soldier going in the line. Neighbours of a man carrying a pick or shovel slipped down the back of the equipment, kept a sharp look-out for a sudden turn on his part in case they lost an eye.

The division was holding a narrow sector with two brigades in the line, the 174th Brigade held from the northern edge of St. Julien on the right for about six hundred yards to the neighbourhood of Triangle Farm, with one battalion in the front line.

On the night of August 28th the front line was taken over by two platoons each of " A " and " D " Companies, each with two platoons in support and with " B " and " C " Companies in the reserve position of the Steenbeek mebuses.

The 7th's journey up the line, everybody well laden, had not been a comfortable one. About half-way along the track the stretcher bearers of " ours " and the 2/10th were busy dressing wounded by the side of the duckboards, part of the normal price a battalion had to pay to get into position. Near Oblong Farm a dump of 18-pounder ammunition was blazing away.

The men found the swampy patch from the Steenbeek to Maison du Hibou extremely bad going, particularly as the Boche was shelling fairly heavily.

The relief of a battalion of the 48th Division being completed, most of our men started to dig in, but soon gave it up as they found they were just digging a drain which filled up as fast as they dug.

For those in the front line and supports it was a semi-isolated existence during the day. Company commanders could only visit them at night and runners rarely got to them, in fact, visitors who might give the positions away were not welcome. The men were strung out four or five to each crater and platoon officers supervised them as best they could from their own craters, each group had its own sentry and those off duty got a little sleep by dozing on the slope of the crater until cold and cramp woke them up.

Rifles and Lewis guns were a trial; in spite of breech covers and old socks, they were in a bad state by the time the men got into position, and constant cleaning was necessary.

Those men in the mebuses were fairly comfortable, in spite of the shelling they received.

Maj. H. S. Green, who was sharing a mebus with Company H.Q. of the 2/10th London Regiment, tried to establish his own H.Q. by having some slit trenches dug at Hammonds Farm, situate on the edge of the village. The effort did not meet with success and Maj. Green decided to share " B " Company's H.Q. at Maison du Hibou. This move was just as well, for a German plane came over next morning ; the observer may have seen the signs of fresh digging or it may have been just chance, but the place was shelled very heavily soon afterwards.

It was soon realised that the area taken over was not exactly a health resort ; the enemy shelled our lines frequently and on the first day in Pte. C. Wickers was killed. On the night of August 30th–31st, during an inter-company relief, " C " and " D " taking over from " A " and " B " Companies, Cpl. A. W. J. Mitchell, who had recently joined " ours " at Simencourt, was killed. Ptes. W. A. Martin and Davison were wounded by a shell which burst right in the entrance of their shelter, the former so seriously that he died at a C.C.S. Pte. Weaver, previously wounded at Vimy while serving with the 1/7th, was also wounded during this relief.

The 2/6th Battalion came up and relieved " ours " on the night of September 1st–2nd, who moved back to the canal dug-outs. Following relief, the main idea of each platoon officer was to get his men out as quickly as possible, but on arrival at the Bath track they found the tall figure of the adjutant, Capt. L. B. Freeston, holding up the men until the distance of one hundred yards separated the platoons.

On the way out Sgt. R. J. Byham was killed. At one point the enemy was sending over 5.9's with clockwork regularity ; platoons waited for a burst and then made a dash through the danger area before the next burst. On arrival at the canal dug-outs the men were glad to receive their rum issue and get down to much needed rest and sleep.

While the battalion was here, carrying parties were on duty nightly, mostly in connection with the R.E.'s, who were engaged in laying a light railway track. Other parties carried ammunition up to Alberta mebus ; on one of these journeys the enemy started searching the track with some heavy stuff. The officer in charge of the 7th party took them off the track to the shelter of some old trenches, where they remained free of casualties, but a company of another unit, which was following, stayed on the track and suffered pretty badly.

There was not much for the men to do during daylight while back at the canal dug-outs : the numerous air fights were, however, watched with interest, as also were the antics of the observation balloons, which were strung out all round and frequently a sudden burst of machine-gun fire from an enemy plane would set the gasbag on fire and the observer would make a graceful descent by parachute.

Visits were made to Dirty Bucket Camp for the purpose of baths, and on the way, near Vlamertinghe, a large scale model in relief showing enemy positions was studied, a pointer of things to come.

On September 5th a move was made to Reigersburg Camp, about a mile further back, but even from here, the everlasting working parties had to be carried out. Many will recall the party engaged on digging a six feet deep trench for the purpose of burying a cable ; water was struck at a depth of two feet and one of our men suggested that the R.E. officer in charge " thought we were divers, not infantry."

A move was made on September 11th to Dambre Camp near Elverdinghe, where very hard training was carried out over a taped course, in preparation for the forthcoming attack. Each night enemy planes dropped bombs in the vicinity of the camp, upon one occasion wounding Ptes. Fiske and Williams.

On September 17th a return was made to Reigersburg Camp. On the way a practice attack was carried out, and to add reality to it the enemy dropped a 5.9 close by. It was at this date that Lieut.-Col. E. N. French left the battalion and Maj. S. L. Hosking assumed command. The day was spent preparing for the line, and there was the usual stripping down to battle order and then the loading up of each man with extra ammunition, bombs, etc.

In the afternoon Maj. S. L. Hosking spoke to all officers and N.C.O.'s on the forthcoming attack, and stressed that lightly wounded men should remain at duty.

On the night of September 18th the battalion, less those sent back as battle surplus, moved forward to occupy assembly trenches, which had been rebuilt, roofed and fitted with seats.

The waiting period throughout the following day and night was very trying ; a battery of field guns near by kept up a non-stop rate of fire which did not improve matters for the waiting troops, who passed the time away sleeping and card playing. The battalion did not escape casualties, Cpl. P. J. Rollings being killed and several wounded.

The original plan of attack had been for the 2/5th and 2/8th battalions to capture Hubner trench, and a battalion of the 173rd Brigade were to capture a cluster of mebuses on the right, while the 2/7th attacked to the left up the Stroombeek valley, with the 2/6th going through to the London Ridge, about eight hundred yards farther on. Owing to the marshy and waterlogged state of the valley it was decided to alter the scheme of attack, by attacking each side of the valley and not through it, consequently the 7th became reserve to the brigade.

The attack, which is known officially as the Battle of the Menin Road Ridge (September 20th-25th), was on a front of eight miles and was covered by the heaviest artillery concentration possible, one gun to every six-and-a-half yards of front.

The weather for some days previously had been fair, and although the going proved heavy in parts, it was found to be better than on the last visit to the line.

Various sectors of the old German line in our area all commenced with " C," California, Calf, etc. Thus we had Calf trench, Calf support and reserve, which were all situate west of the St. Julien-Wieltje-Ypres road and two hundred yards to the right of the Bath track. These were the assembly trenches allotted to " A," " B " and " C " Companies, " D " Company taking over the front line. The battalion got into position and settled down to wait for zero hour, the remaining three battalions of the brigade were to move up on the morning of the attack and go straight into action.

For some time our artillery had been carrying out practice barrages. " Chinese " attacks had been arranged and everything had been done to mystify the enemy, and the final touch came when at 5.40 a.m. on September 20th, our artillery again crashed out. A sheet of flame lit the countryside as with a great roar the barrage began and behind this barrage, described as magnificent in accuracy and volume, went the attacking troops. The German positions were lost to view in the solid wall of smoke and spouting earth created by the barrage.

Eventually came the orders for the 7th to move, and the men filed out of their assembly positions and advanced by half platoons ; the enemy was shelling, and it was not long before the 7th suffered casualties. The men plodded on through the enemy barrage, indeed, it was useless trying to avoid shells, the roar of which going overhead drowned the shriek of one coming extra close.

Still keeping the formation of half platoons at 100 yards distance, the battalion moved on, passing prisoners captured by the 174th Brigade, carrying down the wounded men of the 5th, 6th and 8th Battalions, and past the only tank seen in the action so far, ditched half way between the road and Hubner trench. Fifty yards behind this trench company commanders were standing directing their men into position, and eventually the battalion made a double line of half platoons behind Hubner trench.

This trench had been a very strong position, and although it had received a severe battering, it could still be recognised as a trench ; its late garrison were just a row of dead men along it. Dead and wounded lay about everywhere, and the whole area was being steadily shelled with a terrific barrage. Stretcher bearers of all battalions and a company of the 175th Brigade, attached specially for this duty, were doing their best to get the wounded away.

The men took shelter in shell holes and dug themselves in to obtain some protection from the enemy shelling while waiting for the time to arrive for them to attack the strong points in front of them and the London Ridge beyond. Casualties occurred during this waiting period, and at last the order came to move forward, about two hundred yards round the flank of Hubner to the area of Genoa Farm.

With the advance of the 7th enemy shelling increased, but, despite this, the battalion, retaining the same formation as before, successfully carried out the operation, but under the torrent of shells casualties steadily increased. One shell caught No. 4 platoon, almost immediately killing one man and wounding Sergt. Hooper and five men.

Sergt. Lawson, with his Lewis gun, engaged an enemy plane, which dived down on the 7th with its machine-gun spitting, but fortunately the plane did not do any damage.

Shells continued to fall; Genoa Farm appeared to be a death trap, yet stretcher bearers continued with their work. In normal times the scream of a shell would be sufficient warning to take cover, but here that warning was lost in the general uproar, and the stretcher bearers plodded on, risking their lives with every step in order that unfortunate individuals should receive their attention.

At this time Capt. H. C. Woolner was acting as liaison officer with a neighbouring battalion, and while going forward with the colonel of that battalion a 5.9 fell close by, wounding the colonel in the thigh. Capt. Woolner records: " Later that day our 7th M.O. came over the top with a rough ambulance, a converted lorry, in full daylight, and got the C.O. away. I have always marvelled how any driver got a vehicle so far forward with nothing but shell holes, mud and water everywhere."

Through the barrage Maj. S. Green, followed by his runner, Pte. Page, walked from platoon to platoon. The sergeant who had taken over from Sergt. Hooper, and who had lost four Lewis gunners out of five, begged Maj. Green to arrange for the loan of some more gunners from another platoon. Looking down into the sergeant's shell hole, Maj. Green said : " All right, as soon as we get settled down I will see that you get them," and he then proceeded on to the next platoon situate near Wurst Farm. Within a few minutes Pte. Page came running back and gasped out " Maj. Green is killed." So died a great officer and leader.

Lieut. G. T. Wards immediately took over command of " A " Company and performed the duties of company commander in a most creditable manner under very difficult circumstances. Lieut. Wards subsequently transferred to the Indian Army, and immediately prior to the Second World War was military attaché to the British Embassy in Tokyo with rank of brigadier.

Shortly after this the battalion received orders to get back to the Hubner position, where the shelling was less heavy, but they suffered a further loss here when C.S.M. G. Frost, of " C " Company, was killed.

At dusk came the order to move up to the front line; in one way this was welcomed by the men, as they felt nothing could be worse than their present position. The men of "A," "B" and "D" Companies donned their packs and gathered together tools, water cans, etc., and moved off in file, all glad to leave. "C" Company remained at Hubner.

Many expected the front line would be bad, but, to the surprise of everyone, once past Genoa Farm there was very little shell fire, and the front line on London Ridge was found to be absolutely quiet. After the experiences the men had had, the quietness of the front line seemed too good to be true, and was looked upon as the lull before the storm.

The ridge was well held by the 2/6th London Regiment, who had a line of posts on the crest and others on the forward slope, and the three companies of the 7th filled in the gaps between these posts and dug in, the ground here being dry enough to complete a trench about three feet deep.

The night passed quietly, the only disturbance being a gas alarm, due to some of our own gas shells falling short, one of which caused the death of L/Cpl. R. K. Winter, a keen soldier and a deeply religious man, who was greatly missed.

At dawn "stand to" the men were alert and awaiting an expected counter-attack, but nothing happened. A few Germans were seen a couple of hundred yards out in front, and a burst of rifle fire sent them to cover. This day, September 21st, broke fine, and turned out to be a perfect day as far as the weather was concerned.

The enemy attempted unsuccessfully to filter men through to the Stroombeek valley positions; the garrison of these enemy posts may have been withdrawn during the attack, which had avoided the valley and had swept by on each side, and the enemy may either have been attempting to reoccupy these posts or endeavouring to reinforce any garrison which may have remained.

German infantry, trying to get into position on a line about four hundred yards from the ridge, had no idea that they were under observation until our Lewis gun and rifle fire opened up on them. From the ridge a clear view extended for over a thousand yards, Jerry being visible with the naked eye, and many of our men had a field day sniping. Aviatik Farm, where two planes which had collided in mid-air remained locked together like a big V, could be seen quite distinctly in the distance, the red and white buildings of Poelcappelle stood out clearly.

To the delight of our men a party of the enemy in single file heading for the position of the Stroombeek valley marched into view. This was an opportunity rarely offered to the infantry, and men of the "Shiny Seventh" created havoc among the enemy with Lewis guns and rifles.

Survivors of the murderous fire with which they were greeted speedily went to earth. The attempt to advance was repeated, and was again promptly stopped; the enemy must have found this method costly, as his tactics altered, and they endeavoured to advance with about thirty paces between each man, making spasmodic jumps from shell hole to shell hole, and providing excellent shooting practice for our snipers.

Meanwhile, the enemy was also endeavouring to establish their front line, and a battle of wits ensued between our men sniping and theirs in making use of every scrap of cover available.

During all this, the enemy also had his snipers at work as well as machine-guns, one of which, on our left, was causing trouble. Finally, C.S.M. L. Williams and two N.C.O.'s spotted a German crawling to a small isolated clump of bushes, dragging an ammunition box; he disappeared into the clump, which was evidently the machine-gun post. C.S.M. Williams took a ranging shot, and then he, with the other N.C.O.'s set their sights at twelve hundred yards and poured into the bushes a burst of rapid fire, and so ended the trouble from that machine-gun.

Nearly a mile off, a strip of road was visible and twice a body of enemy troops marching along were seen to be broken up when our rifle fire opened up on them—sniping, the reward of excellent musketry back home.

By mid-day things quietened down: the enemy was now getting wary and few targets were offered, but his snipers increased their activities.

A lull occurred in the early afternoon, which worried our men. The silence seemed ominous and many thought the enemy were preparing a counter-attack. It would appear that the enemy were massing and it is recorded that a message was sent back by a messenger dog and also by a pigeon; the F.O.O. also sent back a message. As a result of these messages our artillery ended the suspense, as with one tremendous ear-splitting crash our barrage fell on the German positions. With thousands of shells, the valley which had previously been sunlit was now a solid wall of H.E., fountains of earth, with a top layer of shrapnel. Simultaneously the Vickers gun teams, which until now had been silent, opened up and poured out a steady stream of bullets.

At first our men crouched in their shell holes, but with no reply from the enemy they gradually stood up to obtain a grandstand view of one of the most extraordinary sights of the war, that of an enemy force and their strongholds being smashed to pieces a few hundred yards away. Bodies of the enemy were hurled 50 feet into the air, turning over and over like a stick as they fell.

Two Germans decided it was too hot and made a bolt for our lines. Some of our over-excited men were apparently going to bump them off, for a 7th officer suddenly jumped up, revolver in hand, and kept order until the Germans reached our lines.

With the end of the barrage excitement faded until the evening, when the enemy shelled our positions on the ridge for the first time.

Soon after dusk a battalion of the 175th Brigade relieved " ours " : the relief was quickly completed and the journey back was fairly quiet. " C " and " D " Companies got a lift back part of the way on a light railway. " D " sustained some casualties when a shell burst near the trucks. " A " and " B " marched back ; Lieut. G. T. Wards headed " A " across country to Boundary Road and then down the Bath track.

On the way back this company followed a company of the Highland Division, who were met by two of their pipers. All the men, thoroughly worn out, had been plodding along, but with the burst of music from the pipers, the Jocks and our men fell into step and swung along in fine style.

Upon reaching Reigersburg Camp in the early hours of September 22nd, the men just dropped their kit and fell sound asleep.

So for the 2/7th ended the Battle of the Menin Road Ridge. The battalion had in this attack gained all its objectives and had every reason to be proud of its success, but at the same time mourned the loss of 120 killed, wounded or missing.

Undaunted, and displaying fine discipline, the officers followed by the men, had advanced despite serious opposition from the strong points which were the objectives. These reinforced strong points, sited to protect the ridge, had each been stoutly defended by well-disciplined and determined troops.

In the course of the assault in this action, as already mentioned, Major H. S. Green, while moving among his men, was killed ; his loss was a severe blow to the battalion. Major H. Green went to the 2/7th at the time of its formation in 1914 and was appointed **adjutant**, an appointment he held until the summer of 1916, when he took over command of " A " Company which he brought to a high state of efficiency. He was one of the finest of many fine officers who gave their lives. He had endeared himself to all ranks by his kindliness and cheerfulness, and his efficiency had been the standard which his juniors admired and to which they strove to attain. He lived always in the hearts of " A " who, right to the end of the war, called themselves " Major Green's Company." A brother officer writes of Major H. Green : " I always felt a sense of solidity and integrity about him and a quiet strength of character which gave confidence to those about him."

It is well worth recording that volunteers were forthcoming, to locate the exact position where Major Green had been buried and to erect a cross to mark the grave. Sergt. H. Lydiart, Pte. Page (who had been Major Green's runner) and Pte. Jukes formed the party and, having collected a cross from the Pioneers, these three set off on the long journey up the line. They succeeded in locating the grave and the cross was firmly and deeply fixed; two bottles containing particulars of Major Green were buried in the grave and a bearing was then taken on the position.

While this party were operating they came in for a hot time, as that morning the attack had been continued by other troops. Nevertheless, these three safely negotiated the nine miles return journey.

Two other officers of the battalion, Lieut. O. A. Keeler, M.C., and 2nd Lieut. J. E. Bishop, were both killed on the same day.

Another casualty was C.S.M. G. T. Frost, of " C " Company. This W.O., extremely popular with all ranks and only in his early twenties, was badly wounded and killed by shell fire before the stretcher bearers could get him away.

The following were among the killed in this action: Cpl. P. J. Rollings, L/Cpl. R. K. Winter and Ptes. W. H. Abbott, S. Cudmore, G. A. Gay, M.M., H. W. Jessup, W. C. Minter, A. H. Morris, J. D. Payne, W. Pope, A. J. Rivers, J. A. Rogers, T. E. Talkington and A. E. Waight. Cpl. Hugh Reed of the Signals was badly wounded and died at the C.C.S. Pte. C. L. Fox, a stretcher bearer, who has seen service with the 1/7th, was also killed.

A. Conan Doyle, writing of this action in his " British Campaign in France and Flanders, 1917," says:

" Next to the Fifty-first Division and covering the ground to the north and east of St. Julien was the Fifty-eighth Division, a new unit of second line London Territorials which had done a good deal of rough service in the line, but had not yet been engaged in an important advance. Their advance was a brilliant one and attained its full objective, taking upon the way the strongly fortified position of Wurst Farm. Nowhere in the line was the ground more sodden and more intersected with water jumps. It was a magnificent battle début and their coolness under fire was particularly remarkable, for in facing the difficult proposition of Wurst Farm they avoided making a frontal attack upon it by swinging first left and then right with all the workmanlike precision of veterans."

Maj. S. L. Hosking, who had been responsible for the detailed organisation and had commanded the battalion throughout this attack, to the great delight of everyone, received promotion to rank of Lieut.-Colonel and was given command from that date.

The XVIIIth Corps Commander, Lieut.-Gen. Sir. Ivor Maxse, congratulated the brigade in the following order to Brig.-Gen. Higgins :

> " Please convey to all ranks under your command my thanks and admiration for their great efforts on the 20th and 21st September which ended in such an unqualified success. The fighting spirit and discipline shown by the whole brigade in capturing and holding this important position against determined attacks was beyond all praise."

It was on Sunday, September 23rd that the battalion moved to Brake Camp near Dirty Bucket Corner, where it stayed until the 27th. The " Goods " concert party gave a show here, but the spectacular event was the massed pipes and drums of a brigade of the 51st Highland Division near by playing " Retreat."

The battalion marched to Elverdinghe on September 27th and entrained for Audruicq in the Pas de Calais area. For the first time since landing, packs were carried by lorries and thus lightened, the battalion marched along in fine style to Bonningues, a small village about seventeen miles from Calais.

The men enjoyed their first real rest among civilians and occupied good billets ; a river near by offered excellent bathing facilities. Parades finished at dinner time and the weather was pretty good.

Writing of the river, Sergt. Lydiart's diary records the following :

> " The river was well stocked with fish, but has been rather spoilt by the troops throwing hand grenades into the deep parts and collecting the fish killed by concussion."

It was about this time that the M.O., Capt. H. J. Fry, left the battalion to take up an important position in connection with research work. Before leaving, he threw a party for the stretcher bearers section, which will long be remembered by those fortunate enough to have participated.

The rest which the battalion had enjoyed ended on October 20th, when we moved off again for Poperinghe, which was reached about 8 p.m. and empty houses just off the square were occupied.

Another move was made on the 24th to Siege Camp near Elverdinghe, and on the following day back to the old dug-outs in the canal bank of the Yser, near Boesinghe.

While the battalion had been out at rest, further advances had been made and the front line advanced to some three hundred yards in front of Poelcappelle village, which was a nest of mebuses standing among the wrecked houses. Bad weather during recent weeks had made the ground for miles around a quagmire.

To get to the line, after crossing the canal the Langemarck road was followed for about fifteen hundred yards to a dismal clump of Nissen huts at the cross roads known to all as Kempton Park. Heavy artillery abounded at this spot, which was used as an advanced infantry resting place, and was situate on the site of what was once the village of Pilckem, which had been a very strong enemy position. The whole area was now a waste of dilapidated trenches and flooded craters; except for the foundations of a house here and there, no other signs that a village once existed were visible.

From the cross-roads the left fork led to Poelcappelle; a quarter of a mile farther on a duckboard journey led direct into the village.

Continuing straight along the main road from the cross-roads, one came to Minty Farm, a large mebus, now used as a dressing station, and from here a track led to Pheasant Trench on the near side of the Poelcappelle-St. Julien road, a few hundred yards south of the former village.

The actual front line was some five hundred yards beyond the end of the tracks. It was this last five hundred yards which caused all the trouble to the troops making their way either into or out of the front line. The foregoing is a brief description of the route to the line, and on October 26th the battalion left the dug-outs of the canal bank, each man carrying two days' rations, and moved to the area of Cane Trench near Kempton Park.

The attack made by the 173rd Brigade over treacherous ground had not been as successful as had been anticipated, in short, the attack had become "bogged." Tracas Farm had been captured but not Papa Farm.

The battalion moved on to Pheasant Trench; this was as far as it could go in daylight and in fact it was only poor visibility due to a steady rain which enabled it to get that far.

At dusk the journey forward was continued, the route being just a track winding along the crater lips, a track made ten times worse by the passage of hundreds of men so that progress was at a crawling pace. Every now and then a man would stick helplessly in the mud and the nearest to him would grab his hand or equipment, or pass him a rifle butt and pull until he got free. Speed was essential, for while this work of extricating a man was going on, others were steadily sinking and often on these occasions several more would have to be pulled out. A man would slither into a crater, often up to his neck, and then there was the same delay and struggle.

The route of the battalion led over Gloucester Farm mebus, literally over it, for it was a tiny place about only three feet above the ground and only big enough to hold about six men.

Finally the line was reached and the 2/2nd London Regiment relieved, " C " and " D " taking over the front line with " A " and " B " in support.

In these last moves towards the line everyone met with trouble in getting over the mud. Many got hopelessly bogged, one man being in the mud for over five hours before he was pulled out; this mud had to be endured to appreciate fully what a journey up the line in this area meant. Capt. P. B. Berliner records the following, which gives an excellent impression as to the state of the going underfoot at this time:

> " The condition of the ground on October 26th, when the 173rd Brigade had attacked, was appalling. Completely honeycombed as it was by shell holes, the entire area had become a morass over which the rate of progress for infantry was at the best about fifteen yards per minute. It was seldom possible to go straight forward round the edges of the shell holes, as these often merged into each other and were half full of water. If a man in battle order slipped on the edge of a shell hole partially filled with water and fell in, which was an extremely easy thing to do, it would often take several men to get him out again ; in some cases ropes pulled over beams had to be used as the shell hole sometimes behaved like a quicksand, if the initial effort to get out was not successful."

As previously mentioned, the 173rd Brigade had attacked east of Poelcappelle and had suffered heavy casualties in the assault on Papa Farm and Tracas Farm. " D " Company took over this pillbox and Capt. P. B. Berliner records the following :

> " On taking over from the 173rd Brigade, the pillbox at Tracas Farm was found by " D " Company to contain some forty stretcher cases of both sides, with considerably more lying outside and in the neighbourhood. Owing to the state of the ground only a very small number could be evacuated until carrying parties could be got up from the rear, and in the meantime the pillbox was only able to be used as a dressing station."

Throughout this turn in the line, the men had to make the best of it in shell holes and it was a case of " if you know of a better 'ole, go to it."

One platoon of " A " took over Beek House mebus on the Lekkerbotterbeek, now a vast swamp, the name translated by Lieut. Shannon, a South African, as " Sweet Butter River." The mebus was low lying and flooded to the top, so the men dug in in the rubble round it.

That night everyone was very much on the alert, as the positions held were new and everything was strange and the distance and position of adjoining troops unknown. Dawn arrived with a thick mist which persisted for some hours, so that it seemed " stand to " would never end.

Throughout the day both sides kept up a steady rate of shell fire and at dusk " A " and " B " Companies were ordered to take over from a battalion at Poelcappelle. This meant a journey back through the mud to Pheasant Trench, during which Sergt. Goodall was wounded, and then on to Norfolk House at the near end of Poelcappelle.

The journey safely accomplished, " B " took over the front line with " A " in support, Company H.Q. being at the famous mebus known as Poelcappelle Brewery.

One Lewis gun section of " A " Company on the left in a support position at the far end of the remains of the ruined village of Poelcappelle were glad to occupy a pillbox which had, while in German occupation, received a direct hit from one of our heavies, penetrating right through one wall and jamming several Germans in the doorway, who were all killed by concussion. Not very pleasant, but any form of shelter was appreciated.

Nothing much happened during that night and on the following day, Sunday October 28th, shelling and continual rain are all that is recorded.

The stretcher bearers had a most difficult task and worked like Trojans getting away the wounded. It was sheer hard work and at times they were reduced to pushing the stretchers over the mud like boats, often in full view of the enemy, who on this occasion made no effort to interfere.

On the night of the 28th the 2/6th London Regiment relieved " ours," who struggled back to the huts of Kempton Park. Everyone was showing signs of exhaustion after this very severe and trying turn in the line, during which time the rain had simply poured down for most of the time. Those of the battalion who experienced this journey will not forget it in a hurry. A report on the general conditions had been sent back to B.H.Q. during the tour and resulted in calling off a proposed attack by the 2/8th which was to have taken place within a few days.

No further attacks were made from this point during the rest of the year, but to the south-east, where the ground was higher, they were continued until the capture of Passchendaele.

It was during the early hours of October 29th that the battalion reached the canal dug-outs and from here they moved farther back, on the following day, to Siege Camp, the accommodation being a mixture of Nissen huts and " walled " tents.

Earlier in the year the battalion had assisted in building this camp. The method adopted in connection with the tents had been to drive into the ground a double circle of stakes, about nine inches apart, to which expanded metal was fixed and the space packed with earth to a height of about thirty inches. On this wall of earth the tent was pitched, the centre pole being extra long; these tents gave more headroom and afforded some protection from bombing.

Rain continued to fall and the men had little opportunity of drying out and it was difficult to get clean, let alone keep clean, but these obstacles were in the main overcome, as the clean rifles and bright buttons on the bedraggled uniforms proclaimed.

Added to the discomfort of rain and mud, were the vermin ; baths were not too frequent, change of underclothing made little difference, and it was not possible to keep free from the pests.

On November 3rd some three hundred of the battalion returned to the canal dug-outs to dig a cable trench ; three days later the remainder of the men joined them.

Preparations for a trip up the line commenced and the usual extras were issued to the men and on the night of November 8th the battalion moved off.

The journey up to the near end of Poelcappelle was accomplished without difficulty. Guides of the 2/10th London whom the 7th were relieving, instead of taking the route the battalion had previously used, led the men along a duckboard track to the left of the village. This last three hundred yards was one of the worst experiences of the battalion, a real nightmare. The track had been hurriedly laid under difficulties, the duckboards had been just placed on top of the mud, and consequently tipped at various angles and time after time men slithered off the slippery boards into the adjacent mud and had to be pulled out. The pitch black night added to the difficulties ; platoon officers and the men had literally to feel their way and throughout the relief the enemy shelled intermittently. Fortunately the shells caused little damage as they went well into the mud before exploding, with the result that a huge fountain of slush covered anyone near by.

By the time the end of the track was reached, everyone was feeling the strain of the journey and all were well soaked and covered with mud. From this point, those of the 7th booked for the front line still had another three hundred yards to cover and this, if anything, was worse than the journey just completed.

The front line consisted of a series of craters, the ground in front almost impassable, thus making the front fairly secure from attack. " A " Company took over a line beyond the village, with its left flank at Racquette Farm, adjoining the 57th Division.

With the relief completed, the men endeavoured to settle down, those in the front line bracing their feet in the opposite side of the shell hole they occupied in order to keep them out of the water, those in support being more fortunate, as they occupied some mebuses.

Fortunately for the 7th, the infantry fighting had died down and it was chiefly a case of making the best of extremely bad conditions, which were not improved by the continual rain which fell throughout the two days the line was occupied.

One great blessing was the Tommy cookers which had been issued and another was, of course, the rum issue. During the first day in the line some liveliness occurred away on the right and the enemy shelling extended to the 7th front line, causing casualties.

Brigade Headquarters required information as to whether the enemy were holding a position known as Spider Cross Roads situate in Westroosbeke village, the next hamlet in advance of Poelcappelle, so that night a patrol of an N.C.O. and two men went out. Upon approaching the cross-road they came under machine-gun fire from a mebus and after standing waist deep in water until the firing died down, the patrol returned well satisfied that the cross-roads were held by the enemy.

The well-known and famous order in connection with " whale oil and the feet " was revived with great strength, but as far as the troops in the front line were concerned, they were unable to comply with the order owing to the conditions under which they existed.

On the night of November 10th the battalion was relieved by the 2/6th London Regiment and " A " and " B " Companies took the original route out through the village, preferring to wade through the knee-deep flooded road rather than tackle the duckboards again. Many of the men were suffering from exposure and had to be helped to the nearest mebus and left for the stretcher bearers to attend to them on the following day.

Once clear of the village the journey out was slow owing to the congested state of the track, caused by meeting a relief for another sector. Eventually the troops were able to get along a little quicker, but even so the men were played out and it was with relief that at one point a rum issue was made to each man as he passed by. This tonic temporarily improved matters.

Further along the homeward route the battalion was met by a party of details from transport lines, who had come up to meet the battalion, and these relieved the worst cases of their equipment and helped to carry back the Lewis guns, etc.

Kempton Park was reached and hot soup was served while the men waited for the lorries to take them back to Siege Camp, where upon arrival, hot tea, well laced with rum, and porridge were immediately issued. In each tent were new sets of underclothing laid out and the men lost no time in getting rid of their muddy khaki and getting down to sleep. Blessings on the company quartermasters!

The following day was spent cleaning up. Many of the men were suffering with trench feet and could not get their boots on, some being so seriously affected that they were sent to hospital.

After spending a week at Siege Camp the battalion moved off on November 17th and entrained at Elverdinghe for Proven, where another train carried the men to Herzele. Here the troops were accommodated in barns and tents.

While here several of the men were delighted to meet Sergt. Hooper, who, having recovered from his wounds, was now serving on the staff of the Divisional Training School.

After a week at Herzele, during which time only routine parades had been held, the battalion, on the 25th, marched to a camp two miles beyond Proven, from where, on the following day, they entrained for Wizernes.

Everyone was in high spirits at the prospect of a long rest out of the line, and when the battalion moved off, one company started " Here's to good old beer," and four hundred throats roared out the many verses as they marched along.

A few hours' march and the battalion reached Bayenghem-lez-Seninghem, where the night was spent. On the following day a further move was made to Selles, the companies being billeted in and around the village.

In the matter of billets here, some were more fortunate than others, as one billet is described as being " a very smelly stable, the ' Gee-Gee ' and several rabbits having to be shifted before it was taken over."

The stay at Selles was not over-enjoyed ; the billets were cramped and the weather pretty miserable. Normal training was commenced, and the battalion settled down to what was expected to be a nice " cushy" time out of the line.

The men received a rude awakening on December 6th, when the news spread that they were booked to return to Ypres. The rumour was only too true, for on the 7th the battalion moved off in F.M.O., complete with one blanket per man, to Bayenghem-lez-Seninghem, which was reached in the early afternoon.

Orders were given for the men to rest and sleep immediately, as a further move was to be made at midnight. Subsequently at 2.30 a.m. on the 8th, the battalion marched off to Wizernes, where it entrained for Elverdinghe, and from the latter place marched to Dirty Bucket Camp and spent the night in huts.

On the next day a move was made in the pouring rain to Kempton Park. For nearly a month the battalion remained here, performing carrying parties and providing some 200 men for working parties in the Pheasant Trench area of Poelcappelle, digging dug-outs.

The weather had changed to snow and ice, but on the whole life for those of the 7th was not too bad.

During Christmas there was plenty of snow about and the men made themselves comfortable and, despite a working party on Christmas Day, they all spent a very cheerful Christmas.

The officers of " C " and " D " Companies, Capts. Jackson and Berliner, were exceptionally fortunate, as they managed to take over from some gunners a palatial corrugated iron structure for use as a joint mess. These premises were known as " Myobb " ; those inquiring the meaning of this name being told " Mind your own b—— business." Captain Berliner, who shortly after Christmas would be celebrating his twenty-first birthday, had made suitable preparations for the event, and was quite prepared to make an early start in the way of celebrations, and this, no doubt, caused " Myobb," apart from its comfort, to be the chief centre of social activities and a great rallying point. More especially at 11 a.m., when a biscuit taken with one of the drier wines did not come amiss.

About the middle of January, 1918, the battalion bade farewell to Ypres and its mud. They left behind them many dear friends, and others had departed owing to wounds. There were large gaps in the ranks of those who had set foot in France just a year ago, and many names of the 2/7th men are recorded on the panels of Tyne Cot Cemetery, Passchendaele, where Major H. Green was subsequently buried.

The battalion spent one night at Proven where, except for H.Q., everyone was in bell tents, and it was considered by all to be just about the coldest spot in the world. After a train journey the battalion found itself in the very pleasant town of Moreuil, some ten miles south-east of Amiens.

After a week at Moreuil, a move was made to Domart-sur-la-Luce, which the battalion were to see in flames as they went into the line at Hangard Wood in the following April.

At this time, February, 1918, the reorganisation of infantry brigades into three battalion brigades instead of four, took place, the 2/5th Battalion (L.R.B.) being disbanded, part of the unit going to their first line battalion in the 56th Division.

The 1/7th Battalion were at this time also disbanded, and on February 2nd, at 2.30 p.m., those officers and men of the 1/7th who were to join the 2/7th arrived at Domart and were met and welcomed by Lieut.-Col. S. L. Hosking.

From this date the 2/7th Battalion ceased to exist and became the 7th Battalion, The London Regiment.

CHAPTER TWENTY-NINE

February—April 3rd, 1918

AMALGAMATED BATTALION

FOLLOWING the influx of officers, N.C.O.'s and men from the 1st Battalion, the combined 7th quickly settled down, and among the N.C.O.'s and men old friendships were revived and new ones made.

A situation which was understandably difficult was handled with tact and sympathy by Lieut.-Col. S. L. Hosking and the officers of the 2/7th, and everyone of the 1st Battalion at various times has testified to the personal kindliness with which they were met.

The first move of the newly amalgamated battalion was to take over the line from the French opposite St. Gobain, where a series of isolated posts were held along the edge of a wide clearing in the forest in front of Servais.

For the first ten days here, all was quiet and peaceful, " a peace that passeth all understanding," so it had been forecast, and so it was until a battery of French 75's, which was being pulled out, shot off all their ammunition rather than carry it away, and stirred up the Huns into being nasty.

It was on the left of this position that a cider apple orchard was discovered ; the apples had been left unpicked and had fallen under the trees but were in the main sound. For a considerable time the troops had them raw or in puddings, stewed or baked, until all had a real surfeit, and even too much so. The following is recorded by Capt. J. G. H. Budd :

> " Someone discovered an old cider press in a cottage and, as a result of their efforts, were successful in inducing violent diarrhoea in a large number of the company. Raw apple juice apparently being an excellent purgative."

From Servais the 7th moved via Autreville to Barisis, which was situated in the extreme south of the divisional sector and immediately on the left of the French. Several of our officers had some pleasant meals with their opposite numbers of the French left company and, naturally, there was much fraternisation with the French and the 7th, brisk business being carried out in the exchange of excess commodities.

While in this area the whole of the defence system had to be re-sited and reconstructed in accordance with British ideas, including the laying of a cable to the rear. Poor old working parties ! Work on the forward and battle zones was completed prior to the German attack on March 21st.

Sandbags in which to carry rations were a real source of trouble to Q.M.'s, and they were for ever on the search and scrounge for spare sandbags. The issue was small, consequently Q.M.'s had to " win " large numbers from the various dumps. C.Q.M.S. F. Scothorne (" B " Company) records the following :

> " On one occasion Norie (C.Q.M.S. " D " Company) and I had appropriated about three thousand bags from a neat pile, when a voice came from inside ' What the hell, etc., etc.,' and out came a furious sentry. We had half pulled down his house. Fortunately, he turned out to be a 7th man, but detached, and a tot of rum and a hand in restoring some semblance of a house finished the matter."

While on the subject of " winning," it would appear that great rivalry existed among the Q.M.'s and Transport as to whose parties were the champions, at one time competitions were held, and to this day disputes are still carried on. For instance, Transport Sergt. T. Scholey will always declare that his party were greater scroungers than the storemen of R.Q.M.S. F. Smith, and vice versa. But the company Q.M.'s had them all beaten to a frazzle.

The battalion took over the line at Barisis from the Post Office Rifles on March 18th, and everything was normal until the afternoon of the 20th, when, from a prisoner captured on another part of the front, it was gathered that an attack was being made either that night or at dawn on the 21st.

From 3 p.m. on the 20th, the whole battalion had been " standing to," and at 4.15 a.m. on the 21st, away on the left a heavy bombardment was heard. At 5.25 a.m. our front line was heavily shelled and mortared with considerable accuracy, this shelling lasting until about 10 a.m., fortunately with comparatively light casualties among those holding the line.

Several raids were beaten off and prisoners taken, but one raiding party succeeded in getting a prisoner from one of our posts.

On the afternoon of the 20th Sergt. R. Richards and a party of four others were sent to the H.Q. of the 215th French Regiment for liaison work, and during the ten days which followed messages were relayed each way, and each evening Sergt. Richards reported back to 7th H.Q.

The disposition of the division on the 21st was 173rd Brigade, holding a front line of five miles from Travecy south to the River Oise, and 174th Brigade from the river, south to Barisis, a further distance of six miles. Against 173rd Brigade the Germans advanced at 6.10 a.m., and by 9 a.m., in thick fog, heavy fighting was proceeding. All day visibility was limited, and fierce fighting continued until nightfall north of the Oise, when the 173rd Brigade, owing to casualties, had little further fighting strength left, and during the course of that night were withdrawn across the Crozat Canal.

No attack developed south of the Oise, and it was not until the 22nd that something became known of the difficulties on the north side of the river.

The weather was fine on the whole, with morning mist which lasted until about 10 a.m. in the Barisis sector, and during this mist it seemed quite safe to walk about in No-man's-land. Apparently the Boche thought so, too, as on the 24th a German officer walked through our forward area and was taken prisoner by one of our posts in the support line. So sure was this officer that we had retired that he was unarmed.

Second Lieut. R. R. Walker, who came out with the battalion, was killed on March 23rd near Noyon, while on a course at a Corps School. An ex-ranker of the Fusiliers, 2nd Lieut. Walker was killed while leading a composite unit from the school. Sergt. T. D. Lush, M.M., of the L.R.B. (afterwards Major T. D. Lush), expressed the opinion that he was one of the finest active service soldiers he had the pleasure to serve under.

On the 26th the battalion vacated the Barisis position and moved back into a line in front of the Forest of Coucy, this line being heavily shelled by the enemy on the 28th with 5.9's.

The 6th London relieved " ours " on March 30th, and the 7th moved back to St. Paul-au-Bois, where they arrived at 6 a.m. on the 31st. At noon the same day another move was made, this time to take up positions on the River Ailette.

About this time the battalion lost the services of its adjutant, Capt. L. B. Freeston, who was invalided home and later went to the U.S.A. as a member of the British Military Mission.

The battalion moved again at noon on April 2nd ; after marching about six miles French lorries took the troops to Vic-sur-Aisne, where they found belated correspondence and parcels. At 8 p.m. that night they entrained for Longeau, near Amiens, which was reached at noon on the 3rd, and then on foot to Boves, where they were billeted for the night.

CHAPTER THIRTY

April, 1918

VILLERS BRETONNEUX

ON April 4th, in the pouring rain, the battalion at noon moved off to reserve positions at Bois L'Abbe, just in front of Villers Bretonneux, where it relieved the remains of several battalions who had fought the whole way back from the St. Quentin positions and were completely exhausted.

The 7th remained in this area for the next ten days, and during this sojourn several fine stews were made by the men, as in Villers Bretonneux was a huge warehouse full of tinned food, wine, candles, etc., and a heap of other things which were in short supply. L/Cpl. W. Horley, M.M., records the following:

> "There were many expeditions to this warehouse, which was guarded by Australians, who, if they wanted a bottle of wine themselves, and not having a corkscrew, would line up the bottles at the far end of the building and shoot off the necks of the bottles with a bullet."

While at Bois L'Abbe, R.S.M. F. Payne received a shoulder wound from a shell splinter. He still marched away as if on a parade ground, although his arm was in a sling.

It was from here about this time that another stalwart departed from the battalion; Capt. V. H. Raby left to join the 22nd London Regiment and subsequently became their adjutant and the recipient of a Military Cross.

On the night of the 13th "ours" relieved the 6th London, and it was while on the way up through Villers Bretonneux—a key point in the critical military situation—that Sergt. W. Robertson was so seriously wounded that he eventually had to have his leg amputated. Sergt. Robertson had originally crossed over with the first battalion and had served throughout.

The 7th took over a close support position in a sunken road at Bois d'Aquenne, where bivouacs were occupied; these were not too comfortable owing to the sodden state of the ground and the enemy shelling.

Each night from here working parties were engaged wiring the front line, and at this time Pte. J. Harris was killed. He was an original 1st Battalion man and had been awarded the M.M. while serving with them. C.S.M. L. W. Everson, one of the best all-round sportsmen of the battalion, was also seriously wounded, and shortly afterwards succumbed.

On April 16th the battalion took over the front line in advance of Villers Bretonneux, B.H.Q. being situated in the village. It was on this day that 2nd Lieut. H. E. Benstead was killed, as also was L/Cpl. H. M. Erwin, brother of Pte. R. R. Erwin, who had been accidentally killed a year previously.

The night passed quietly for the 7th in the line, but not entirely without casualties. At this time Pte. P. H. Coles, M.M., another 1st Battalion man, was killed.

On the morning of the 18th the enemy, commencing at 5 a.m., put 15,000 mustard gas shells into Villers Bretonneux. This tremendous concentration of gas shells absolutely saturated the village and knocked out the entire B.H.Q. and most of the 6th B.H.Q. who were also in the village. Maj. W. Hunt (2/11th London) came up from battle surplus to take command, but he himself absorbed a considerable amount of gas and had to go to hospital shortly after the 7th were relieved.

It would appear that soon after the gas shelling commenced B.H.Q. were awakened and respirators donned and worn throughout the shelling, which persisted until 8 a.m. Efforts were made to prevent gas entering B.H.Q., and everyone was set to work trying to clear the dug-out of the gas which had already penetrated. The work was rendered useless, as B.H.Q. received a direct hit and the occupants crawled out and established a new H.Q. in a lime kiln not far away.

The day proved fine and sunny, and the new H.Q. soon became hot and stuffy; early in the forenoon the occupants all began to complain of body burns and of blisters on the neck and wrists. Later the eyesight of some became affected. What had really happened was that in the atmosphere of H.Q. everyone was gassing everyone else with the gas being given off their own clothing. Practically all the staff of H.Q. were laid low; Lieut.-Col. S. L. Hosking was among those temporarily blinded and was so badly gassed that he was eventually evacuated to " Blighty." Lieut. J. H. Wilson and 2nd Lieut. R. E. Stevenson also went down the line with gas.

Lieut.-Col. S. L. Hosking had come to the 7th in 1909 as a second lieutenant, and was posted to " B " Company. He was promoted lieutenant in 1910 and captain in 1912, crossing over with the battalion as second-in-command and becoming its commanding officer in September 1917. Col. Hosking's departure was greatly regretted by all ranks of the battalion, to whom he had greatly endeared himself. He had led the battalion most ably for the previous nine months during good times and bad and both officers and men while under his command were happy and contented.

Among the men who were killed or died of wounds were: Pte. E Emmett, M.M., Pte. A. F. Meader, M.M., Cpl. R. G. Newton, M.M., and Cpl. W. Norford, M.M. The last three had all seen active service with the 7th since March 1915.

Quite a number of our men died as a result of this murderous gas shelling and many more suffered in various degrees; many lives of 7th men have been cut short as a direct result of being gassed on this day.

On the night of April 19th the 2nd Battalion Middlesex Regiment relieved the 7th, who were glad to make a move back to Boutillerie. On the way back while halted at the cross roads near the church at Gagny, two platoons of " A " Company were bombed and suffered many fatal and other casualties, among whom were Capt. A. A. Shearman and Lieut. C. D. Metcalf.

The loss of these officers was a severe blow. Capt. Shearman, who came out with the 2/7th, was pure Irish and spoke with a delightful brogue. He was always cheerful and full of fun and a first-class officer, liked by all and generally voted one of the best. Lieut. Metcalf had, with the 1st Battalion, established himself as a soldier of quality and his death caused his many friends much grief.

At this time Capt. G. G. Jackson became second-in-command, with Capt. P. B. Berliner as adjutant.

The gas shelling now began to take effect on most of the men; several lost their voices and the majority could speak only in a whisper, while many had raw blisters on their bodies where the poison had come into contact with their skin.

Practically all company cooks had become casualties and all cooking equipment had become affected by gas, so cooking arrangements had to be improvised with borrowed dixies lent to C.Q.M.S. Scothorne by Lieut. Simons, a former 7th officer, at this time serving with the R.A.S.C., and met accidentally in Cagny. What a happy reunion!

Following a medical inspection, the worst of the gas cases were sent down the line and the remainder carried on.

On the night of the 21st a patrol in front of Villers Bretonneux captured a German sergeant-major of the 4th Guards Division, from whom information was obtained after special examination, that an attack was impending on Villers Bretonneux. Further examination elicited the statement that the attack had been planned for the morning of the 23rd, but would probably be delayed for a day or so owing to his capture. This proved to be correct and the battalion, having stood to at dawn on April 23rd and 24th, moved up to a point near Cachy switch line early on the 24th under Capt. G. G. Jackson.

The morning of the 24th was very foggy and the enemy opened up with a heavy bombardment at 3.45 a.m. More gas shells fell on our back areas during the shelling, which continued for over two hours.

On this morning the disposition of the division was as follows: The 173rd Brigade (Brig.-Gen. R. B. Worgan) was in the line; behind them was the 175th Brigade (Brig.-Gen. M. E. Richardson) and the 174th Brigade (Brig.-Gen. C. G. Higgins) was in Divisional Reserve at Cagny.* As previously stated, the 7th had at dawn moved forward to Cachy switch.

The divisional front was from the junction with the French at Hangard Wood to just short of the Monument, the latter being a French memorial to the fallen of Villers Bretonneux (La Lallue) fought on the 23rd–24th December, 1870; a plantation of trees round the Monument became known as Monument Wood.

At dawn on the 24th, visibility was at first about 30 yards and enemy tanks, covered by the noise of the barrage, reached our front line; these tipped the scale in favour of the enemy, as without tanks the German infantry would have been beaten. During the course of the day, many of the battalion saw our whippet tanks chase several heavy German tanks around the south side of Bois L'Abbe, which was about half a mile away.

The enemy penetrated our lines for a depth of about a mile on a four-mile front, and the village of Villers Bretonneux was lost to us. The safety of Amiens depended upon the recapture of the village and a vigorous and determined counter-attack was made, which resulted in Villers Bretonneux and Bois d'Aquenne being almost encircled and most of the ground lost being regained, although the old front line was nowhere reached.

Although the battalion was not itself engaged this day, their position was not too comfortable and they suffered several casualties, among whom was Capt. L. E. Bishop, M.C., wounded. The 7th were warned for a counter-attack on Villers Bretonneux that night, but this was eventually carried out by the 13th and 15th Australian Brigades on the north and south sides of the village respectively, with units of the 8th Division, with results as previously mentioned.

During the day Lieut.-Col. A. A. Hanbury Sparrow, D.S.O., M.C., of the Royal Berkshire Regiment, who had already been three times wounded, assumed command of the battalion, which moved into the line that night, through Domart to a position opposite Hangard Wood, B.H.Q. itself being situated in a spot which had been used by them earlier in the year as a 30-yards range.

---
* British Official History.

The 7th remained in the line here for 48 hours and during this time there was a good deal of activity by both sides, as the line between Hangard Wood and the Monument had been recovered but could not be held, but by the night of the 26th this had been almost entirely accomplished. The battalion's role during this operation was to give covering fire on to Hangard Wood, where machine-guns had been holding up the attack.

On the night of April 27th–28th, the battalion, which had suffered fairly heavy casualties, were relieved by a regiment of Zouaves of the French Moroccan Division, and moved back to Amiens and bussed to Caours, near Abbeville, where a draft of officers and men awaited the much depleted battalion.

Between April 5th and 27th the losses of the 58th Division were 153 officers and 3,377 other ranks killed, wounded and missing.*

Dealing with this period, the following is taken from the diary of L/Cpl. W. Horley, M.M.:

"On the morning of the 23rd, we all stood to from 1 a.m. to 6 a.m. On the 24th the order " stand to " was repeated, and our chaps decided to have something tasty to eat at stand down. Accordingly, a lot of army biscuits were ground up with the aid of a coffee grinder and mixed with a pot of jam. The whole was put into a pillow slip from one of the houses and put to boil in a dixie. It was calculated that it would be cooked by 6 a.m., but before that time we received orders to move up the line, so the roly-poly to which we had looked forward, was not eaten by us."

Capt. K. O. Peppiatt, who had arrived back from England, took over the adjutancy from Capt. P. B. Berliner, who resumed command of " D " Company, the other company commanders at this time being : " A," Capt. J. G. H. Budd ; " B," Capt. J. H. Jackson ; and " C," Capt. G. G. Jackson.

---

* British Official History.

CHAPTER THIRTY-ONE

May 2nd—July 31st, 1918
HENENCOURT AND BAISIEUX

AFTER Villers Bretonneux, the 7th were withdrawn to Caours, and on May 2nd were visited by the divisional commander, Maj.-Gen. A. B. E. Cator, D.S.O. At this time the men were still incomplete as regards equipment, etc., after their long spell in the line.

The weather was now glorious, and on the 3rd the battalion took part in some range firing, marching many miles to carry out this practice.

On the 6th buses carried the 7th to Molliens-au-Bois, and on the route some very encouraging sights were seen; many thousands of colonial troops and much artillery were passed and also loads of Americans. As Capt. K. O. Peppiatt records in his diary, " Everywhere stiff with troops of all kinds."

The following day a move was made to Mirvaux, a small village about ten miles due west of Albert, the latter place at this time being in German hands.

A move was made on the 9th to Contay, where the troops occupied bivouacs amidst surroundings very rural and pleasant. The following day the 7th moved to Warloy, and while here, were delighted to receive a visit from Lieut.-Col. C. J. Salkeld Green, D.S.O., M.C., who was at this time commanding the 22nd London (47th Division), which lay not far away.

The officers took a trip up the line to have a look round, ready for the future. They were particularly interested in Henencourt Chateau, which the 7th had been detailed to counter-attack in the event of it being lost.

The time came for the battalion to return to the line, and on May 15th " ours " relieved the 21st London Regiment of the 47th Division at Millencourt, just over two miles west of Albert. The relief was completed about midnight, with artillery on both sides active throughout the change-over. The Post Office Rifles relieved the 7th on the night of the 19th, and the battalion returned to Henencourt, none the worse for the trip in the line, and occupied the old cellars.

Generally in this area the defence was in zones; behind the front line were carefully selected positions to check any attempt to advance, and in the rear of these positions was a reserve zone, from which, if necessary, counter-attacks would be made.

As the enemy were expected to perform, the battalion moved forward and " stood to " at 3 a.m. on the 21st, but nothing happened, so it trudged back. German artillery shelled the area occupied by the 7th, and their planes were very active dropping bombs; in addition some gas shells came over, mixed with H.E., necessitating respirators being worn.

On the 23rd the battalion relieved the 6th London in a line much different from what some of the " old timers," who had returned, were used to; here cornfields took the place of craters between the trenches.

Lieut. Freeman, a South African, who made a hobby of night patrolling, was at this time battalion scout officer, and in charge of the fighting patrol which so many times brought in much valuable information. In the early hours of the morning of May 26th, Lieut. Freeman and his patrol, without opposition, advanced right up to the German front line, arriving just in time to see a German carrying a large box, which he placed on the ridge in front of the patrol. The patrol were signalled to return, and to get into our line they had to go over the brow of a slight rise and, as they did so, the contents of the box opened up; it was a machine-gun. Unfortunately, one of the patrol was killed and Lieut. Freeman had a very narrow escape.

In the London Gazette of May 25th the following were " Mentioned in Dispatches ": Lieut.-Col. C. J. S. Green, D.S.O., M.C., Lieut.-Col. S. L. Hosking, Lieut. F. C. Pettigrew, and Capt. L. E. Rundell, M.C. (died of wounds).

The 9th London Regiment relieved the battalion on the 27th, who moved back to bivouacs in Henencourt Wood. While here the men had baths, respirators were tested and practice attacks were carried out.

A large working party was provided by the 7th on the night of the 30th, and this proved a stroke of luck for many, as those left behind were subjected to an extremely heavy bombardment by the enemy, who scored a direct hit on one of the cookers and shelled the wood with mustard and tear gas mixed with H.E.'s for hours. Those who could, evacuated their bivouacs and occupied some near-by trenches. The night proved extremely unpleasant, and the battalion suffered 27 casualties, among them C.Q.M.S. W. M. C. Norie, of " D " Company. But for the working party, the casualties would have been much heavier.

On June 1st the battalion carried out a practice attack in gas helmets, and on the following day, after more gas shelling at night, marched to Baisieux; enemy shelling still persisted, and transport had seven horses killed.

The next move was to Round Wood, near Franvillers, and while here most of the time was spent in carrying out practice attacks.

On June 10th the battalion moved to Picquigny-sur-Somme—rumour had it en route for the Italian front, recently disrupted—and on the 15th, in the afternoon, battalion sports were held ; these included a bare-back mule race, which caused considerable amusement.

Maj.-Gen. A. B. E. Cator, D.S.O., having gone sick in May, the division had since been under the temporary command of Brig.-Gen. C. G. Higgins, C.M.G., D.S.O., and for a time under Maj.-Gen. N. M. Smyth, V.C., K.C.B. On June 13th Maj.-Gen. F. W. Ramsay, C.M.G., D.S.O., assumed command of the division, an appointment he retained until the end.

Buses on the 17th took the troops to a reserve position at Baisieux. Here an epidemic of trench fever, or what was commonly known as " Spanish Flu," came over the battalion. The second-in-command, chaplain, two company commanders and five other officers went to hospital, and any amount of the men also went down ; the trouble was rife on both sides of the line. On the 18th the battalion moved forward to take over the line from the 19th London Regiment of the 47th Division. Was this relief a stroke of coincidence or was it friendly foresight on the part of the staffs of the two divisions ?

When the 1/7th were broken up in February 1918, 14 officers with a large number of N.C.O.'s and men were transferred to the 19th London and here they were, being relieved by the 7th. There were many scenes of conviviality at the reunion of so many friendships. Many officers and sergeants of the 19th who had come from the 7th handed over on relief to their opposite number in the 7th. What was probably a unique experience was that Headquarters of the 19th was handed over by the adjutant, Capt. L. E. Peppiatt, M.C., to the 7th London adjutant, Capt. K. O. Peppiatt ; one might almost say an unparalleled event of the war for two brothers.

While in the line the 7th suffered a few casualties among the men while wire cutting, two officers were slightly wounded and two others went down the line sick ; during this tour of the line some Americans were attached to " ours " for instruction.

The 7th were relieved on June 24th and moved back to the deserted village of Baisieux. Capt. H. S. P. Symonds went down with " Spanish Flu," making the third company commander to go, and the same complaint laid low all the battalion runners.

During the night of the 27th the enemy bombed the 7th three times, thus spoiling for many what might have been a good night's sleep.

The first day of July found the 7th back in the line again ; this time they were in trenches cut out of chalk and while here the men performed many working parties, mostly wiring. The battalion were relieved on the 5th only to return on the following night on a working party.

At this time the command of the 174th Brigade was assumed by Brig.-Gen. A. Maxwell, C.B., C.M.G., D.S.O. (late Post Office Rifles), who retained command until the end of the war, vice Brig.-Gen. C. G. Higgins.

A very welcome draft of officers arrived on the 8th and the next day the 7th took over the line; the journey going up was very " sticky " and the battalion suffered casualties. The men had a pretty rough time of it in the line and the climax was reached on July 12th when one officer and 12 men became casualties. Following relief, the battalion moved back to Baisieux.

Trench fever or " Spanish Flu " was still taking toll of the battalion and it was about this time that the commanding officer became affected and went down the line. Lieut.-Col. A. A. Hanbury Sparrow had commanded the battalion since Lieut.-Col. S. L. Hosking had been gassed. There is no doubt that Lieut.-Col. Sparrow was a real soldier, a strict disciplinarian and very efficient ; his decorations, all gained since 1914, spoke for his bravery. In 1932 he wrote a book called " The Land-Locked Lake " and followed this in 1934 with another entitled " The Gilt Edged Insecurity." The former deals with the war and is exceedingly good reading.

On the 18th the battalion found its way back into the line again, having carried out a relief in almost record time, this time just west of Albert.

This turn in the line proved to be very lively and the battalion suffered several casualties. On July 21st 2nd Lieut. A. Fraser was wounded and on the night following Lieut. Freeman and ten of his fighting patrol became casualties ; 2nd Lieut. W. V. Lort was wounded while helping to get in the wounded. On the 25th 2nd Lieut. F. R. A. Dansey was killed, as also was 2nd Lieut. H. J. Alexander ; on the same date Lieut. Miller was wounded.

The trenches were extremely muddy and the battalion, which was not at all comfortable, was looking forward to being relieved. This, however, did not mature and matters were not improved when on the 25th the Post Office Rifles carried out a raid from our lines and the enemy retaliation, caused, in addition to the officers already mentioned, several casualties among the other ranks.

A corporal of " ours " records that on the day when the P.O.R.'s made their raid from our line, one of our 7th men should have been awarded the V.C. He writes :

" This man went into No-man's-land to bring in a wounded man of the P.O.R.'s, who had made a daylight raid. On the way back with the wounded man he was fired upon and hit. He dropped his man but picked him up again and although wounded himself, brought his man to the parapet, where he was hit again and killed, but he got his man in. He lost his own life saving another."

After ten days in the line the battalion were relieved by the Americans and a move was made back to Round Camp. While here Lieut.-Col. C. E. Johnston, M.C., of the 5th London Regiment, assumed command of the battalion; he had for a time been commanding the 8th London Regiment.

Albert, Somme: Notre Dame de Brebieres

CHAPTER THIRTY-TWO

August 2nd—August 13th, 1918

MALARD WOOD AND CHIPILLY RIDGE

Lieut.-Col. C. E. Johnston, M.C., found the battalion situate at Round Wood, near Franvillers. The constitution of the 7th at this time was Maj. C. W. Armitage, second-in-command; Capt. K. O. Peppiatt, adjutant; Capt. J. H. G. Budd, O.C. " A " Company with Capt. H. S. P. Symonds, second-in-command; Capt. J. H. Jackson, O.C. " B " Company with Capt. Halley-Jones, M.C., second-in-command; Capt. G. G. Jackson, O.C. " C " Company; and Capt. P. B. Berliner, O.C. " D " Company; Capts. Budd and J. H. Jackson being on battle surplus; the four officers actually commanding companies were Capts. Symonds, Halley-Jones, G. G. Jackson and Berliner.

The weather had now turned gloriously fine and the enemy consequently resumed his bombing attacks at night. On August 2nd " ours " moved by bus and then marched many miles to Halloy, near Vignacourt. Three weeks' rest was anticipated by the division, but on the 3rd the C.O. attended a conference at which he was informed of the part the battalion was to play in the great attack on August 8th which was to be launched by Allied Forces under the direction of Marshal Foch.

On August 4th the C.O. accompanied Brig.-Gen. A. Maxwell, his acting brigade major, Capt. Berkeley, and Lieut.-Col. C. B. Benson, commanding the 6th London Regiment, to a point near Vaux-sur-Somme to reconnoitre the ground in front of Malard Wood ; great secrecy as to the coming attack was to be observed.

Buses on August 5th took the battalion on a long journey, during which they were held up many times by convoys of tanks, finally debussing at 4 a.m. at La Houssoye and, after a short sleep in some barns at Bonnay, again went forward and marched into a valley near Vaux ; a little bluff on the enemy.

Reconnaissances of approach routes were carried out on the 6th. The scheme of attack with the co-operation of tanks was briefly as follows : The 58th and 18th Divisions, the left of the attack, were north of the Somme, Australians were on our right south of the river, and beyond them the Canadians and French. Malard Wood was the first objective of the 174th Brigade, assisted by the 2/10th Battalion, who were to take the village of Sailly Laurette, and the 173rd Brigade were then to pass through and take Chipilly Ridge ; the 175th Brigade, less 2/10th Battalion, were in reserve. The 6th and 7th Battalions were to assault, with the 8th Battalion, who were to take over the front line trenches beforehand, in support.

The attack on August 8th had a great effect on the German High Command and from this day onwards, which Ludendorf afterwards referred to as " the black day of the German Army," the enemy acted generally on the defensive.

In this great attack the " Shiny Seventh " played a most important role, attacking vigorously and with great determination ; the battalion pressed home its attack and gained all its objectives.

Zero hour was set for 4.20 a.m. on August 8th and at 10.30 p.m. on the 7th the approach march was begun ; the route was very congested, and assembly positions were reached at 3.30 a.m. with just sufficient time for the rum issue. At 4 a.m. a dense fog came on, and for some time after zero hour visibility was not more than 25 yards.

Malard Wood, the further edge of which lay about a couple of miles from the forming-up positions, was rectangular in shape and measured 2,000 yards north to south and 1,000 yards east to west ! The objective of the 7th was the high ground N.E. of Malard Wood, to gain which a deepish ravine leading out of the N. side of the wood had to be crossed. " D " Company was to occupy the N.W. corner of the wood. The 6th Battalion were to pass round the N. and S. end of the wood and take the high ground east of the wood, The 8th Battalion were to follow behind to mop up and reinforce, and were to occupy the western edge of the wood. No one was to pass through the wood. The order of assembly from left to right was as follows :—

" A " Coy.	" B " Coy.	Two Coys.	" D " Coy.	Two Coys.
7th London		6th London	7th London	6th London
" C " Coy.				
174th T.M.B.			8th London	
			173rd Infantry Brigade	

Crump Lane, a communication trench, was the boundary on our left, and here touch was made with the 36th Infantry Brigade. B.H.Q. was in a trench at Lonetree Cemetery and the 173rd Brigade, who were assembled in the rear of our brigade, were to pass through us one hour after our objective was taken.

At 4.20 a.m. promptly, down came our barrage and the assault was launched. A thick mist lay upon everything, platoons were soon separated and sense of direction was difficult, particularly by the tanks, who did not really take the full part intended in the action.

Parties of the 6th, 7th and 8th were very soon all mixed up, and although the attack proceeded well, it became necessary to collect the men of the battalion together. Several officers and N.C.O.'s had become casualties, and Lieut.-Col. C. E. Johnston, M.C., together with Capt. K. O. Peppiatt, went forward and as the history of the 6th London records, " no time was lost in sorting out the different units all congregated along the high ground north of the wood, and putting it into a state of defence. This they did at 7.15 a.m."

Having found elements of four companies of the 7th under Capt. Halley-Jones, M.C., these were reorganised and sent forward under that officer to hold the high ground east of the ravine, and to gain touch with troops on either flank.

Capt. P. B. Berliner and Capt. H. S. P. Symonds were both wounded early on. Other parties lost direction in the fog, and it was a very good performance of the remainder to have found their way to the ravine.

This ravine, full of shelters, showed signs of a hasty flight, a consignment of undistributed Iron Crosses was found there, together with many M.G.'s, rifles and equipment. A very good aid post subsequently became B.H.Q. on August 9th. Some men of the 6th and 8th Battalions attached themselves to us, and were organised as the support line on the western edge of the ravine.

The 173rd Brigade had become hopelessly scattered in the fog and were not in a position to carry out the role of taking Chipilly Ridge. Parties of them were posted on our left flank, which was in the air; in the afternoon this line was made good by the 36th Brigade, and occupied in continuation of our left flank.

With improved visibility, the enemy began to shell the ravine from Gressaire Wood. Touch was obtained with a party of the 6th London on the east side of the wood at the quarry.

Supply tanks brought up rations and dumped them at the corner of Malard Wood, and ammunition was dropped by aeroplanes.

The situation appeared to be well in hand, and the 173rd Brigade took over the frontage of Malard Wood, from which position they launched an attack at 5 p.m. in an endeavour to capture Chipilly Ridge. The attack was abortive, as the enemy had moved men and machine-guns forward and it withered away under heavy machine-gun fire.

On August 9th our front was heavily shelled, and we suffered casualties; tanks assembling in the ravine had attracted the attention of enemy artillery.

The 7th hoped for relief that night, but orders were received to continue the attack, which was to be made at 5.30 p.m. to take Gressaire Wood and Chipilly Ridge ; American troops were to operate on our left. No written orders were issued in connection with this attack as far as the 7th were concerned ; Lieut.-Col. C. E. Johnston, M.C., received verbal orders and arrived with just sufficient time to make the bare essential arrangements before the barrage began.

The ravine was full of tanks and American troops arriving were hardly ready to follow the barrage; their men were still getting into position and throwing off their packs after the attack had begun.

Heavy enemy machine-gun fire met our lads as they advanced, and caused many casualties. Capt. Halley-Jones, M.C., fell mortally wounded early on; later, Lieut. E. W. Pinnock, also wounded, managed to struggle back to B.H.Q. to report that no officers of the 7th were left. Capt. G. G. Jackson was sent forward by the C.O. and he found the remnants of the battalion at the south end of Gressaire Wood, and he carried them on to capture the ridge overlooking the Somme, finally reaching this objective with less than 40 other ranks; in this advance he was wounded in the leg.

Lieut.-Col. C. E. Johnston, M.C., together with Capt. K. O. Peppiatt and H.Q. Lewis gunners, followed up the advance and joined Capt. G. G. Jackson. Americans were clearing Gressaire Wood and posts were organised on the ridge.

Two Boche machine-guns on the left were causing trouble to our men and quoting from the diary of the C.O. " Capt. K. O. Peppiatt led some parties of Americans to clear out these guns, which he effected with great enterprise and gallantry, capturing 11 prisoners."

Chipilly Ridge, which looked so formidable, had been stormed and won, and on the night of August 10th, the battalion were relieved by Australians and moved back to Malard Wood.

On the following day a further move to the rear was made, and on August 13th the battalion marched back, via Heilly, to Round Wood.

The casualties of the 7th had been heavy; in the two days' fighting the battalion suffered over 300 casualties—but the results were splendid; all objectives had been gained and many machine-guns, prisoners, and much equipment had been captured. August 8th and 9th had been two hectic days; much ground had been covered, and without a doubt the 7th had put up a wonderful show, as the following from the diary of Capt. K. O. Peppiatt indicates :

"In two days we had captured 500 prisoners, 10 T.M.'s, 25 light machine-guns, 10 heavy M.G.'s, 3 5·9 Hows. and 4 field guns. Not too bad. Our casualties pretty heavy; 4 officers killed, 10 wounded and over 300 casualties among the men."

As already stated, Capt. P. Halley-Jones, M.C., was killed; this officer had crossed to France with the battalion. At Ypres he had displayed great bravery, which resulted in his winning the M.C. He was struck down while gallantly leading his men into action.

2nd Lieuts. W. E. Constance and F. A. Roberts, two most popular officers, were killed, and the following were wounded:

Capts. P. B. Berliner, W. F. Clarke, H. S. P. Symonds, G. G. Jackson, Lieut. E. W. Pinnock, 2nd Lieuts. K. B. Hartley, W. J. Wakerell, R. L. Read, V. L. Robinson, H. Marks.

How severe were the losses among N.C.O.'s will be realised by the number killed, among whom were:

Sergts. G. Angus, H. P. Bartlett, A. Chapman, M.M., F. Cripps, T. Folley, E. R. Jenkinson, W. J. Mason, D. J. Miller, Cpls. W. S. Crisp, A. Jones, W. F. Prior, L/Cpls. H. W. Hopcraft, A. Tilley.

A severe loss to the battalion was Sergt. Bill Neben, M.M., who succumbed to the wounds he received on August 8th. A colleague writes:

"Bill was an old 3rd London and a pre-war 7th man who, like many others, returned to the fold in 1914 and soldiered all the way through with the 2/7th. His soldierly bearing and proverbial good humour were indeed sadly missed."

Accounts of heroism are absent, due, as so often happened, to witnesses subsequently becoming casualties.

Lieut.-Col. C. E. Johnston, M.C., received the D.S.O. for the part he played and the following officers received the M.C.: Capts. P. B. Berliner and K. O. Peppiatt, Lieuts. A. C. Fraser and E. W. Pinnock. Twenty-four Military Medals were awarded to other ranks in connection with these two days' fighting.

Cpl. J. Chetland in the course of the action at Chipilly Ridge found himself in sole charge of his platoon, all officers and senior N.C.O.'s having become casualties. Cpl. Chetland displayed courage, initiative and devotion to duty and was the recipient of an M.M., the ribbon being presented to him by Brig.-Gen. A. Maxwell, at Peruwelz.

CHAPTER THIRTY-THREE

August 13th—September 26th, 1918
WAR OF MOVEMENT

THE whole of the front was now on the move and August 13th found the battalion at Round Wood, refreshed and with its strength made up by large drafts of officers and 290 men transferred from the Staffords and Lincolns. Capts. J. G. H. Budd and W. D. Coleridge had both rejoined during the last day or so. Companies were now commanded as follows : " A," Capt. J. G. H. Budd ; " B," Capt. J. H. Jackson ; " C," Lieut. C. B. Moylan ; " D," Lieut. J. H. Walsh, D.C.M.

Those who had been through the recent actions had rested and were restored to a normal atmosphere, being able to have a good wash and a shave, with a general clean up. Only a soldier can understand and appreciate the benefit of " Spit and Shine."

Sir Douglas Haig visited the battalion and congratulated it on what it had done. The G.O.C. of the Division inspected the battalion and afterwards Brig.-Gen. A. Maxwell addressed the 7th, thanking one and all for their excellent performances.

Intense training was resumed, and following the visits of many " brass hats " it came as no surprise when on the 21st a move was made to a reserve position ; all knew that there was something in the air and that big things were afoot.

It was at this time that 2nd Lieut. P. L. Smout, who had crossed overseas with the 1/7th as a private and had been twice wounded, was upholding 7th traditions while serving with the 2/20th London Regiment, being again wounded and subsequently being awarded an M.C., the citation for which was as follows :

> " 2nd Lieut. P. L. Smout, 1/7th Bn. Attd. 2/20th Lond. R. He led his men with great gallantry against a strong point, when the company was held up by barbed wire. He found a small gap, and dashed through alone in face of withering machine-gun fire, and although wounded, he jumped up and got into the enemy trench. His courageous leadership resulted in the capture of the strong point and 30 prisoners."

At 6 a.m. on August 22nd " ours " were off again in fighting order, this time to occupy a ridge north-west of Heilly. Apart from a little sneezing gas, the day was quiet. On the 23rd another move was made to Darwin Reserve, and on the following day the battalion found itself occupying shell holes for the night south of Morlancourt.

On the 25th the 7th moved again at 1.30 a.m. to support an attack of another brigade. Apparently their services were not required, as at 8 a.m. they were off again and eventually came to rest in Happy Valley, just north of the Somme, assembling there at 7 p.m.

Three hours later, in a blinding thunderstorm, a move forward was made in pitch darkness, going through a small wood; everyone became saturated and all were slipping about on the clay soil, some fell over and rifle muzzles became clogged. Eventually, after advancing nearly two miles, the battalion reached its position anything but fighting fit, and dug in on the other side of Billon Wood.

All these moves had naturally made everyone weary, but there was no rest. Orders arrived for an attack to be carried out at 4.55 a.m. on the 26th to gain ground forward towards a line south of Maricourt. The move forward the previous night had been very trying and difficult and was not completed without casualties. Capt. Budd had performed good work throughout these moves.

The attack carried out on August 26th was a huge success as far as the advance went, but our casualties were again heavy, the enemy fighting well with machine-guns and artillery; but those of his infantry taken prisoners were poor specimens.

The 7th went forward in the face of heavy enemy machine-gun fire and gained 1,000 yards, getting as far as " D " Copse. The Australians on our right and the 173rd Brigade on our left, although gaining some ground, were not in touch with us.

A gallant stand was made by our men at " D " Copse under Capt. J. H. Jackson, " B " Company, and Lieut. L. H. Walsh, D.C.M., of " D " Company. Several attempts to encircle them were beaten off, and Lieut. Walsh worked his way back through machine-gun fire to report the position to B.H.Q. at Nigger Copse.

Meanwhile Lieut. C. B. Moylan and 2nd Lieut. Cockcroft, with part of " C " Company, had been cut off on the left flank and made prisoners.

Capt. Budd's " A " Company were rather scattered, and there were remnants left on the edge of Billon Wood. H.Q. Lewis gunners were sent up under 2nd Lieut. Edwards-Trollip to reinforce these, and the adjutant made a reconnaissance of the forward position.

" Ours " were unable to get into touch with the 173rd Brigade, who were reported at " B " Copse.

As the 7th maintained their position at " D " Copse, the Australians were enabled to make a sweeping movement up the valley on our right in the afternoon. Without our occupation of " D " Copse this move would have been impossible and it was beyond all doubt a most gallant performance on the part of 7th officers and men. Many of the latter were untried soldiers and their behaviour was most praiseworthy. C.S.M. T. Archdeacon was awarded the D.C.M., and Sergt. Precious the M.M. for gallant conduct upon this occasion. The citation for the D.C.M. of C.S.M. T. Archdeacon read:

> "With an officer and 18 men, he secured a commanding position about 1,000 yards in front of the main line. The party was subjected to heavy enfilade machine-gun fire, the officer and 12 men becoming casualties. He immediately took command . . . and beat off an enemy counter-attack. He subsequently held on for eight hours."

The battalion suffered nearly 100 casualties before nightfall, when the situation eased and preparations were made for the intended assault on the Maricourt line the following morning. 2nd Lieut. J. Edwards-Trollip was sent to take charge of " C " Company. Australians were again to co-operate on the right of 174th Brigade, with one company of the 8th London between us and the Australians; the remainder of the 174th Brigade front was: 7th on the right, 6th on our left, to capture Maricourt village, with the 173rd Brigade beyond, the objective being the old British front line.

Behind a well placed barrage the 7th went into the assault at 4.55 a.m. The attack again went well and progress was rapid; some machine-guns caused trouble but were speedily dealt with.

The 7th, sadly depleted owing to the previous day's attack, again did exceptionally well and gained the whole of the old British front line.

This fresh attack drained the battalion again of officers and N.C.O.'s, to say nothing of the heavy casualties among the ranks. Among the officers killed were the following: 2nd Lieuts. W. A. Tyler, C. L. Moore, E. H. Maule-French, and J. Edwards-Trollip.

Capt. L. H. Walsh, M.C., D.C.M., a South African, was so seriously wounded that he succumbed to his wounds on the 29th. This very active officer had been with the battalion in all its actions. He was a fine soldier, and a gallant gentleman, and was undoubtedly " as hard as nails." He had taken over " D " Company after Capt. P. B. Berliner, M.C., had been wounded.

2nd Lieut. E. H. Maule-French was killed and 2nd Lieuts. W. A. Tyler and C. L. Moore, who had only recently joined the battalion, were both killed within a day of each other.

2nd Lieut. J. Edwards-Trollip, a South African, who was also killed, was a most popular officer, whose conversation usually turned to farming. He was described as being fifteen stone of cheerfulness, humour and efficiency.

Among the officers wounded, in addition to Capt. Budd, who, as he himself says, " was hit for six," were Lieut. G. E. Bradfield, and 2nd Lieuts. Sydenham, Stocker and Edkins.

L/Cpl. W. Horley, M.M., was so seriously wounded that he had to have his leg amputated; he had crossed over with the 1/7th and had served throughout.

The 7th remained in support in the old British front line, while the 6th and 8th Battalions continued the advance on August 28th and that night, following relief, the battalion moved back to the scene of its earlier action and were joined by battle surplus.

There was not much rest for the men and before they had hardly time for a general clean up they were off up the line again, in a very weak state, returning on the night of the 30th by bus to Hem Wood, from where a march was made to Junction Wood. At this time the company commanders were: " A," 2nd Lieut. F. B. Milne, who had recently arrived; " B," Capt. J. H. Jackson; " C," Lieut. A. C. Fraser, M.C.; and " D," Capt. Mortlock.

It was anticipated that the 7th would only be in reserve, but these ideas were shattered when at 1.30 a.m., on the 31st, orders arrived for the battalion to support an attack which was to be carried out that morning at 5.10 a.m. on Marrieres Wood.

On this occasion Capt. K. O. Peppiatt, M.C., guided the battalion into its assembly position, which was reached at 4.40 a.m. on the 31st. A 5·9 fell close to Capt. Peppiatt; fortunately he was only slightly wounded in the leg and was able to carry on. Contact was established with the battalion on our right but on our left we were in the air; the battalion that should have been there was missing.

The 6th, who were also in this attack, apart from company commanders, had only two other officers. When the 6th advanced, they did so with the addition of three officers lent by the 7th.*

The assault was to be delivered by the 6th and 8th battalions passing through the 175th Brigade. The Australians were on our right and the 47th Division on our left. The 7th were in support of the 6th and 8th Battalions.

Zero, as stated, was 5.10 a.m. and at this time barrage and counter-barrage opened together. The attack went exceedingly well and as Capt. K. O. Peppiatt, M.C., records, " More prisoners than I've seen for days. Unfortunately Fraser was killed and Harbott badly wounded." The following is quoted from the diary of Lieut.-Col. C. E. Johnston, D.S.O., M.C.:

" Two platoons of ' C ' Company under 2nd Lieut. R. B. Cooke (who was afterwards awarded the M.C. for this action) carried right

---
* 6th London History.

through the wood with the assault and ultimately led it across the valley east of the wood and beyond the objective to a quarry on the far slope. This unpremeditated gain of ground was a great tactical success."

Lieut. A. C. Fraser, M.C., a South African who had proved himself a gallant, fearless and first-class fighting officer, was killed here. A sniper was giving trouble and he went out to snipe him and was himself sniped. A most gallant action in an endeavour to make the position safe for the men of his company.

2nd Lieut. R. B. Cooke took command of " C " Company and " A " and " B " were moved forward to Marrieres Wood, under Capt. J. H. Jackson.

It should here be mentioned that throughout all these moves and attacks of the battalion since Villers Bretonneux, Capt. K. O. Peppiatt, M.C., who had borne a charmed life, had remained with the battalion and at this time was the only front-line officer with this distinction. Capt. Peppiatt had previously served with similar good fortune for a year with the 1/7th Battalion. Very popular with all ranks, he was quite fearless and would never ask anyone to go where he would not go himself ; he got a great kick out of war and on many occasions his dry humour relieved tense situations.

On September 1st the 74th Division took over and in the evening the 7th moved back about two miles to a position between Battery Copse and Hem Wood, and spent the next few days cleaning up, making shelters in shell holes and refitting.

On the 5th a brigade practice attack took place and in the evening a fearful thunderstorm occurred, the men in their shell-hole shelters were quickly swamped out. This storm led to amazing scenes of activity, the men swarming all over the place collecting old pieces of corrugated iron and building new homes.

On September 6th buses took the 7th up to Moislains, from where the battalion marched to Nurlu Wood, arriving at their new positions at 5 a.m. on the 7th, in a support line, to relieve the 24th London Regiment of the 47th Division. The following night the battalion moved into position at Saulcourt, west of Epehy, the companies reaching the assembly positions at 3 a.m. on September 8th in preparation for an assault on Epehy, so whacked that they fell straight off to sleep. Company commanders were : " A," Lieut. E. W. Pinnock, M.C. ; " B," Capt. J. H. Jackson ; " C," 2nd Lieut. R. B. Cooke, M.C. ; and " D " Lieut. G. E. Bradfield.

At 7.30 a.m. on September 8th the 7th assaulted the enemy and met with very stiff opposition from machine-guns in Epehy, some prisoners were taken and the battalion finished up in a sunken road south-west of the village, where they were relieved on the night of the 9th by the 6th London.

The resistance at Epehy was greater and more determined than any the battalion had encountered since the beginning of the attack, and moreover, " ours " were very weak in numbers and we had lost many experienced officers and men ; the place was held strongly by the enemy and consequently the battalion suffered many casualties.

In this attack Capt. Jackson was rather badly hit, but was brought in safely to our lines. 2nd Lieut. R. S. Hewton took command of " B " Company. 2nd Lieuts. R. A. Bradford, Leigh and J. M. Fraser were also wounded.

Following relief, the 7th moved back to Guyencourt Saulcourt and at 11.30 p.m. again moved, this time to a concentration point, from where at 1.30 a.m. on September 10th, they marched off in an appalling downpour on a cross-country journey, and it was at 5 a.m. when the 7th arrived at its new position, only half an hour before zero.

The 173rd Brigade were making an attack and the role of the 7th was to protect their right flank. Men and rations were sodden, and the shell-hole positions occupied by the men were held throughout the day in pouring rain. The battalion was now so reduced that it was organised as one company under Lieut. G. E. Bradfield, each company forming one platoon.

" Ours " were relieved at night by a company of the Suffolk Pioneer Battalion and moved off to the rear, occupying some old huts at Lieramont, where it arrived at 2 a.m. on September 11th. Following a general clean up, the battalion was at once reorganised and refitted.

While here, Capt. W. D. Coleridge and other officers rejoined. This deserved rest was rudely interrupted on the 15th by a sudden return to the support position in front of Epehy. The companies were all in isolated spots and cut off from communications, the positions being held to facilitate future operations.

The night was overcast and a terrific storm broke, which quickly saturated the men, and, to make things more miserable, the rum issue failed to arrive. The day which followed was quiet, but the night proved to be another wet one, and conditions were not improved by the fact that rations failed to turn up.

On the 18th Epehy was again attacked, and again considerable resistance was met with by our troops. The 7th was withdrawn at 3.30 p.m., and moved back to some broken huts, which they reached at 5 p.m. wet and exceedingly hungry, as they had been without food since the previous night.

Cleaning up and further reorganisation was continued, but again interrupted, when on September 21st, in the middle of the night, orders came to move again, the battalion marching off at 7.30 p.m. to a recently captured railway cutting, where they lay and froze till the morning.

On the 22nd, at 5 p.m., the battalion moved forward to Ronnsoy, a little village just captured, and here the men occupied the cellars where, after recent positions, they felt comparatively safe.

For bravery in the face of the enemy in recent actions, C.S.M. F. Haxell was awarded the M.M.

The enemy shelled the village on the following day, and again on the night of the 24th. The 7th were relieved by Americans and marched back to its old embankment positions, where buses picked up the men and drove them some miles back in a long drive through the rain.

At long last it was realised that the 7th were departing from the devastated Somme area. They were leaving behind them many who had forfeited their lives; those who had carried on since the gas days of Villers Bretonneux and still remained were few. However, it was with a certain amount of relief that the battalion entrained on the 26th.

Thus ended two very hectic months of moves, attacks and counter-attacks, with very brief rests for refitting and reorganising.

Truly a war of movement, throughout which, despite all losses and changes, the spirit of the battalion remained.

C.Q.M.S. Scothorne records an interesting event which occurred a few days before this move, in fact, " manna from heaven." He was acting as B.Q.M. for reasons he describes as " leave and discipline," when an instruction arrived to draw 800 new suits. He advised D.A.D.O.S. that he could find no record of any such requisition, but he was told to fetch them and say no more about it, and, reporting the good luck to the C.O., was directed to bring the whole stock, suitably sized, to a valley just behind the line at 3 p.m. the next day. This was done, and the whole battalion, officers and men alike, had a new suit at one and the same time, a very pretty parade indeed.

The old suits were dumped in blocks according to condition, but before they could be sent back to ordnance the move was ordered, and the C.Q.M. says that as far as he knows some 700 part-worn, lousy suits still adorn the fields of France. His record finally says :

" I felt quite a hero for a time, as probably the only Q.M. in the field (and acting at that) who was able to reclothe the whole battalion, almost without moving a finger. I was quite sure dear old economical Gallagher would have had a heart attack if the same experience had happened to him."

CHAPTER THIRTY-FOUR

October—November, 1918

FINAL MONTHS

THE beginning of October, 1918, found the battalion north of Lens, with H.Q. in Hythe tunnel, which was very comfortable. However, the 7th were soon on the move again, as on October 2nd the Boche, having in mind no doubt the extent of our advance in the south, started to retreat in this sector also. Strong enemy rearguards were encountered, but the battalion advanced some two miles and captured a few prisoners.

Capt. K. O. Peppiatt, M.C., reported back to brigade at 11 p.m. that night the advanced position of the 7th, and came away with orders for the battalion to carry on with the attack the following morning. There was no time for written orders, and as Capt. Peppiatt was the only one who knew the position of the 7th, there was nothing else he could do than to make his way back to where he had left the battalion. In the pouring rain he returned and moved them into the jumping-off positions, and at 5.45 a.m. on October 3rd, " over the top " they went again.

Capt. Peppiatt received a bullet through the back of his tin hat which grazed his head, and as his diary records, " tumbled me down an embankment like a shot rabbit."

The attack proceeded well, and from this time onwards it became a case of the British being almost continually on the move, following up the retreating enemy and beating down his rearguards.

For his excellent work throughout September, and particularly the past two days, Capt. K. O. Peppiatt, M.C., was recommended for a D.S.O., but received a bar to his M.C., an award which was thoroughly deserved. 2nd Lieut. R. S. Hewton had also greatly distinguished himself and was awarded an M.C. Lieut. F. Glenton, acting as intelligence officer, was Mentioned in Dispatches.

The battalion spent a few days' rest at Champs Grenelles, having been relieved by the 2/10th London Regiment, and moved off on October 12th from the area of Lievin, marching through Lens, which was at this date a vast heap of rubble, and on to Sallaumines, where cellars were occupied. The stay was of short duration, as within 15 minutes the men were on the move again.

In full marching order the battalion marched for hours in the pouring rain, and about midnight relieved the Queens of the 12th Division, taking over a series of isolated posts near Courrierres, with the left flank of " A " Company resting on the Souchez River ; the river joined the Canal de la Haute Deule, which was situate three kilos in front of Courrierres.

The rain continued to pour down all night, and on the following morning orders came to push forward, and patrols advanced through a wood about 150 yards to Courrierres. Sergt. H. Lydiart, M.M., and his patrol were fired at by machine-guns and a sniper ; the position of the enemy was checked and reported back to Lieut. E. W. Pinnock, M.C.

The Germans were shelling the village, and all the men could do was to dig in. " B " Company's H.Q. in a cellar was shelled very heavily, and they moved " toute de suite." No sooner had they done so when enemy shells scored direct hits—a lucky escape.

" A " Company had one man killed and half-a-dozen wounded, one of whom was Sergt. E. Wharram.

That night, October 13th, the Post Office Rifles relieved the 7th, who marched back to Billy Montigny, where the troops were billeted in pillboxes and cellars.

On October 15th the men handed in their greatcoats, and nobody was surprised when orders came for them to move to Courrieres, where the cellars were occupied. Extra ammunition and bombs were issued, and at midnight the men moved forward, " A " to occupy some trenches about 600 yards ahead of the village, while the other companies established a line in front of the village of Oignes.

The R.E.'s were busy building a bridge over the canal, which Jerry shelled throughout the day.

The village of Oignes was searched for snipers ; this was ticklish work, as Jerry had planted plenty of booby traps, and the cross-roads were found to be mined.

It was now a case of brigade leapfrogging brigade and ever advancing and at 4 a.m. on October 17th the battalion moved forward, " A " passing through " C " to Gartuelle and on to Thumeries.

The battalion were now passing through country undisturbed by war, with civilians quite close to the front line positions. The civilians of Thumeries and other villages gave the men of the 7th a great welcome, waving and yelling ; they hung out all their flags and many provided coffee, wine and food for the troops.

Many of the men were in huts built by Jerry but it is recorded that " Les. Williams and we three sergeants managed to get a billet. Will sleep on a bed to-night."

At Mons-en-Pevele, where the battalion moved to on October 18th, the inhabitants gave the troops a wonderful welcome ; the band played in the street and after they had rendered the Marseillaise the people showered them with flowers.

That night another move was made to the area of Vincourt, where barns were occupied; the following morning an early breakfast was provided and the battalion moved off just after 5 a.m.

Marching throughout the day, the battalion made many halts, as distance had to be kept behind the advancing front-line troops and towards the end of the day everyone was thoroughly tired out but all were very cheerful and in excellent spirits.

A position near Ouvignies station was reached; here several buildings had been set on fire by the Boche and the 173rd Brigade passed through the outpost lines held by the 6th and 7th London; the 7th then marched back to Auchy, where they arrived just after dusk and occupied billets.

The following day, October 20th, the 7th moved to Nomain; this was quite a decent village and the billets were exceptionally good; at one, madame supplied black coffee, saying "the Boche had won her last two cows." The inhabitants were all agog with excitement, Jerry had left hurriedly and apart from cutting down telegraph poles, blowing up railway lines and mining roads here and there, he had not caused a great deal of damage to property.

These were very busy days for Q.M. and transport; it was no mean task for them to keep pace with all the moves. They had their work cut out to keep the advancing companies supplied with food and, despite the efforts of the enemy in placing concrete obstructions in the roads and in places mining the cross-roads, transport overcame all these difficulties and succeeded in getting rations up to them wherever they were.

The enemy was at this time using a considerable amount of gas, and in addition to looking after the troops, the medical officer and his staff had to give considerable attention to the civilian population.

Elderly people and children continued to arrive from the forward villages carrying their worldly possessions in bundles, and on barrows and carts. The A.S.C. performed a good job of work in helping these unfortunate people to get away in their wagons and lorries.

The battalion was enjoying a rest, being in Divisional Reserve; it was a great change these days to stay in one place for any length of time.

On October 27th the battalion moved off and after marching some distance, the move was cancelled, so the battalion had dinner and returned to billets. The following day this move was repeated but on this occasion the battalion did not return and after dinner rested in a wood, much needed as the march had been a long and trying one.

At dusk a move forward was made and at Cense de Choques the battalion relieved the 2/10th London on October 28th. "A," "B" and " C " Companies occupied the front line from right to left in that order, of the Maulde Sector, " D " Company being back in reserve at Cense de Choques. Company commanders were as follows : " A," Lieut. F. Glenton ; " B," Lieut. H. C. Woolner ; " C," Lieut. A. G. McLeod ; and " D," Lieut. G. W. M. Hare.

Opposite, the enemy had several machine-gun posts in the woods and houses and while here the battalion carried out many patrols, the river being crossed on rickety rafts of floats and duckboards fixed up by the R.E.'s.

Lieut. Davison, Sergt. Lydiart, M.M., and two men took part in one of these patrols and returned safely just before dawn. Not all patrols were so fortunate and the battalion suffered several casualties.

An inter-company relief took place on the night of the 29th. " D " Company came up and took over from " A," who were detailed to cross the river and attack the Chateau de Mortagne and another strong point close by, known as Le Fort.

At this time the operations of the battalion were being directed by Lieut.-Col. C. E. Johnston, D.S.O., M.C., with Capt. W. D. Coleridge as acting adjutant in the absence of Capt. K. O. Peppiatt, M.C., on leave. All bridges having been destroyed the difficulty was to get 150 men over the water ; R.E.'s fixed a wire from bank to bank and on the night of October 30th " A " Company under Lieut. F. Glenton crossed the river about 1.30 a.m. on rafts in groups of ten, and formed up on the far side ; thick mist favoured the venture, but the men found it very damp and cold.

Advancing carefully, the men took up a position on the edge of the road facing the chateau. Jerry apparently had wind of the coming attack and left a few machine-gunners to cover the retreat of his main body to the village.

2nd Lieut. Edkins, following up the retreating enemy, was seriously wounded when quite close to an enemy post, and Cpl. A. H. Kingsnorth, while dressing his wound, was shot dead. Efforts were made at dusk to try to get his body in, but without success.

The chateau was found to be in ruins ; machine-gun and sniping positions were found and cleared ; the men dug in and while doing so were mortared with considerable accuracy by the enemy, one man was killed and one of the M.G. Corps attached to " A " Company for the attack was wounded.

An inter-company relief took place and this was followed by the Post Office Rifles relieving the 7th on November 1st, and the battalion moved back to Cense de Choques, where billets of empty houses were occupied.

The enemy shelled daily and four sergeants of " D " Company were wounded, Sergt. D. R. Harrison succumbing later to the wounds he received.

While here the men enjoyed the pleasure of a bath and change of underclothing; both were very much needed and the usual parades and inspections filled in the time.

The enemy were at present holding a position on the far side of the Escaut and the battalion went into training for the purpose of making the necessary assault. The Escaut, a main waterway from Tournai to Valenciennes, had for some days provided the enemy with a natural fortification, deeply dredged and with a width of about 50 yards.*

Rafts were the only means of crossing and the battalion put in much practice on the moat of a chateau, using rafts capable of bearing four or five men and constructed of tarpaulin sheets and brushwood. Great difficulties were found in landing from these; several practices were carried out in the dark and few favoured the chances of success when the actual attack would be launched.

To the great relief of many, the enemy obliged by retiring, and on November 8th the battalion moved off in full marching order to Maulde, and then crossed the Escaut over a rickety bridge which had been hastily constructed of tubs and planks. Still, several thought this a much better way to cross than on rafts in the darkness.

The enemy continued to shell the area the battalion were now in and for a few moments things were very warm. One shell-burst killed Pte. J. Daniels and wounded Pte. Page. This was the last shelling the battalion experienced in the war.

The 7th carried on, eventually digging in in a cabbage field; later a move was made back to the cellars in Mortagne. Here there were plenty of booby traps about, "flying pigs" and shells with wires attached to them.

On the following day, November 9th, the battalion moved off and passed through the outpost lines of the 6th London, crossing in single file over the wreckage of the Pont de Callenelle, and then across the Antoing Pommeroeul Canal.

At dusk the village of Brasmenil was reached, and the men, who were by now very tired, were glad to get down to rest and sleep.

The following morning, November 10th, the battalion were off again as advance guard, and in full marching order covered a considerable distance to reach the small town of Beloeil, where it was intended that billets should be occupied for the night.

At Beloeil, the inhabitants gave the 7th a royal welcome, for no sooner

---
* 6th London History.

were the men in billets than the people came along and took all the men into their own houses for supper. Flags of all nations were flying from the windows. The inhabitants certainly showed their joy in being liberated after over four years of life under enemy occupation.

The town band was on duty; it was said their instruments had lain hidden throughout the war; this band, with every good intention, managed to " wheeze out," in very slow time, our National Anthem, and kept on playing it time after time.

After passing Beloeil the battalion marched on to Grosages and just as everyone had got nicely settled down, sudden orders came for another move. Sergts. Byron and Lydiart were about to enjoy a chicken which was being cooked for them by one of the inhabitants. Owing to the sudden orders they each had to be content with tearing off a leg of the chicken, grabbing a piece of bread and making tracks.

The move was not far, a matter of a few hundred yards to La Biderie, where fresh billets were taken over and two companies formed outposts at Grosages.

The following morning, Monday, November 11th, the men were on parade waiting for the 8th London to pass through, when Lieut. F. Glenton came running down the road to " A " Company with the great news that an armistice had been signed. The boys just gave a yell; their first reaction towards the news was to change their tin hats for soft caps.

Four men promptly disappeared for about five hours and were put " on the peg " when they returned.

Whilst everyone was greatly relieved that the fighting was over and began looking forward to a speedy return to " Blighty," it seemed too good to be true, perhaps an enemy trick.

Two days later the battalion returned to Beloeil, and on November 14th took part in a brigade Thanksgiving Service.

Parades and inspections filled in the time until November 18th, when the battalion marched to Peruwelz.

CHAPTER THIRTY-FIVE

PERUWELZ

THE story of the stay at Peruwelz could cover many pages, most of which would be devoted to the hospitality of the inhabitants.

Generally Peruwelz, bereft of machinery and artificial light, except military candles, has pleasant memories for most of the 7th. The mornings were devoted to education and training, as few guards as possible were mounted and fatigues were infrequent, occasional route marches were held, and on Sundays the battalion fell in for church parade.

It was here that the men of " C " Company subscribed for a gold watch, which was presented to C.Q.M.S. F. Heale for the personal consideration and kindness which he had shown to the men of the company. C.Q.M.S. F. Heale is described as being " a wonderful and popular quarter-bloke." In fact Lieut.-Col. Hosking once described his C.Q.M.S.'s as the best in the army.

Normally, work was over by midday and the afternoons were given over to sports, and in the evenings the " Goods " gave nightly concerts.

Football, inter-unit sports and cross-country runs were all the rage. A football match between " ours " and the 6th London, in the final of a competition, ended in a draw of two goals each.

Capts. H. C. Woolner, H. Symonds, Sergt. Goodman, M.M., and nine other ranks were dispatched to London to bring out the King's and Regimental Colours.

The sergeants held a dinner to celebrate several events, including :

> The Trouping of the Colours at Peruwelz, January 27th, 1919.
> The Amalgamation of the 1st and 2nd Battalions, February, 1918.
> The second anniversary of the landing of 2nd Battalion in France, January 27th, 1917.
> " 1918 "—A glorious climax to the magnificent record of the " Shiny Seventh " during 1915–16–17.

Maj. R. J. F. Danford Thomas turned up for this dinner. He had been in charge of Corps Reinforcements Camps, and the last note in his diary reads as follows :

> " On the whole I did my job behind the lines to the best of my ability and tried to make others as comfortable as I could. It was a great study of my fellow-men in all ranks.
> " Finis after four-and-a-half years. Thank God."

A torchlight tattoo was held, which proved a great success and was followed by singing and dancing, which lasted throughout the night. Writing of the tattoo, Pte. K. M. Wood records :

> "There was a considerable amount of daylight rehearsal under R.S.M. F. Payne, M.C. I actually took part in some, and on the eventful night there were a large number of lanterns of various hues and colours scrounged, and also a large number of poles, which had been immersed in pitch or tar, to the detriment of the person marching behind."

The inhabitants of Peruwelz presented the 174th Brigade with a Flag, and for the occasion of the presentation the battalion provided the Guard of Honour and a detachment.

In March, H.M. King George V, accompanied by H.R.H. The Prince of Wales, visited Peruwelz. The whole place was thronged and to the delight of everyone, the King passed through the waiting crowds on foot. At the Hotel de Ville came a spontaneous cheer that must have been heard for miles around.

R.S.M. F. Payne, M.C., records the following :

> "During this period, which was an unsettled one for the army overseas waiting to come home, I am certain that every officer, W.O., N.C.O. and man of the 7th was proud to have served with the battalion and to have helped to carry on the traditions of the Regiment."

A draft of some 200 of all ranks of the battalion left to join the 6th London Regiment, who formed a composite battalion from the 174th Brigade, for service with the Army of Occupation on the Rhine, and by this time quite a number had been demobilized.

Eventually, in June, the cadre returned from Leuze to London with the Colours, where they were met and welcomed by Col. E. Faux, C.M.G., V.D., and marched to Sun Street headquarters with Colours flying.

In conclusion of this chapter, herewith the final paragraph from the diary of Capt. K. O. Peppiatt, M.C. :

> "I'm afraid I must be written down as one of those who enjoyed the war. I loved the battalion and the life. The chief fascination to me was the men, most of them Cockneys—nearly always grousing and swearing when in billets, but amazingly cheerful and incredibly gallant in battle."

CHAPTER THIRTY-SIX

7th (Reserve) Battalion, The London Regt.

THE Reserve Battalion was formed in April, 1915, Maj. (subsequently Lieut.-Col.) Sir Pieter C. van B. Stewart-Bam from the 2/7th being appointed to command on formation and remaining in command throughout ; for his services he was awarded the O.B.E.

Maj. W. Mudford, T.D., was the first second-in-command, being succeeded by Maj. L. E. Peppiatt, who in turn was succeeded by Maj. J. Nicol, V.D.

The adjutants were successively Capts. L. E. Peppiatt, P. Ludbrook, and J. P. Scothorne. Capt. H. M. Ryland was quartermaster.

R.S.M. E. Cruwys, M.S.M., was appointed on formation and retained his appointment throughout. He was one of the original permanent staff instructors of the 1/7th, having been attached to them from the Coldstream Guards, and no one did more than he to make the Reserve Battalion an efficient and happy unit. After the war he became chairman of the Old Comrades' Association, a position he held until his death, which occurred in 1934. The regimental quartermaster-sergeant was R.Q.M.S. T. Middleton from the 2/7th, an old 3rd London sergeant. He performed splendid work throughout.

Lieut.-Col. Sir P. Stewart-Bam was a South African of Dutch descent. During the Boer War he served in the Cape Garrison Artillery and had come into close contact with officers of the 3rd London serving with the C.I.V.'s. He was an officer of outstanding energy and, owing in a large measure to a strenuous recruiting campaign which he carried out in London, the strength of the Reserve Battalion rapidly rose until it reached the figure of 1,800.

One of his most important contributions to the Regiment was the arrangement he made with the High Commissioners of the various Dominions, and with the full approval of the Director-General of the Territorial Force, whereby young men from the Dominions and Colonies, with the necessary qualifications, coming to England to serve in the Forces during the war, were commissioned in the 7th London.

In this manner the Regiment received officers of a high standard at a time when the normal channels for the training of officers were hard put to it to replace the casualties caused by the fighting in France. There were at times as many as 70 officers in training with the Reserve Battalion, and at one time no less than 37 from South Africa.

The duty of the Reserve Battalion was to train and despatch drafts to replace casualties in the 1/7th, 2/7th and other units overseas.

By July, 1916, nearly 80 officers and 3,300 men had been sent to the front and this number increased as the war proceeded. A great number of the officers served with distinction in the 1st and 2nd Battalions and in other regiments in France; and at home and in many parts of the Dominions to-day, men in leading positions are to be found who are proud to have served in the " Shiny Seventh " during the war. Drafts were also sent to the King's African Rifles, so that for the second time in the history of the Regiment, its representatives fought in Africa.

During a visit of South African delegates to the Reserve Battalion, Mr. Becker (Chief Government Whip of General Botha), after congratulating Sir P. Stewart-Bam, said: " The success of the ' Shiny Seventh,' with its Colonial officers, is the biggest lesson in the Empire which I have yet met with."

The battalion commenced its training at Sun Street headquarters, and in September, 1915, moved into a brewery at Orpington. In January, 1916, a move was made into a hutted camp at Fovant, and while here, the regimental badge of the 7th was carved in the chalk of the Downs, and still remains to this day, being cared for by the British Legion at Salisbury. A photograph of this carving to-day adorns the walls of the sergeants' mess at B.H.Q. of the 32nd Searchlight Regiment, R.A.

In July, 1916, sports were held at Sutton Mandeville, at which the 2/7th were guests. The late Lady Stewart-Bam presented prizes to the winners of the 24 events. The arrangements for the day were in the hands of Maj. W. Mudford, T.D., and 2nd Lieut. H. B. Smith. Among those acting as judges were Lieut.-Col. C. W. Berkeley, T.D., Maj. J. Nicol, V.D., Capt. H. M. Ryland, 2nd Lieuts. H. A. Brown, L. E. James, C. V. Hosken, C. Cartwright, R.S.M. E. Cruwys, and C.S.M.'s G. Lehrs, J. Hawes, and A. Hounsell. Sideshows were under the direction of R.Q.M.S. T. Middleton.

January, 1917, found the battalion in billets at Dartmouth, where the friendliest relations were established with the R.N. College and with the residents, the mayor being particularly active in plans for entertaining the troops and making their training at Dartmouth as pleasant as possible.

While here, the second anniversary of the formation of the Reserve Battalion was celebrated by a Sports Day, arrangements being in charge of 2nd Lieut. R. W. Thomas. The regimental silver band performed under Bandmaster H. W. Crane, and sideshows were again in the charge of R.Q.M.S. T. Middleton.

The battalion made a further move in March, 1917, to a hutted camp at Blackdown, Aldershot, where they remained until demobilization.

CHAPTER THIRTY-SEVEN

1914–1918

EPILOGUE

THE total enlistments to the Regiment during 1914–18 were 8,631 all ranks. It is recorded with proud regret that 88 officers and 1,430 other ranks made the supreme sacrifice. Nine of our men died in captivity.

A number were taken prisoner and for the benefit of these a Prisoners of War Committee was formed with Col. E. C. Stevenson as chairman and Capt. Prince as secretary, while Mrs. Salkeld Green acted as treasurer for about six months until her health made it necessary for her to give up the work.

Subsequently when it became necessary for the secretary to devote whole time to the work, Mrs. Peppiatt became honorary secretary and treasurer with the assistance of Miss Sutton. The packing department was under Mrs. Davis, with the assistance of Mrs. Salkeld Green after she ceased to be treasurer.

A number of the wives and mothers of officers in the Regiment worked during the whole time in the packing room. The committee was given invaluable help by Sergt. Farmer—whom many will recall as caretaker at headquarters.

Between December 1915 and November 1918 this committee dispatched over 20,000 food parcels and other comforts to 7th London officers, N.C.O.'s and men at a cost of over £11,000.

Both the prisoners and the Regiment as a whole were deeply grateful to the ladies who so unselfishly gave up so much of their time to do this work.

For many years prior to the 1914–18 war the well-known tune " Austria " had always been played as the Regimental March, but in 1914, as the tune was the same as " Deutschland uber alles," the tune of " My Lady Greensleeves," which had been in use for some years as a second Regimental March tune, was adopted. The earliest mention of this tune which has already been credited to the Train Bands when it was played in slow time, is 1580 in the register of the Stationers' Company. The music played in quick time by the Regimental drum and fife band was inspiring and became well-known to the many thousands that passed through the Regiment.

Shakespeare, in the " Merry Wives of Windsor " twice mentions the tune, Act II, Scene I, Mrs. Ford : " But they do no more than adhere and keep pace together than the hundredth psalm, to the tune of Green

Sleeves." Act v, Scene v, Falstaff: "Let the sky rain potatoes, let it thunder to the tune of Green Sleeves."

When the 1st Battalion was out of the line in Flanders the drums used to beat " Retreat " and the programme always finished with :

  1. " Greensleeves."   2. " The Marseillaise " (in France) or " Brabanconne " (in Belgium).   3. "God Save the King."   4. " Abide With Me."

During the command of the Regiment by Lieut.-Col. C. J. Salkeld Green, D.S.O., M.C., T.D., it was customary at any presentation of medal ribbons for gallantry to play the first few bars of " Greensleeves " as the medal ribbon was pinned on the recipient in recognition of the fact that the award was an honour to the Regiment as well as to the winner.

In recent years the British Broadcasting Corporation have frequently included " Greensleeves " in their programme, the most used version being one by Vaughan Williams, as used in his opera " Sir John in Love." The song is published separately by the Oxford University Press and two popular recordings are one by the Jacques String Orchestra on Columbia D.X.825, and by the Queen's Hall Orchestra on Decca K.222. Long live " Greensleeves."

The discipline of the 7th was well to the fore when a troopship was torpedoed in the Mediterranean in December, 1917. The boat was rapidly sinking, but along with other drafts the 7th men fell in on deck as steadily as if on parade, and as the boat went down they sang " My home in Kentucky."

Regarding this the officer in charge wrote the battalion as follows: " I particularly wish to state that the discipline amongst the men was beyond all praise and well worthy of being noted in the records of the battalion." Six members of the 7th draft were lost in this disaster.

CHAPTER THIRTY-EIGHT

1920–1935

POST-WAR ACTIVITIES

IN 1920 the Regiment was reformed and came under the command of Lieut.-Col. C. E. Johnston, D.S.O., M.C., and an outstanding event of this year was the presentation of the 1914–15 Star by Maj.-Gen. Sir C. Pereira, K.C.B., C.M.G., to members of the Regiment

At this time the following officers held appointments:

Maj. L. E. Peppiatt, M.C., was second-in-command
Lieut. R. J. Hunt was signalling officer

" A " Company	" B " Company
Maj. K. O. Peppiatt, M.C.	Capt. H. G. Head
Capt. G. B. Slater	Capt. J. Chatterton, M.C.
Lieut. J. F. Preston, M.C.	Lieut. S. J. King
Lieut. A. E. Clarke	Lieut. P. L. Smout, M.C.

" C " Company	" D " Company
Capt. P. Ludbrook	Capt. P. B. Berliner, M.C.
Capt. E. Vaus	Capt. L. E. Bishop, M.C.
Lieut. J. Pryer	Lieut. H. R. Gibb
Lieut. J. B. White, M.C.	Lieut. C. F. Rofe

Officers at that time who were not appointed were Lieuts. A. E. Hope, A. G. Coulson, A. C. Robinson, and G. H. G. Ross.

During the war the battalion had, in 1916, become affiliated to the Middlesex Regiment, who provided the adjutant and permanent staff of the reformed battalion. This corrected the position of a line unit being affiliated to a rifle regiment. Although in the past affiliated to the K.R.R. Corps, the Regiment had always been a line unit and brass buttons adorned the uniform throughout and not the black buttons customary to a rifle unit.

This, no doubt, is the real reason for the nickname " Shiny Seventh "; there are many versions as to the origination of this title, but when the Regiment was brigaded with three rifle regiments, who all wore the black buttons, the 7th were the only regiment in the brigade with brass buttons, hence " Shiny Seventh."

On November 12th, 1920, the London Troops Memorial at the Royal Exchange was unveiled by H.R.H. Duke of York, K.G., on behalf of H.R.H. the Duke of Gloucester, K.G., K.T., K.P.

In 1921 Princess Mary presented Colours to the battalion on the Horse Guards parade ground. These were received by Maj. L. E. Peppiatt, M.C., and were deposited at the Guildhall, where they remain to this day.

In 1922 the 7th London was amalgamated with the 8th City of London (Post Office Rifles) and Lieut.-Col. J. Stewart, D.S.O., took over command of the Regiment.

The 8th London was originally raised from the employees of the General Post Office who had acted as special constables during the Fenian troubles of 1868. Previous to becoming the 8th City of London they were known as the 24th Middlesex Rifle Volunteers. In 1882 the unit proceeded overseas with the Egyptian Expeditionary Force and operated the entire postal services, earning the battle honour " Egypt 1882," the first overseas battle honour to be conferred on a non-regular unit.

Recruiting became brisk and the Regiment stood first in the order of strength of infantry units in the 56th (1st London) Division, T.A. Later on recruits had to go on a waiting list.

In 1924 Felixstowe was visited for camp, and Aldershot or Shorncliffe seems to have been the popular choice for camps between 1925 and 1929.

The Osborne Cup which was competed for throughout the division for the best M.G. platoon was won five years in succession by Capt. R. J. Hunt's platoon and he received the congratulations of the G.O.C. of the 56th Division.

Sport was now taking a major part in the unit and there were regular football and billiards fixtures and a boxing champion was produced in 1923, when Pte. Scot of " B " Company won the bantam-weight championship of the 56th Division, and he again brought credit to the Regiment when, in 1925, he won the T.A. fly-weight championship at Cardiff.

In 1924 Lieut.-Col. and Bt.-Col. W. Bernard Vince, D.S.O., O.B.E., M.C., took over command from Lieut.-Col. J. Stewart, D.S.O.

Lieut.-Col. Vince in his Christmas greetings, asked all members " to make the battalion worthy of the traditions of the past years and above all, worthy of our comrades of the Great War."

Prize distributions were again instituted and in 1925 the Guildhall, so well known to the older members for these events, was again the scene of enthusiasm which always goes with prize distributions.

During annual training in 1928 the battalion met with great success, winning the Divisional Transport Cup, Inter-Unit Relay Race, and Territorial Swimming Championship. The following year more credit came to the battalion when Pte. Lazarus won the bantam-weight championship. C.S.M. Lee had the distinction of winning the Grannard

Challenge Cup, the Du Platt Taylor Cup, and the W.O.'s and Sergeants' Cup.

The twenty-first anniversary of the Territorial Association was celebrated in 1929 and H.M. the King sent the battalion a letter of congratulation.

Sir W. Waterlow, K.B.E., J.P., took the salute in 1929 upon the occasion of a Regimental Church Parade when the service was conducted by the Rev. Smissen, M.C., M.B.E., C.F., T.A.

Falmer was the scene of camp in 1931 after an Easter camp at Colchester; this year the prizes were distributed by Gen. Sir Hubert de la Poer Gough, G.C.M.G., K.C.B., K.C.V.O.

The Regimental drums had the honour of being engaged in 1931 and 1932 at the Royal Military Tournament.

The flourishing state of the Regiment at this time was no doubt largely due to the additional interest shown by the C.O., Bt.-Col. E. E. F. Baker, D.S.O., M.C., who took over the command of the Regiment in 1931. Bt.-Col. Baker, who was in the summer of 1914 representing his Public School, had shot for the Ashburton Shield and won the Spencer Cup; won the M.C. in 1917, and in 1918 a bar to his M.C. During the latter part of the war he commanded the 2nd Middlesex Regiment; early on he had a narrow escape at Neuve Chapelle when he was wounded by a bullet which passed through the peak of his cap at the front and emerged from the side.

He played a large part in the capture of Douai and assisted in the supervision of hoisting the Union Jack and the French National Flag over the Hotel de Ville. In 1919 he was the recipient of the D.S.O. In 1935 he received the Territorial Decoration and in 1938 was made a C.B.E. The County of Middlesex honoured him in 1938 by making him a Deputy Lieutenant; the following year he attained the rank of brigadier and in 1941 had the honour of being made A.D.C. to H.M. the King.

Great attention in the Regiment was again being paid to shooting and among the stars of this period were Sergts. Ellis and Delaney; among the prizewinners of the Old Comrades were Messrs. J. Shepherd, B. Hooper, and W. Lennard.

In 1932 the Maj. H. D. Barnes prize was won by Sergt. Summers and Ptes. Payne and Powell. Capt. L. S. Davis, O.C. of " A " (M.G.) Company, had the honour of winning the Battalion Challenge Cup, the Lord Napier Cup, Miniature Range Cup and Curtis Cup which were presented at the prize distribution by the Hon. Colonel of the Regiment, Brig.-Gen. Sir A. Maxwell, C.M.G., D.S.O., T.D., who had the previous year inspected the Regiment while in camp.

On the sporting side the unit was as strong as ever and the Postmaster-General, The Right Hon. Sir H. Kingsley Wood, presented a boxing ring to the Regiment.

The boxing team won nine out of fifteen fights against the 2nd Battalion Devon Regiment, and against the 12th London scored fourteen points against seven.

In the shooting results of 1933 the names of Joel, Merlini and Shepherd appear as winners for the Old Comrades. Sergt. Ellis had the highest aggregate, Sergt. Delaney was the best shot of the Regiment, and Bt.-Col. E. Baker the best shot of the officers.

Upon the occasion of the opening of Faraday House by the Lord Mayor in the company of H.R.H. the Prince of Wales, the Regiment had the privilege of providing a Guard of Honour.

The Regiment suffered the loss of a former commanding officer in 1931 when Lt.-Col. J. Stewart, D.S.O., passed away and four years later received another blow, by the death of its Hon. Colonel, Brig.-Gen. Sir A. Maxwell, K.C.B., C.M.G., D.S.O., T.D., after holding that office for 12 years. He was succeeded by Col. J. Trevor. who prior to the South African War had served in the London Rifle Brigade. Too old for service in the First World War, Col. Trevor took an active part in the National Guard. During the Second World War he created and commanded the 10th Battalion of the Home Guard.

A keen supporter of the Territorial Army, Col. Trevor has devoted much of his time to recruiting suitable individuals for the Territorials, his good work in this direction having been acknowledged by the War Office.

Upon the occasion of the opening ceremony in 1934 of the reconstructed Sorting Office, Mount Pleasant, by H.R.H. the Duke of York, in company with the Duchess, the Guard of Honour was furnished by the Regiment.

In 1935 Sergt. Ellis received the congratulations of the G.O.C. for his individual success during the Bisley meeting. G. Addison took the Old Comrades prize which this year, together with the Regimental prizes, was presented by Maj.-Gen. P. R. C. Cummings, C.B., C.M.G., D.S.O.

CHAPTER THIRTY-NINE

1935–1939
FURTHER REORGANISATION
BY LIEUT.-COL. L. S. DAVIS, T.D.

GREAT and far-reaching changes took place throughout the whole of the Territorial Army in 1935 and the following years. The effect was soon felt by the battalion and the infantry role so long held was abandoned for that of A.A. employment to meet the changing needs of national defence. The title of the battalion was altered in 1936 to 32nd (7th City of London) A.A. Battalion, R.E., T.A., and in the early part of the year Bt.-Col. E. E. Baker, D.S.O., M.C., handed over command to Bt.-Col. H. G. Murgatroyd, M.C., T.D. Other notable changes were that all privates became sappers: the red sashes worn by warrant officers and sergeants disappeared and Royal Engineer buttons, badges and shoulder titles replaced those of the 7th City of London. This conversion was accepted with the feeling that the demands of the times made such a change of arm imperative and, if the infantry role was relinquished with regret, it was with the determination to strive to add laurels in the new sphere.

The plan for the A.A. defence of the capital necessitated considerable reorganisation. A larger recruiting area was also desirable and during the latter part of 1936 the battalion moved to fresh headquarters.

The new headquarters were at Grove Park, Lewisham, and with Battalion H.Q. were 329 and 330 Companies. 328 Company remained at the old Sun Street headquarters and a new 331 Company was raised with headquarters in Bexley Heath. Whilst the new H.Q. was being built the new companies used an adjacent house and grounds, No. 255, Baring Road. The headquarters at Grove Park were named Napier House in memory of the former Hon. Colonel. The Lord Mayor of London performed the opening ceremony on January 20th, 1939, in the presence of a distinguished gathering. In company with a detachment of serving members forming a Colour party bearing the King's Colour and the Regimental Colour, a party composed of Old Comrades, with their standard, formed the Guard of Honour on this memorable occasion. After the opening ceremony by the Lord Mayor, a pageant of seven episodes depicting the history of the Regiment since its early days was presented by Lieut. A. E. F. Barnes and this was followed by an All Ranks Ball.

At the Jubilee of Their Majesties King George V and Queen Mary the Regiment lined the route for the drive to St. Paul's. The section allocated to the Regiment was Ludgate Hill. The Colours were carried on this occasion and once again the Regiment was paraded within the City for duty on a notable occasion.

In 1936, on the passing of King George V, the Regiment provided a party to line the route taken by the cortege. The party, under the command of Capt. L. S. Davis, was stationed in Oxford and Cambridge Terrace near Paddington Station.

The annual camp in this year took place at Mytchett, near Aldershot, the first camp in the new role of searchlights. The equipment used was of an early pattern, but the customary fortnight saw much useful work accomplished and the Regiment returned on the conclusion of the training with a greater appreciation of the requirements of the new task.

In 1937 efforts were made to recruit the greater numbers required to fill the establishment of the Regiment in its new role and during this year the strength of the Regiment was doubled.

A noteworthy event was the presence of the Regiment on the occasion of the Coronation of Their Majesties King George VI and Queen Elizabeth. A detachment was provided to march in the Coronation procession and the remainder of the Regiment lined the route in Northumberland Avenue.

In July the Regiment proceeded to a camp at Ingrave, Essex. The deployment in this area was governed by the possible war deployment which the Regiment might be called upon to take up if the need arose. Modern equipment was then becoming available and by the end of the annual training the new role of the Regiment was being fast assimilated by all ranks.

The annual camp of 1938 took place at Orsett, Essex, an area very near the camp of the previous year.

The Munich crisis in September resulted in the embodiment of the Regiment, which proceeded to its war stations on the north bank of the Thames, and it was deployed over an area from Shoeburyness to Canvey Island with headquarters near Purfleet.

The Munich deployment was of short duration and the Regiment returned to the drill halls with the benefit of the experience gained in the move to war stations.

By the year 1939 the Regiment had reached a state of training and preparedness for mobilization which provided confidence that if the war clouds, which were gathering so rapidly throughout Europe, should result in a conflict then the Regiment would be ready for whatever tasks might be allotted to it.

In April of this year 331 Company was severed from the Regiment and was regimented with another searchlight unit. With the fast deterioration of international relations the policy of siting anti-aircraft defences of the country at their war stations was begun. This commenced in June and resulted in the companies of the Regiment proceeding in turn to an area covering Laindon, Southend-on-Sea, and adjoining parts of Essex.

330 Company commenced the deployment and 328 Company followed in July. The final company of the Regiment, 329 Company, took station during August, and in the middle of this month the war deployment area of the Regiment was altered to comprise most of the County of Suffolk. A reconnaissance was made to form the basis of the fresh mobilization scheme and the equipment for the Regiment was placed in readiness at Hadleigh Mobilization Store. On August 24th the Regiment was again embodied for service and proceeded throughout the night to the new war stations in Suffolk.

Within a few days the Second World War broke out in Europe.

CHAPTER FORTY

1939–1945

SECOND WORLD WAR

BY LIEUT.-COL. L. S. DAVIS, T.D.

THE battalion commenced its deployment with Battalion H.Q. at Framlingham, Suffolk, and the companies deployed in areas around that headquarters with 328 Company at Bildeston, 329 Company at Framlingham and 330 Company at Saxmundham.

Lieut.-Col. L. F. S. Dawes, M.B.E., relinquished command of the Regiment on his return to an important post in the War Office and Maj. S. N. Beall was appointed to command.

The first months of the war were generally quiet and, apart from slight enemy reconnaissance over the battalion area, there was little activity. The first Christmas was spent in unaccustomed conditions, but all ranks made merry, despite the severe weather.

On April 11th, 1940, Lieut.-Col. C. J. Woolley, M.C., took over command from Lieut.-Col. S. N. Beall.

The equipment of the battalion comprised modern 90 cm. searchlight projectors with sound locators mainly of an early pattern. On the night of 7/8th June, 1940, the battalion scored its initial distinction by being the first searchlight unit to bring down an enemy plane on British soil. A Heinkel 115 on reconnaissance came over the east coast near Aldeburgh: it was illuminated by a detachment at Rendlesham, with the result that the pilot and crew, dazzled by the beam, lost control and the aircraft crashed near the site.

A notable success was scored on the night 18/19th June, 1940, when a strong raid by enemy aircraft crossed the coast at Harwich and flying towards London, flew through the battalion area. Spitfires from day squadrons took off to intercept. Many illuminated targets were presented and the pilots, unassisted by scientific means of detection, shot down seven of the raiders. This successful engagement proved the value of searchlights in co-operation with night-fighter aircraft as a means of harrying and destroying the night raiders.

A contemporary writer has written of this night's action:

> " It was on the night of June 18th, 1940, a clear sparkling night with everything illuminated brightly by a moon almost at the full, when the enemy sent about 30 bombers at intervals up the Thames estuary. They began to drop their bombs and dozens of searchlights swept the skies and held them in their beams as the guns

started to boom out. The bombing continued and for some time the pilots on Squadron-Leader Malan's station watched the searchlights picking up and holding the Germans. As they watched the enemy bombers coming over, they chafed to get into their Spitfires to attack, but the area was so heavily defended by guns that it was considered inadvisable for any pilots to fly there. Conditions were so ideal for attacking the raiders from the air, however, that permission was granted to send up one aircraft and Squadron-Leader Malan was selected as the pilot.

"According to an eyewitness he called for his fitter and rigger, who happened to have turned in for the night. Without waiting to dress, they pushed their feet into gum-boots, slung their rifles over their shoulders, put on their tin hats and reported for duty in their striped pyjamas. No one seemed to take much notice of their incongruous appearance. More vital things claimed their attention. Along with the squadron-leader they were rushed out to the aircraft dispersal post.

"While the rigger and fitter worked swiftly to start up the Spitfire, the pilot methodically buckled on the harness of the parachute. By the time he had got his gear on, the engine had started, so he climbed into the cockpit and strapped himself in before opening up the throttle to warm the engine up a bit.

"Meanwhile he looked up and tried to pick out a target ahead and saw a Heinkel 111 at 6,000 ft. being held by the searchlights. It was making a straight run directly across him. A second glance at the approaching bomber made him decide that discretion was the better part of valour and that the engine was quite capable of warming itself up. Leaping out of the cockpit with his parachute on, he made a dive for a little trench close at hand. When the Heinkel had passed over, he got in and cracked off and made straight for the same Heinkel, which was obviously blinded by the searchlights. Heading for the coast and climbing quickly, he intercepted it just as it was on a slow climb crossing the coast. The beams of the searchlights made things very deceptive. The first thing he knew he was about 50 yds. from it. One moment it looked like a moth in a candle flame, the next the wings suddenly took shape and he realised he was very close.

"He gave signs to the guns to stop firing directly he was in a position to attack, and they at once stopped firing—the whole thing worked like a charm—and in he went. He pressed the trigger, but after a three-second burst he had to jam his stick forward to avoid colliding with the enemy. In this short time his screen was covered with oil from the bomber, which spiralled out of the searchlights and soon crashed on the beach, half in and half out of the water.

"As the South African pilot returned to his base he looked back and saw another Heinkel 111 held by the searchlights. Climbing in a spiral below the enemy he signalled the guns to hold off. Then he moved in to attack at 16,000 ft. This time he was a lot more cautious, and determined not to overrun the enemy, so he opened fire at 200 yds. and closed to 100 yds. As he passed, the Heinkel burst into flames and a parachute became entangled near the tail. Then the enemy aircraft went down in a steep spiral well on fire. The pilot of the Spitfire saw it crash in a vicar's garden near Chelmsford with a terrific sheet of flame that was seen all the way from Southend.

"So Squadron-Leader Malan, in 20 minutes, brought down two of the enemy bombers out of the seven destroyed by British fighters that night. The following night three more of the enemy bombers were shot down by British fighters and directly the German bombers learned that the fighters were up they began to turn off to sea. The losses suffered by the Germans on these occasions curtailed their night attacks for some time."*

From June 1940 the tempo of the war rapidly increased, and the battalion saw much action on the northern fringe of the Battle of Britain which was in the main fought out to a successful conclusion in the skies above Kent and Essex.

On June 8th, 328 Company moved to headquarters at Friars Hall, Hadleigh. The new headquarters replaced the early and scattered accommodation previously occupied at Bidleston.

The Regiment was transferred from 41st A.A. Brigade to 6th A.A. Brigade on July 4th; it still remained in 2nd A.A. Division for a short time but within a few weeks was transferred to 6th A.A. Division.

With the advent of September the major night-bombing attacks upon the country commenced, and anti-aircraft units in Suffolk saw much action as on many nights enemy aircraft proceeded to attack London and the Midlands. Long hours of duty were usual, and all ranks strove to assist in destroying the enemy. Successes were gained and at last the enemy retired temporarily to reorganise for a resumption of the attacks.

Co-operation between Royal Air Force night fighter squadrons and searchlight units was rapidly becoming closer as it became increasingly

---

* Reproduced by special permission of David Masters from his book "So Few." Copyright strictly reserved.

328 SEARCHLIGHT BATTERY H.Q. STAFF, 1944

LT.-COL. L. S. DAVIS T.D.

COL. J. TREVOR

apparent that, until the scientific measures then pending were perfected, fighter aircraft at night were wholly dependent on searchlights to indicate and illuminate the enemy aircraft which they were endeavouring to intercept.

The value of the Territorial Army system by which many fresh units could be formed quickly from existing ones was strikingly demonstrated in the months of 1940 commencing in May. The urgent need for new units could best be met by the selection of trained cadres to form the basis of the new units; three cadres were provided from the Regiment to form new searchlight companies. The many demands for man-power were met by reinforcements of men called to the Colours. At first all companies trained their reinforcements, but with the arrival of approximately 400 recruits, a Regimental Training Centre was established at Brandeston Hall, Suffolk. The recruits arrived on September 15th, 1940, and received six weeks' initial training and were posted at the conclusion to the three batteries.

On November 2nd, 1940, the Regimental Training Centre was closed down, its task completed, and Regimental H.Q., at that time situated at Monewden Hall, was transferred to Brandeston Hall and 329 Battery remained on at the former hall. The move of Regimental H.Q. was followed on November 6th by a re-deployment of the batteries: 328 Battery moved from Friars Hall to Monewden Hall, 329 to Carlton Hall, Saxmundham, and 330 from Saxmundham to Friars Hall at Hadleigh.

Improved scientific sound location methods had supplanted the aural methods which had been used for some time, but they could not keep pace with the improvement in general design of aircraft. For some time it had become increasingly apparent that the improvements in aircraft necessitated essential improvements in methods of anti-aircraft defence and in April of 1941 radiolocation, adapted to the requirements of searchlight equipment, made its appearance. In the later months of the year quantities of the new equipment fitted with Radar began to be received by the battalion. The efficiency of the equipment was soon appreciated by the detachments which were operating these sets. The difficulties of sound location in relation to fast-bombing aircraft were gone; science had provided an answer by immediate detection. The battalion commenced to train hard to master the new technique of operating the equipment.

During the year there had been internal changes in the deployment of the battalion, but it remained in Suffolk. In August a further change took place by transfer from Royal Engineers to the Royal Artillery; this change was introduced to facilitate the administration of all anti-aircraft units by placing them all in one corps.

As spring approached, the expected invasion gave all ranks a great deal of work in preparing to meet it. It appeared highly probable at that time that the effort which was expected in the previous September would be made in the coming spring. The Regiment was holding a particularly vulnerable part of the coast extending from south of Lowestoft to Southwold and there was every reason to expect that, should the anticipated attack be made, at least part of the effort would fall upon part of the coast line held by the Regiment. The expectation of the Regiment that it might be engaged within a comparatively short time in defending its native soil lent enthusiasm and impetus to the preparatory work. The attack upon Russia which was made in the middle of the year altered the situation, but it was not until some time later that the possibility of invasion finally became improbable.

On December 12th, 1940, Maj. E. A. Parr-Dudley, the Regimental second-in-command, was posted to command a light-aircraft regiment, and Maj. L. S. Davis was appointed second-in-command. Capt. A. E. F. Barnes was promoted to command 328 Battery. It was fitting indeed that Maj. H. D. Barnes' son should attain field rank to comman the original Sun Street company. Within a few months Lieut.-C C. J. Woolley, M.C., gave up command of the Regiment on his promotion to full colonel in command of the Gun Operations Room at Malta. On August 28th, 1941, Maj. L. S. Davis was appointed to command the Regiment; this further promotion of an officer who commenced his commissioned service with the Regiment came within 16 years of his posting as 2nd Lieut. to " B " Company of the battalion in July 1926.

It was in this year that the Regimental flash was introduced for wear by all ranks. The flash was $1\frac{1}{2}$ in. square and in Regimental colours of scarlet and buff on a black background; the 7th grenade in gold was superimposed on this background. This visible link with the old insignia of the Regiment was immediately popular with all ranks; it served to remind them of the past traditions of the Regiment, add to the already strong *esprit de corps,* and act as an encouragement to enhance the traditions of which all were proud and also as an incentive to add further laurels to those won in earlier days.

Long periods of routine duties were interrupted at times by action when the keenly awaited raiders came within range. On the nights 12/13th and 14/15th May two Heinkel 111's were engaged with light automatic fire by sites DNO54 and DNO6 and claims for their probable destruction were admitted.

On July 2nd, 1941, a new battery, 562, joined the Regiment. It had been formed from a cadre provided by the Regiment, to which had been added the war establishment of men called to the Colours in 1941.

The battery was posted to the Regiment and proceeded to Brettenham Hall, near Hadleigh, to undergo training. On completion of the training period the battery moved to operational deployment and took station in the Hadleigh area. The men had come from a young class and were in the main aged 20.

Throughout 1941 the production models of Radar equipped searchlights were being received: these were 90 cm. projectors. This caused considerable re-deployment, as the needs of the scientific weapon required siting in localities that would produce the best Radar results. During the latter half of 1941 the Regiment worked hard in changing the location of the searchlight detachments and perfecting its personnel in the new technique. Day raiders had become more common and sites were often engaging the enemy by day, sometimes with success.

Early in 1942 the Regiment extended its deployment to the south and part of Essex came under operational command. 328 Battery moved from Monewden Hall to new headquarters at Felix School, Felixstowe, whilst 330 Battery moved from Hadleigh to Lawford Place, Manningtree. The area covered by the former battery was Felixstowe-Bawdsley-Ipswich, whilst 330 Battery covered Shotley Naval Training Establishment, Harwich Naval Base, and south to Frinton and Brightlingsea.

562 Battery also moved to an area including Colchester and Marks Tey and to a point a few miles north of Chelmsford. They extended to the coast from Brightlingsea and Mersea Island. 329 Battery remained in the old area and covered the coast from Aldeburgh to Southwold.

This re-deployment necessitated a change in sector control. Previously all batteries had been working through Debden Operations Room but this was changed to place 328, 330 and 562 Batteries under North Weald Operations Room, leaving 329 Battery remaining under Debden Control.

In January 1942 the 562 Battery Commander, Maj. W. Gartell, left the battery on posting to another command and his place was taken by Maj. C. W. Cronin, T.D.

It soon became apparent that re-deployment of batteries to a point farther south necessitated a change of Regimental H.Q. and, in September, Brandeston Hall was vacated and Regimental H.Q. moved to Manningtree where it was sited in a property known as "Aldhams."

Part of the commitments of 328 Battery were a group of searchlights at Martlesham known as a "Canopy." The object of these lights was to form a circular deployment round the airfield and to assist in homing aircraft by forming a cone of searchlights over the aerodrome. This was part of a bigger scheme by which searchlights on receipt of certain signals, or on the initiative of detachment commanders when aircraft in distress were detected, were to indicate the way to the nearest airfield. Pilots were thus enabled to fly in the direction indicated by the searchlight beam and sight the cone of searchlight units over the airfield. Throughout the war a great number of aircraft were successfully homed and the crews saved by this method. It was one of the many tasks carried out by searchlights and cordial recognition was paid by the Royal Air Force for the value they obtained from this service. This canopy maintained by 328 Battery continued until the 8th American Army Air Force took over Martlesham as one of the many airfields they occupied throughout the Eastern Counties and by that time the big airfield at Woodbridge, which had been constructed partially for the purpose of homing aircraft in distress, was in operation. The only other "Canopy" which the Regiment operated was the one at Wattisham airfield which operated during April, May and June 1941.

Improvements in equipment were constantly being made and the 90 cm. projectors were giving way to the larger 150 cm. searchlights. This equipment had the advantage of a longer and more intense beam. The battle of aircraft and anti-aircraft was constantly in progress; raiders flew higher and at 25,000 ft. they attempted to elude the defences, but scientific detection was advancing faster than improvements in aircraft. The best phase of the war for searchlights was commencing: night-fighter aircraft were equipped with Radar to enable them to proceed to illuminated targets or targets indicated by intersections of beams provided by Radar equipped searchlights and the pilots knew that if they proceeded to investigate such targets, with the assistance of their own detection methods, successful interception should take place.

Mutual confidence between the Royal Air Force and searchlight crews increased and aircraft crews knew that if the ground controlled interceptions were not made over the sea, then searchlights would pick up raiders as they crossed the coast and illuminate them throughout the searchlight belts, and there was a strong chance of successful combat.

The day-flying Spitfires used by night in the early part of the war, together with the night-flying Hurricanes then used, gave way to the fast twin-engined heavily armed night fighter, the Beaufighter, and this aircraft, which successfully carried on the battle, was soon to be superseded by the Mosquito

The success of searchlights was dependent upon close co-operation with night-fighter squadrons. The squadrons with which the Regiment mainly co-operated was 85 Squadron, equipped with Havocs and afterwards with Mosquitos commanded by Wing-Commander Rafael, D.S.O., D.F.C., 29 Squadron equipped with Mosquitos, commanded by Wing-

Commander Mack, D.F.C., and afterwards by Wing-Commander Arbon, D.F.C., and 488 Squadron.

85 Squadron operated from Hunsdon airfield, whilst the other two units operated from Bradwell Bay. The majority of the close co-operation was with these squadrons, but other squadrons of the Royal Air Force were operational in the Regimental area throughout.

In 1943 there was much movement throughout Anti-Aircraft Command of searchlight units, necessitated by the saving of man-power, as the building up and training of the armies for the coming invasion of the Continent increased in effort. The Regiment still remained deployed in the same area and the enemy continued his attacks, but the sustained attempts of the earlier years were giving way to more isolated phases. Notable efforts by the enemy were low-level attacks by fighter aircraft mainly directed against the south coast towns. Minor efforts were made against the east coast and the Regiment obtained successes in engagements. The big re-deployment of anti-aircraft artillery resulted in complete success against this effort and the Germans gave up the attempt as their losses were too high to be sustained. A further phase was the attacks at night by F.W.190's flying at a high altitude and carrying a single bomb. These fast aircraft were difficult to combat, but this phase passed as the enemy found that the effort was non-productive of results.

Throughout 1943, so far as the Regimental areas were concerned, the enemy's efforts were disappointing, and it began to appear that the German Air Force was faltering in its efforts and that really strong concentrated efforts were lacking.

By comparison with the mighty efforts which were then commencing to be delivered by the Royal Air Force in Germany the attacks by the German Air Force were insignificant, but throughout the year the Regiment were at their posts dealing with the spasmodic attempts by the enemy.

May of this year provided a month with typical operational actions in which the Regiment were engaged. On the night of the 13/14th, between 01.40 and 03.50 hours, scattered raids took place over East Anglia with Chelmsford as the main target. The enemy aircraft flew at varying heights and took violent evasive action when engaged by searchlights. The aircraft engaged were mainly Do.217 and Ju.88's Some enemy aircraft flew very low and appeared to act as decoys; these aircraft were engaged by a number of sites with light automatic and twin Vickers fire. NWO515 and NWO543 engaged an enemy aircraft with searchlights with the result that the light anti-aircraft site at Bawdsey were able to shoot it down. The enemy dropped bombs at scattered places in country districts, undoubtedly due to the harrying effect of the defences.

This raid was followed by another attack on the night of the 15th. At 21.30 hours 20 F.W.190 and Me.109's made scattered raids on the Southwold and Felixstowe coasts. Raiders flying very low dropped bombs which caused damage and casualties in both towns. NWO515 engaged an Me.109 with twin Vickers fire; this aircraft was destroyed and a Category 1 claim shared by 328 Battery with 426 and 427 Light A.A. Batteries. A further attack took place on the 30th; NWO422 and NWO423 engaged the enemy with fire and two claims were allowed in co-operation with L.A.A.

The Regiment had often to wait a long time for opportunities to engage the enemy but it unfailingly seized every occasion when the enemy came within range.

In the latter half of 1943 562 Battery moved from Marks Tey back to the former headquarters at Friars Hall, Hadleigh.

During the summer of this year two members of the Regiment were awarded the British Empire Medal for their successful efforts in rescuing an American pilot whose aircraft crashed near the searchlight site at Brampton. The aircraft had force-landed, turned completely over and burst into flames. Amongst exploding ammunition and flames the searchlight detachment endeavoured to release the pilot, who was injured and helpless inside the machine. They were successful in doing so and were undoubtedly instrumental in saving the pilot's life.

These incidents were of frequent occurrence throughout the Regiment, as it carried out the tasks allotted to it as part of the anti-aircraft defences.

Early in 1944 562 Battery, which had served so well and enthusiastically since it joined the Regiment in 1941, was withdrawn for disbandment and the reposting of personnel to infantry units. The men were well suited for this change of employment and in January the battery left the Regiment.

The Regiment were operationally busy during January, February and March and amongst other activities the following actions took place:

21st/22nd January. Forty to 50 aircraft operated over S. and S.E. England. Enemy aircraft used technical devices to foil the defences but searchlights were only partially hampered. R.A.F. fighters went directly for enemy aircraft in searchlight beams; this was an opportunity for which searchlights had been waiting and the results were very satisfactory to both the R.A.F. and the Army. In a later phase commencing at 04.16 hours a further 40 aircraft crossed the coast in bad weather; 11 aircraft crossed the Regimental areas at heights from 10,000 to 18,000 ft. A total of 16 aircraft were shot down during the night.

13/14th February. Thirty-five to 40 enemy aircraft, with Harwich and London as objectives, made landfall between Southwold and Deal. Weather was favourable for searchlight work and results were good in spite of enemy efforts to jam the defences. The following types of aircraft were recognised in searchlight beams—Do.217, Me.410 and Ju.88. At 21.50 hours one aircraft was picked up north of Ipswich and carried from NWO5 and NWO6 areas, illuminated and recognised as a Ju.88; a fighter on orbit saw this plane held in seven beams and shot it down as the enemy crossed the coast north of the Orwell. This enemy aircraft was credited as a Category 1—searchlight aided interception to 328 and 329 Batteries. Once again a large number of flares were dropped, mainly around Harwich and Clacton, and a number of incendiaries were dropped in the Clacton area.

20th/21st February. Forty aircraft attacked London, making landfall between Southwold and Dover; visibility was good. At 21.36 hours jamming was reported out at sea just before the enemy aircraft made landfall in the Harwich and Clacton areas. Later, low cloud hampered searchlights but nevertheless they did good work. At 21.56 hours a target was taken over north of Stowmarket flying south-east and a fighter from Coltishall sector made contact and the aircraft was shot down. Shortly afterwards NWO631 and NWO632 engaged an Me.410 at 500 ft., and hits were seen on the tail and fuselage.

22nd/23rd February. Of a force of approximately 100 enemy aircraft with London as the target only 25 eluded the defences. In the Regimental area NWO5 illuminated a Do.217, which was shot down by a Coltishall fighter four miles north of Saxmundham.

14/15th March. In a raid on London the enemy aircraft approached over East Anglia and returned over Kent. There were many long illuminations in which He.111, Do.217, Ju's.88 and 188 and Me.410 were identified. Three Ju.88's were shot down in the sector as a result of engagements initiated in the Regimental area. About 300 incendiaries were dropped round Orbit Z in NWO5 area, and it would appear that the orbit was the target; there was no damage to personnel or equipment.

21st/22nd March. Sixty to 80 aircraft attacked London from the north-east simultaneously with a force attacking from the south. The main body of the force made landfall between Felixstowe and Southwold. Searchlight results were again good. Fighters manning sector orbits made seven contacts, six being visual, and destroyed five and probably destroyed one. Of the five enemy definitely destroyed in the sector, two were Ju.188 and three Ju. 88. During the attack eight aircraft were shot out of searchlight beams.

As the first half of this year passed the threat of new weapons which was frequently being made by the Germans was coupled with the impending invasion of the Continent. One of the first flying bombs despatched against England fell near Saxmundham and, within a short time, the Southern Counties were being subjected to a bombardment by these weapons which was to call for a very strong effort to combat.

The Regiment was actively engaged during July to October in assisting the operations against this weapon. The majority of the flying bombs which approached the Regimental area were launched from aircraft operating from the Dutch coast.

On July 8th, 1944, Lieut.-Col. L. S. Davis left the Regiment on being appointed to command another regiment. He had commanded the Regiment through three of the major war years and had received the Territorial Decoration in the previous May. His place was taken by Lieut.-Col. G. W. Hogsflesh, T.D. Maj. K. J. Pearce was promoted to command a regiment; he had risen from a subaltern with 329 Battery at Grove Park, Lewisham, to Regimental second-in-command. His place was taken by Maj. Woods.

Lieut.-Col. G. W. Hogsflesh remained in command until February 27th, 1945, when he handed over command to Lieut.-Col. V. C. Ritchie, M.B.E.

In 1945 members of the Regiment were honoured by the award of decorations; Lieut.-Col. Hogsflesh received the O.B.E.; the second-in-command, Maj. Woods, the M.B.E., and Junior-Commander King in command of the A.T.S. attached to the Regiment for duty, the M.B.E. This mark of recognition to the A.T.S. who had rendered such good service to the Regiment in their many roles as plotters, drivers, telephonists, clerks, and in other employment, was most fitting. R.S.M. G. Jolland received the M.B.E. and Staff-Sergt. Law of 328 Battery, the B.E.M.

In 1945 as victory in Europe approached, the anti-aircraft task was completed. The Luftwaffe had ceased to be operational and the tasks and duties at which the Regiment had toiled through the years 1939 to 1945 were virtually completed. Earlier events had called the Regiment to a new sphere and it had loyally responded by playing its part in the defeat of the German Air Force.

The Regiment was dispersed to fresh duties of an administrative nature and, during the remainder of 1945, fresh units formed from the Regiment staffed release centres at Oxford and Reading and assisted in carrying out the requirements of the demobilization scheme.

Early in 1946 the Regiment, which had been withdrawn to Derby as a holding unit, ceased this function.

The pages of history written in the second great conflict were completed.

CHAPTER FORTY-ONE

THE OLD COMRADES' ASSOCIATION

President:
*Maj. H. D. BARNES, O.B.E., T.D., D.L.

Vice-Presidents:
Brig. E. E. F. BAKER, C.B.E., D.S.O., M.C., T.D., D.L., A.D.C.
Lieut.-Col. L. S. DAVIS, T.D.
*Lieut.-Col. C. J. SALKELD GREEN, D.S.O., M.C., T.D.
*Lieut.-Col. S. L. HOSKING
Maj. ALLAN D. LAURIE, T.D.
Lieut.-Col. K. J. PEARCE
Maj. Sir K. O. PEPPIATT, K.B.E., M.C.

Hon. Treasurer:	*Hon. Secretary:*	*Asst. Hon. Secretary:*
Capt. H. M. RYLAND	G. S. ADDISON	C. DIGBY PLANCK

"OUR PRESIDENT"
Maj. HAROLD DOUGLAS BARNES, O.B.E., T.D., D.L., F.S.A.

HAROLD DOUGLAS BARNES, born in the year 1876, the only son of Edmund Barnes, D.L., J.P., first mayor of St. Pancras, was educated at Malvern College and displayed early tendencies to soldiering by becoming a bombardier in his school cadet corps.

Articled to the late C. O. Humphreys, Esq., the father of the present judge, Maj. Barnes was admitted to the Roll of Solicitors in 1901.

In the year 1911 he was appointed Clerk to St. Pancras Justices, which office he still holds, although he has retired from practice as a solicitor.

Nearly half a century ago, in 1898 to be precise, he was gazetted to the 3rd London V.R.C. as a second lieutenant and was promoted captain in 1900 and major in 1914.

Those who knew him then, very quickly realised what a keen soldier he was and no one could be long with him in the officers mess without realising his aptitude for music and song; at gatherings it would be he who would " get the table in a roar."

As officer commanding the old " B " Company he rarely missed a parade and was never absent from camp. He went overseas with the battalion in March 1915 with the rank of major.

* Trustees

All his friends in the Regiment sympathise with him in his long and trying disability, suffered owing to his severe wound received at Festubert, but even this has never been allowed to interfere with his equable temperament.

In December 1916 he joined the office of the Judge Advocate-General and later was appointed staff-captain and D.A.A.G. (War Office Staff), being finally demobilized in 1923.

Maj. Barnes is a Deputy Lieutenant for the County of London and was the recipient of the Territorial Decoration and awarded the O.B.E. (Military Division).

As a hobby, he derives great pleasure from archeology, he is an authority on arms and armour, of which he possesses a very fine collection ; he is also a Fellow of the Society of Antiquaries.

Many will recall the final wind-up of the 3rd London, when just before midnight everyone was asked to stand and Maj. Barnes rendered a parody, " D'ye ken John Peel, you'll be 7th Territorials in the Morning."

Maj. Barnes is indeed a fellow of " infinite variety," and has long been a trustee of the O.C.A. He is the oldest surviving officer of the Regiment.

Upon many occasions he has proved his keenness and has done much to inspire and sustain the traditions of the Regiment, his ever ready help to the O.C.A. on many occasions proving very valuable.

His son, Maj. A. E. F. Barnes, following in his footsteps, commanded the 328th Battery of the 32nd S.L. Regiment, R.A., and was subsequently promoted to the rank of lieutenant-colonel, and served on Allied Military Control in Germany.

The Old Comrades have every reason to be proud and happy to have Maj. Barnes as their president.

GENERAL ACTIVITIES

UP to the outbreak of the Second World War, Old Comrades have each year attended the annual Regimental church parade on Armistice Sunday upon the invitation of the commanding officer. On the nearest Sunday to each anniversary of the Battle of Loos (September 25th) a church parade has been held, at the conclusion of which a wreath has been laid on the Royal Exchange Memorial for London troops.

At twelve noon on each anniversary of the landing of the Regiment in France (March 18th, 1915), a wreath has been laid on the Cenotaph, Whitehall, and throughout the recent war the ceremony was performed as usual.

Old Comrades in good strength took part in the Royal Review at Hyde Park in 1937, and also each of the parades held by the Federation of

O.C.A.'s of the London Territorial units upon the Horse Guards, and the Remembrance Parades of the Ypres League.

Reunion dinners have been held, and they have also organised New Year's Eve dances, several cinderella dances and film shows.

For many years running Mr. C. D. Planck organised tours to the battlefields for the benefit of the O.C.A. These were always well supported and the scenes of former actions of the Regiment were all visited at some time or other.

Reports of these tours, written by Mr. C. D. Planck, were published by the Ypres Times, and reprints of the articles were sent each year to all members.

Each year, upon the anniversary of the departure of the battalion for France, Old Comrades meet upon the steps of St. Martin-in-the-Fields and, on the Saturday evening preceding Armistice Sunday, Old Comrades attend a dinner known as the " 2nd/7th Rally."

The committee meets officially six times a year for the purpose of carrying on the activities of the Association, and no opportunity is lost which offers a chance of bringing Old Comrades together. Cases of comrades in distress always receive the earnest attention of the committee and a great deal of good work has been quietly and efficiently carried out in this direction.

During the Second World War all fit members again served their country; several went straight back to H.M. Forces and served throughout. Others immediately joined the ranks of Civil Defence, but the great majority enlisted in the Home Guard.

Following much work by the committee, in 1943 an alteration was made in the rules which permitted serving members of the Regiment to become enrolled as honorary members of the O.C.A. This alteration had the full approval and support of the commanding officer, Lieut.-Col. L. S. Davis, T.D.

A Report and Balance Sheet are issued annually and every effort is made to make the former interesting to all and the latter satisfactory to everybody.

The general funds of the Association are in a sound condition and are invested in government stock in the joint names of the trustees. The invested moneys, which include £100 left to the Association by the late Mr. H. Wickham, have remained untouched since invested.

For a considerable number of years the committee has carefully and diligently carried out its duties and all expenses have been met by the interest on investments, together with the amount of subscriptions paid annually by members.

As a result of the appeal for the Old Comrades' Standard being oversubscribed, a Benevolent Fund came into being.

This fund, which is controlled by the committee, enables assistance to be given to members of the Regiment who are not members of the Association. How useful this fund has been can be better appreciated when it is realised that only members of the Association can be assisted out of the General Funds; consequently prior to the Benevolent Fund many deserving cases could not be assisted as the individuals concerned were not members of the Association. With the General Fund and the Benevolent Fund the committee is now in a position to assist any past member of the Regiment.

Under the guidance of Lieut.-Col. L. S. Davis, T.D., the Regiment has given great assistance to this fund since 1943.

The late Lieut. J. H. B. Fletcher, before proceeding overseas in 1915, made provision in his will for a sum of money " to be controlled by the officer commanding the 1/7th London Battalion, or by a person appointed by him, in trust to use at his discretion, towards the relief of any non-commissioned officers or men serving abroad with the above battalion, who may be wounded or disabled in the present war, or for the relief of the families or dependants of any who may be killed or die in the war." This fund is known as " The Fletcher Fund."

We are affiliated to the Federation of O.C.A.'s of The London Territorial Units. Only a few know of the good work done by this Federation, which operates quietly and efficiently.

Our secretary and assistant secretary, Mr. G. Addison and Mr. C. D. Planck respectively, represent us on the committee of the Federation, and have attended all meetings since its formation.

Our Association is also affiliated to the British Legion. It is through this agency that the plot of ground at Westminster Abbey is reserved for the Regiment during Armistice Week, when Haig poppies are planted in memory of departed comrades, the proceeds going to the aid of ex-Servicemen.

Committee :

G. HILL, M.C., D.C.M. (Chairman).

W. HORLEY, M.M.	F. MANNOCK	F. EVANS
F. RICH	W. ROBERTSON	H. EMBLIN
C. CARTER	W. HILLS	G. CAMBDEN
S. JEANES	C. LUCK	W. PYE
B. FRYER	R. RAYNER	N. WILLIAMS

Hon. Auditors :

| C. P. LORD | S. J. LEE | W. PURSSORD |

APPENDIX A
HONORARY COLONELS OF THE REGIMENT

Sir William de Bathe, Bt.	1861–1868
Field-Marshal Lord Napier of Magdala, G.C.B., G.C.S.I.	1868–1890
H.R.H. Duke of Clarence and Avondale, K.G., K.P., A.D.C.	1890–1892
Colonel R. P. Laurie, C.B., V.D., M.P., J.P.	1892–1904
Colonel E. C. Stevenson, V.D.	1904–1921
Colonel E. Faux, C.M.G., V.D.	1921–1923
Brig.-General Sir A. Maxwell, K.C.B., C.M.G., D.S.O., T.D.	1923–1935
Colonel J. Trevor	1935

APPENDIX B
REGIMENTAL COLOURS AND BATTLE HONOURS

THE TEMPLE BAR AND ST. PAUL'S ASSOCIATION.
KING'S COLOUR. Union Jack, 6 ft. square.

REGIMENTAL COLOUR. 6 ft. square. Blue, with replica of the west front of St. Paul's in gold, silver and colours. On reverse: Temple Bar, in wreaths of oak leaves, inscribed "Temple Bar and St. Paul's Association."

NOTE. The Jacks of above have the crosses of St. George and St. Andrew only, having been given before the union with Ireland.

3rd REGIMENT OF LOYAL LONDON VOLUNTEERS.
CAMP COLOUR. Blue, with 3rd L.L.V. in gold on red oval centre.

NOTE. These Jacks have the three crosses of England, Scotland and Ireland, having been presented after the union.

7th (CITY OF LONDON) BATTALION THE LONDON REGIMENT.
KING'S COLOUR. Union Jack, 6 ft. square.

REGIMENTAL COLOUR: The west front of St. Paul's is still retained and is carried out in scarlet and buff. This Colour carries the Honour, "South Africa, 1900–1902." After the amalgamation in 1922 with the Post Office Rifles, the following Honour was added: "Egypt, 1882." After the Great War 1914–1918 the following Battle Honours were inscribed on the King's Colour:

FESTUBERT, 1915.	LOOS.	FLERS COURCELLETE.
BULLECOURT.	MESSINES, 1917.	PASSCHENDAELE.
CAMBRAI, 1917.	VILLERS BRETONNEUX.	AMIENS.
	PURSUIT TO MONS.	

The following table gives the official names of the battles and other engagements as they appear in the Report of the Battles Nomenclature Committee; these were approved by the Army Council and published in 1921. Principal engagements classified as "Battles," "Actions," or "Affairs"; the relative importance of "Battles" is indicated by size of type. With the assistance of the Historical Section of the War Cabinet an endeavour has been made to adjust Battle Honours to 1/7th, 2/7th, and the Amalgamated Battalion of the 7th London. The chronological limits are fixed for each engagement.

REGIMENTAL COLOURS AND BATTLE HONOURS

1/7th BATTALION.

Summer Operations, 1915:

Battle of Festubert	May 15–25
LOOS	Sept. 25–Oct. 8
Subsequent Actions of Hohenzollern Redoubt	Oct. 13–19

Local Operations:

German Attack on Vimy Ridge	May 21, 1916

Operations on the Somme, 1916:

SOMME	July 1–Nov. 18
Flers-Courcellette	Sept. 15–22
Transloy Ridges	Oct. 1–18

(Including capture of Eaucourt L'Abbaye and attacks on the Butte de Warlencourt.)

The Flanders Offensive, 1917:

MESSINES	June 7–14
*YPRES	July 31–Nov. 10

The Cambrai Operations, 1917:

Cambrai, 1917	Nov. 20–Dec. 3
The German counter-attacks	Nov. 30–Dec. 3

2/7th BATTALION, 1917.

Bullecourt	May 3–17
YPRES:	
Menin Road Ridge	Sept. 20–25
Passchendaele	Oct. 26–Nov. 10

AMALGAMATED BATTALION (7th London), 1918.

The First Battles of the Somme, 1918:

St. Quentin	March 21–23
Ancre with subsequent action of Villers Bretonneux	April 24–25
AMIENS	Aug. 8–11

The Second Battle of the Somme, 1918:

Albert	Aug. 21–23

The Battles of the Hindenburg Line, 1918:

Epehy	Sept. 18
PURSUIT TO MONS	

---

*The battalion did not take part in any major operations during this time, although its period of line duty prior to the Battle of the Menin Road Ridge, Sept. 20–25, was among the most unpleasant of its experiences, and included a successful attack on a position which subsequently became known as "Cryer Farm."

APPENDIX C

OFFICERS AND MEN WHO DIED IN THE GREAT WAR
1914-1918

"Roll of Honour"

Abbott, R. P. J., Pte.
Abbott, W. H., Pte.
Aber, A. T., Pte.
Adair, A. L., Pte.
Adams, D. S., L/Sergt.
Adams, H. J., Pte.
Adams, S. V., L/Cpl.
Adams, W. J., Pte.
Addison, W. J., Pte.
Addlestone, C. R., Drm.
Ager, F. G., Pte.
Ainsworth, A., Pte.
Aitkens, A. R. K., 2/Lt.
Alabaster, W., Pte.
Aldred, H. E., Pte.
Alexander, H. J., 2/Lt.
Allan, J. K., Pte.
Allcraft, A., Pte.
Allen, A., L/Cpl.
Allen, H., Pte.
Allen, H. F., Cpl.
Allen, J., Pte.
Allen, J. S. F., Pte.
Allsop, A. C., Pte.
Amos, J., Pte.
Anderson, G., Pte.
Anderson, H., Pte.
Anderson, H. A., L/Cpl.
Anderson, J. H., Pte.
Andrews, G. H., Pte.
Angus, G., Sergt.
Angus, J. W., Cpl.
Anthony, J., Pte.
Appleton, A., Pte.
Arden, R. W., Pte.
Arnold, E. W., Pte.
Ashley, E., Pte.
Ashplant, J. H., Pte.
Ashton, E. A., Pte.
Atkin, A. R., Pte.
Ayling, C. W., Pte.

Babbs, A. H., Pte.
Bacon, H. R., Pte.
Bailey, A. H., Cpl.
Bailey, C. F., Lieut.
Bain, W. J., Pte.
Baker, A. G., Sergt., M.M.
Baker, A. J., L/Cpl.
Baker, C., Pte.

Baker, H. J., Cpl.
Baker, J. S. M., Pte.
Balaam, P., Pte.
Ball, A. E., Pte.
Bancroft, T. O., Pte.
Bareham, B. E. V., Pte.
Barker, F. T. S., Pte.
Barker, H., Pte.
Barker, R. A., Pte.
Barnard, W. E., Pte.
Barnes, W. J. V., Pte.
Barnett, G. J., Pte.
Barnitt, F. W. J., Pte.
Barrand, M. S., Pte.
Barry, A., Pte.
Bartlett, H. P., Sergt.
Bartlett, J., Pte.
Barton, A., Cpl.
Barton, J., Pte.
Batchelor, W. C., Pte.
Batstone, E. M. T., Pte.
Battell, W. E., Cpl.
Beasley, L., Pte.
Beavis, E., L/Cpl.
Becklake, A., Sergt.
Bell, S., Pte.
Belsey, E. E., L/Cpl.
Bennett, G., Pte.
Bennett, J. H., Pte.
Benstead, H. E. 2/Lt.
Bentall, G. N., Pte.
Betsworth, H. S., Pte.
Bezley, W., Pte.
Bicknell, M., L/Sergt.
Bingham, C. F., Pte.
Bint, P. A., Pte.
Birch, H. W., Pte.
Birchfield, J., Pte.
Bird, A., Pte.
Bird, A. G., Pte.
Bird, R. L., Pte.
Bishop, H., Pte.
Bishop, J. E., 2/Lt.
Bishop, W. H., Pte.
Bivand, G., L/Cpl.
Black, L. J. V., Pte.
Blake, A. G., Pte.
Blake, F., Pte.
Bloomfield, J. J., L/Cpl.
Blyther, A., Pte.

Boag, A., 2/Lt.
Boakes, F. J., Pte.
Boast, B. B., Pte.
Boden, B., Pte.
Boecker, W. E. B., Pte.
Boeckler, F., Pte.
Boita, E. H., Pte.
Bolam, R. H., Pte.
Bolton, W. F., L/Cpl.
Bone, J., Pte.
Boon, J., Pte.
Boord, O. E., Pte.
Bosher, C. W., Cpl.
Bosher, F. N., Pte.
Bosher, R. F., Cpl.
Bowden, F. S., Sergt.
Bowers, C. C., Sergt., D.C.M., M.M.
Bowers, W., Pte.
Bowles, S. W., Pte.
Boyer, E. A., 2nd Lt.
Boyten, H. G., L/Cpl.
Brabham, A. H., Sergt.
Branch, W. H., Pte.
Brand, E. H., Sergt.
Brandon, C. T., L/Cpl.
Brandon, E. W., Pte.
Bremer, A., Pte.
Brett, P. E., Pte.
Brice, C., Pte.
Bridge, J. E., Pte.
Bridger, J. H., Pte.
Bridges, E., Pte.
Bright, A. G., Pte.
Brill, R., L/Cpl.
Brimfield, E. G., 2/Lt.
Brindley, G. F. W., L/Cpl.
Brinn, V., Pte.
Bristow, F. L., L/Cpl.
Britten, T. W., Pte.
Brittle, B., Pte.
Brooke, H. D., Pte.
Brooker, A. E., Pte.
Brooks, W., Pte.
Brotherhood, F. S., Pte.
Brouard, W., L/Cpl.
Brown, A. F., Pte.
Brown, H. E., Pte.
Brown, H. J., Sergt.
Brown, J. F., Pte.

ROLL OF HONOUR

Brown, W. H., Pte.
Brown, W. T., Pte.
Brundritt, N. W., Pte.
Brunning, E., Pte.
Bruty, C. H., Pte.
Bryant, A. H., Pte.
Bubb, T. B., L/Cpl.
Bubear, G., Pte.
Buckingham, H. F., Pte.
Bull, J., Pte.
Bullock, L. S., Pte.
Bultitude, W., L/Cpl.
Bunce, F. A ., Pte.
Burbedge, A., Pte.
Burden, S. R., C.S.M., M.M.
Burdett, F. B., Pte.
Burford, G. P., Pte.
Burfutt, B. C., Pte.
Burgess, E. W., Pte.
Burgin, C., Sgt.
Burnand, W. A., Pte.
Burnside, J., Pte.
Burrell, R. G., Cpl.
Burton, H. J., Pte.
Burton, W., Pte.
Bush, G. A., Pte.
Bush, W. J., Pte.
Butcher, G. H., Pte.
Butler, C. V., Pte.
Butler, E. G., Pte.
Butler, F., Pte.
Butler, W. J., Pte.
Byham, R. J., Sgt.

Cakebread, R., Pte.
Callam, R., L/Cpl.
Cambridge, A., Pte.
Cameron, D. M., L/Cpl.
Campbell, W., Pte.
Candy, L., Pte.
Cannon, H. W., Sgt.
Capham, P. W., Pte.
Carew, E. W., Pte.
Carpenter, W. G., Sgt.
Carrington, R. L., L/Cpl.
Carter, A., L/Cpl.
Carter, S. G., Pte.
Casson, W., Maj., T.D.
Cate, G. J., Pte.
Cauchefert, H. C., Pte.
Cawkell, J., Pte.
Chalk, J. W., Pte.
Chambers, A. W. D., Cpl.
Chambers, E., L/Cpl.
Chambers, J. T., Pte.
Chance, W., Pte.

Chapman, A., Sgt., M.M.
Chapman, C. L., Pte.
Chapman, G. B., Cpl.
Chapman, H. J., Pte.
Chapman, J. G., Pte.
Chapman, J. G., Cpl.
Chapman, W. J., Pte.
Chappell, S., Pte.
Cherrington, J., Pte.
Chicken, R., Pte.
Chittock, F. E., Pte.
Chizlett, T. C., Pte.
Christmas, H. C., Pte., M.M.
Chudley, C. L., Pte.
Church, A., Pte.
Clark, A., Pte.
Clarke, C. A., Pte.
Clarke, J. A., Pte.
Clarke, T., Pte.
Clarke, T. H., Pte.
Clarke, W. A., Pte.
Clarke, W. J., Cpl.
Clarkson, L., Pte.
Claydon, H. L., Pte.
Clayton, G. E., Pte.
Clements, A. L., Pte.
Clements, J. B., Pte.
Cliffe, K., Pte.
Clifford, S. P., Pte.
Clover, F. G., Pte.
Cockman, W. W., Pte.
Codling, W. G., Pte.
Cole, E., Pte.
Cole, E. H. T., Pte.
Cole, H. W., Pte.
Cole, S., Cpl.
Cole, W. G., Pte.
Cole, W. J., Pte.
Coles, W. P. V., 2/Lt., M.M.
Coles, P. H., L/Cpl., M.M.
Coleman, L. H., Sgt.
Collier, W. E., L/Cpl.
Collins, F. L., Pte.
Collins, J., Pte.
Collinson, W. H., Pte.
Colquhoun, H., Pte.
Commins, A. E., Pte.
Connelly, B., Pte.
Conningsby, T. L., Pte.
Connolly, W., Pte.
Connor, W., Pte.
Constance, W. E., 2/Lt.
Cook, C. T., Pte.
Cook, H. M., 2/Lt.
Cook, J. J., Pte.
Cook, W., Pte.

Cook, W. R., Pte.
Cooley, J. W., Pte.
Cooper, A., Pte.
Cooper, J. C., Pte.
Corps, A., Pte.
Cosburn, E. A., Pte.
Costello, W. S., Pte.
Costerd, T. R., Pte.
Costin, A. G., Pte.
Cottle, J., Pte.
Cottrell, W. G., Pte.
Coulson, L., Cpl.
Cowling, E., Pte.
Cownden, S., Pte.
Cox, G. B., 2/Lt.
Cracknell, G. E., Pte.
Cranham, W. I., Pte.
Craven, R., Pte.
Crawfurd, R., Pte.
Cray, J. E., Pte.
Cripps, W. F., L/Sgt.
Crisp, W. S., Cpl.
Crocker, C., Pte.
Crockett, H., Pte.
Croft, V. S., Pte.
Cronin, E., Pte.
Cronin, H. G., Pte.
Crosier, V. S., 2/Lt.
Cross, A. L., Pte.
Crossingham, C. L., L/Cpl.
Crouch, H., Pte.
Crudgington, G. H., Pte., M.M.
Crump, T. J., Pte.
Cryer, B. N., 2/Lt.
Cudmore, S., Pte.
Culpin, A. E., Pte.
Cunningham, T., Pte.
Curtis, W., Pte.

Dace, E. M., Pte.
Daly, D., Pte.
Daniels, J., Pte.
Dansey, F. R. A., 2/Lt.
Darling, T. E., Pte.
David, J. J., Pte.
Davidson, A. B., Pte.
Davies, H., Pte.
Davies, J., Pte.
Davies, W. B., Pte.
Davis, B. C., 2/Lt.
Davis, A. A., Pte.
Davis, H. C., Pte.
Davison, E. H., Pte.
Davison, R. A. P., Pte.
Dawson, H., 2/Lt.

ROLL OF HONOUR

Day, A. E., Pte. D.C.M.
Daykin, H. J., Pte.
Deeble, J., Pte.
Deegan, L., Pte.
Dew, V. W., Pte.
Dickens, G. R., L/Cpl., M.M.
Diggins, E. J., Pte.
Dignum, R., Pte.
Dixon, H., Sgt.
Donaldson, D. H., 2/Lt.
Doney, J. G., Pte.
Donovan, R. H., Pte.
Doody, W., Pte.
Dormer, T., Pte.
Dorsett, A., Pte.
Doughty, A., L/Cpl.
Douglas, T., Pte.
Downer, R., Pte.
Downey, J. C., Pte.
Dowsett, G., Pte.
Drabble, T. A., Pte.
Drake, C. J., Pte.
Draper, L. H., Pte.
Duck, H. C., Pte.
Duffy, S. O., Pte.
Dunkerley, J., Pte.
Dunkley, W. H., Pte.
Dunn, H. A., Pte.
Dunn, M., Pte.
Dyall, A. E., Pte.

Eady, A. D., Pte.
Eagles, P. G., Pte.
Earl, A. H., Pte.
Earl, A. S., Cpl.
Eastoe, F. H., L/Cpl.
Eaton, S. S. C., L/Sgt.
Edgar, S., 2/Lt.
Edmondson, G. A., Pte.
Edwards, E. R., Pte.
Edwards, G., Sgt., M.M
Edwards, G., Pte.
Edwards, G. G., Pte.
Edwards, H. H., Pte.
Edwards, R. D., Pte.
Edwards, W., Sgt.
Edwards, W., Pte., M.M.
Edwards, W. T., Pte.
Edwards-Trollip, 2/Lt.
Eggleton, W., Pte.
Elderton, F. W., Pte.
Elledge, N. H., Pte.
Elliott, H. L., Pte.
Ellis, C. F., Pte.
Ellis, F., Pte.

Ellis, G., L/Cpl.
Elms, A. J., L/Cpl.
Elson, P., Pte.
Emmett, R., Pte., M.M.
Endall, P. G., Cpl.
Endersby, W., Pte.
English, L. W., Pte.
English, M. S., Pte.
Ennor, R. C., Pte.
Erwin, H. M., L/Cpl.
Erwin, R. R., Pte.
Evans, G. W., Pte.
Evans, J. T., Pte.
Evans, T. C., Pte.
Everett, S., Pte.
Evers, J. W., Pte.
Eversfield, W., Pte.
Evershed, P. D., Lieut.
Everson, L. W., C.S.M.
Ewens, W., Pte.

Farmer, P. G., Pte.
Favell, W. G., Pte.
Fearnside-Speed, R. N., Lieut.
Feast, H. A. J., Pte.
Feaveryear, A. G., 2/Lt.
Feder, E., Pte.
Fenn, R. C., Pte.
Ferguson, A. A., Lieut.
Ferrett, R., Pte.
Ferris, B. L., Cpl.
Fessey, H. F., Pte.
Field, F. D., Pte.
Fink, H. B., Pte.
Fink, W. A., Pte.
Findlayson, A. D., L/Sgt.
Finn, G. H., Pte.
Fisher, J., Pte.
Flaherty, T. H., Pte.
Fleming, F. C., Pte.
Fletcher, J. H. B., Lieut.
Fletcher, W., Pte.
Flower, L. A. L., Capt.
Folley, T., Sgt.
Forge, D. F., Pte.
Forsyth, R., Pte.
Fowler, J., Pte.
Fox, C. L., Pte.
Francis, B., Pte.
Francis, C. F., Pte.
Francis, E., Pte.
Franklin, H. W., Sgt.
Fraser, A. C., 2/Lt., M.C.
Fraser, A. A., Pte.
Fraser, A. G. R., Pte.

Fraser, R., Pte.
Freeman, T. G., Pte.
French, W., Pte.
Frost, G. T., C.S.M.
Frost, J. H., Pte.
Fuller, F. T. F., Pte.
Fuller, W., Pte.
Fulton, K. W. F., Cpl

Gadd, W. J., Pte.
Galton, F. J., Pte.
Gardiner, J., L/Cpl.
Garland, C., Pte.
Garland, J., Pte.
Garnham, L., L/Cpl.
Garrad, B., Pte.
Garrad, H., L/Cpl.
Garraway, W., Pte.
Garrett, B., Pte.
Garrett, C. G., Pte.
Garrett, H. G., L/Cpl
Gartner, A., Dmr.
Gates, E. F., Pte.
Gay, G. A., Pte., M.M
Gee, E. R., Pte.
Geer, A. J., Sgt.
Geis, B. A., Cpl.
Gibbs, A., Pte.
Gibbs, H., Pte.
Gilbert, J. S., Pte.
Gilbert, S., Pte.
Gill, J., Pte.
Gilles, A. F., Pte.
Gillham, C. F., Pte.
Ginelack, L. F. L., Pte.
Ginsberg, J., Pte.
Gladwin, G. H., Pte.
Glassup, S. W., Pte.
Glen, J. F.
Goddard, E., Pte.
Goddard, G., Pte.
Goddard, W. T., Pte.
Godfrey, A., L/Cpl.
Godfrey, E. C., L/Cpl.
Godfrey, J. T., L/Cpl.
Godfrey, W. H., Pte.
Godier, H., Pte.
Goldsmith, V. E., Pte.
Golland, A. W., Cpl.
Goodall, J. A., Pte.
Goodfellow, A. R., Pte.
Goodridge, H. H., Pte.
Gordan, F., Pte.
Gorton, J., L/Cpl.
Gough, W. C., Sergt.
Gould, G. E., Pte.

247   S

ROLL OF HONOUR

Gourley, W. H., Pte.
Gover, G. F., Pte.
Graham, A. G., Pte.
Graham, W., Pte.
Grainger, S. J., Pte.
Graves, S. A., L/Cpl.
Gray, J. T., Pte.
Gray, T. W., Pte.
Gregg, C., Pte.
Green, H. S., Maj.
Green, R., Pte.
Green, W., Cpl.
Greenslade, W. C., Pte.
Greenwood, J. T., Pte.
Greenyer, T., Cpl.
Grieg, H. E., Pte., M.M.
Grierson, C. J., Pte.
Grinstead, G. H., Pte.
Grose, W. J., Pte.
Groves, A., Pte.
Gurd, H., Pte.
Gurney, G. T., Pte.
Guy, F., L/Cpl.
Gyde, H. C., Pte.

Haddy, E., Pte.
Hall, H. T. I., Pte.
Hall, S. H., Pte.
Hallett, W., Pte.
Halley-Jones, P., Capt., M.C.
Hallworth, C. A., Pte.
Halsey, E. C., 2/Lt.
Halsey, J. D., Pte.
Hammerton, G. H., Pte.
Hancock, A. L., 2/Lt.
Hann, C. J., Pte.
Hanson, F., Pte.
Harding, L. V., Pte.
Harding, W. Pte.
Hardy, H. W., L/Cpl.
Harradine, F. C., Cpl.
Harris, E., L/Cpl.
Harris, E. J., Pte.
Harris, F., Pte.
Harris, J., Pte.
Harris, J., Pte., M.M.
Harris, W., L/Cpl.
Harrison, D. R., Sergt.
Harrison, H. E., L/Cpl.
Hart, E. J., Pte.
Harvey, H. W., Pte.
Harvey, L., Pte.
Harvie, A. J., Pte.
Hatch, R., Pte.
Hatchett, A. G., Pte.

Hawkins, A. S., Pte.
Hawkins, G. W., Pte.
Hayes, W. H., Pte.
Haygarth, J. W., L/Cpl.
Haynes, V. A. E., Pte.
Heath, W., Pte.
Heatley, F., L/Cpl.
Hedges, W. S., Pte.
Hemmings, J. F., Pte.
Hempstead, H. A., Sergt.
Hendon, J., Pte.
Hendry, H. O., L/Cpl.
Hersant, W., Pte.
Hewins, J. H., Pte.
Hewlett, A. V., Pte.
Higgins, A. J., Pte.
Higgins, F., Pte.
Higginson, P., Pte.
Higley, E., Pte.
Hilburn, W. J., Cpl.
Hill, D. E., Pte.
Hill, W., Pte.
Hills, E. E., Pte.
Hislop, W. M., Sergt., M.M.
Hobbs, A. E., Cpl.
Hockley, F. C. A., Pte.
Hodgkinson, W. G., Pte.
Hogben, J. J., Pte.
Hogg, S., Pte.
Holland, T. H., Pte.
Holloway, A. E., Pte.
Holloway, H., Pte.
Holm, J. B., L/Cpl.
Holmes, A., Sergt.
Holmes, A. E. H., L/Cpl.
Hooker, G., Pte.
Hopcraft, H. W., L/Cpl.
Horne, J. E., Pte.
Horne, T., Pte.
Horwood, G. E., Pte.
Horsford, A., Pte.
Hosken, V. F., 2/Lt.
Hotten, J. A., Pte.
Hounslow, W., Pte.
Housden, P. R., Pte.
House, H. W., Cpl.
Howard, G. A., L/Cpl.
Howell, R. P., Cpl.
Howes, A. E., L/Cpl.
Howes, W. G., C.S.M.
Hoy, W. R. G., Pte.
Hubbard, H. C., Pte.
Hubbard, L. S., Pte.
Hudgell, J. T., Pte.
Hudson, H., Pte.
Huggins, O., Cpl., M.M.

Hughes, A. J., Pte.
Hughes, E., Pte.
Hughes, E. G., Pte.
Hughes, T., Pte.
Hull, G., Pte.
Hulland, H. H., Pte.
Humber, J. H., Sergt.
Humphrey, J. W. C., L/Cpl.
Hunt, T. A., Pte.
Hurst, E., Pte.
Hutton, W. W., 2/Lt.
Hutton, A. J., Cpl.
Huxtable, W. A., Pte.
Hyde, J. S., Pte.
Hyder, H. A. S., Pte., M.M.
Hymas, G. A., Pte.

Innocent, J. C., Pte.
Ivey, C. G., Pte.

Jackman, J. P., Pte
Jackson, A. J., Pte.
Jackson, G., Pte.
Jackson, W. C., Pte
Jacobs, A., Pte.
Jacquest, J., Pte.
James, H., Pte.
James, J. T., Sergt.
Janson, W. F., Pte.
Jacques, A. E., Pte.
Jay, P. G., Pte.
Jennett, C. H., Pte.
Jenkinson, R. R., Sergt.
Jennings, A. R., L/Cpl.
Jepps, A. G., Pte.
Jesshop, E. O., Pte.
Jessup, J. H. W., Pte.
Jiggins, W. H. J., Dmr.
Jilbert, W. F., Pte.
Johnson, A. H., Pte.
Johnson, G. W., Pte.
Johnson, H. R., Sergt.
Johnson, S., Pte.
Johnson, T. G., Pte.
Johnson, W., Pte.
Johnston, E., Pte.
Johnstone, W. J., Capt.
Johnstone, G. D., 2/Lt.
Jolley, W. H., Pte.
Jones, A., Cpl.
Jones, A. B., Pte.
Jones, A. W., Pte.
Jones, H., Pte.
Jones; H. O., Pte.
Jones, P. J., Pte., M.M.
Jones, T., Pte.

ROLL OF HONOUR

Jordan, V. H., Capt.
Joseph, N., Pte.
Judd, D. K., Pte.
Jury, G. R., 2/Lt.

Keeler, O. A., 2/Lt., M.C.
Keeling, A. E., L/Cpl.
Keene, E., Pte.
Kees, F. H. D., Pte.
Kelly, A., Pte.
Kemble, W. T., Pte.
Kemp, W. H., Pte.
Kench, J., Sergt.
Kendle, F., Pte.
Kenealy, M., L/Sergt.
Kennett, T., Pte.
Kent, P., Pte.
Keough, J., Pte.
Kerr, J., Pte.
Kersley, C. W., Pte.
Kiddle, R., Sergt.
Kiggins, F. E., Pte.
Kilbey, A. J., Pte.
Kimber, A., Pte.
Kimber, J. W., Pte.
King, C. R., Pte.
King, E., Cpl.
King, E. S., Pte.
King, F. V., Pte.
King, H.. Pte.
King, C. W., Pte.
King-Church, C. E., Capt.
Kingsman, W. F., Pte.
Kingsnorth, A. H., Cpl.
Kinnersley, A., Pte.
Kirk, R. L., 2/Lt.
Kirk, A. A., Pte.
Kirkpatrick, C., Pte.
Kitson, H. J., Pte.
Knight, A., Pte.
Knight, A., Pte., M.M.
Knight, F., Pte.
Knight, S. W., Pte.
Knightley, E. H., Pte.
Kolnetz, M., Pte.

Lacey, W., Pte.
Lambert, H. C., Pte.
Lane, D., Pte.
Lang, G. F., Pte.
Langham, A., Pte.
Lavey, W. F., Pte.
Lawrence, M. H., Pte.
Lawrie, H. A., Pte.
Lay, A. F., Pte.
Lazarus, M., Pte.

Leatch, A. J., Pte.
Ledwith, W. D., Pte.
Lee, J. W., Sergt.
Leftley, S. J., Pte.
Lemmon, A. D., Pte.
Lench, J. H., Pte.
Lentz, E. G., Pte.
Leserve, L. A., Cpl.
Lester, T. H., Pte.
Lewington, R. H., Pte.
Lewis, H. B., 2/Lt.
Lewis, J. W., Pte.
Lewis, L., Pte.
Lewsey, F. C., Pte.
Linnell, H. J., Pte.
Lippiatt, C. A., Pte.
Livock, H. W., Pte.
Lloyd, E. W., Pte.
Lloyd, J. T., Pte.
Lloyd, W. R., Pte.
Lock, A. L., Cpl.
Locker, E. J., Pte.
Long, H. D., 2/Lt.
Longley, F. A. J., 2/Lt.
Lord, R., L/Cpl.
Lovelock, H. W., L/Sergt., M.M.
Lovesay, L. A. J., Pte.
Lowing, J. J., Pte.
Lockhurst, W. A., Pte.
Lutzen, J., Cpl.
Lynch, E., Pte.
Lynn, R. P., Pte.

Macey, F., Pte.
Macken, G. A., Pte.
Macpherson, J., Cpl.
Maguire, H. M., Pte.
Maguire, P. P., Sergt.
Mair, J. B., Pte.
Malcolm, A. E., Pte.
Male, W., Pte.
Manning, A., Pte.
Mantle, A., Lieut.
Mapp, W., Pte.
Marchant, E. H., Pte.
Marchant, G. T., Pte.
Margetts, F., Pte.
Marks, J., Pte.
Marshall, A., L/Cpl.
Marshall, C. J., Pte.
Marshall, J. F., Pte.
Marston, F. G., Pte.
Martin, A. V., Pte.
Martin, H. W. B., Pte.
Martin, W. A., Pte.

Mason, W. J., Sergt.
Matthews, C. H., Pte.
Matthews, G. J., Pte.
Matthews, H. C., Pte.
Maule-French, E. H., 2/Lt.

May, A., Pte.
McBean, W., Pte.
McCann, H. O., Pte.
McCarthy, D., L/Cpl.
McCarthy, W., Pte.
McCormac, J., Pte.
McHardy, S. J., 2/Lt.
McKechnie, H. W., L/Cpl.
McKeon, F. B., Pte.
McClaren, A., 2/Lt.
McLoughlin, W., Pte.
Meade, W., Pte.
Meader, A. F., Pte.
Meale, G. A., Pte.
Mees, A. C., Pte.
Meltzer, D., Pte.
Merchant, W. J., 2/Lt.
Merry, E., Pte.
Messenge, R. J. S., Pte.
Messenger, T. W., Cpl.
Metcalf, C. D., Lieut.
Metcalf, A. H., Pte.
Michelmore, A. G., L/Cpl.
Middleton, W. G. E., Pte.
Midson, G., Pte.
Mileman, V. W., Lieut. (A/Capt.) M.C.
Miles, W., Pte.
Miles, W. W. H., L/Cpl
Milford, F. G., Pte.
Miller, W. E., 2/Lt.
Miller, D. J., L/Sergt.
Miller, H., Pte., M.M.
Miller, J., Pte.
Mills, G., Pte.
Mills, J., Dmr.
Mills, J. E., Pte.
Mince, A., Pte.
Minter, W. C., Pte.
Minty, W., Pte.
Missions, A. S., L/Sergt., M.M.
Mitcham, J. H., L/Cpl.
Mitchell, A. W. J., Pte.
Mitchell, C. H., Pte.
Mitchener, D. W. A., Pte.
Monger, W. J., Pte.
Montgomery, I. D., 2/Lt.
Montier, D. H., L/Cpl.
Moody, T. A., Cpl.

ROLL OF HONOUR

Moore, C. L., 2/Lt.
Moore, A. J., Pte.
Moore, C., Pte.
Moore, G. H. J., Pte.
Moore, H. C., Pte.
Moore, O. J. A., Pte.
Morgan, F. L., 2/Lt.
Morgan A. E., Pte.
Morgan, H., Pte.
Morgan, H. W., Pte.
Morley, W. F., Pte.
Morris, A. H., Pte.
Morris, F., Pte.
Morris, G. F., L/Cpl.
Moses, N., Pte.
Moss, H. W., L/Cpl.
Moxon, T. H., Sergt.
Mudd, H. W., Cpl.
Musgrave, A. J., Pte.
Mutton, J. F., Pte.
Myers, G., Pte.
Myhill, B. R. H., L/Cpl.

Naylor, W. G., 2/Lt.
Neale, W. G. V., Cpl., M.M.
Neben, W., Sergt., M.M.
Neville, S. W., 2/Lt.
Newble, W. H., Pte.
Newell, T., L/Cpl.
Newman, H. G., L/Cpl.
Newman, S., L/Sergt.
Newton, A. J., Pte.
Newton, J. W., Pte.
Newton, R., Pte.
Newton, R. G., Cpl., M.M.
Newton, W. G., Pte.
Nicholson, W. D., L/Cpl.
Nisbett, N. M., Cpl.
Noad, W. C., Pte.
Noakes, T. G., Pte.
Nodder, J., Pte., M.M.
Norford, W., Cpl., M.M.
Norris, G., Pte.
North, H. C., Pte.
Northam, A. R., L/Cpl.
Nugent, F. J., Cpl.
Nugus, A. G., Cpl.

O'Brien, A. B., Pte.
O'Brien, T. W., Pte.
O'Connor, J., Pte.
Odd., F. J., Cpl.
O'Donoghue, W. F., L/Cpl.
O'Hara, A. M., Pte.
Oman, D. J. M., Pte.
Opet, I. H., 2/Lt.

Orridge, J., L/Cpl.
Orridge, J. W., Pte.
Orson, A. E., Cpl.
Overton, A. E., L/Cpl.
Owttrim, P., Pte.

Pack, C., Pte.
Page, F., Pte.
Page, L. G., Pte.
Page, S., Pte.
Palmer, C. S. B., L/Cpl.
Palmer, F. J., Pte.
Palmer, H. W., Sergt.
Pariset, A., Pte.
Parker, A. E., L/Sergt.
Parker, A. W., Pte.
Parker, L., L/Sergt.
Parker, S., Pte.
Parmenter, T. W., Pte.
Parr, A., Pte.
Partridge, T. J., Pte
Partt, A., Cpl.
Patient, H., Pte.
Patrick, J. S., Pte.
Payne, A. A., Pte.
Payne, J. D., Pte.
Pays, W. H., Pte.
Peak, A. E., Pte.
Pearce, A. H., Pte.
Pearce, H., Pte.
Peek, F. J., Pte.
Pegram, R., Cpl.
Pennell, A. V., Pte.
Pennett, H. F., Pte.
Peters, H. R., Pte.
Peters, H., Pte.
Phillips, A., Pte.
Phillips, J., Pte.
Phillips, R. J., Pte.
Philott, G., Pte.
Philpott, H. W. A., Pte.
Philpot, J., Pte.
Pickrill, W., Pte.
Pige, H., Cpl.
Piggott, P., Pte.
Pitt, F. J., Pte.
Pizey, C. W., Pte.
Pleece, L., Pte.
Pole, L., Pte.
Polge, W. E., 2/Lt.
Poole, G. F., Pte.
Pope, A. W., Pte.
Pope, H., Pte.
Porter, A. J., Pte.
Potter, A., Pte.

Poulden, F. A., Pte.
Powell, H. J. E., Pte.
Pratt, A. W., Pte.
Pratt, P. H. J., Pte.
Press, H., Cpl.
Price, A. E., Pte.
Price, F. R., Pte.
Price, H., Pte.
Prince, J. S., Lieut.
Prior, W. T., Cpl.
Pritchard, H. A., Pte.
Proctor, W., Pte.
Puddicombe, W. H., Pte.
Pulham, H. F. C., L/Sgt.
Purdon, E., Pte.
Purdy, J. J., Pte.
Purnell, N. J., Pte.
Puttock, S. V., L/Cpl.
Pye, A., Pte.
Pym, J. W., 2/Lt.

Quartermain, F. J., Pte.
Quellhorst, A. H., L/Cpl.
Quinn, R. E., Pte.

Radford, A. J., Pte.
Raggett, A., Pte.
Raggett, C. A. E., Pte.
Ralph, J. G., 2/Lt.
Ralph, G. B., Pte.
Ramm, W. H., Pte.
Rance, R. E., Cpl.
Randall, C. J., Pte.
Ranger, H. T. S., Pte.
Ransom, G. W., Pte.
Ranson, W., Pte.
Rason, W. T., Pte.
Ratcliffe, A. W., Pte.
Rayner, J., Pte.
Razzell, A., Pte.
Read, E. S., Cpl.
Reece, P. H., Cpl.
Reed, A. A., Pte.
Reed, W. E., Pte.
Reader, A., Pte.
Rennell, C. E., Pte.
Reynolds, A. V. G., Pte.
Rhodes, A. A., Pte.
Ridgway, H. C., 2/Lt.
Rice, R., Pte.
Richards, C., Pte.
Richardson, A., Pte.
Richardson, A., Pte.
Richmond, W., Pte.
Rider, J. R., Pte.
Riggs, W. C. L., L/Cpl.

ROLL OF HONOUR

Rinder, C. H., 2/Lt.
Rist, J. F., Pte.
Rivers, A. J., Pte.
Roach, W. R., Pte.
Robbins, A. A., Pte.
Roberts, H. O. B., Lieut., M.C.
Roberts, F. A., 2/Lt.
Roberts, A. E., Pte.
Roberts, C., Pte.
Roberts, C. J., Pte.
Roberts, E. R., Pte.
Roberts, J. H., Pte.
Roberts, W. E., Pte.
Robertson, C. W. A., L/Sgt.
Robertson, H. A., Pte.
Robertson, W. J., L/Cpl.
Robinson, A. T., Pte.
Robinson, F. G., Pte.
Robinson, H., Pte.
Robinson, J. A., Pte.
Robinson, R. B., Pte.
Rogers, J. A., Pte.
Rogers, P., Pte.
Rollings, P. J., Cpl.
Rolls, G., Pte.
Roots, P. W., 2/Lt.
Rose, G. W., Pte.
Ross, A. J., Pte.
Rowe, A. E., L/Cpl.
Rowe, D., Pte.
Rowe, J., Pte.
Rowe, J. T., Pte.
Rowell, A. M., L/Cpl.
Rowlatt, J. J., Pte.
Rowson, W. W. T., Pte.
Ruel, A. H., L/Cpl.
Rundell, L. E., Capt., M.C. and Bar
Rushworth, T., Capt.
Russell, E., Pte.
Russell, H. E., Pte.
Russell, S. J., Pte.
Rust, T., Pte.
Rutter, H., Pte.
Rymer, W., Pte.
Sage, J. A., Pte.
Salter, H. A., 2/Lt.
Sanders, A., L/Cpl.
Sanders, F., Pte.
Sandford, A., Pte.
Sangorski, R., Pte.
Sard, F. E., Pte.
Saunders, H. A., Pte.
Saunders, W., Pte.

Saunders, H. E., Pte.
Savill, L. G., L/Cpl.
Saywell, E. H., Pte.
Scholey, W. H., Pte.
Scott, A., Cpl.
Scott, N. E., Pte.
Scott, S. H., Pte.
Scranney, R., Pte.
Scriven, H. J., Pte.
Sealy, R. G., L/Cpl.
Sears, C. J., Sergt.
Seary, A., Pte.
Seddon, J. H., Sergt., M.M.
Sell, F. J., Pte.
Servant, H. F., L/Cpl.
Shadwell, A. G., Sergt., D.C.M.
Sharman, W., Pte.
Sharp, M., 2/Lt., M.C.
Sharp, C. J., Pte.
Sharpe, F. T., Pte.
Sharpe, E. A., Pte.
Shepherd, G. H., Cpl., M.M.
Shepherd, L. G., Pte.
Sheppard, A. E., Pte.
Shearman, A. A., Capt.
Shilling, H., Pte.
Shipton, G., L/Cpl.
Short, A. W. C., Cpl.
Shorter, A. E., Pte.
Silver, W. R., Pte.
Simmonds, R. D., 2/Lt.
Simmonds, S. B., Pte.
Simmons, A. C., Pte.
Skinner, J., Pte.
Slade, C. S., Pte.
Slate, G. S., Pte.
Smee, A. C., Pte.
Smith, A. J., T/Lt.
Smith, H. B., 2/Lt.
Smith, A., Pte.
Smith, C., Pte.
Smith, E. A., L/Cpl.
Smith, F., Pte.
Smith, G., Pte.
Smith, G. W., Pte.
Smith, H. S., Pte.
Smith, H. H., Sergt.
Smith, H. G., L/Cpl.
Smith, H. C., Pte.
Smith, J. C., Pte.
Smith, J. H., Pte.
Smith, J. W., Pte.
Smith, M., Pte.
Smith, W. E., Pte.

Smyth, R., Pte.
Snelling, H. J., Pte.
Soloman, J. H., 2/Lt.
Southgate, W., Pte.
Spalding, S., Pte.
Spears, A. A., Pte.
Spencer, G. H., Pte.
Spice, T., Pte.
Spicer, C. E., Pte.
Spillane, W. E., Pte.
Spink, H., Pte.
Spokes, R., Pte.
Squire, L. C. H., 2/Lt.
Stacey, F., Pte.
Staines, E. J. A. G., Pte.
Staines, F. H., Pte.
Stallwood, I. E., Pte.
Stannard, G. E., Pte.
Stark, C. H., Pte.
Stevens, C. W. F., Pte.
Stevens, W. T., L/Cpl.
Stocks, F. C. M., Pte.
Stonehouse, W. T., Pte.
Storey, A. E., Pte.
Stroman, T. A., Pte.
Strong, J., Pte.
Stubbs, H., Pte.
Such, T. G., Pte.
Sullivan, J., Pte.
Sumner, F., Pte.
Sursham, T. K., L/Cpl.
Sutton, J. W., Pte.
Swedloff, S., Pte.
Swindells, J., Pte.

Talkington, T. E., Pte.
Tanner, E. S., Pte.
Tansley, T. H., Pte.
Tapps, B., Pte.
Taylor, F. V. A., L/Cpl.
Taylor, J., Pte.
Taylor, R. A., L/Cpl.
Taylor, W. E., Pte.
Tench, C. A., Pte.
Tester, A., Pte.
Thackham, J. W., Pte.
Thain, A. R. A., L/Cpl.
Thain, E., Pte.
Thain, E. V., Pte.
Thaine, H. T., Pte.
Thatcher, E., Pte.
Thirgood, A. J., Pte.
Thomas, C. A., L/Cpl.
Thompsett, C., Pte.
Thompson, A. E., Pte.
Thompson, S. E., Pte.

ROLL OF HONOUR

Thorn, R. H., **Pte.**
Thorn, V. W., Pte.
Thurnell, W. G., 2/**Lt.**
Thurston, P. W., **Pte.**
Tickel, H. V., L/Cpl.
Tilley, A., L/Cpl.
Tilt, W. C., L/Cpl.
Tomalin, A. W. J., **Pte.**
Tombs, V., L/Sergt.
Tomkins, R. W., Pte.
Tomlin, F. A., Pte.
Thompson, A. S., 2/Lt.
Toulmin, E. C., Pte.
Tournay, H. J., Pte.
Trebilcock, V. B., **Pte.**
Tregurtha, P. H., Pte.
Tremlett, F., Pte.
Triggs, G. A. A., Pte.
Tucker, H. J., Pte.
Tungatt, L., Pte.
Turner, G., Pte.
Turtle, A. E., Pte.
Tweed, H. W., Pte.
Tyler, W. A., 2/Lt.
Tyson, A. S., L/Sergt.

Ungratte, D., L/Cpl.
Urquhart, J. D., Pte.

Vanner, R. S., Pte.
Varney, J. G., Pte.
Veniard, F. L., Pte.
Vening, E. F., Pte.
Vicars, S. E., Pte.
Vincent, H., Pte., M.M.

Wade, S., Pte.
Wade, T., Pte.
Wager, C. H., Pte.
Waight, A. E., Pte.
Wakelin, J. B., L/Cpl.
Wakely, H. J., Pte.
Walden, H. J., Pte.
Walden, J., Pte.
Walding, A. G., Pte.
Wale, T. F., Pte.
Walker, R. R., 2/Lt.
Walker, A. H., Pte.
Wall, F. H., Pte.
Walsh, L. H., A/Capt., M.C., D.C.M.
Walsh, J., Pte.
Walsh, T. K., Pte.

Walters, H., Pte.
Walton, W. T., L/Cpl.
Wannell, S. E., Cpl.
Warby, A. T., Pte.
Ward, A. J., Sergt.
Ward, T. C., Pte.
Ward, W., **Pte.**
Ware, W. H. S., Pte.
Warman, C. N., Pte.
Warner, A. A., Pte.
Warner, G. H. J., Pte.
Warner, R. F., Pte.
Warren, J. W., Pte.
Warren, P. D., Cpl., M.M.
Wass, M. E., Pte.
Waters, A. J., Pte.
Watson, C. T., 2/Lt.
Watts, F. J., Pte.
Watts, H. J., Pte.
Watts, W. H., Pte.
Way, J. G., Pte.
Wayth, S. A., Pte.
Weatherilt, H., Pte.
Webb, J., Pte.
Webb, W., Pte.
Webster, S. N., Cpl.
Weeks, S., Pte.
Welch, F. T., Pte.
Welch, H. E., Pte.
Wells, F. T., Pte.
Wells, J. F., Pte.
Wells, J. G., Pte.
Wenham, H. C., **Pte.**
West, A. C., Pte.
West, F., Pte.
West, G. S. W., Pte.
Westover, W. G., Pte.
Westwood, S. H., Sergt.
Wheeler, A. G., Pte.
Wheeler, B., Pte.
Whitby, W., Pte.
White, B., Pte.
White, C., Pte.
White, E., L/Cpl.
White, E., Pte.
White, G. P., Pte.
White, J., Pte.
White, J. T., Pte.
Whitehead, G., Pte.
Whitfield, F. J., **Pte.**
Whiting, G., Pte.
Whitlock, B., Pte.

Whowall, G., **Pte.**
Whowell, A. J., Pte.
Wickes, C. A. J., **Pte.**
Wickers, C., Pte.
Wilkes, G. L., 2/Lt.
Wilkinson, A. C., Pte.
Wilkinson, J. W., **Pte.**
Wilkinson, W., Pte.
Willcocks, A. W., Pte.
Williams, C. B., 2/Lt.
Williams, A. L., Pte.
Williams, E. S., L/Cpl.
Williams, F., Pte.
Williams, J., Pte.
Williams, T. J., **Pte**
Williams, Z., Pte.
Willingale, F., Pte.
Willis, C. H., Pte.
Wilson, E. B., Pte.
Wilson, H., Pte.
Wilson, J. E., Pte.
Wilson, T., Pte.
Wilson, W. J., Pte.
Winbledon, C., Pte.
Windebank, W. H., Pte.
Winn, J. N., Pte.
Winter, R. K., L/Cpl.
Wiseman, J. M., L/Cpl.
Witchurch, A. R., Pte.
Wood, B. R. P., 2/Lt.
Wood, H. H., Pte.
Wood, H., Pte.
Wood, P., Pte.
Woodhouse, C. W., Pte.
Woods, F., L/Cpl.
Woolhead, W. A., **Pte.**
Woolhouse, R., Pte.
Woolsey, R. J., Pte.
Worboys, S., Pte.
Worley, G. A., L/Cpl.
Wormull, A. G., Pte.
Wright, J. A. L., Pte.
Wyles, F. G., Pte.

Yates, H. G., Pte.
Yellop, W. W. R., **Pte.**
York, H. J., Pte
York, J., Pte.
Yorke, S. J., Pte.
Young, C. L., Pte.
Young, F. C., L/Cpl.
Young, R. A., Pte.

Officers killed while attached to 7th London:
Capt. H. PETLEY (2/1st London).
Lieut. H. F. STAPLETON (2/1st London).
2/Lieut. A. K. SANDERSON (Middlesex).
Lieut. J. TIPLADY (Middlesex).

APPENDIX D

HONOURS LIST 1914—1919

1/7th BATTALION THE LONDON REGIMENT
140th BRIGADE.   47th DIVISION

Compiled mainly from Supplement to the Monthly Army List, October 1919, and 47th Divisional History.

† Already the recipient of M.C. prior to joining the Regiment.
*Name appears elsewhere in this Appendix.
Rank shown is that as at date of award.

ORDER OF ST. MICHAEL AND ST. GEORGE
*Faux, Col. E.   Companion.

DISTINGUISHED SERVICE ORDER
*Salkeld Green, Lieut.-Col. C. J.

MILITARY CROSS AND BAR
Rundell, Capt. L. E.

BAR TO M.C.
†Palmer, Lieut. C. R.

MILITARY CROSS

Bishop, Lieut. L. E.
Blackhurst, Lieut. S.
Chatterton, Lieut. J.
Cook, Lieut. R. J.

Eve, Lieut. R. N.
Goldsbury, Lieut. C. M.

*Salkeld Green, Capt. C. J.
Harman, 2nd Lieut. H. H.
*Juriss, Lieut. M.
King, Capt. H. H. (att. from P.O.R.'s)
Mileman, 2nd Lieut. V. W.
Preston, Lieut. J. F.

Roberts, Lieut. H. O. B.
Sutton, Capt. D.
Taylor, 2nd Lieut. R. E.
Thomas, Lieut. R. W.

Wigney, Lieut. C. R. D'A
Wright, J., R.S.M.

DISTINGUISHED CONDUCT MEDAL

Allan, F. M., Pte.
*Bacon, C. W. C., Sergt.
Baker, A., Sergt.
*Bowers, C. C., Sergt.
*Brooks, F. G., Cpl.
*Collins, H., C.S.M.
Crisford, J. E., L/Cpl.

Day, A. E., Pte.
Gilder, T. H., Sergt.
Hayward, T., Sergt.
*Hill, G., C.S.M.
Hodge, J., L/Cpl.
Jeffries, S., C.S.M.
King, J., Sergt.
Warner, S., L/Cpl.

*Monck, H., Sergt.
Moon, F., Sergt.
Newnham, A. E., Pte.
Powell, H. J. H., Sergt
Shadwell, A., Sergt.
Steele, G. W., Cpl.
*Taylor, A. J., Sergt.

MILITARY MEDAL AND BAR

Baker, W. M., Pte.

Bond, R. E., Pte.

Huntley, J. C., Pte.

MILITARY MEDAL

*Bacon, C. W., L/Cpl.
Baker, A., L/Cpl.
Baker, H. A., Cpl.
Barclay, G., Pte.
Betts, W. C., Pte.

Edwards, W., Pte.
Fairman, C. D., Pte.
Foster, C. C., Pte.
Fuller, C. E., L/Cpl.
Gadd, C., Pte.

Mills, T., Pte.
Missions, A., Cpl.
*Monck, H., Sergt.
Newton, C., Pte.
Newton, R. G., L/Cpl.

HONOURS LIST 1914-1919

Military Medal—(continued)
*Bowers, C. C., Sergt.
*Brooks, F. G., Cpl.
Browning, W. G., Pte.
Brownsall, A., Pte.
Burden, S., Sergt.
Chalk, F., Pte.
Christmas, H. C., Pte.
Claydon, W. A., Sergt.
Coles, P. H., Pte.
Coles, W. P. V., Sergt.
Cook, J. A., Pte.
Cornell, A., Pte.
Crudgington, G. L., L/Cpl.
Davey, W. H., Cpl.
Dickens, G. R., L/Cpl.
Dilley, W., Pte.
Downs, G. H., Pte.
Duck, H., Sergt.
Edwards, G. E., Sergt.

Gill, H. V., Pte.
Gordon, E. J., Pte.
Griffen, E. T., Pte.
Halls, G., Pte.
Harris, J., Pte.
Hendry, H. O., L/Cpl.
Honig, H., Pte.
Horley, W. E., Pte.
Huggins, P., Pte.
Hyder, H., Pte.
Jones, P., Pte.
Knight, A., Pte.
Leary, W., Cpl.
Lovelock, H. W., L/Cpl.
Luton, J., Pte.
McCullum, S., L/Cpl.
Marr, G., Sergt.
Marson, G., L/Cpl.
Meader, F., Pte.

Nodder, J., L/Cpl.
Norford, W., Cpl.
Pettitt, G., Pte.
Pilley, E. C., Sergt.
Sage, W., Pte.
Seddon, J. H., Sergt.
Shepherd, G., L/Cpl.
Shepherd, W., L/Cpl.
Steele, A., Pte.
Sumner, H. J., Pte.
Taylor, F. G., Pte.
Vincent, H., Pte.
Vivian, E. T. J., Pte.
Warren, P., Pte.
Wilcox, H., Pte.
Wilson, J. A., L/Cpl.
Winter, E., Cpl.
Winter, W., Pte.

M.S.M.
*Collins, H., C.S.M.   Hughes, H. J., C.Q.M.S.   Norton, A., Sergt.

CROIX DE GUERRE, FRENCH
Pearse, 2nd Lieut. E. W.   *Taylor, A., Sergt.

CROIX DE GUERRE, BELGIAN
*Salkeld Green, Lieut.-Col. C. J.   Brooks, H., Pte.   Coleman, R., Sergt.

DECORATION MILITAIRE, BELGIAN
*Bowers, C. C., Sergt.

2/7th BATTALION THE LONDON REGIMENT. 174th BRIGADE
7th BATTALION THE LONDON REGIMENT. 58th DIVISION
1917-19

DISTINGUISHED SERVICE ORDER
† Johnston, Lieut.-Col. C. E., M.C.

MILITARY CROSS AND BAR
Peppiatt, Capt. K. O.

MILITARY CROSS
Berliner, Capt. P. B.
Cooke, 2nd Lieut. R. B.
Fraser, Lieut. A. C.
Halley Jones, Capt. P.

Hewton, 2nd Lieut. R. S.
Michell, Lieut. L.
Pinnock, Lieut. E. W.
Payne, F. R.S.M.

Shannon, Lieut. S. B.
Walsh, Capt. L. H., D.C.M.
Wilson, Lieut. J. H.

DISTINGUISHED CONDUCT MEDAL
Archdeacon, J., C.S.M.   Williams, L., C.S.M.

MILITARY MEDAL
Brooks, L/Cpl.
Chapman, A., Sergt.

Gay, G. A., Pte.
Haxell, F., Sergt.

Miller, H., Pte.
Neben, W., Sergt.

HONOURS LIST 1917-1919

Military Medal—(*continued*)
Chetland, J., Cpl.
Emmett, R., Pte.
Edwards, Sgt.
Goodman, T., Sergt.
Grieg, H., Pte.
Hislop, W. M., Sergt.
Kerr, M., Sergt.
Leman, A., Pte.
Long, V., Pte.
Lonon, J., Cpl.
Lydiart, H., Cpl.
Neale, W. G. V., Cpl.
Precious, Sergt.
Ross, G., Pte.
Townsend, L/Cpl.
Woodcock, Dmr.

M.S.M.
Heale, F., C.Q.M.S.

MEDAILLE D'HONNEUR
Scothorne, F., C.Q.M.S.

CROIX DE GUERRE, FRENCH
Scholey, F., Sergt.
Marsden, Cpl.

HONOURS AND AWARDS WON BY MEMBERS OF THE 7th BATTALION, THE LONDON REGIMENT, WHILE SERVING WITH OTHER UNITS

O.B.E. (MILITARY DIVISION)
Stewart-Bam, Sir P. (Reserve Battn.)
Barnes, Maj. H. D.
* Juriss, Lieut. M.

MILITARY CROSS AND ONE BAR
Peppiatt, Capt. L. E., 1/19th Lon. Regt.
Hodgson, Lieut. F., 50th M.G. Battn

MILITARY CROSS
Brewer, Capt. E. B., 140th T.M.B.
Lucas, 2nd Lieut. J., Royal Fus's.
*Hill, Lieut. G., Tank Corps
James, Lieut. L. E., K.R.R.C.
Keeler, 2nd Lieut. O. A., K.R.R.C.
Keey, Lieut. C. W., 2/10th Lon. Regt.
Peate, Lieut. E. W., 4th R.W.F.'s
Raby, Capt. V. H., 1/22nd Lon. Regt.
Smout, 2nd Lieut. P. L., 2/20th Lon. Regt.
White, 2nd Lieut. J. B., 1/19th Lon. Regt.
Winterflood, 2nd Lieut. L. W., 1/19th Lon. Regt.
Williams, 2nd Lieut. N. O., K.R.R.C.
Bold, 2nd Lieut. A. L. D.
Dryden, 2nd Lieut. S. G.
Foord, Lieut. B. A.
Hasslacher, Lieut. A. J. E
Jones, Lieut. G. E.
Lort, Lieut. W. V.
Randall, Lieut. C. J.
Shilcock, 2nd Lieut. H. G.
Urquart, Lieut. W.

MILITARY MEDAL
Ferris, B., L/Cpl., 140th T.M.B.
Rasberry, M., Cpl., 140th T.M.B.
Phelan, S., L/Cpl., 1/22nd Lon. Regt.

M.S.M.
Field, R. J., S.M., 140th T.M.B.

CHEVALIER DE LA LEGION D'HONNEUR
Enoch, Maj. C. D.

Every effort has been made to ensure the accuracy of these lists and any corrections, omissions or additions would be welcomed for record purposes.

APPENDIX E
MEMORIALS AND STANDARDS

47th DIVISION

In the first instance, a wooden cross was erected at High Wood, this was later substituted by a stone cross with a canopy and ashlar surround of stone.

The site it occupies measures seven metres by five metres, is in the commune of Combles and a short distance east of " London Cemetery," High Wood.

The monument received the approval of the Battle Exploits Memorials Committee of the War Office, and was unveiled by Major-General Sir William Thwaites, K.C.B.. K.C.M.G., on September 15th, 1925, and is inscribed:

To the Glorious Memory
of the
GALLANT OFFICERS, N.C.O.'s and MEN
of the
47th (LONDON) DIVISION
who lost their lives in the capture of High Wood,
SEPTEMBER 15th, 1916

The Divisional Memorial at Martinpuich takes the form of loggia and entrance gateway to the school playground. This was originally handed over to the Maire of the commune. Both memorials are under the care of the Imperial War Graves Commission for normal maintenance.

58th DIVISION

At Chipilly, eleven kilometres south of Albert, is a Memorial consisting of a drinking trough surmounted by a sculptural group of a British soldier holding the head of a dying charger.

It was erected on communal land in 1923 under the auspices of General Ramsay. The architect was a Frenchman, Monsieur Guillaume, and the sculptor, also French, Monsieur H. Gauquie. The inscription on the memorial is as follows:

Aux Morts de la 58eme Division Britannique
London Division

La 58eme Division Britannique fut une des seules Divisions Anglaises qui en cooperation avec l'Armée Francaise et les Corps d'Armée Australiens et Canadians reussit a penetrer les défenses Allemands entre le Quesnoy et Montidier le 8e Aout, 1918, déterminant le commencement de la retraite Allemande qui se termina par l'Armistice du 11 Novembre, 1918.

In the entrance hall at Sun Street Headquarters is a memorial plaque recording the casualties of the Regiment in the Great War 1914–1919.

STANDARDS

A silk standard, 4 ft. by 3 ft., carried out in Regimental colours—scarlet background with buff edging and blue lettering.

The 7th City of London badge in gold occupies the central position and the following words appear in ornamental scrolls:

7th (City of London) Battalion
The London Regiment
To the Glory of God in Memory of all Ranks
who fell in the Great War 1914–1918

This Standard was provided by members of the Old Comrades' Association and presented to the British Church of St. George, Ypres, and on May 16th, 1937, was unveiled by Lieut.-Col. C. J. Salkeld Green, D.S.O., M.C., T.D., in the presence of a large number of Old Comrades. A replica of this standard is carried by the Old Comrades on suitable occasions.

APPENDIX F

Copy of Letter written to Lt.-Col. C. J. S. Green by Brig.-Gen. the Right Hon. Viscount Hampden on giving up the command of the 140th Infantry Brigade

No. 10 Stationary Hospital,
St. Omer.
May 18th, 1917.

My Dear Green,

I am to be evacuated to the Base this morning and I presume from there to England. There are no words to express my feelings. It is an unlucky moment to break down, but there it is—the fortune of war. I hope to be right again in a few weeks and at it again, but I shall have lost my brigade and many friends.

I can't go without putting on paper my thanks to you and those under you in the 7th for all the help which has been given to me in the past ten months. It has been a pleasant task to command the 140th Brigade, and everything from my side has appeared to work smoothly. I hope you feel the same.

I shall follow your doings and those of the gallant 7th with more than deep interest and I wish you the highest degree of success. After all these months in the Ypres Salient and the trials and discomforts your officers and men have put up with so uncomplainingly, they deserve to achieve a glorious victory, and I have every confidence that they will do more than their share when called upon.

A final word as regards yourself—I recall to mind that one of the first public acts which I performed on taking command was to inspect the 7th Battalion. I congratulated you then on the appearance of the battalion and, speaking from hearsay, on its gallantry in the past. Now, after a knowledge based on the fighting at the Somme and a winter in the Ypres Salient, I can again say that you should be a proud man to command such a battalion—and, after all, in war particularly, the efficiency of the battalion is entirely dependent on the efficiency and energy of the C.O. You have had, like others, much to contend with in the way of new officers and men, etc., but I am quite sure that when you turn your head eastwards at the end of this month you will have under your command as well trained a lot of men as possible under the circumstances. As regards their fighting qualities, they will follow in the footsteps of the men of the 7th who have gone before them. I am sure of that—and what more could you ask?

I should be grateful if you would convey to all your officers and men my deep disappointment and regret at leaving them, and I wish them all fortune in the future, wherever they are.

Yours very sincerely,
HAMPDEN.

APPENDIX G
REGIMENTAL TITLES, DATES, AND COMMANDING OFFICERS

1798 THE TEMPLE BAR AND ST. PAUL'S ASSOCIATION.
Lt.-Col. J. Atkinson.
1803 THIRD REGIMENT OF LOYAL LONDON VOLUNTEERS.
Col. Kensington.
1860 3rd CITY OF LONDON RIFLE VOLUNTEERS.
Col. Sir William De Bathe, Bt. 1861
Col. Bates Richards 1861–1867
Col. R. P. Laurie, C.B. 1867–1892
Col. Gerald E. Boyle 1892–1895
Col. Mortimer Hancock, V.D. 1895–1900
Col. E. C. Stevenson, V.D. 1900–1904
1904* 3rd (CITY OF) LONDON VOLUNTEER RIFLE CORPS.
Col. T. C. Ekin 1904
1908 7th (CITY OF LONDON) BATTALION THE LONDON REGT.
Col. T. C. Ekin 1912
Lt.-Col. G. A. A. Viscount Hood 1912–1914
1914 1/7th (CITY OF LONDON) BATTALION THE LONDON REGT.
Col. E. Faux, V.D. 1914–May 1916
Major C. J. Salkeld Green, M.C. .. .. .. May 1916–Aug. 1916
Col. E. Faux, C.M.G., V.D. .. .. Aug. 1916–Sept. 1916
Lt.-Col. C. J. Salkeld Green, D.S.O., M.C. .. Sept. 1916–Feb. 1918
1914 2/7th (CITY OF LONDON) BATTALION THE LONDON REGT.
Lt.-Col. C. W. Berkeley, T.D. .. .. .. Oct. 1914–April 1917
Lt.-Col. E. N. French .. .. April 1917–Sept. 1917
Lt.-Col. S. L. Hosking .. .. Sept. 1917–Feb. 1918
1918 7th (CITY OF LONDON) BATTALION THE LONDON REGT.
Lt.-Col. S. L. Hosking .. .. Feb. 1918–April 1918
Lt.-Col. A. A. Hanbury Sparrow, D.S.O., M.C. April 1918–July 1918
Lt.-Col. C. E. Johnston, D.S.O., M.C. .. .. .. July 1918–1921
(Including post-war reformed Battalion).
3rd/7th (CITY OF LONDON) RESERVE BATTALION THE LONDON REGT.
Lt.-Col. Sir P. C. van B. Stewart-Bam, O.B.E. 1915–1918
1922 7th CITY OF LONDON REGT. (POST OFFICE.)
Lt.-Col. J. Stewart, D.S.O. 1922–1924
Lt.-Col. and Bt. Col. W. B. Vince, D.S.O., O.B.E., M.C. .. 1924–1931
Bt. Col. E. E. F. Baker, D.S.O., M.C. 1931–1935
1936 32nd (7th CITY OF LONDON) ANTI-AIRCRAFT BATTALION, R.E. (T.A.)
Bt. Col. H. C. Murgatroyd, M.C., T.D. 1936–1939
Major L. F. S. Dawes, M.B.E., R.E. (T.) .. Sept. 1939–Oct. 1939
Lt.-Col. S. N. Beall .. .. .. Oct. 1939–April 10, 1940
1940 32nd SEARCHLIGHT REGT. R.A. (7th CITY OF LONDON T.A.)
Lt.-Col. C. J. Woolley, M.C. .. .. April 11, 1940–Aug. 27, 1941
Lt.-Col. L. S. Davis, T.D. .. .. .. Aug. 28, 1941–July 8, 1944
Lt.-Col. G. W. Hogsflesh, O.B.E., T.D. .. July 9, 1944–Feb. 27, 1945
Lt.-Col. V. C. Ritchie, M.B.E. .. .. Feb. 27, 1945–May 8, 1945
Major D. C. Bowman .. .. .. May 9, 1945–Jan. 1946

* Information obtained from District Orders dated April 20th, 1904.
Battalion Orders previous to 1904 are headed "Third City of London Rifles," and also "Third London Rifles."

APPENDIX H
32nd SEARCHLIGHT REGT., R.A. (7th CITY OF LONDON, T.A.)

Commanding Officers, Seconds-in-Command, Battery Commanders, Adjutants and Quartermasters. September 3rd, 1939, to May 8th, 1945

COMMANDING OFFICERS

Lt.-Col. L. F. S. Dawes, M.B.E.	Sept. 3, 1939–Oct. 1939
Lt.-Col. S. N. Beall	Oct. 1939–April 10, 1940
Lt.-Col. C. J. Woolley, M.C.	April 11, 1940–Aug. 27, 1941
Lt.-Col. L. S. Davis, T.D.	Aug. 28, 1941–July 8, 1944
Lt.-Col. G. W. Hogsflesh, O.B.E., T.D.	July 9, 1944–Feb. 27, 1945
Lt.-Col. V. C. Ritchie, M.B.E.	Feb. 27, 1945–May 8, 1945

SECONDS-IN-COMMAND

Major E. A. Parr-Dudley	Oct. 7, 1940–Dec. 12, 1940
Major L. S. Davis, T.D.	Dec. 13, 1940–Aug. 27, 1941
Major K. J. Pearce	Aug. 28, 1941–Aug. 20, 1944
Major J. Woods, M.B.E.	Aug. 21, 1944–May 8, 1945

BATTERY COMMANDERS

328 Battery.

Major L. S. Davis, T.D.	Sept. 3, 1939–Oct. 14, 1940
Major W. F. J. Gartell	Oct. 14, 1940–April 17, 1941
Major A. E. F. Barnes	April 18, 1941–Nov. 29, 1944
Major J. E. G. Quick	Nov. 30, 1944–May 8, 1945

329 Battery.

Major S. N. Beall	Sept. 3, 1939–Oct. 1939
Major Penney, M.B.E.	Oct. 1939–April 4, 1940
Major K. J. Pearce	April 5, 1940–Aug. 27, 1941
Major The Hon. R. E. O. Long, T.D.	Aug. 28, 1941–Oct. 17, 1942
Major V. C. Green, M.C.	Oct. 18, 1942–May 8, 1945

330 Battery.

Major E. A. Parr-Dudley	Sept. 3, 1939–Sept. 14, 1940
Major C. Pryor	Sept. 15, 1940–Nov. 22, 1941
Major G. Blake	Nov. 23, 1941–Nov. 10, 1943
Major N. A. Straker	Nov. 11, 1943–May 8, 1945

562 Battery.

Major W. F. J. Gartell	July 2, 1941–Nov. 14, 1941
Major C. W. Cronin T.D.	Nov. 15, 1941–Nov. 16, 1942
Major K. Stockell	Nov. 17, 1942–April 4, 1944

ADJUTANTS

Captain W. J. Alywin, R.E.	Sept. 3, 1939–Oct. 1939
Captain C. Pryor	Oct. 1939–Sept. 14, 1940
Captain J. R. L. Nicholson	Sept. 15, 1940–Sept. 1941
Captain N. A. Straker	Sept. 1941–Sept. 14, 1942
Captain G. T. Hollebone	Sept. 15, 1942–June 11, 1944
Captain D. B. Burrage	June 12, 1944–May 8, 1945

QUARTERMASTERS

Captain V. H. A. Holdich	Sept. 3, 1939–June 1, 1940
Major G. Norman, R.A.	June 2, 1940–May 8, 1945

INDEX

Abbott, Pte. W. H., 175, **245**
Addison, C.Q.S.M. G., 70, 224, 239, 242
Albert, 77, 88, 192, 244, 256
Aldred, Pte. E., 152, 245
Alexander, Lieut. J., 195, 245
Aitkens, Lt. A., 16, 24, 245
Allan, Pte. F. M., 37, 50, 253
Allan, Pte. J. K., 19, 245
Amalgamated Battalion, 184
Angus, Sergt. J. W., 82, 245
Angus, Sergt. G., 201, 245
Anti-Aircraft Battalion, 225
Archdeacon, S.M. J., 145, 149, 204, **254**
Arras, 128, 151, 164, 165
Aryton, Capt. B. F., 91, 104
Ashley, Pte. E., 163, 245
Atkinson, Lieut.-Col. J., 2
Aubyn, Lieut. J. K., 96, 120, 126
Auchel, 17, 19
Bacon, Sergt. C., 81, 116, 253
Bailey, Lieut. C. F., 152, 245
Baisieux, 192, 194, 195
Baker, Lieut-.Col. E. E. F., 223, 224, 225, 258
Baker, L/Cpl. A., 116, 253
Baker, Sergt. A., 126, 253
Baker, Pte. W. M., 81, 116, 253
Baker, Cpl. H., 119, 253
Balaam, Pte, P., 109, 245
Bam, Lieut.-Col. S., 217, 218, 255, **258**
Barisis, 184, 185, 186
Barclay, Pte. G., 67, 253
Barnes, Maj. H. D., 10, 13, 14, 15, 19, 21, 23, 223, 232, 239, 255
Barnes, Lieut.-Col. A. E. F., 225, 232, 240, 259
Barter, Maj. Gen. Sir C., 13, 14, 17, 23, 59, 60, 83
Bartlett, Sergt. H. P., 201, **245**
Battle Honours, 11, 243
Beall, Maj. S. N., 228, 258, 259
Bell, Capt. A., 16, 23, 38, 41, 42
Beloeil, 213, 214
Bennett, Maj. C., 6
Benstead, Lieut. H. E., 188, 245
Berkeley, Lt.-Col. C. W., 7, 8, 9, 143, 146, 148, 156, 218, 258
Berliner, Capt. P. B., 149, 155, 158, 160, 178, 183, 189, 191, 197, 199, 201, 204, 221, 254
Berles, 151, 153
Betts, Pte. W. C., 90, 95, 253
Bethune, 18, 19, 23, 26
Bezley, Pte. W., 109, 245
Bishop, Lieut. L. E., 91, 103, 126, 139, 190, 221, 253
Blackhurst, Lieut. S., 108, 116, 142, 253
Boast, Dmr. B., 27, 245
Bond, L/Cpl. H., 43, 48
Bond, Pte. R. E., 87, 90, 95, 126, 253
Bosher, Pte. F. N., 19, 245
Bosher, Cpl. C. W., 44, 245
Bosher, Pte. R. F., 44, 245
Bourlon Wood, 130, 132
Bowers, Pte. W., 44, 245
Bowers, Sergt. C., 110, 116, **135**, 142, 245, 253, 254
Bowles, Pte. S. W., 19, 245

Boyce, Col. A., 6, 8
Boyle, Col. C. E., 6, 8, **258**
Brabham, Sergt. A. H., 121, 245
Brebis, 29, 31, 32, 36, 49
Brewer, Capt. E. B., 44, 107, 255
Brooks, Cpl. F. G., 126, 127, 135, 253, 254
Brooks, Lieut. W. V., 65
Brooks, Pte. H., 142, 254
Brooks, L/Cpl., 163, **254**
Browning, Pte., W. G., 131, 135, 139, 254
Brownsall, Pte. A., 90, 95, 254
Bubb, L/Cpl. T., 28, 246
Buckingham, Pte. H., 44, 246
Budd, Capt. J. G. H., 15, 21, 59, 73, 136, 142, 184, 191, 197, 202, 203, 205
Bull, Pte. J., 52, 246
Bullecourt, 157, 159, 243, 244
Burden, C.S.M. S., 50, 81, 91, 246, **254**
Burgin, Sergt. C., 77, 246
Butte de Warlencourt, 12, 83, 85, 89, 95, 244
Byham, Sergt. R., 168, 246
Caestre, 91, 112, 117, 128
Cambrai, 129, 243, 244
Canopy, 233, 234
Carency, 57, 58, 60
Carew, Pte. E. W., 19, 246
Carter, L/Cpl. A., 154, 246
Cartwright, Capt. C., 87, 88, 96, 99, 116, 218
Casson, Maj. W., 14, 15, 20, 33, 35, 37, 42, 43
Cator, Maj.-Gen. A., 192, 194
Cawston ; Lieut.-Col., J., 6
Chalk, Pte. F., 117, 254
Chapman, Pte. J. G., 31, 246
Chapman, Sergt. A., 201, 254
Chatterton, Lieut. J., 44, 47, 52, 53, 221, 253
Cherisy, 162
Chetland, Cpl. J., 201, 255
Chipilly, 197, 199, 201
Chizlett, Pte. T. C., 52, 246
Christmas, Pte. H. C., 90, 254
Clarke, Pte. T., 154, 246
Claydon, Sergt. W. A., 67, 254
Coles, Lt. W., 67, 83, 89, 254
Cole, Cpl. S., 97, 246
Coleman, Sergt. R., 142, 254
Colerdige, Capt. W. D., 149, 155, 158, 202, 207, 212
Collins, C.S.M. H., 73, 95, 102, 253, 254
Constance, Lieut. W. E., 201, 246
Cook, Lieut. R. J., 91, 116, 253
Cook, Pte. J. A., 119, 254
Cooke, Lt. R. B., 205, 206, 254
Cornell, Pte. A., 135, 254
Cownden, Pte. S., 161, 246
Craven, L/Cpl. R., 124, 246
Cripps, Sergt. F., 201, 246
Crisford, L/Cpl. J., 52, 54, 253
Crisp, Cpl. W. S., 201, 246
Crossman, Col. A., 3, 6
Crossingham, L/Cp. C. P., 27, 246
Crudgington, L/Cpl. G., 135, 246 254
Cryer, Lieut. B. N., 110, 125, 246

Cryer Farm, **122, 125, 126**
Cudmore, Pte. S., 175, 246
Culverwell, Lieut. W., 16, 38
Cunnington, L/Cpl. T., 122, 246
Cuthbert, Brig.-Gen., G. J., 13, 29, **47, 58,** 74
Daniels, Pte. J., 213, 246
Dansey, Lt. F., 195, 246
Davenport, Lieut. G. C., 96, **99**, 109, 135
Davey, Cpl. W. H., 116, 254
David, Pte. J. J., 52, 246
Davis, Lieut. B. C., 142, 246
Davis, Lieut. F. M., 15, 35, 37, 52, 56, 61, 65, 142.
Davis, Lieut .-Col., L. S., 223 226, 228, 232, 238, 239, 241, 242, 258, 259
Dawes, Lieut.-Col., L. F. S., 228, 258, 259
Day, Pte., A. E., 25, 253
Daykin, Pte. H. J., 52, 247
Dickens, L/Cpl. G., 81, 254
Dilley, Pte. W., 116, 254
Doll, Maj. R., 6, 9, 10
Donaldson, Lieut. D., 43, 247
Downs, Pte. H., 135, 254
Duck, Sergt. H., 66, 254
Dunham, Pte. F., 97, 102, 108, 117, 119, 132, 138
Eady, Pte. A. D., 21, 247
Eastoe, L/Cpl. F. H., 44, **247**
Ecksteen, Lieut. A., 149, 158
Edgar, Lieut. S., 84, 89, 247
Edwards, Sgt. G. E., 135, 254
Edwards, Pte. W., 95, 102, 135, 247, **253**
Edwards-Trollip, Lt., 203, 204
Ekin, Col. T. C., 7, 11, 258
Elms, L/Cpl. A. J., 135, 247
Elvy, S.M. A., 145, 149, 159
Emmet, Pte. E., 189, **255**
Endall, Cpl. P., 161, 247
Enoch, Maj. C. D., 10, **14, 15,** 20, 23, 29, 32, 45, 255
Epehy, 206, 207, 244
Epilogue, 219
Erwin, Pte. R., 154, **247**
Erwin, L/Cpl. H. M., 188, **247**
Eve, Capt. R. N., 91, 116, **253**
Evershed, Lieut. P. D., 106, 108, 139, 141, 247
Everson, C.S.M. L. W., 187, 247
Fairman, Pte. C., 135, 253
Faux, Col. E., 7, 12, 15, 20, 29, 36, 37, 43, 45, 49, 50, 56, **58**, 60, 63, 76, 83, 216, 243, **253** 258
Faux, Capt. C. L., 148, 152
Fearnside Speed, Capt. D., 148, 150, 158, 159, 160
Fearnside Speed, Lieut. R., 27, 35, 38, 41, 247
Feast, Pte. H., 52, 247
Feaveryear, Lt. A., 141, 247
Ferris, L/Cpl. B., 67, 247
Ferguson, Lieut. A. A., 24, 27, 35, 37, 247
Festubert, 12, 18, 21, 22, 164, 243, 244
Fisher, Pte. J., 45, 247
Fletcher, Lt., 15, 22, 23, 242, 247

Flower, Capt. L. A. L., 16, 17, 24, 27, 35, 59, 88, 247
Folley, Sergt. T., 201, 247
Foret Farm, 114, 118
Foster, Pte. C., 126, 139, 253
Foster, Capt. R. T., 8, 15, 37, 46
Fox, Pte. C. L., 175, 247
Fraser, Lieut. A. C., 195, 201, 205, 206, 247, 254
Freeston, Capt., 148, 168, 186
French, Lord, 17, 41, 146
French, Lieut.-Col. E. N., 156, 158, 169, 258
Frost, C.S.M. G. T., 149, 171, 175, 247
Fry, Capt. B., 148, 160, 176
Fryer, Col/Sgt. B., 9, 242
Fuller, L/Cpl. C., 90, 95, 253
Fuller, Pte. F., 162, 247
Gallagher, Lieut., 143, 148, 208
Gardiner, L/Cpl. J., 104, 247
Gay, Pte. A., 175, 247, 254
Gibson, Lt. A., 96, 104, 106, 108
Gilder, Sgt. T. H., 37, 50, 253
Gill, Pte. H. V., 81, 254
Gladwin, Pte. G., 48, 247
Glenton, Capt. F., 119, 209, 212, 214
Godfrey, L/Cpl. A., 42, 247
Godfrey, L/Cpl. E. C., 42, 247
Godson, Capt. M. W., 145, 149
Goodman, Sgt., 215, 255
Goldsbury, Lieut. C. M., 96, 118, 119, 253
Gordon, Pte. J., 117, 254
Gorringe, Sir F. G., 95, 112, 139
Green, Maj. H. S., 143, 146, 148, 167, 171, 174, 175, 183, 248
Green, Lieut.-Col. C. J. S., 14, 15, 19, 20, 24, 25, 26, 33, 35, 37, 38, 42, 45, 46, 49, 56, 58, 60, 63, 65, 68, 72, 75, 80, 83, 95, 97, 98, 107, 108, 112, 113, 116, 125, 133, 140, 141, 142, 143, 192, 193, 220, 239, 253, 254, 257, 258
Greensleeves, 1, 60, 128, 219, 220
Greenyer, L/Cpl. T., 42, 248
Griffen, Pte. E. T., 81, 254
Haddy, Pte. E., 18, 248
Hadleigh, 230, 231, 233, 236
Haig, Sir D., 19, 72, 131, 202
Halls, Pte. G., 116, 254
Hally-Jones, Capt. P., 144, 149, 197, 199, 200, 248, 254
Halsey, Lt. E., 149, 162, 248
Hallworth, Pte. C., 101, 248
Hampden, Lord, 74, 90, 91, 95, 98, 112, 257
Hampton, Lieut. O. A., 61, 64, 67
Hancock, Col. M., 6, 8, 10, 258
Hancock, Lieut. A. L., 65, 248
Hangard Wood, 183, 190, 191
Hankey, Capt. G. F. B., 8
Hardy, R.S.M., 14, 46
Harris, Pte. F., 53, 248
Harris, Pte. J., 117, 187, 248, 254
Harrison, Sgt. D., 213, 248
Harwich, 228, 237
Hartley, Capt. J., 27, 35, 38, 56, 61, 79, 95, 96
Haxell, C.S.M. R., 208, 254
Hayes, Pte. W. H., 45, 248
Hayward, Sergt. T., 24, 25, 253
Heale, C.Q.M.S. F. J., 149, 215, 255
Head, Lieut. G. L., 107, 141

Head, Lieut. J. L., 16, 44, 73
Head, Capt. H. G., 15, 20, 221
Hendry, L/Cpl. H., 81, 254
Henencourt Wood, 89, 192
Hepworth, Maj. J., 6
Hewton, Lt. R., 207, 209, 254
High Wood, 12, 77, 84, 89, 90, 136, 256
Higley, Pte. C., 152, 248
Higgins, Brig.-Gen. C., 155, 176, 190, 194, 195
Hill, C.S.M. G., 37, 242, 253, 255
Hill 60, 93, 114, 121
Hodge, L/Cpl. J., 52, 54, 253
Hogsflesh, Lt.-Col. G., 238, 258
Hohenzollern Redoubt, 44, 47, 48, 244
Honig, Pte. H., 117, 254
Honorary Colonels, 243
Honours List, 253, 254, 255
Hood, Lord, 11, 12, 258
Hooper, Sergt., 145, 171, 182
Hopcraft, L/Cpl. H., 201, 248
Horley, L/Cpl. W. E., 28, 42, 87, 90, 95, 187, 191, 205, 242, 254
Hosken, Lieut. V. F., 83, 89, 248
Hosking, Lieut-Col. S. L., 142, 143, 148, 169, 175, 183, 184, 188, 193, 195, 215, 239, 258
Howes, C.S.M. W., 27, 248
Huggins, Pte. P., 116, 254
Hughes, C.Q.M.S. H., 28, 254
Hunt, Pte. H., 17, 44, 53
Huntley, Pte. J., 116, 135, 253
Hyder, Pte. H., 117, 254
Ingram, Dr. W., 19
Ipswich, 146, 233
Jackson, Lieut. J. H., 38, 40, 81, 191, 197, 202, 203, 205, 206
Jackson, Lieut. G. G., 149, 189, 191, 197, 200, 201
Jacobs, Pte. A., 144, 248
Jay, Pte. G., 23, 248
Jenkinson, Sergt. R., 201, 248
Jenner, Capt., L. C. D., 8, 10
Jennings, L/Cpl. R., 51, 248
Jessup, Pte. H., 175, 248
Jones, Pte. P., 126, 254
Jones, Cpl. A., 201, 254
Johnston, Lieut.-Col. C. E., 196, 197, 199, 200, 201, 205, 212, 221, 254, 258
Johnson, Sergt. H. R., 42, 248
Johnstone, Capt. W. J., 119, 120, 135
Jolland, R.S.M. G., 238
Jordan, Capt. V., 44, 86, 89, 248
Juriss, Lieut. M., 49, 61, 253, 255
Jury, Lieut. G. R., 77, 248
Keeler, Lieut. O. A., 175, 248
Keeling, L/Cpl. A. E., 24, 248
Kempton Park, 177, 179, 181
Kennedy, Brig.-Gen. H., 112
Kerr, Sergt. W., 144, 255
Kettle, Cpl. R., 113
Kiddle, Sergt., 42, 249
King, Sergt. J., 116, 253
King-Church, Capt. C. E., 15, 33, 34, 35, 38, 41, 249
Kingsnorth, Cpl. A. H., 212, 249
Knight, Pte. A., 135, 254
K.R.R.C., 8, 27, 58, 221
Lang, Capt. L. H., 148, 154, 162
Laurie, Col. R. P., 2, 3, 5, 6, 243, 258
Laurie, Col. R. M., 5
Laurie, Capt. K. S., 5

Laurie, Maj. A. D., 5, 14, 15, 18, 23, 24, 33, 35, 37, 41, 239
Laurie, Mr. R. A., 6
Laurie, Maj.-Gen. P. R., 6
Leary, Cpl. W., 97, 139, 254
Lewis, Lieut. H. B., 135, 249
Lillers, 46, 54, 55, 58
Light, Lieut. A. D., 30, 38
Long, Capt. W. J., 8, 10
Long, Lieut. H. D., 58, 61, 62, 65
Loos, 12, 31, 164, 243, 244
Lord, L/Cpl. R., 135, 249
Lovelock, L/Cpl. H., 64, 67, 88, 254
Lucas, Lieut., 62, 131
Luck, Col.-Sergt. C., 9, 242
Luton, Pte. J., 109, 110, 254
Lydiart, Capt. H. E., 14, 16, 25, 35, 37, 41, 46, 56, 58
Lydiart, Sergt. H. E., 151, 153, 155, 159, 160, 162, 164, 175, 176, 210, 212, 214, 255
Maguire, Sergt. P., 135, 249
Mailley-Maillet, 154, 158
Maisnil Bouche, 60, 75
Malard Wood, 197, 198, 199
Mantle, Lieut. A., 148, 159, 249
Manningtree, 233
Maret-Tims, Lieut. R. D., 15, 22
Maroc, 28, 30, 35, 49
Marrieres Wood, 205, 206
Marr, Sergt. G., 67, 254
Marson, L/Cpl. G., 116, 254
Mason, Sergt. W. J., 201, 249
Matthews, Pte. H. C., 53, 249
Maule-French, Lt. E., 204, 249
Maxwell, Brig.-Gen. A., 195, 197, 201, 202, 223, 224, 243
McConnel, Lt. G., 145, 146, 148
McCullum, L/Cpl. S., 117, 254
McGrigor, Brig.-Gen. C., 145, 146, 155
Meader, Pte. F., 69, 102, 117, 189
Memorials, 256
Merchant, Lieut. W., 89, 249
Messines, 114, 243, 244
Metcalf, Lieut. C. D., 95, 110, 114, 142, 189
Michell, Lieut. L., 149, 158, 159, 160, 254
Michelmore, L/Cpl. G., 77, 249
Middleton, Pte. W., 52, 249
Middleton, R.Q.M.S., T., 9, 143, 217, 218
Mileman, Lt. V. 61, 68, 86, 88, 89, 90, 95, 126, 249, 253
Miller, Sergt. D. J., 201, 249
Mills, Pte. T., 139, 253
Mince, Pte. A., 57, 249
Minter, Pte. W., 175, 249
Mitcham, L/Cpl. H., 154, 249
Mitchell, Cpl. A., 168, 249
Mitchener, Pte. D., 116, 249
Missions, Cpl. A., 135, 253
Monck, Sergt. H., 90, 95, 109, 114, 128, 253
Monro, Gen. Sir C., 54, 55, 72
Moon, Sergt. F., 85, 119, 253
Moore, Lieut. C. L., 204, 249
Morris, Pte. A., 175, 249
Moses, Pte. N., 108, 249
Moxon, Sergt. T., 42, 249
Mudford, Maj. W., 7, 10, 143, 217, 218
Mudge, Sergt. E., 20
Murgatroyd, Bt.-Col. H. G., 225, 258

261

Napier, Lord, 4, 243
Neben, Sergt. W., 163, 201 250, 254
Newnham, Pte. A., 126, 127 253
Newton, L/Cpl. R., 67, 189, 253
Newton, Pte. C., 81, 95, 253
Nisbett, Cpl. N. M., 44, 250
Noad, Pte. W., 128, 250
Nodder, L/Cpl. J., 117, 250 254
Norford, Cpl. W. F., 113, 116 189, 250, 254
Norie, C.Q.M.S.W., 149, 185, 193
Norton, Pte. H., 42
Norton, Sergt. A., 95, 254
Nouex-les-Mines, 36, 46 48, 50
Odd, Cpl. F. J., 21, 250
O'Hara, Pte. A., 104, 250
Old Comrades' Association, 239
Palmer, Lt. C., 133, 139, 141, 253
Parker, L/Sergt. A., 51, 250
Parker, Lieut. G. V., 84, 89, 135
Passchendaele, 91, 165, 179 183, 243, 244
Patrickson, Col/Sergt. J., 9
Payne, R.S.M. F., 143, 144, 145, 146, 149, 187, 216, 254
Payne, Pte. D., 175, 250
Payne, Pte. A., 22, 250
Pearce, Lieut.-Col. K. J., 238 239, 259
Pearse, Lieut. E. W., 73 83 87, 89, 104, 113
Peppiatt, Capt. K. O., 91, 96 101, 103, 109, 116, 118, 120, 142, 191, 192, 194, 197, 199, 200, 205, 206, 209, 212, 216, 221, 254
Peppiatt, Capt. L. E., 139, 140, 141, 194, 217, 221, 222 255
Peruwelz, 201, 214, 215
Petley, Capt. H., 79, 252
Pettigrew, Lieut. F. C., 77, 88 113, 193
Pettitt, Pte. G., 126, 254
Philosophe, 29, 36
Pilley, Sergt. E. C., 135, 254
Pinnock, Lieut. E. W., 200, 201 206, 210, 254
Pitt, Pte. F. J., 50, 250
Planck, C. D., 239, 241, 242
Poelcappelle, 165, 172, 176, 177 179, 180, 181, 182
Pollock, Lieut.-Col. D., 6
Pope, Pte. H., 57, 250
Potter, Capt. R. F., 149, 163
Powell, Sergt. J., 37, 50, 75, 253
Precious, Sergt., 204, 255
Preston, Lt. J., 96, 108, 115, 116, 117, 119, 123, 124, 221 253
Price, Sergt. H., 9
Prince, Lieut. J., 16, 22, 25, 35 37, 40, 250
Prince, Capt. A., 143, 219
Prior, Cpl. W., 201, 250
Purdon, Pte. E., 53, 250
Pursuit to Mons, 243, 244
Pym, Lieut. J. W., 72, 73, 250
Raby, Lieut. V. H., 104, 140, 142, 187, 255
Ralph, Lieut. J. G., 72, 250
Ramsay, Maj.-Gen. F., 194
Rasberry, Cpl. M., 117, 255
Reader, Pte. A., 65, 250
Redway, Sergt. F., 46, 69
Regimental Colours, 2, 11, 225 243

Regimental Flash, 232
Rendlesham, 228
Reserve Battalion, 217, 258
Rhodes, Pte. A., 154, 250
Richards, Col. A. B., 3, 258
Richardson, Pte. A., 97, 250
Ridgway, Lieut. H., 89, 250
Ritchie, Lieut.-Col. V. C., 238 258, 259
Rivers, Pte. A., 175, 251
Roberts, Lieut. F. A., 201, 251
Roberts, Lieut. H., 16, 25, 35 36, 37, 40, 242, 251, 253
Robertson, Sergt. W., 69, 82 187, 242
Robertson, L/Cpl. C., 154, 251
Roche, Lieut. G. D., 14, 16, 19, 23, 38, 46, 56, 57, 70, 73, 96
Rogers, Pte. A., 175, 251
Rollings, Cpl. P., 169, 175, 251
Roots, Lieut. P. W., 116, 251
Rundell, Capt. L. E., 16, 27, 44 52, 53, 56, 61, 66, 81, 103, 107, 132, 136, 193, 251, 253
Rushworth, Capt. T., 15, 23 30 59, 61, 63, 65, 68, 72 76, 79, 251
Rushworth, Lieut. H. M., 16, 19, 31, 35, 38
Rust, Pte. T., 52, 251
St. Julien, 165, 166
Sage, Pte. W., 90, 254
Sanderson, Lieut. A. K., 35, 38 41, 252
Saxmundham, 231, 237, 238
Scothorne, C.Q.M.S. F., 144, 149, 150, 185, 189, 208
Sealy, L/Cpl. R. G., 154, 251
Seddon, Sergt. J., 135, 251 254
Shearman, Capt. A., 144, 149, 189, 251
Shepherd, L/Cpl., 67, 117, 254
Shepherd, Pte. L. G., 104, 251
Short, Cpl. A., 117, 251
Simencourt, 129 163, 164, 165
Simons, Lt. E., 144, 145, 189
Slater, Lt. G., 35, 41, 83, 89, 221
Smith, Henry Bates, 2
Smith, Rev. C., 2
Smith, Lieut. A. J., 16, 35, 38 41, 43, 251
Smith, Lieut. W., 16
Smith, R.Q.M.S. F., 149, 185
Smout, Lieut. P. L., 202, 221 255
Southwold, 237
Sparrow, Lt.-Col., 190, 195, 258
Squire, Lieut. L., 16, 22, 23, 251
Staines, Pte. E., 124, 251
Staines, Pte. F. H., 162, 251
Standards, 256
Stapleton, Lieut. H., 81, 252
Steele, Pte. A., 23, 67, 254
Steele, Sergt. G. W., 66, 253
Stevenson, Col. E. C., 10, 219, 243, 258
Stewart, Lieut.-Col. J., 222 224, 258
Stubbs, Pte. H., 44, 251
Such, Pte. T. G., 84, 251
Sumner, L/Cpl. H., 67, 254
Sutton Veny, 147
Sutton, Capt. D., 27, 35, 38, 56, 77, 91, 102, 118, 253
Symonds, Capt. H., 57, 59, 81, 142, 194, 197, 199, 201, 215
Talkington, Pte. T., 175, 251
Tanner, Pte. E. S., 53, 251

Taylor, L/Cpl. F., 31, 251
Taylor, Sergt. A. J., 37, 253
Taylor, Pte. F. G., 135, 254
Taylor, Lieut. R. E., 61, 63 66, 81, 253
Temple Bar and St. Paul's, 1 243, 258
Thistlewayte, Maj. E. W., 8, 14
Thomas, Lieut. R. W., 129, 133 141, 218, 253
Thomas, Maj. D., 145, 149 155, 215
Thompson, Lieut. A. S., 77, 252
Thurnell, Lt. W., 73, 79, 252
Thwaites, Sir W., 256
Tilley, L/Cpl. A., 201, 251
Tiplady, Lieut. J., 30, 35, 38 41, 252
Train Bands, 1, 3
Trevor, Col. J., 224, 243
Tyler, Lieut. W. A., 204, 252
Tyson, Sergt. A., 42, 252
Uniforms, 4
Vacquerie-le-Boucq, 150, 154
Vaus, Capt. E., 81, 103 108, 221
Venn, Lieut.-Col. W., 6
Vermelles, 27, 46, 136
Verquin, 36, 44, 46, 48
Villers-aux-Bois, 55, 57, 58, 60
Villers Bretonneux, 144, 187 188, 189, 190, 206, 208, 243
Vimy, 12, 61, 136, 164, 244
Vincent, Pte. H., 105, 110, 252, 254
Vivian, Pte. E., 126, 254
Vlamertinghe, 165, 166, 168
Voormezeele, 92, 109
Waight, Pte. A., 175, 252
Wakelin, L/Cpl. J. B., 21, 252
Walden, Pte. H., 44, 252
Wallis, Capt. A. R., 45, 61, 66, 69, 103, 115, 116, 117
Walker, Lt. R., 149, 159, 186, 252
Walsh, Lieut. J. H., 202, 203, 204, 252, 254
Ward, Pte. T. C., 101, 252
Ward, Pte. W., 131, 252
Wards, Lieut. G. T., 171, 174
Warren, Pte. P., 81, 254
Wass, Pte. E., 53, 252
Weaver, Sergt. S., 96, 99, 121
Weeks, Pte. S., 22, 252
Welch, Pte. F., 155, 252
West, Pte. A. C., 162, 252
White Chateau, 114, 118, 121
Wickers, Pte. C., 168, 252
Wigney, Lieut. C. R., 81, 95, 253
Wilcox, Pte. H., 126, 254
Willoughby, Capt., 7
Williams, C.Q.M.S. L., 144, 145, 149, 173, 210, 254
Wilson, L/Cpl. A., 135, 254
Winter, Cpl. E., 135, 254
Winter, Pte. W., 135, 254
Winter, L/Cpl. R., 172, 175, 252
Wood, Pte. H., 53, 252
Wood, Lieut. B., 16, 28, 252
Woods, Maj., 238, 259
Woods, L/Cpl. F., 48, 252
Woolley, Lieut.-Col. C. J., 228, 232, 258, 259
Woolner, Lt. H., 162, 171, 212, 215
Ypres, 91, 165, 182, 183, 200 244, 256
Zouave Valley, 59 60, 61